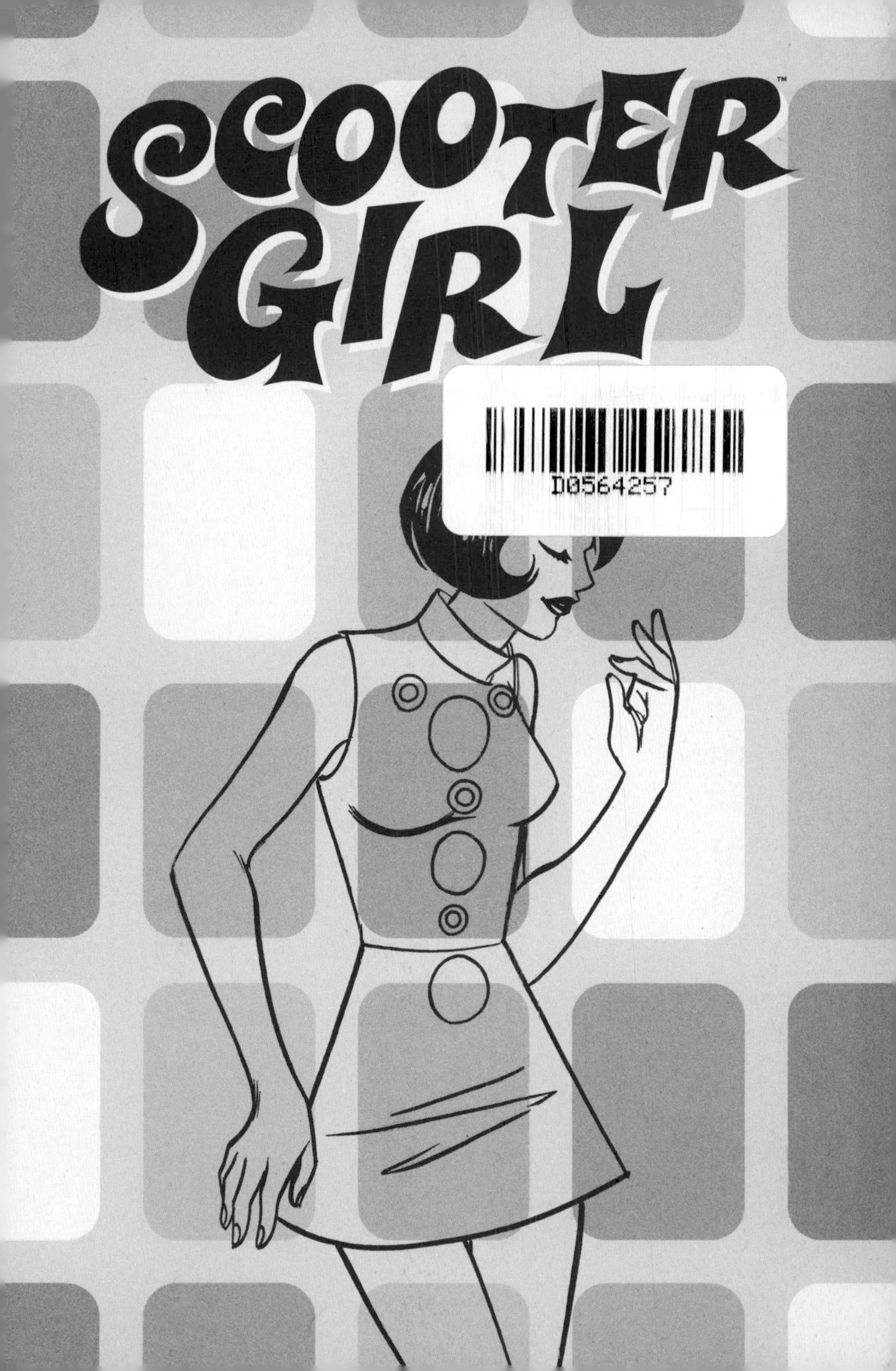
SCOOTER GIRL™

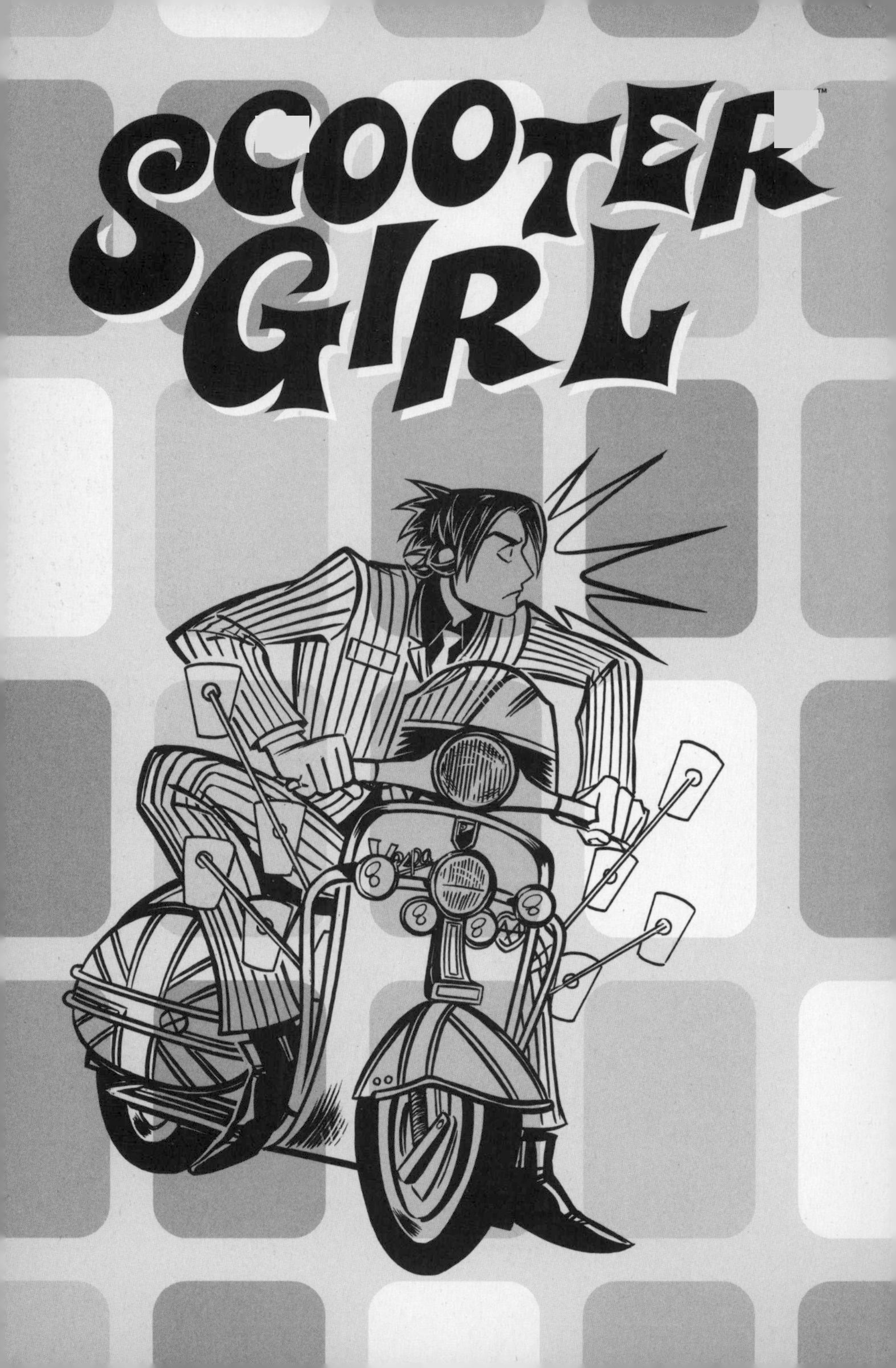
SCOOTER GIRL™

written and illustrated by
Chynna Clugston-Major

cover colors by
Guy Major

lettering by
Bryan Lee O'Malley
with
Christopher Butcher
(chapter 4)

introduction by
Nabiel Kanan

book design by
Keith Wood

dark curses by
Jamie S. Rich

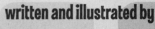

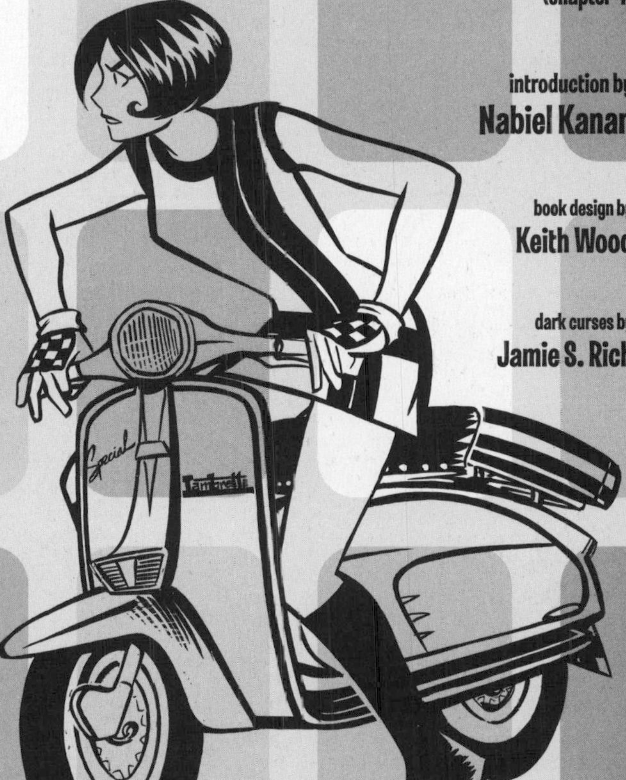

Published by Oni Press, Inc.

Joe Nozemack, publisher

Jamie S. Rich, editor in chief

James Lucas Jones, senior editor

Randal C. Jarrell, managing editor

Ian Shaughnessy, series editorial assistant

This collects all six issues of the Oni Press
comic book series, *Scooter Girl*™.

Editorial soundtrack: Tindersticks, *Working for the Man,*
The Pretty Things, *S.F. Sorrow*

ONI PRESS, INC.
6336 SE Milwaukie Avenue, Suite 30
Portland, OR 97202
USA

www.onipress.com

First edition: May 2004
ISBN 1-929998-88-0

1 3 5 7 9 10 8 6 4 2
PRINTED IN CANADA.

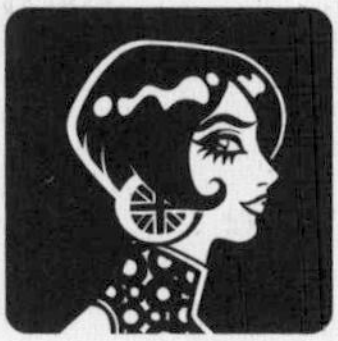

Introduction
by
Nabiel Kanan

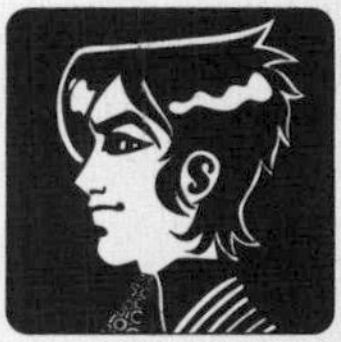

I'm a little anxious.

You see, I've never written one of these introductions before. What if Chynna's fans hate it? What if it's too brief, or too verbose? What if it misses the point completely? Worse still, they might think it's completely unnecessary. God. Anything could happen. They might even read it.

Then it dawned on me. I am one of those fans. So, just write it as a fan. So, I will.

"Teenage dreams, so hard to beat..." And they are, you know. *Scooter Girl* is a teenage dream. On wheels. You know the dream, where you're the most popular person in school? Where all the guys want to be you and all the girls want to be *with* you. You're the jock. You're the BMOC. Yes. You're a real arsehole. Well, Ashton Archer is that guy. He's got it all. The looks, the girls, the grades, the do-I-see-a-flock-of-seagulls-overhead hairdo. Er... Anyway. He's got it made. He's even got some fancy British ancestry. We know this because instead of just *telling* us, Clugston-Major shows us, in a brilliant historical sequence. One that will be reprised, to great effect, later in the novel.

It's never enough though, is it? When first we meet him, Ashton is King Midas. Everything he touches turns to gold. He is supremely confident and supremely satisfied. There is a danger in supreme confidence. Ask Napoleon. Ashton doesn't know it yet, but the snow is coming for him, too. Or at least, the Snow Queen is. There is a dissatisfaction in supreme satisfaction. When bonkers Chilean tennis player Marcelo Rios reached World No.1 in the rankings, he promptly fired his coach. His reason? He wanted to go higher. He hasn't been seen since. Of course, Ashton doesn't *know* he's dissatisfied. That's the beauty of it. Why would he be? He can have anything he wants. *Anything*. Except Margaret.

She hits him like a bolt of lightning (his words, not mine), and I can see why. No one can draw young people like Clugston-Major. She owns the copyright. A few effortless strokes of the pen, a swish of the inkbrush and a living, breathing person is captured on the page. Every time. Margaret is gorgeous. How gorgeous? Even silent screen stunner Louise Brooks would approve. Of course, it's much easier to render fictional faces than it is to capture, say, a real person whom people recognise, like, say, Louise Brooks. I bet it wouldn't be so easy to capture *her* in a few ink li....Damn you, Clugston-Major.

Margaret Sheldon is the new girl in town, and for the first time in his life, Ashton is tongue-tied. Like all truly beautiful girls, Margaret is infuriatingly calm. Ashton is a storm of slapstick around her. All he can see are her eyes, all he can think of are her lips, all he can taste is his foot. He thinks she's a goddess. She thinks he's a tit. She's right.

Pretty soon King Midas is no more. In his place sits King Canute. Margaret is the tide. The oblivious, disinterested tide. He can shout and scream and stamp his feet as much as he wants. The tide is not listening. It will not obey. I don't think it's giving too much away to say that by chapter 4, Ashton is having some seriously psychotic thoughts. To say that Margaret is getting to him would be an understatement of quite epic proportions. It's black, black comedy. It's quite awful to behold. It had me in stitches. You will want to cover your eyes in parts. But you will look. And you will laugh. A lot. And Grandpa Archer. Don't miss Grandpa Archer. He's a hoot.

I know some people find CCM's dialogue a little too close to the bone at times. Offensive, even. Personally, I love it. It's uncommonly witty and uncompromising. If it was watered down it would lose something vital. Or more to the point, the characters voicing it would. She isn't writing the way people *should* talk. She's writing the way they *do* talk. But with funny.

As with Clugston-Major's *Blue Monday* series, music plays a key role in the story, to the extent where a suggested soundtrack accompanies the narrative as you're reading it. You might hear your own soundtrack as you're reading—for what it's worth, a scene late on in the novel involving Kitty and Margaret's brother, Drake, brought the wistful beauty of Slowdive's "Catch The Breeze" to my mind. The truth is, though, the music's already there, in the images. At times they are kinetic. No, your eyes are *not* deceiving you. Margaret *is* actually moving on that dancefloor. That scooter *is* swaying as it wends its crazed, demented path along those low-rise lined streets. You can *hear* the panels. Panels that conjure up a city and its sounds. Its school corridors, its empty lots, and its pulsating nightclubs. I've never been to California, but now I've been to California. And people say they're just comic books.

Ultimately, though, it's the unexpected that makes *Scooter Girl* such a special story. You think you've got it all worked out. You think you know what you're in for. You're wrong. Because the truth is, Ashton is hit not once, but twice, by that lightning bolt. And the second strike reveals something quite unexpected. And quite unexpectedly moving. But don't take my word for it.

Ladies and gentlemen, start your engines.

Nabiel Kanan
Derby, United Kingdom
March, 2004

Nabiel Kanan is the creator of many fine graphic novels, including Exit, The Birthday Riots, *and his most recent,* The Drowners. *Visit him at www.new-flame.co.uk.*

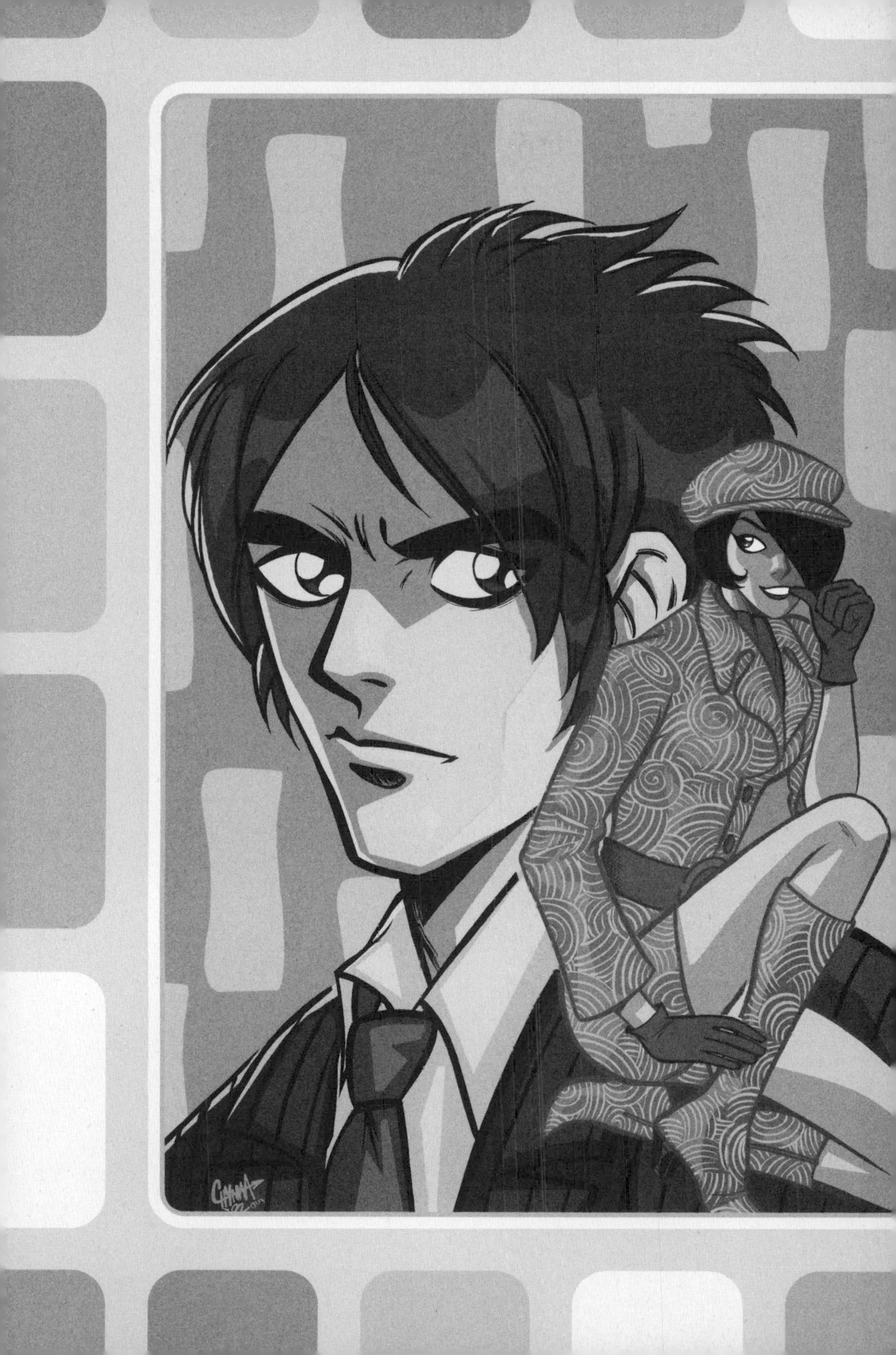

Chapter 1:
"Blow Up!"

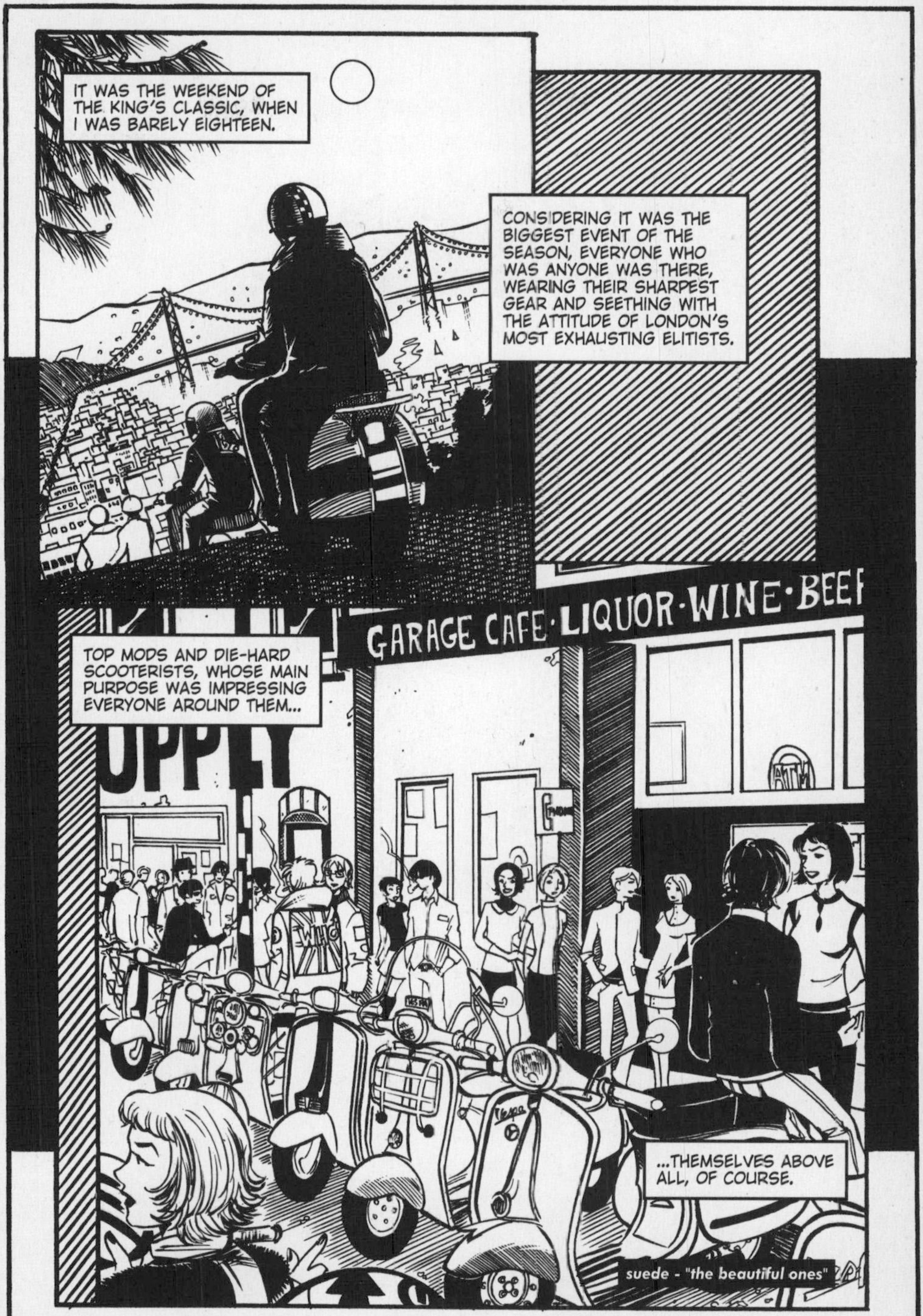
IT WAS THE WEEKEND OF THE KING'S CLASSIC, WHEN I WAS BARELY EIGHTEEN.
CONSIDERING IT WAS THE BIGGEST EVENT OF THE SEASON, EVERYONE WHO WAS ANYONE WAS THERE, WEARING THEIR SHARPEST GEAR AND SEETHING WITH THE ATTITUDE OF LONDON'S MOST EXHAUSTING ELITISTS.
GARAGE CAFE · LIQUOR · WINE · BEE
TOP MODS AND DIE-HARD SCOOTERISTS, WHOSE MAIN PURPOSE WAS IMPRESSING EVERYONE AROUND THEM...
UPPLY
WHO
ATM
Vespa
...THEMSELVES ABOVE ALL, OF COURSE.
suede - "the beautiful ones"

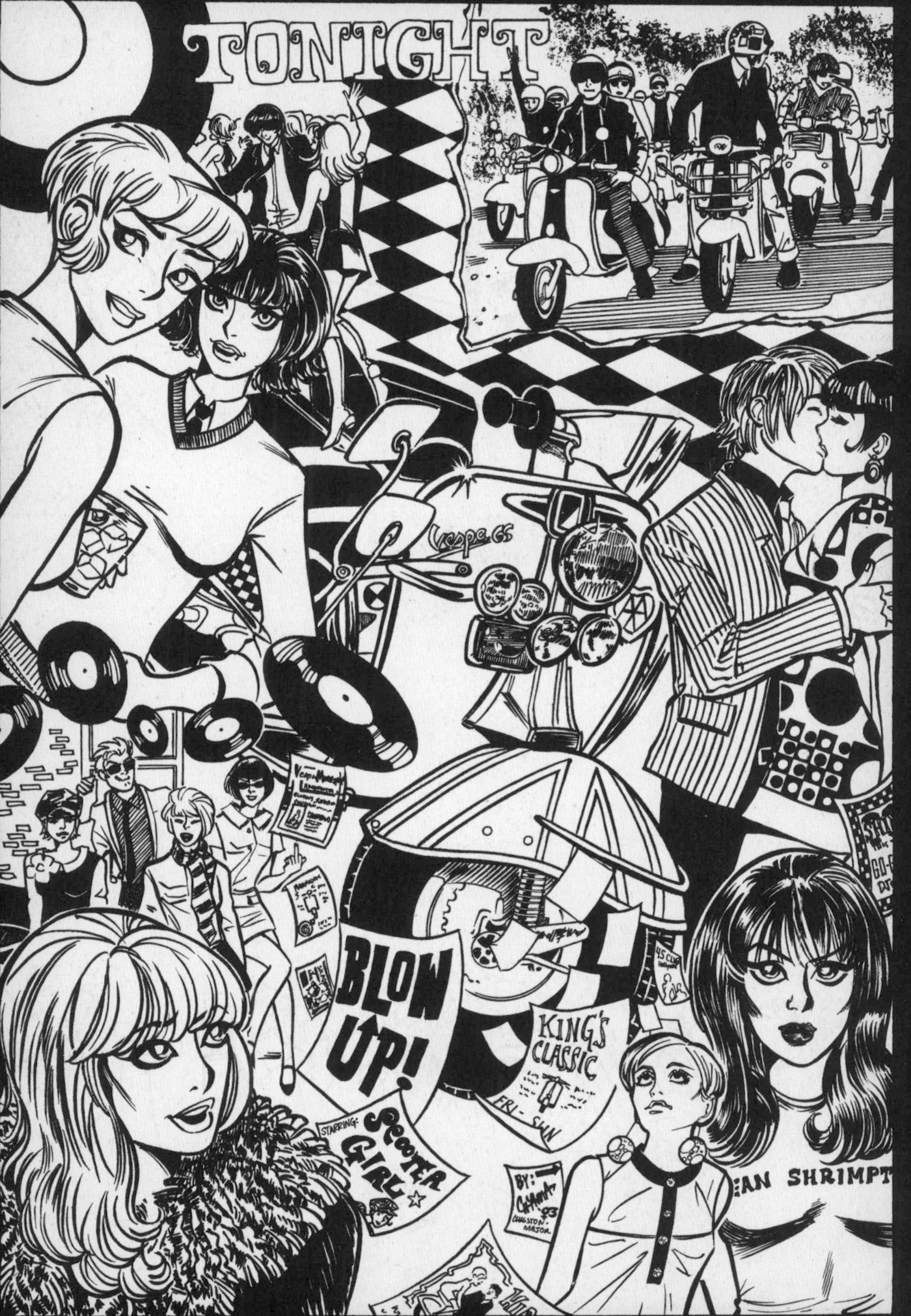

TONIGHT
Vespa 65
BLOW UP!
KING'S CLASSIC
FRI - SUN
STARRING:
SCOOTER GIRL
BY:
'93
CLUGSTON-MAJOR
EAN SHRIMPT

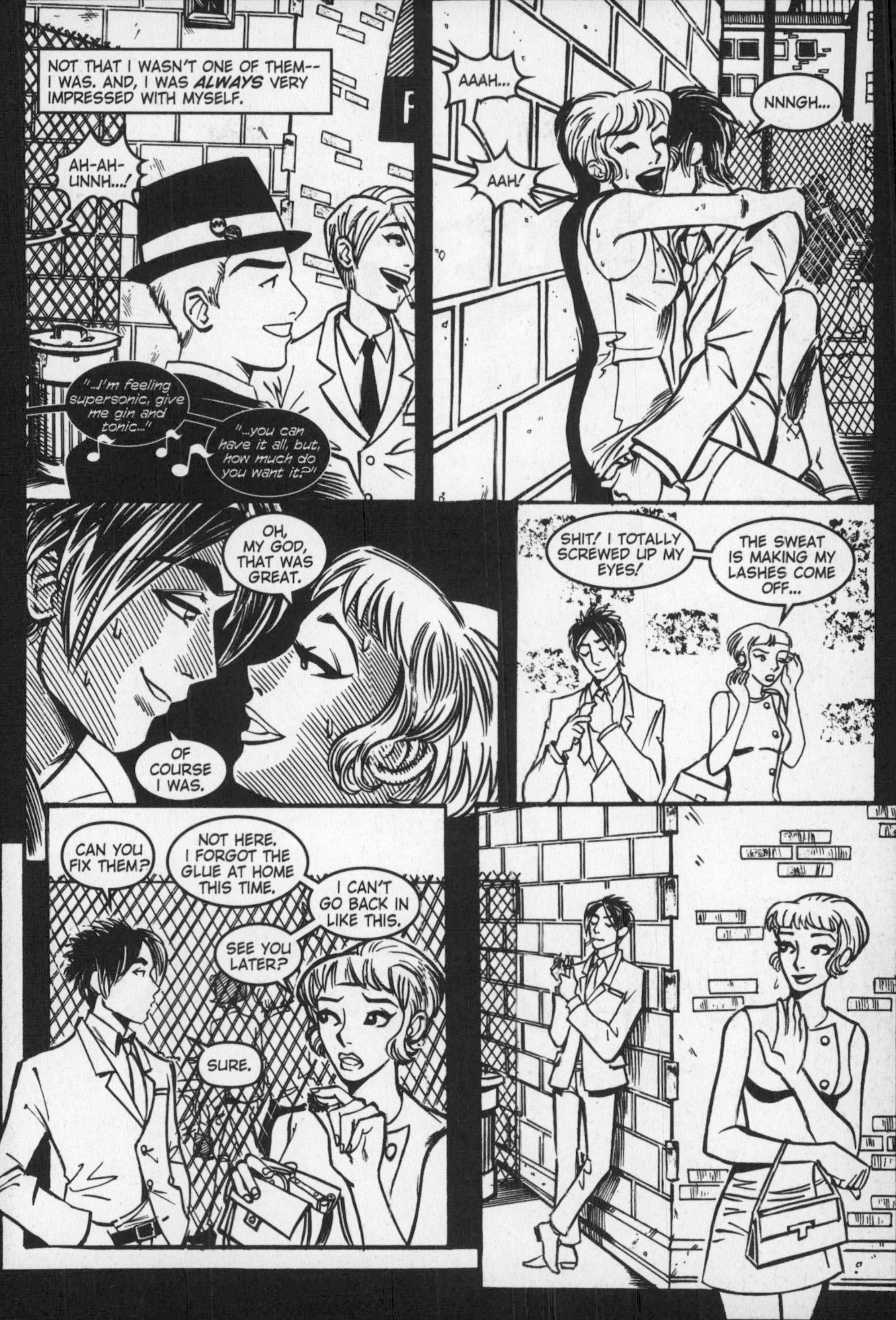
NOT THAT I WASN'T ONE OF THEM-- I WAS. AND, I WAS *ALWAYS* VERY IMPRESSED WITH MYSELF.
AH-AH-UNNH...!
"...I'm feeling supersonic, give me gin and tonic..."
"...you can have it all, but, how much do you want it?"
AAAH...
AAH!
NNNGH...
OH, MY GOD, THAT WAS GREAT.
OF COURSE I WAS.
SHIT! I TOTALLY SCREWED UP MY EYES!
THE SWEAT IS MAKING MY LASHES COME OFF...
CAN YOU FIX THEM?
NOT HERE. I FORGOT THE GLUE AT HOME THIS TIME.
I CAN'T GO BACK IN LIKE THIS.
SEE YOU LATER?
SURE.

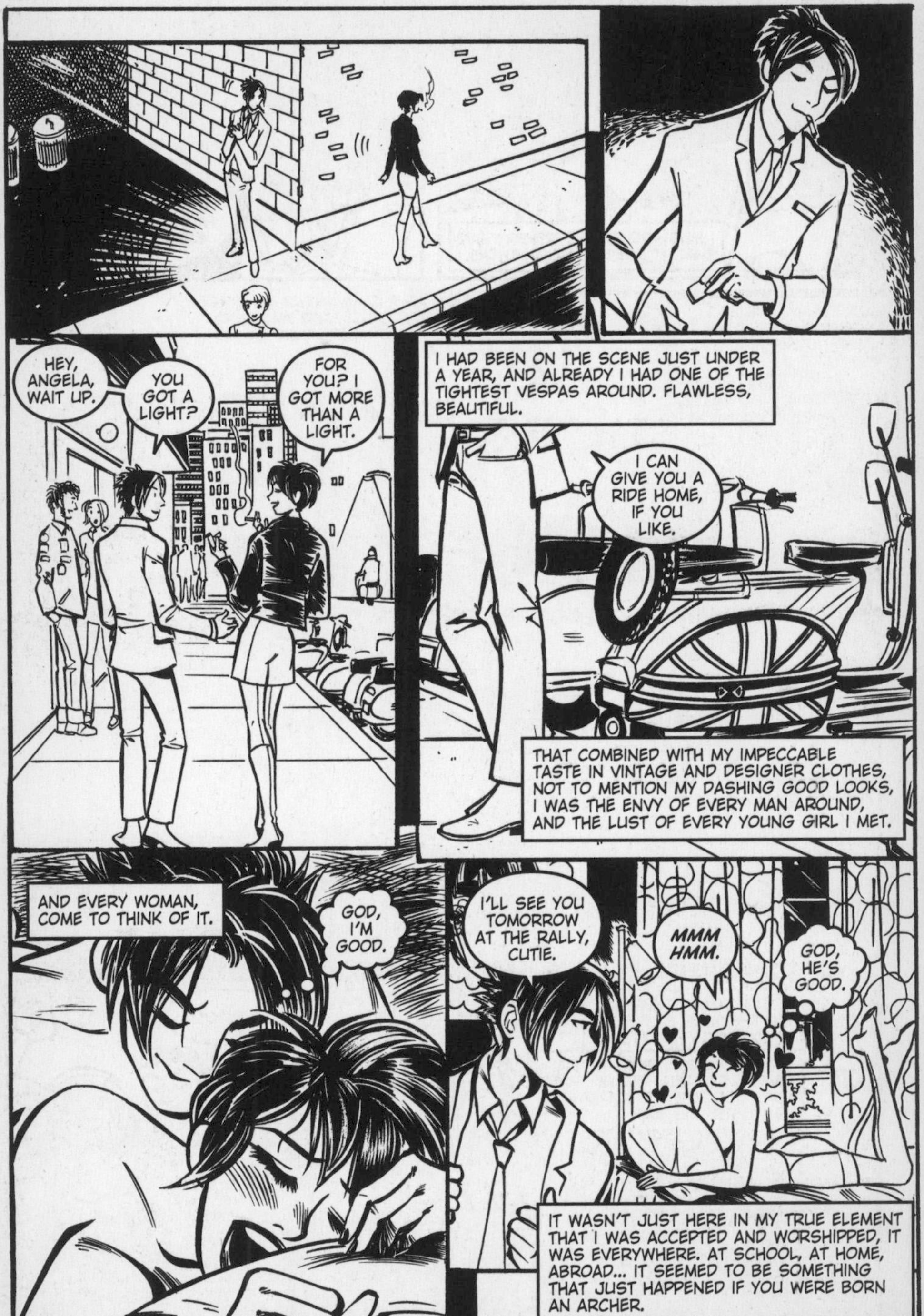
HEY, ANGELA, WAIT UP.
YOU GOT A LIGHT?
FOR YOU? I GOT MORE THAN A LIGHT.
I HAD BEEN ON THE SCENE JUST UNDER A YEAR, AND ALREADY I HAD ONE OF THE TIGHTEST VESPAS AROUND. FLAWLESS, BEAUTIFUL.
I CAN GIVE YOU A RIDE HOME, IF YOU LIKE.
THAT COMBINED WITH MY IMPECCABLE TASTE IN VINTAGE AND DESIGNER CLOTHES, NOT TO MENTION MY DASHING GOOD LOOKS, I WAS THE ENVY OF EVERY MAN AROUND, AND THE LUST OF EVERY YOUNG GIRL I MET.
AND EVERY WOMAN, COME TO THINK OF IT.
GOD, I'M GOOD.
I'LL SEE YOU TOMORROW AT THE RALLY, CUTIE.
MMM HMM.
GOD, HE'S GOOD.
IT WASN'T JUST HERE IN MY TRUE ELEMENT THAT I WAS ACCEPTED AND WORSHIPPED, IT WAS EVERYWHERE. AT SCHOOL, AT HOME, ABROAD... IT SEEMED TO BE SOMETHING THAT JUST HAPPENED IF YOU WERE BORN AN ARCHER.

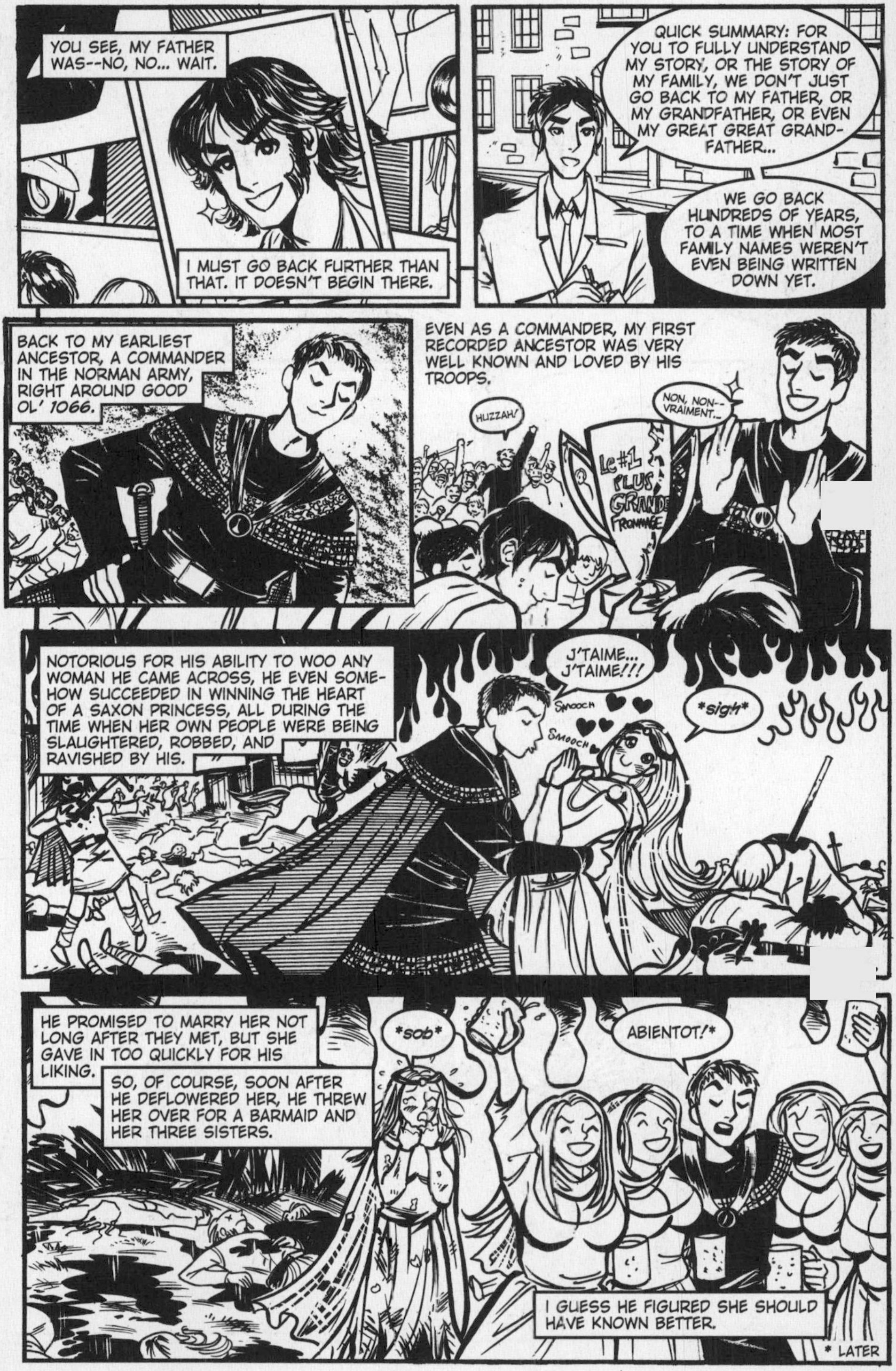

YOU SEE, MY FATHER WAS--NO, NO... WAIT.
I MUST GO BACK FURTHER THAN THAT. IT DOESN'T BEGIN THERE.
QUICK SUMMARY: FOR YOU TO FULLY UNDERSTAND MY STORY, OR THE STORY OF MY FAMILY, WE DON'T JUST GO BACK TO MY FATHER, OR MY GRANDFATHER, OR EVEN MY GREAT GREAT GRAND-FATHER...
WE GO BACK HUNDREDS OF YEARS, TO A TIME WHEN MOST FAMILY NAMES WEREN'T EVEN BEING WRITTEN DOWN YET.
BACK TO MY EARLIEST ANCESTOR, A COMMANDER IN THE NORMAN ARMY, RIGHT AROUND GOOD OL' 1066.
EVEN AS A COMMANDER, MY FIRST RECORDED ANCESTOR WAS VERY WELL KNOWN AND LOVED BY HIS TROOPS.
HUZZAH!
NON, NON-- VRAIMENT...
Le #1 PLUS GRANDE FROMAGE
NOTORIOUS FOR HIS ABILITY TO WOO ANY WOMAN HE CAME ACROSS, HE EVEN SOME-HOW SUCCEEDED IN WINNING THE HEART OF A SAXON PRINCESS, ALL DURING THE TIME WHEN HER OWN PEOPLE WERE BEING SLAUGHTERED, ROBBED, AND RAVISHED BY HIS.
J'TAIME... J'TAIME!!!
SMOOCH
SMOOCH
sigh
HE PROMISED TO MARRY HER NOT LONG AFTER THEY MET, BUT SHE GAVE IN TOO QUICKLY FOR HIS LIKING.
SO, OF COURSE, SOON AFTER HE DEFLOWERED HER, HE THREW HER OVER FOR A BARMAID AND HER THREE SISTERS.
sob
ABIENTOT!*
I GUESS HE FIGURED SHE SHOULD HAVE KNOWN BETTER.
* LATER

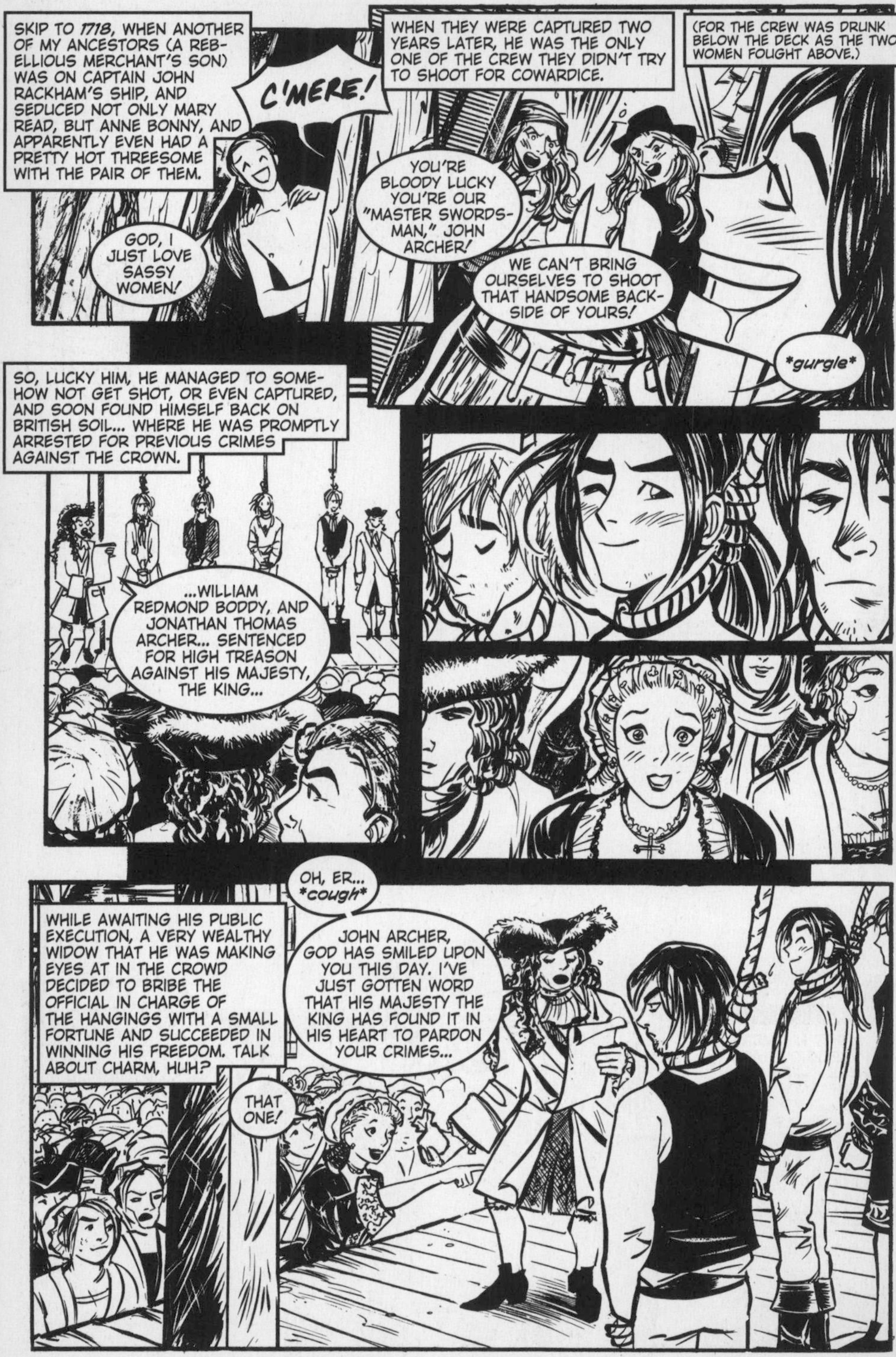
SKIP TO 1718, WHEN ANOTHER OF MY ANCESTORS (A REBELLIOUS MERCHANT'S SON) WAS ON CAPTAIN JOHN RACKHAM'S SHIP, AND SEDUCED NOT ONLY MARY READ, BUT ANNE BONNY, AND APPARENTLY EVEN HAD A PRETTY HOT THREESOME WITH THE PAIR OF THEM.
C'MERE!
GOD, I JUST LOVE SASSY WOMEN!
WHEN THEY WERE CAPTURED TWO YEARS LATER, HE WAS THE ONLY ONE OF THE CREW THEY DIDN'T TRY TO SHOOT FOR COWARDICE.
YOU'RE BLOODY LUCKY YOU'RE OUR "MASTER SWORDSMAN," JOHN ARCHER!
WE CAN'T BRING OURSELVES TO SHOOT THAT HANDSOME BACKSIDE OF YOURS!
(FOR THE CREW WAS DRUNK BELOW THE DECK AS THE TWO WOMEN FOUGHT ABOVE.)
gurgle
SO, LUCKY HIM, HE MANAGED TO SOMEHOW NOT GET SHOT, OR EVEN CAPTURED, AND SOON FOUND HIMSELF BACK ON BRITISH SOIL... WHERE HE WAS PROMPTLY ARRESTED FOR PREVIOUS CRIMES AGAINST THE CROWN.
...WILLIAM REDMOND BODDY, AND JONATHAN THOMAS ARCHER... SENTENCED FOR HIGH TREASON AGAINST HIS MAJESTY, THE KING...
WHILE AWAITING HIS PUBLIC EXECUTION, A VERY WEALTHY WIDOW THAT HE WAS MAKING EYES AT IN THE CROWD DECIDED TO BRIBE THE OFFICIAL IN CHARGE OF THE HANGINGS WITH A SMALL FORTUNE AND SUCCEEDED IN WINNING HIS FREEDOM. TALK ABOUT CHARM, HUH?
OH, ER... *cough*
JOHN ARCHER, GOD HAS SMILED UPON YOU THIS DAY. I'VE JUST GOTTEN WORD THAT HIS MAJESTY THE KING HAS FOUND IT IN HIS HEART TO PARDON YOUR CRIMES...
THAT ONE!

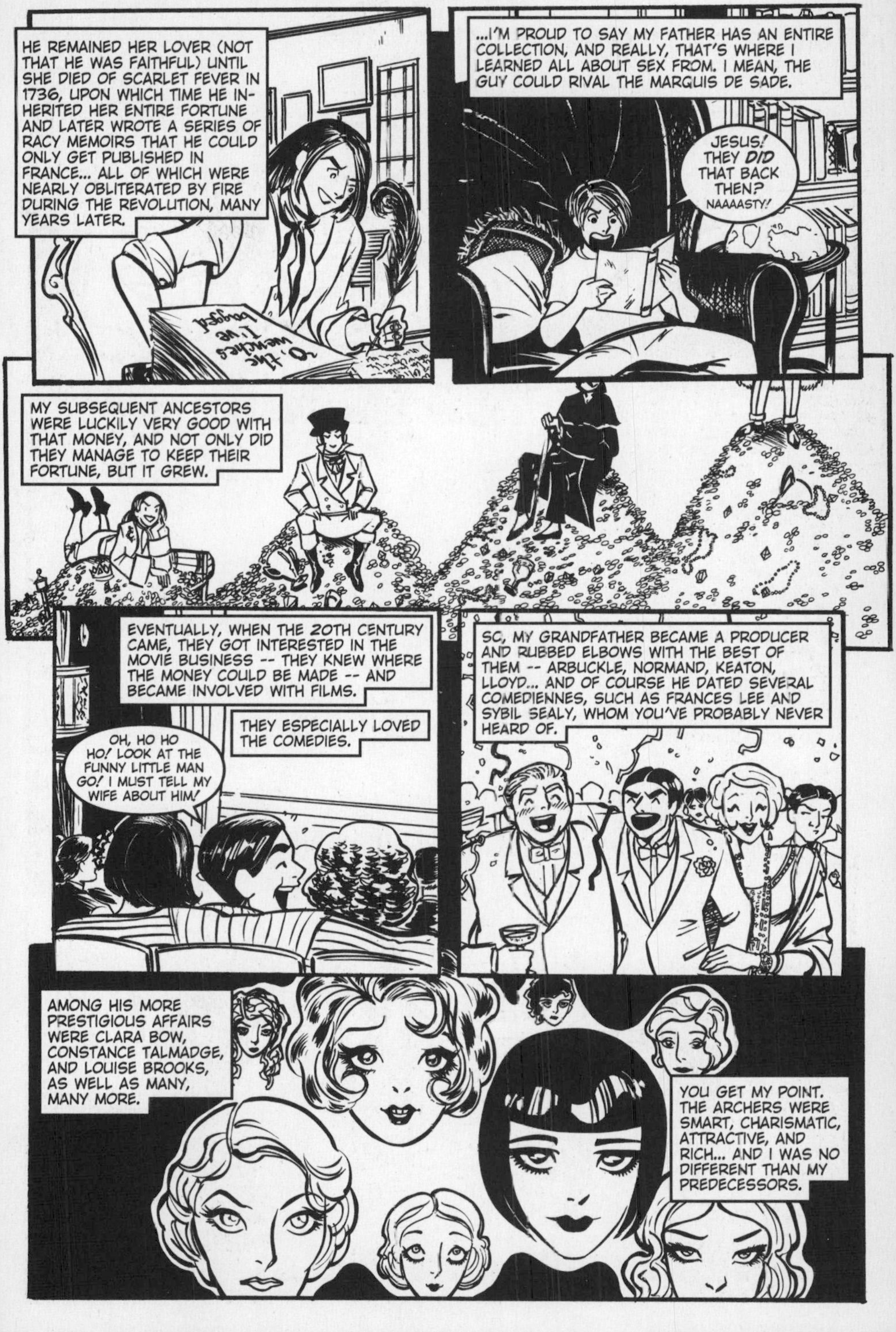
HE REMAINED HER LOVER (NOT THAT HE WAS FAITHFUL) UNTIL SHE DIED OF SCARLET FEVER IN 1736, UPON WHICH TIME HE INHERITED HER ENTIRE FORTUNE AND LATER WROTE A SERIES OF RACY MEMOIRS THAT HE COULD ONLY GET PUBLISHED IN FRANCE... ALL OF WHICH WERE NEARLY OBLITERATED BY FIRE DURING THE REVOLUTION, MANY YEARS LATER.
'O, the wenches I've bagged
...I'M PROUD TO SAY MY FATHER HAS AN ENTIRE COLLECTION, AND REALLY, THAT'S WHERE I LEARNED ALL ABOUT SEX FROM. I MEAN, THE GUY COULD RIVAL THE MARQUIS DE SADE.
JESUS! THEY *DID* THAT BACK THEN? NAAAASTY!
MY SUBSEQUENT ANCESTORS WERE LUCKILY VERY GOOD WITH THAT MONEY, AND NOT ONLY DID THEY MANAGE TO KEEP THEIR FORTUNE, BUT IT GREW.
EVENTUALLY, WHEN THE 20TH CENTURY CAME, THEY GOT INTERESTED IN THE MOVIE BUSINESS -- THEY KNEW WHERE THE MONEY COULD BE MADE -- AND BECAME INVOLVED WITH FILMS.
THEY ESPECIALLY LOVED THE COMEDIES.
OH, HO HO HO! LOOK AT THE FUNNY LITTLE MAN GO! I MUST TELL MY WIFE ABOUT HIM!
SO, MY GRANDFATHER BECAME A PRODUCER AND RUBBED ELBOWS WITH THE BEST OF THEM -- ARBUCKLE, NORMAND, KEATON, LLOYD... AND OF COURSE HE DATED SEVERAL COMEDIENNES, SUCH AS FRANCES LEE AND SYBIL SEALY, WHOM YOU'VE PROBABLY NEVER HEARD OF.
AMONG HIS MORE PRESTIGIOUS AFFAIRS WERE CLARA BOW, CONSTANCE TALMADGE, AND LOUISE BROOKS, AS WELL AS MANY, MANY MORE.
YOU GET MY POINT. THE ARCHERS WERE SMART, CHARISMATIC, ATTRACTIVE, AND RICH... AND I WAS NO DIFFERENT THAN MY PREDECESSORS.

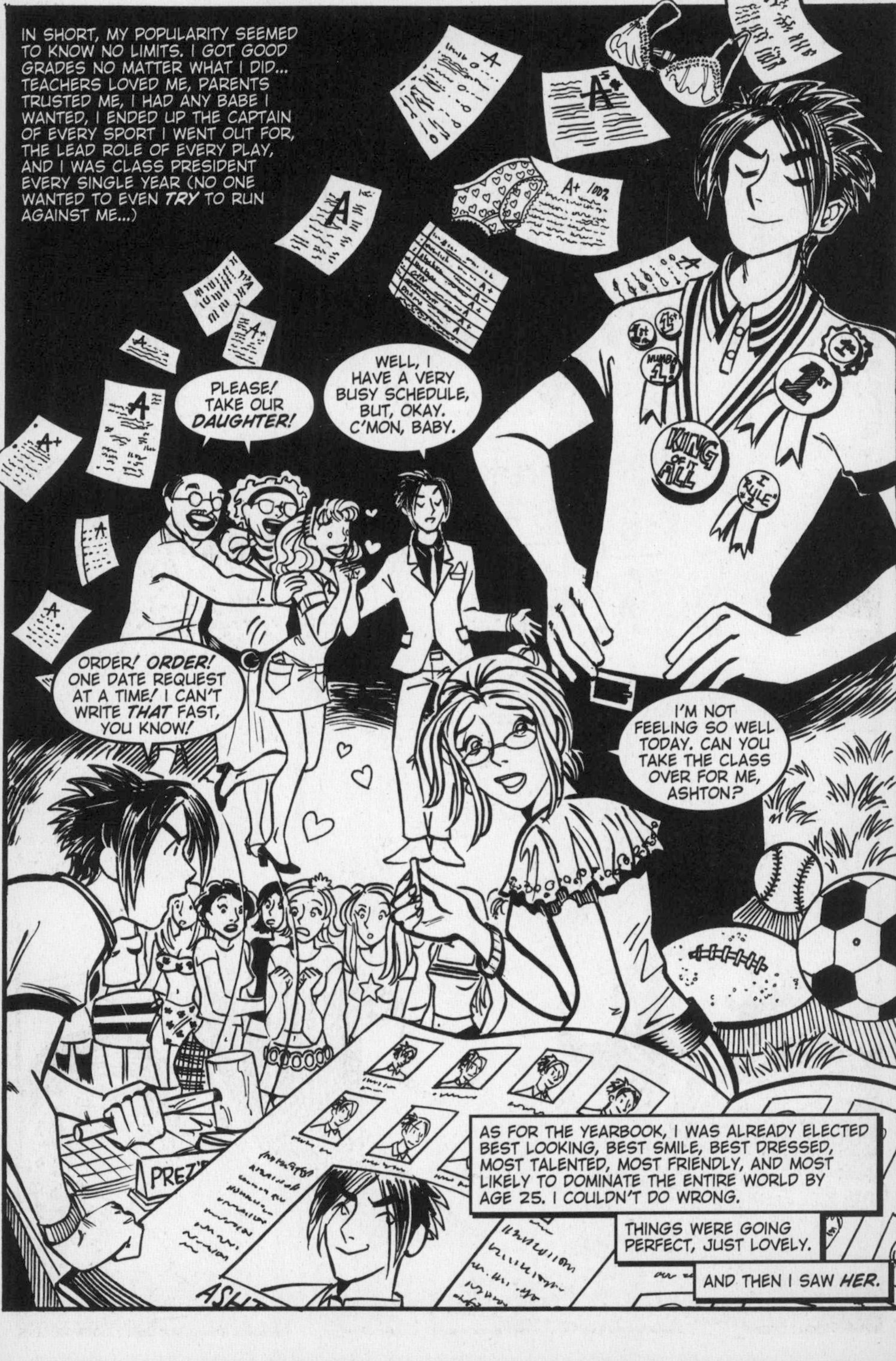
IN SHORT, MY POPULARITY SEEMED TO KNOW NO LIMITS. I GOT GOOD GRADES NO MATTER WHAT I DID... TEACHERS LOVED ME, PARENTS TRUSTED ME, I HAD ANY BABE I WANTED, I ENDED UP THE CAPTAIN OF EVERY SPORT I WENT OUT FOR, THE LEAD ROLE OF EVERY PLAY, AND I WAS CLASS PRESIDENT EVERY SINGLE YEAR (NO ONE WANTED TO EVEN *TRY* TO RUN AGAINST ME...)
PLEASE! TAKE OUR *DAUGHTER!*
WELL, I HAVE A VERY BUSY SCHEDULE, BUT, OKAY. C'MON, BABY.
KING OF IT ALL
ORDER! *ORDER!* ONE DATE REQUEST AT A TIME! I CAN'T WRITE *THAT* FAST, YOU KNOW!
I'M NOT FEELING SO WELL TODAY. CAN YOU TAKE THE CLASS OVER FOR ME, ASHTON?
PREZ
AS FOR THE YEARBOOK, I WAS ALREADY ELECTED BEST LOOKING, BEST SMILE, BEST DRESSED, MOST TALENTED, MOST FRIENDLY, AND MOST LIKELY TO DOMINATE THE ENTIRE WORLD BY AGE 25. I COULDN'T DO WRONG.
THINGS WERE GOING PERFECT, JUST LOVELY.
AND THEN I SAW *HER*.

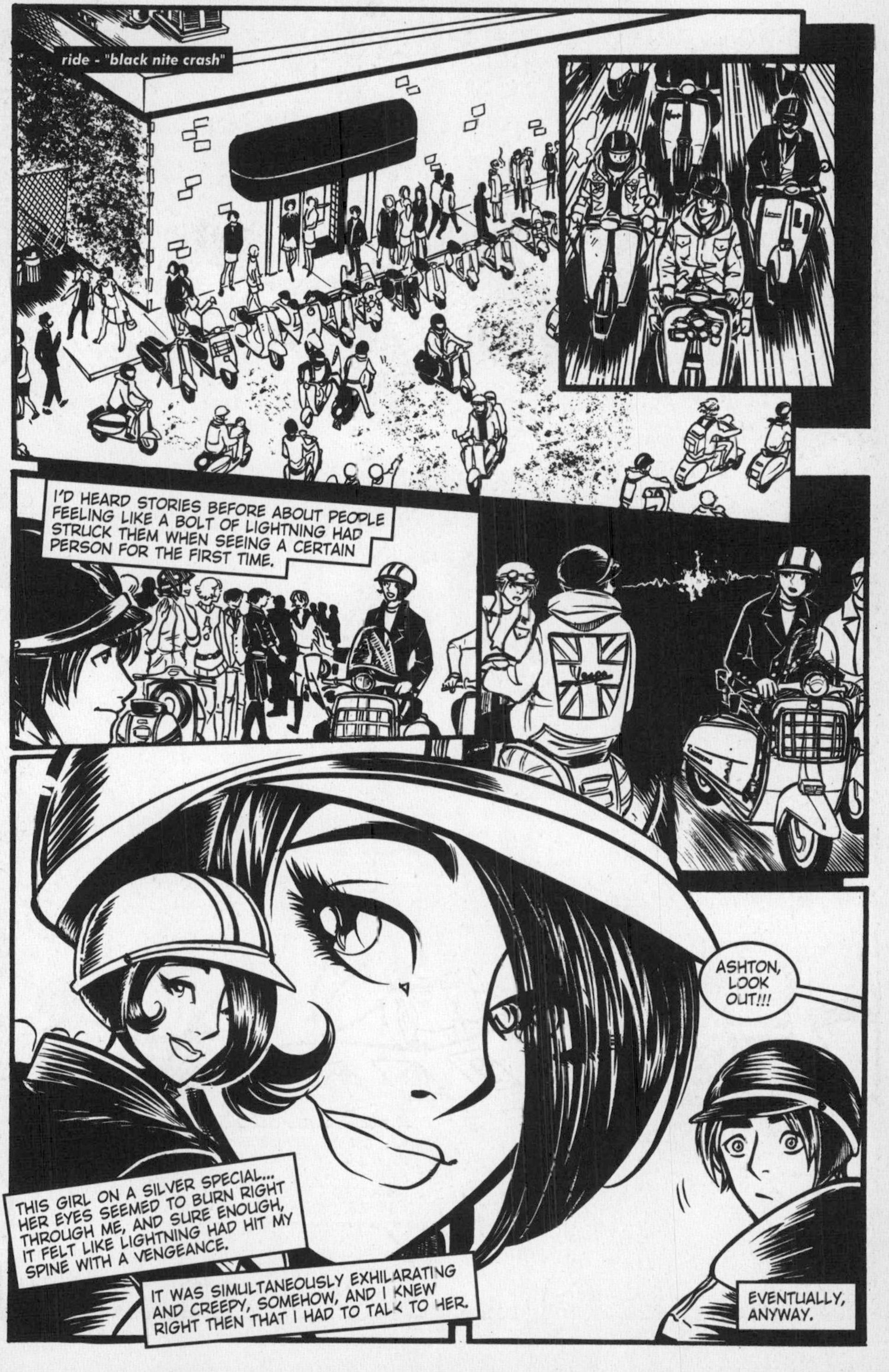
ride - "black nite crash"
I'D HEARD STORIES BEFORE ABOUT PEOPLE FEELING LIKE A BOLT OF LIGHTNING HAD STRUCK THEM WHEN SEEING A CERTAIN PERSON FOR THE FIRST TIME.
THIS GIRL ON A SILVER SPECIAL... HER EYES SEEMED TO BURN RIGHT THROUGH ME, AND SURE ENOUGH, IT FELT LIKE LIGHTNING HAD HIT MY SPINE WITH A VENGEANCE.
IT WAS SIMULTANEOUSLY EXHILARATING AND CREEPY, SOMEHOW, AND I KNEW RIGHT THEN THAT I HAD TO TALK TO HER.
ASHTON, LOOK OUT!!!
EVENTUALLY, ANYWAY.

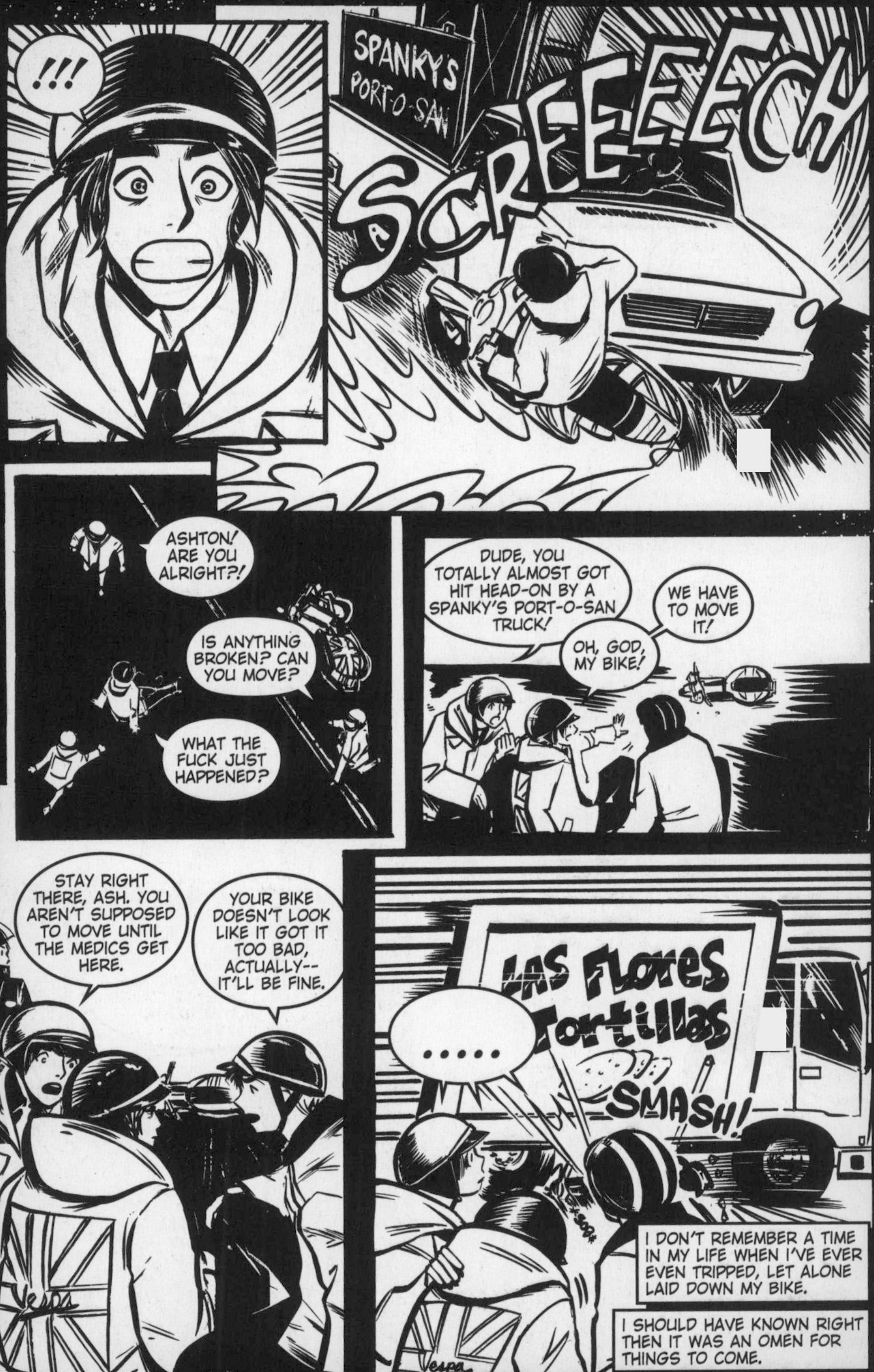
!!!
SPANKY'S PORT-O-SAN
SCREEEECH
ASHTON! ARE YOU ALRIGHT?!
IS ANYTHING BROKEN? CAN YOU MOVE?
WHAT THE FUCK JUST HAPPENED?
DUDE, YOU TOTALLY ALMOST GOT HIT HEAD-ON BY A SPANKY'S PORT-O-SAN TRUCK!
WE HAVE TO MOVE IT!
OH, GOD, MY BIKE!
STAY RIGHT THERE, ASH. YOU AREN'T SUPPOSED TO MOVE UNTIL THE MEDICS GET HERE.
YOUR BIKE DOESN'T LOOK LIKE IT GOT IT TOO BAD, ACTUALLY-- IT'LL BE FINE.
LAS FLORES TORTILLAS
......
SMASH!
I DON'T REMEMBER A TIME IN MY LIFE WHEN I'VE EVER EVEN TRIPPED, LET ALONE LAID DOWN MY BIKE.
I SHOULD HAVE KNOWN RIGHT THEN IT WAS AN OMEN FOR THINGS TO COME.

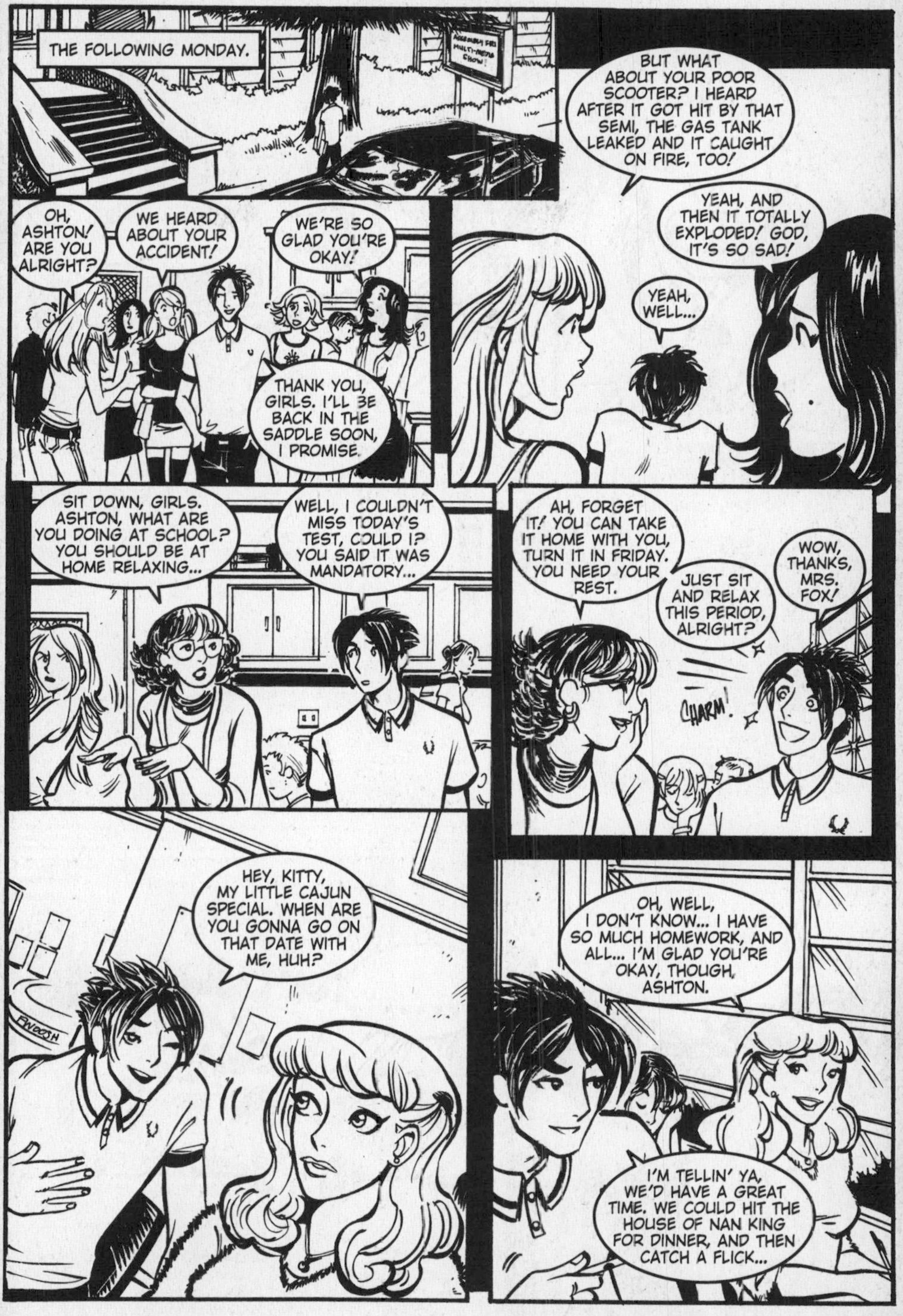
THE FOLLOWING MONDAY.
BUT WHAT ABOUT YOUR POOR SCOOTER? I HEARD AFTER IT GOT HIT BY THAT SEMI, THE GAS TANK LEAKED AND IT CAUGHT ON FIRE, TOO!
OH, ASHTON! ARE YOU ALRIGHT?
WE HEARD ABOUT YOUR ACCIDENT!
WE'RE SO GLAD YOU'RE OKAY!
THANK YOU, GIRLS. I'LL BE BACK IN THE SADDLE SOON, I PROMISE.
YEAH, AND THEN IT TOTALLY EXPLODED! GOD, IT'S SO SAD!
YEAH, WELL...
SIT DOWN, GIRLS. ASHTON, WHAT ARE YOU DOING AT SCHOOL? YOU SHOULD BE AT HOME RELAXING...
WELL, I COULDN'T MISS TODAY'S TEST, COULD I? YOU SAID IT WAS MANDATORY...
AH, FORGET IT! YOU CAN TAKE IT HOME WITH YOU, TURN IT IN FRIDAY. YOU NEED YOUR REST.
JUST SIT AND RELAX THIS PERIOD, ALRIGHT?
WOW, THANKS, MRS. FOX!
CHARM!
HEY, KITTY, MY LITTLE CAJUN SPECIAL. WHEN ARE YOU GONNA GO ON THAT DATE WITH ME, HUH?
FWOOSH
OH, WELL, I DON'T KNOW... I HAVE SO MUCH HOMEWORK, AND ALL... I'M GLAD YOU'RE OKAY, THOUGH, ASHTON.
I'M TELLIN' YA, WE'D HAVE A GREAT TIME. WE COULD HIT THE HOUSE OF NAN KING FOR DINNER, AND THEN CATCH A FLICK...

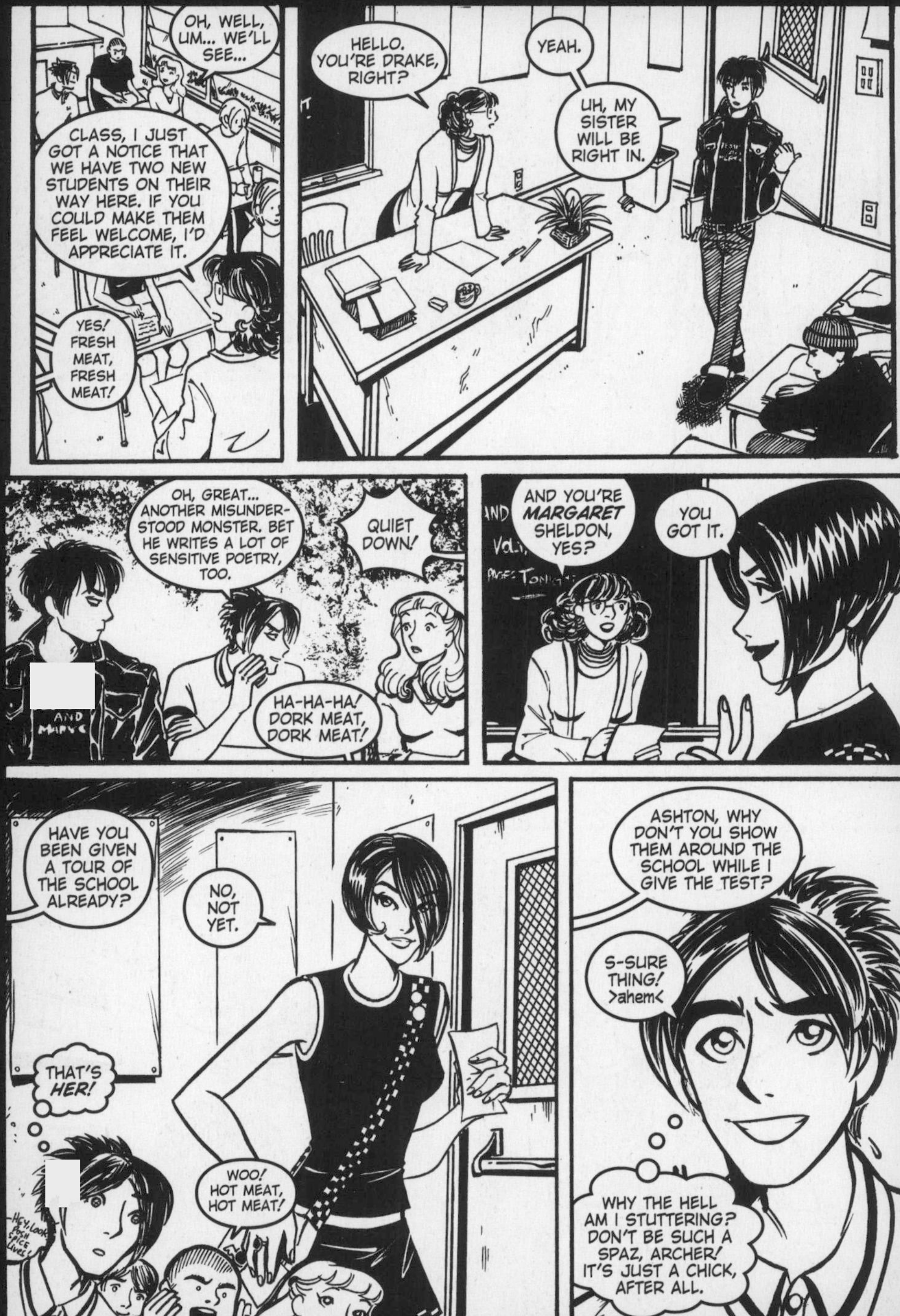
CLASS, I JUST GOT A NOTICE THAT WE HAVE TWO NEW STUDENTS ON THEIR WAY HERE. IF YOU COULD MAKE THEM FEEL WELCOME, I'D APPRECIATE IT.
YES! FRESH MEAT, FRESH MEAT!
OH, WELL, UM... WE'LL SEE...
HELLO. YOU'RE DRAKE, RIGHT?
YEAH.
UH, MY SISTER WILL BE RIGHT IN.
OH, GREAT... ANOTHER MISUNDER-STOOD MONSTER. BET HE WRITES A LOT OF SENSITIVE POETRY, TOO.
QUIET DOWN!
HA-HA-HA! DORK MEAT, DORK MEAT!
AND YOU'RE MARGARET SHELDON, YES?
YOU GOT IT.
HAVE YOU BEEN GIVEN A TOUR OF THE SCHOOL ALREADY?
NO, NOT YET.
THAT'S HER!
WOO! HOT MEAT, HOT MEAT!
HEY, LOOK! POSH SPICE LIVES!
ASHTON, WHY DON'T YOU SHOW THEM AROUND THE SCHOOL WHILE I GIVE THE TEST?
S-SURE THING! >ahem<
WHY THE HELL AM I STUTTERING? DON'T BE SUCH A SPAZ, ARCHER! IT'S JUST A CHICK, AFTER ALL.

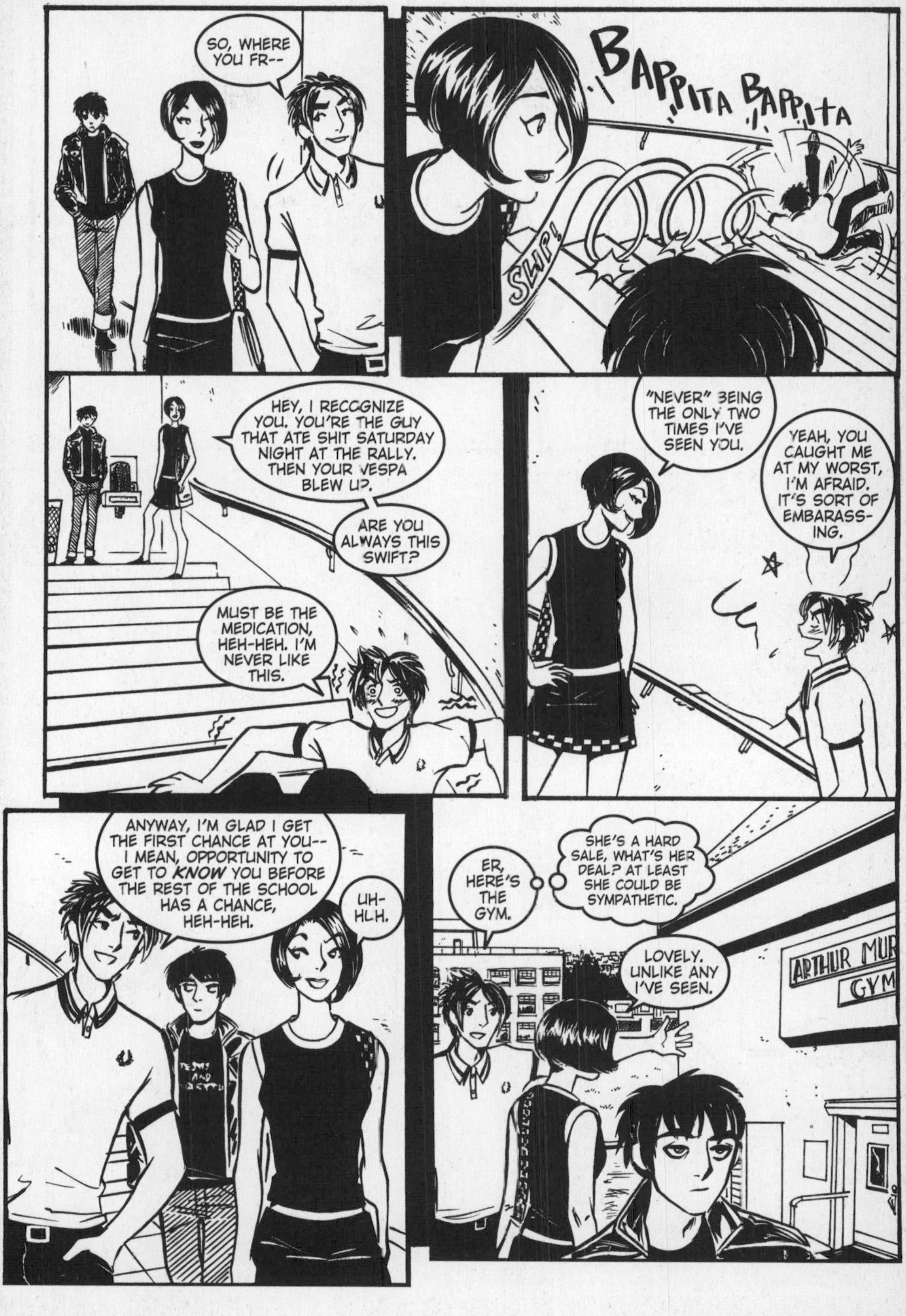
SO, WHERE YOU FR--
BAPPITA BAPPITA
SWIP!
HEY, I RECOGNIZE YOU. YOU'RE THE GUY THAT ATE SHIT SATURDAY NIGHT AT THE RALLY. THEN YOUR VESPA BLEW UP.
ARE YOU ALWAYS THIS SWIFT?
MUST BE THE MEDICATION, HEH-HEH. I'M NEVER LIKE THIS.
"NEVER" BEING THE ONLY TWO TIMES I'VE SEEN YOU.
YEAH, YOU CAUGHT ME AT MY WORST, I'M AFRAID. IT'S SORT OF EMBARASS-ING.
ANYWAY, I'M GLAD I GET THE FIRST CHANCE AT YOU-- I MEAN, OPPORTUNITY TO GET TO KNOW YOU BEFORE THE REST OF THE SCHOOL HAS A CHANCE, HEH-HEH.
UH-HUH.
ER, HERE'S THE GYM.
SHE'S A HARD SALE, WHAT'S HER DEAL? AT LEAST SHE COULD BE SYMPATHETIC.
LOVELY. UNLIKE ANY I'VE SEEN.
ARTHUR MUR
GYM

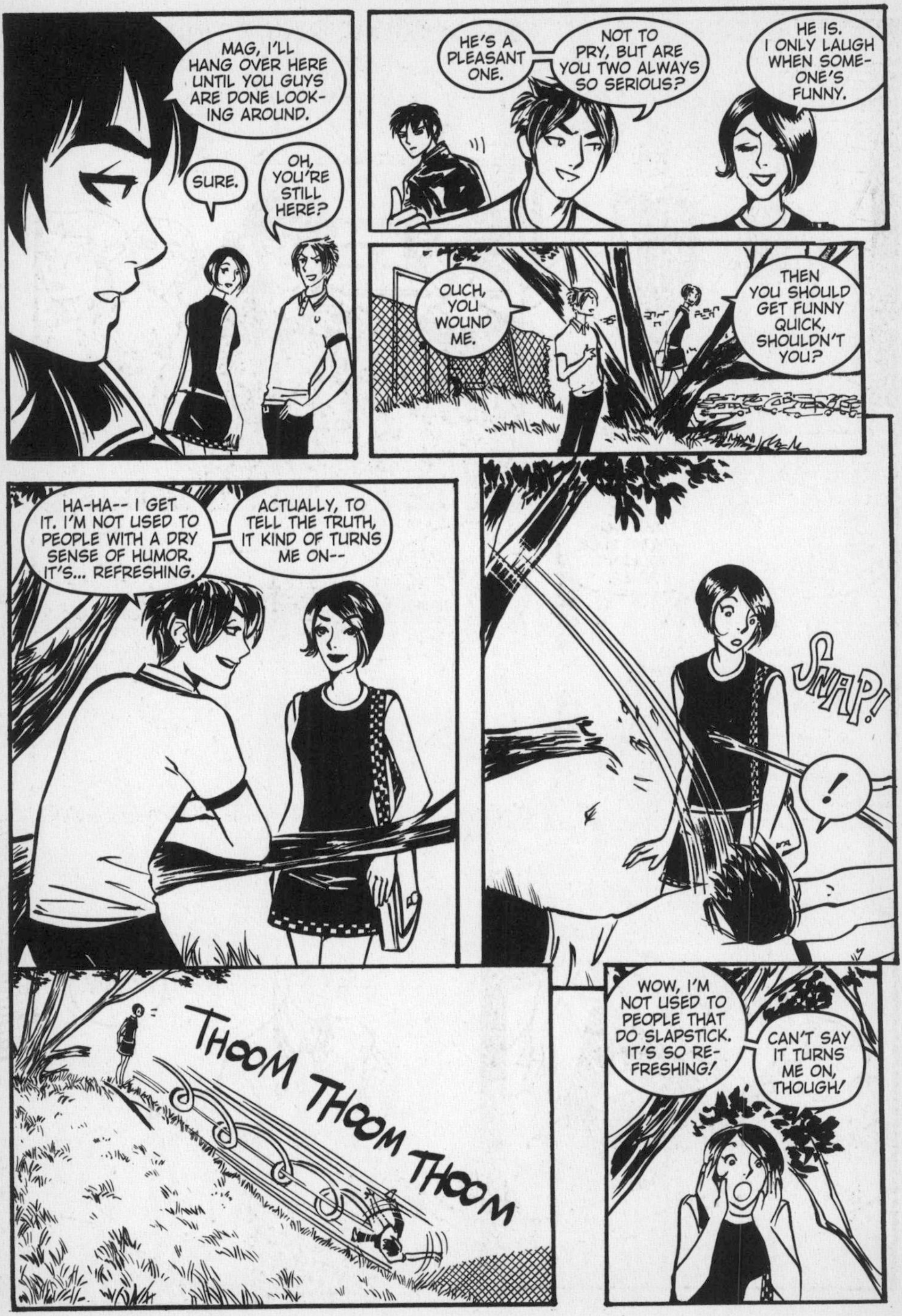
MAG, I'LL HANG OVER HERE UNTIL YOU GUYS ARE DONE LOOKING AROUND.
SURE.
OH, YOU'RE STILL HERE?
HE'S A PLEASANT ONE.
NOT TO PRY, BUT ARE YOU TWO ALWAYS SO SERIOUS?
HE IS. I ONLY LAUGH WHEN SOMEONE'S FUNNY.
OUCH, YOU WOUND ME.
THEN YOU SHOULD GET FUNNY QUICK, SHOULDN'T YOU?
HA-HA-- I GET IT. I'M NOT USED TO PEOPLE WITH A DRY SENSE OF HUMOR. IT'S... REFRESHING.
ACTUALLY, TO TELL THE TRUTH, IT KIND OF TURNS ME ON--
SNAP!
!
THOOM THOOM THOOM THOOM
WOW, I'M NOT USED TO PEOPLE THAT DO SLAPSTICK. IT'S SO REFRESHING!
CAN'T SAY IT TURNS ME ON, THOUGH!

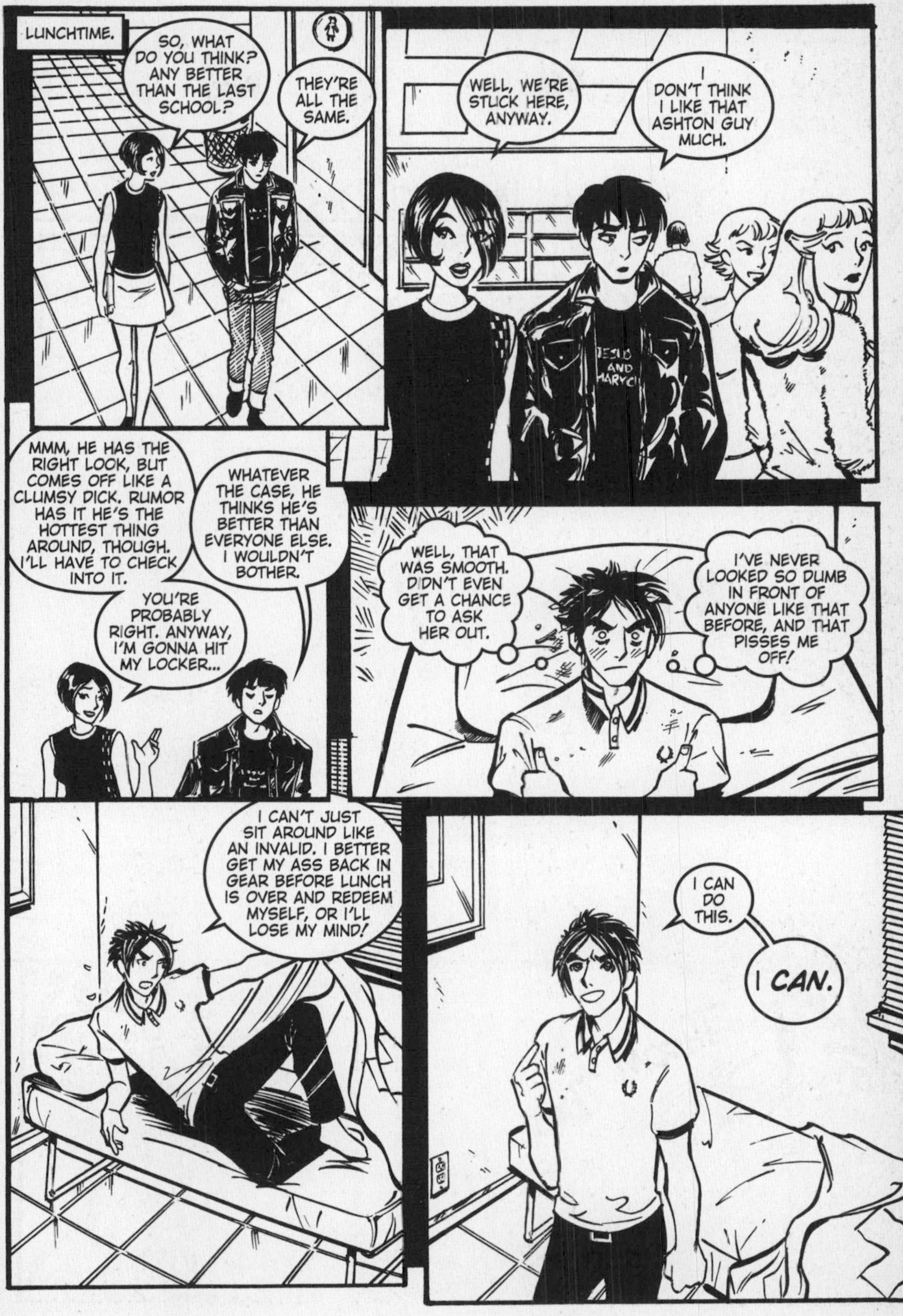
LUNCHTIME.
SO, WHAT DO YOU THINK? ANY BETTER THAN THE LAST SCHOOL?
THEY'RE ALL THE SAME.
WELL, WE'RE STUCK HERE, ANYWAY.
I DON'T THINK I LIKE THAT ASHTON GUY MUCH.
MMM, HE HAS THE RIGHT LOOK, BUT COMES OFF LIKE A CLUMSY DICK. RUMOR HAS IT HE'S THE HOTTEST THING AROUND, THOUGH. I'LL HAVE TO CHECK INTO IT.
WHATEVER THE CASE, HE THINKS HE'S BETTER THAN EVERYONE ELSE. I WOULDN'T BOTHER.
YOU'RE PROBABLY RIGHT. ANYWAY, I'M GONNA HIT MY LOCKER...
WELL, THAT WAS SMOOTH. DIDN'T EVEN GET A CHANCE TO ASK HER OUT.
I'VE NEVER LOOKED SO DUMB IN FRONT OF ANYONE LIKE THAT BEFORE, AND THAT PISSES ME OFF!
I CAN'T JUST SIT AROUND LIKE AN INVALID. I BETTER GET MY ASS BACK IN GEAR BEFORE LUNCH IS OVER AND REDEEM MYSELF, OR I'LL LOSE MY MIND!
I CAN DO THIS.
I *CAN.*

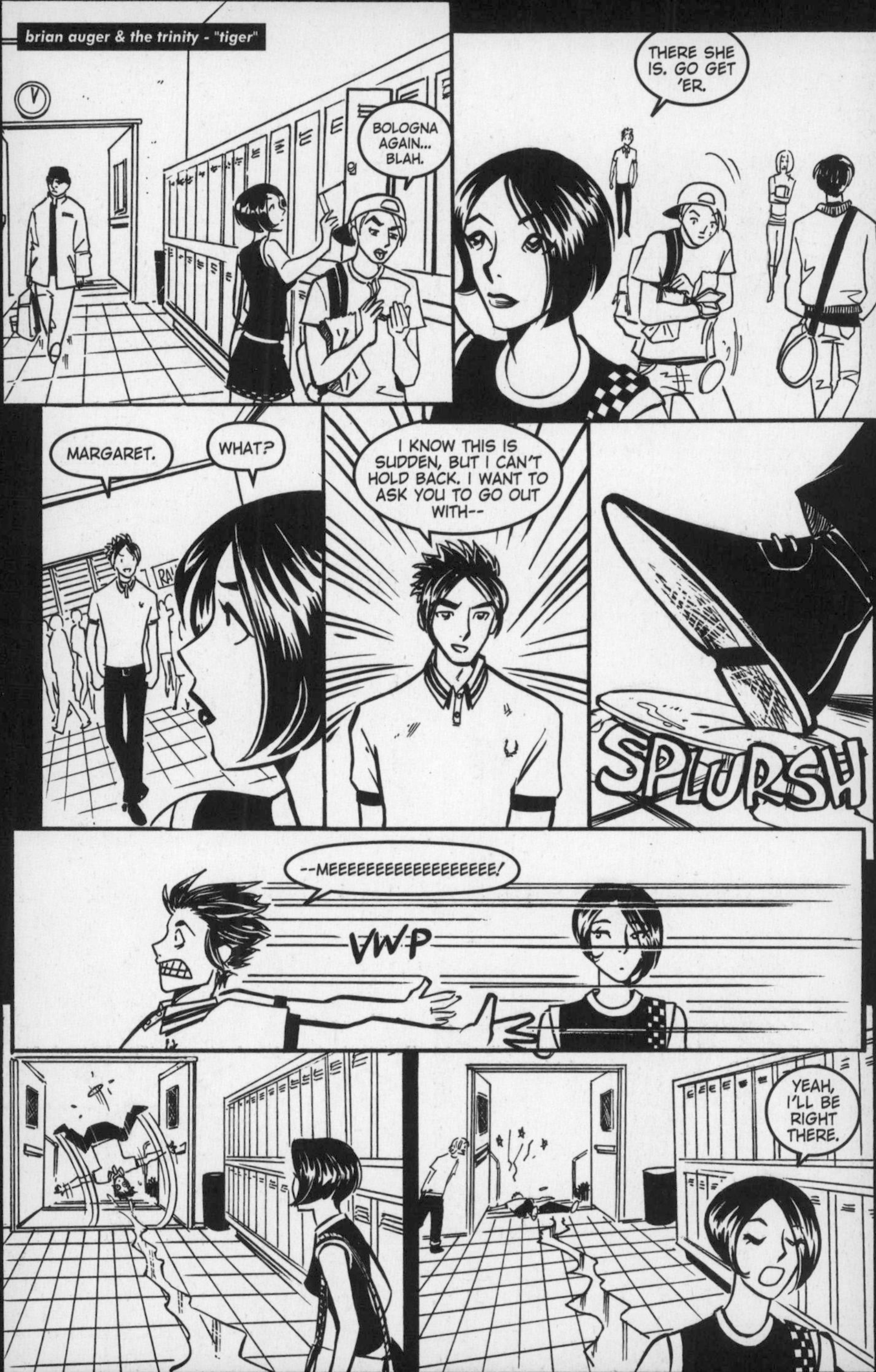
brian auger & the trinity - "tiger"
BOLOGNA AGAIN... BLAH.
THERE SHE IS. GO GET 'ER.
MARGARET.
WHAT?
I KNOW THIS IS SUDDEN, BUT I CAN'T HOLD BACK. I WANT TO ASK YOU TO GO OUT WITH--
SPLURSH
--MEEEEEEEEEEEEEEEEE!
VWP
YEAH, I'LL BE RIGHT THERE.

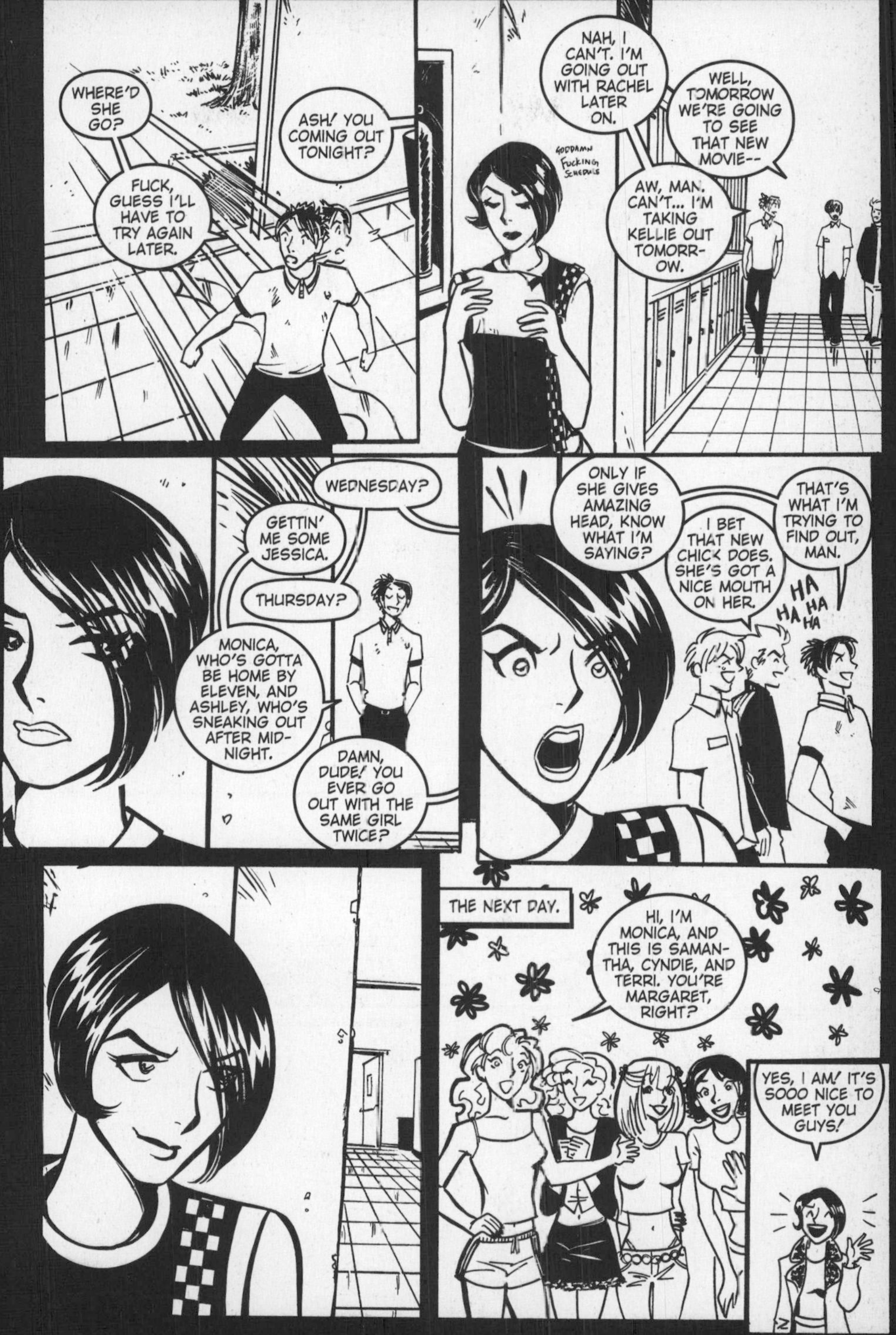
WHERE'D SHE GO?
FUCK, GUESS I'LL HAVE TO TRY AGAIN LATER.
ASH! YOU COMING OUT TONIGHT?
NAH, I CAN'T. I'M GOING OUT WITH RACHEL LATER ON.
GODDAMN FUCKING SCHEDULE
WELL, TOMORROW WE'RE GOING TO SEE THAT NEW MOVIE--
AW, MAN. CAN'T... I'M TAKING KELLIE OUT TOMORR-OW.
WEDNESDAY?
GETTIN' ME SOME JESSICA.
THURSDAY?
MONICA, WHO'S GOTTA BE HOME BY ELEVEN, AND ASHLEY, WHO'S SNEAKING OUT AFTER MID-NIGHT.
DAMN, DUDE! YOU EVER GO OUT WITH THE SAME GIRL TWICE?
ONLY IF SHE GIVES AMAZING HEAD, KNOW WHAT I'M SAYING?
I BET THAT NEW CHICK DOES. SHE'S GOT A NICE MOUTH ON HER.
THAT'S WHAT I'M TRYING TO FIND OUT, MAN.
HA HA HA HA
THE NEXT DAY.
HI, I'M MONICA, AND THIS IS SAMAN-THA, CYNDIE, AND TERRI. YOU'RE MARGARET, RIGHT?
YES, I AM! IT'S SOOO NICE TO MEET YOU GUYS!

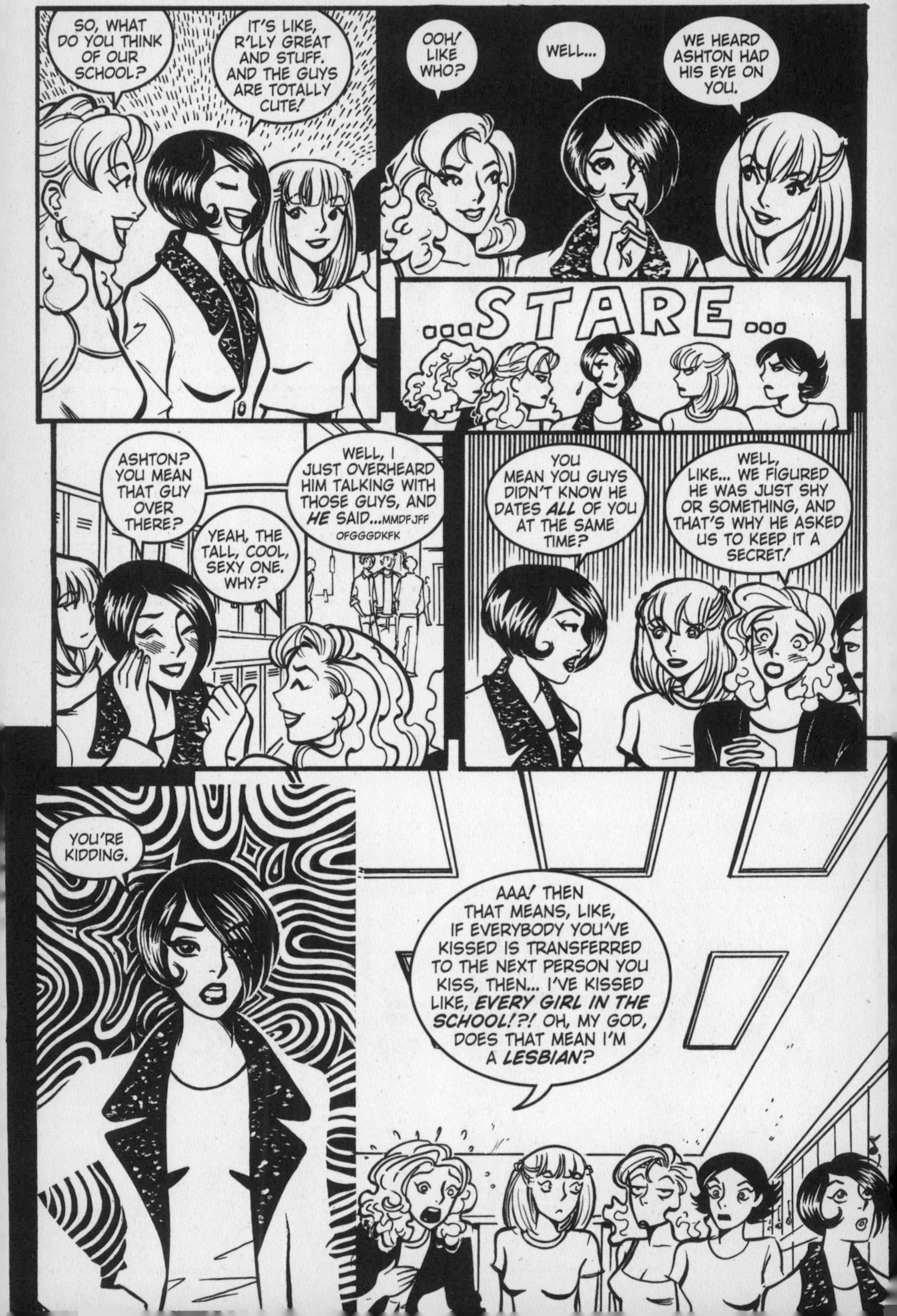
SO, WHAT DO YOU THINK OF OUR SCHOOL?
IT'S LIKE, R'LLY GREAT AND STUFF. AND THE GUYS ARE TOTALLY CUTE!
OOH! LIKE WHO?
WELL...
WE HEARD ASHTON HAD HIS EYE ON YOU.
...STARE...
ASHTON? YOU MEAN THAT GUY OVER THERE?
YEAH, THE TALL, COOL, SEXY ONE. WHY?
WELL, I JUST OVERHEARD HIM TALKING WITH THOSE GUYS, AND HE SAID...MMDFJFF OFGGGDKFK
YOU MEAN YOU GUYS DIDN'T KNOW HE DATES ALL OF YOU AT THE SAME TIME?
WELL, LIKE... WE FIGURED HE WAS JUST SHY OR SOMETHING, AND THAT'S WHY HE ASKED US TO KEEP IT A SECRET!
YOU'RE KIDDING.
AAA! THEN THAT MEANS, LIKE, IF EVERYBODY YOU'VE KISSED IS TRANSFERRED TO THE NEXT PERSON YOU KISS, THEN... I'VE KISSED LIKE, EVERY GIRL IN THE SCHOOL!?! OH, MY GOD, DOES THAT MEAN I'M A LESBIAN?

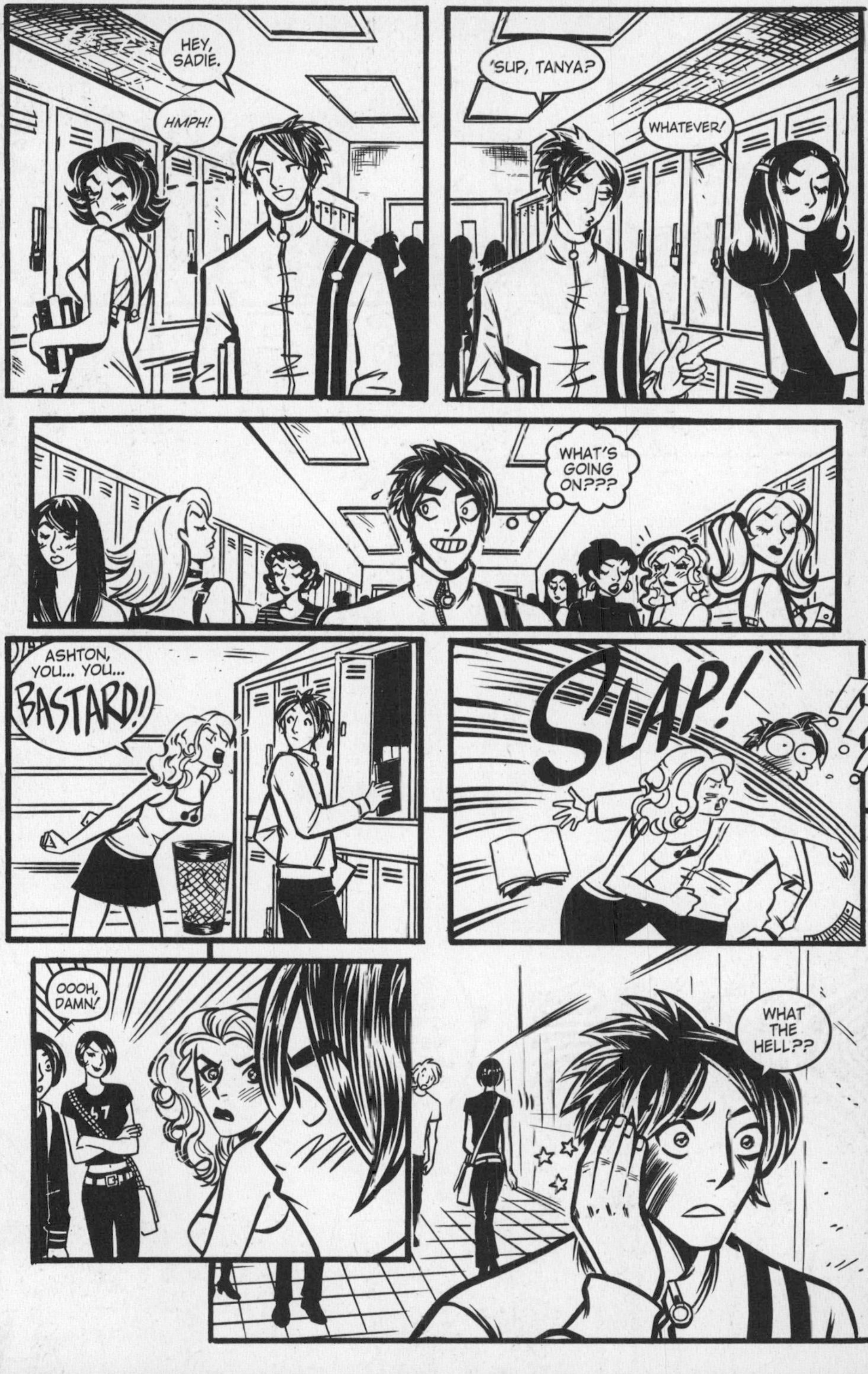
HEY, SADIE.
HMPH!
'SUP, TANYA?
WHATEVER!
WHAT'S GOING ON???
ASHTON, YOU... YOU... BASTARD!
SLAP!
OOOH, DAMN!
WHAT THE HELL??

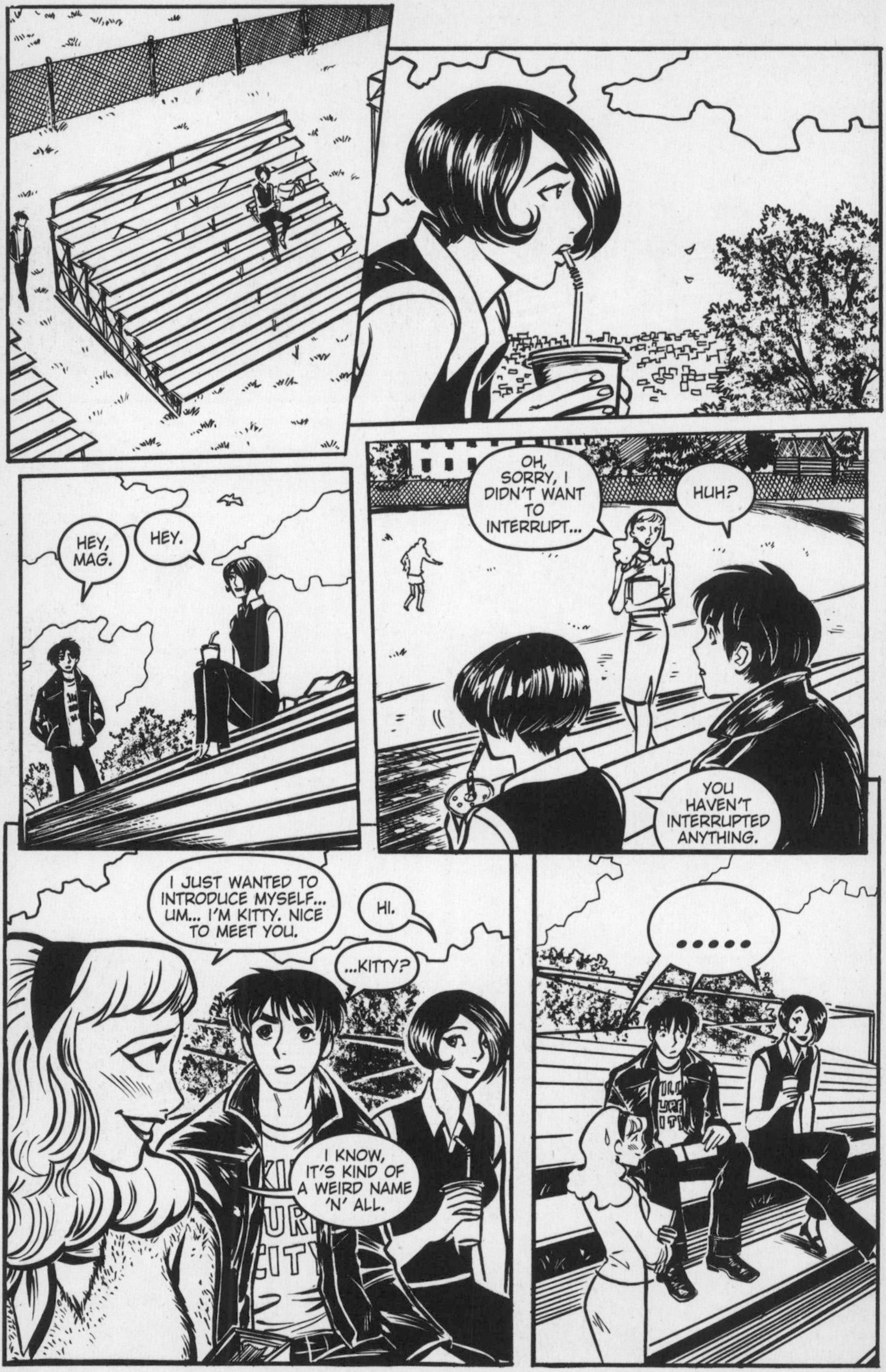
HEY, MAG.
HEY.
OH, SORRY, I DIDN'T WANT TO INTERRUPT...
HUH?
YOU HAVEN'T INTERRUPTED ANYTHING.
I JUST WANTED TO INTRODUCE MYSELF... UM... I'M KITTY. NICE TO MEET YOU.
HI.
...KITTY?
I KNOW, IT'S KIND OF A WEIRD NAME 'N' ALL.
.....

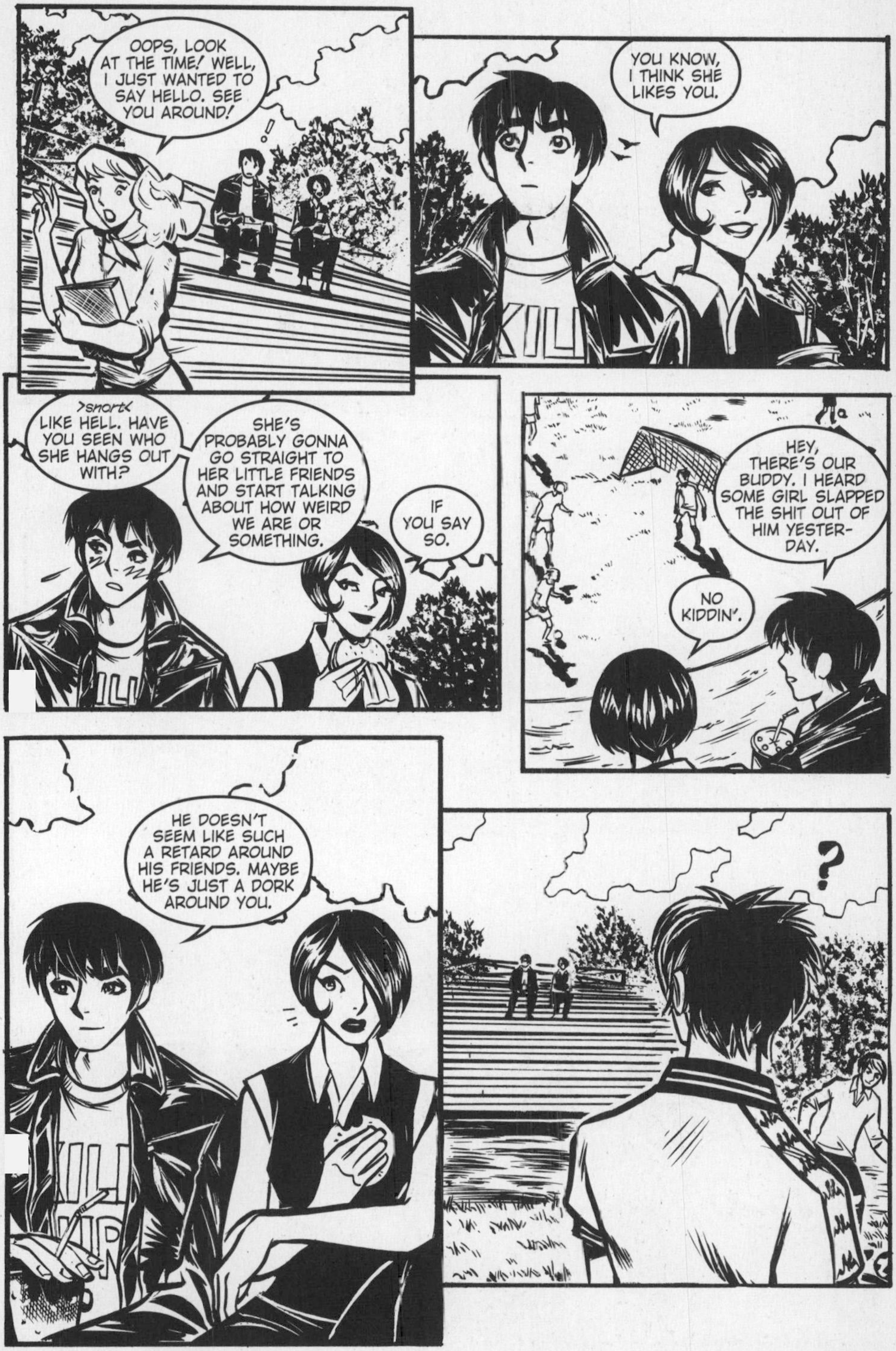
OOPS, LOOK AT THE TIME! WELL, I JUST WANTED TO SAY HELLO. SEE YOU AROUND!
!
YOU KNOW, I THINK SHE LIKES YOU.
>snort<
LIKE HELL. HAVE YOU SEEN WHO SHE HANGS OUT WITH?
SHE'S PROBABLY GONNA GO STRAIGHT TO HER LITTLE FRIENDS AND START TALKING ABOUT HOW WEIRD WE ARE OR SOMETHING.
IF YOU SAY SO.
HEY, THERE'S OUR BUDDY. I HEARD SOME GIRL SLAPPED THE SHIT OUT OF HIM YESTER-DAY.
NO KIDDIN'.
HE DOESN'T SEEM LIKE SUCH A RETARD AROUND HIS FRIENDS. MAYBE HE'S JUST A DORK AROUND YOU.
?

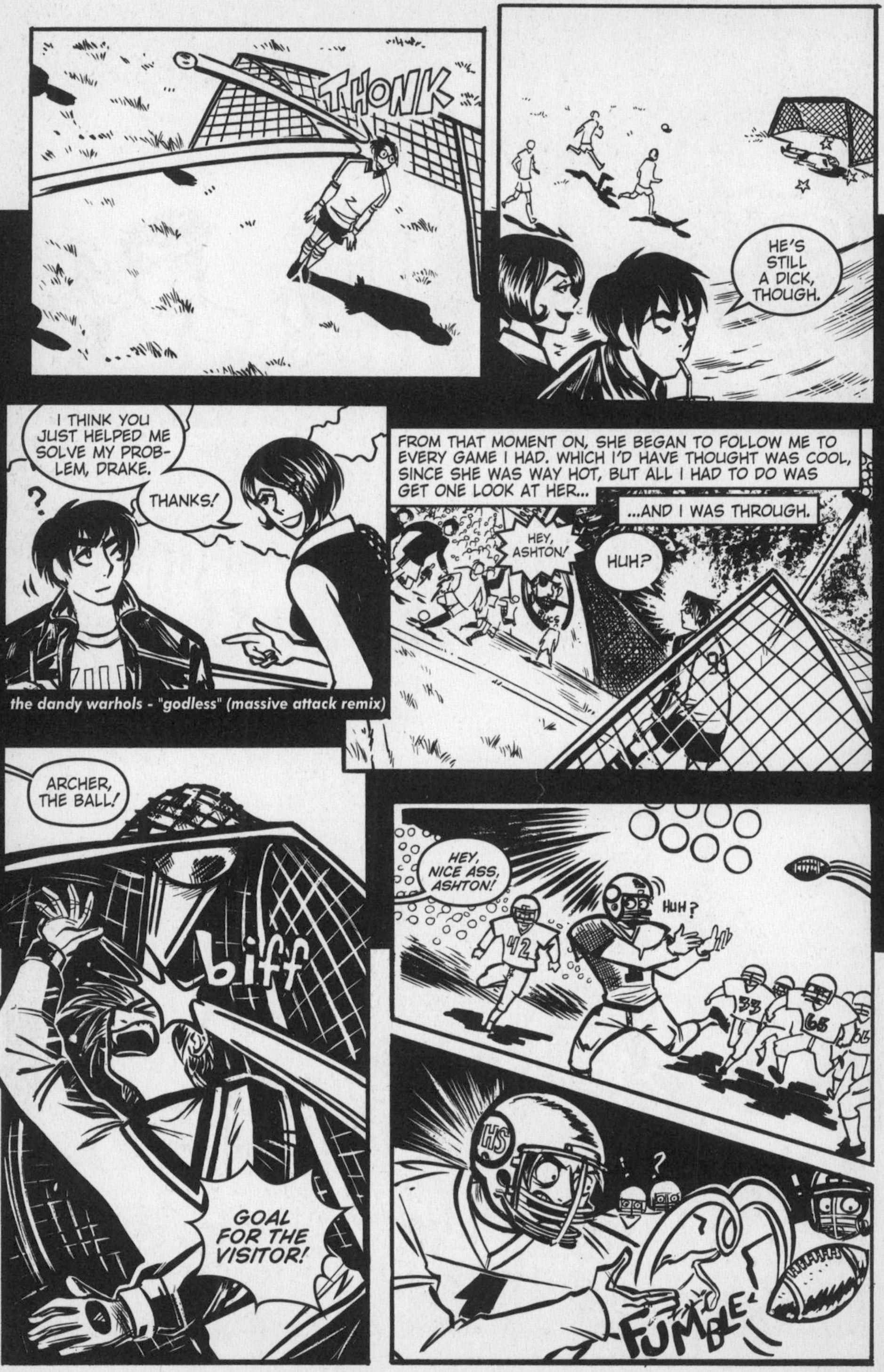
THONK
HE'S STILL A DICK, THOUGH.
I THINK YOU JUST HELPED ME SOLVE MY PROB-LEM, DRAKE.
?
THANKS!
the dandy warhols - "godless" (massive attack remix)
FROM THAT MOMENT ON, SHE BEGAN TO FOLLOW ME TO EVERY GAME I HAD. WHICH I'D HAVE THOUGHT WAS COOL, SINCE SHE WAS WAY HOT, BUT ALL I HAD TO DO WAS GET ONE LOOK AT HER...
...AND I WAS THROUGH.
HEY, ASHTON!
HUH?
ARCHER, THE BALL!
biff
GOAL FOR THE VISITOR!
HEY, NICE ASS, ASHTON!
HUH?
FUMBLE!

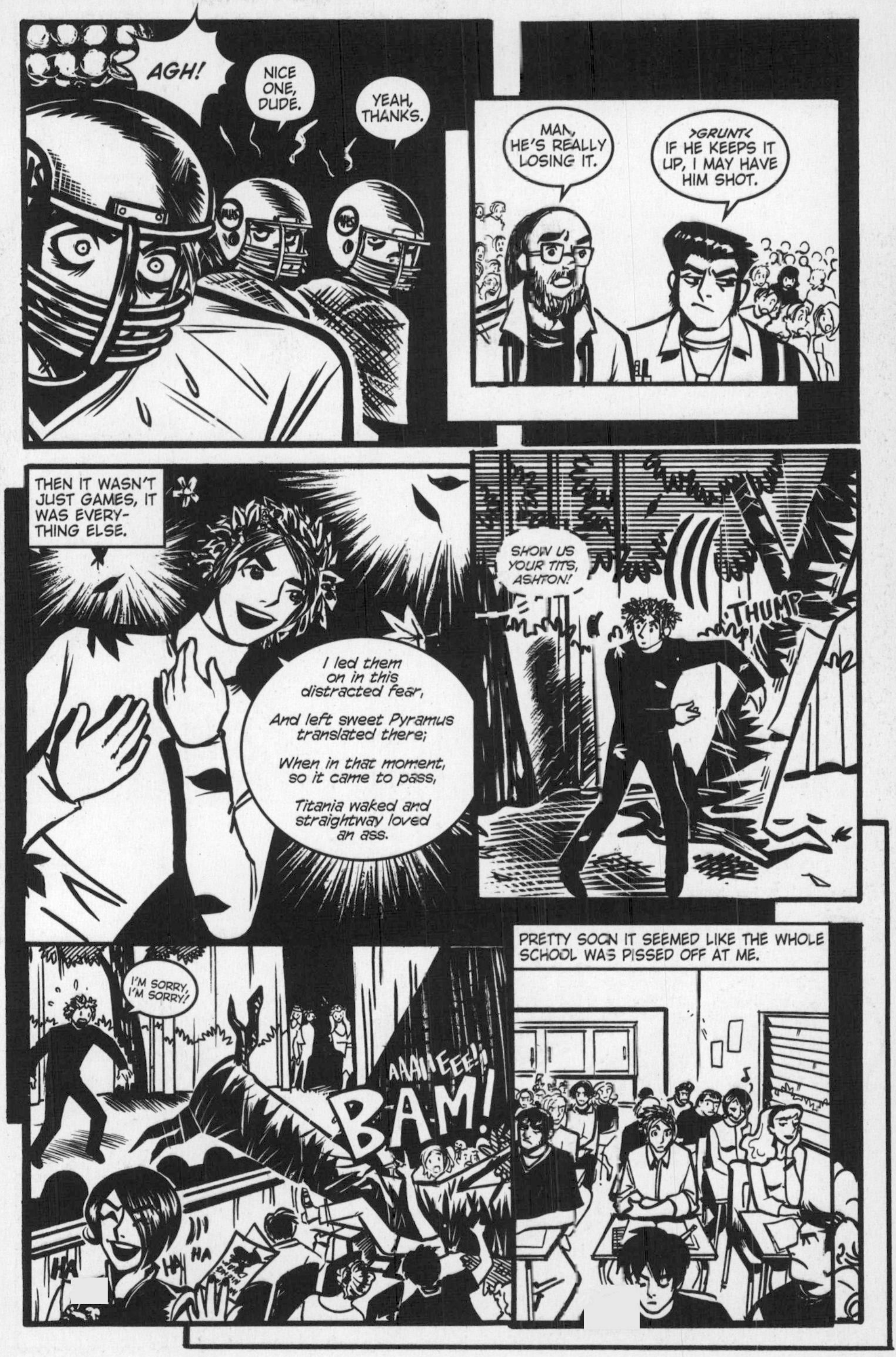
AGH!
NICE ONE, DUDE.
YEAH, THANKS.
MAN, HE'S REALLY LOSING IT.
>GRUNT< IF HE KEEPS IT UP, I MAY HAVE HIM SHOT.
THEN IT WASN'T JUST GAMES, IT WAS EVERY-THING ELSE.
I led them on in this distracted fear,
And left sweet Pyramus translated there;
When in that moment, so it came to pass,
Titania waked and straightway loved an ass.
SHOW US YOUR TITS, ASHTON!
THUMP
I'M SORRY, I'M SORRY!
BAM!
HA
HA
PRETTY SOON IT SEEMED LIKE THE WHOLE SCHOOL WAS PISSED OFF AT ME.

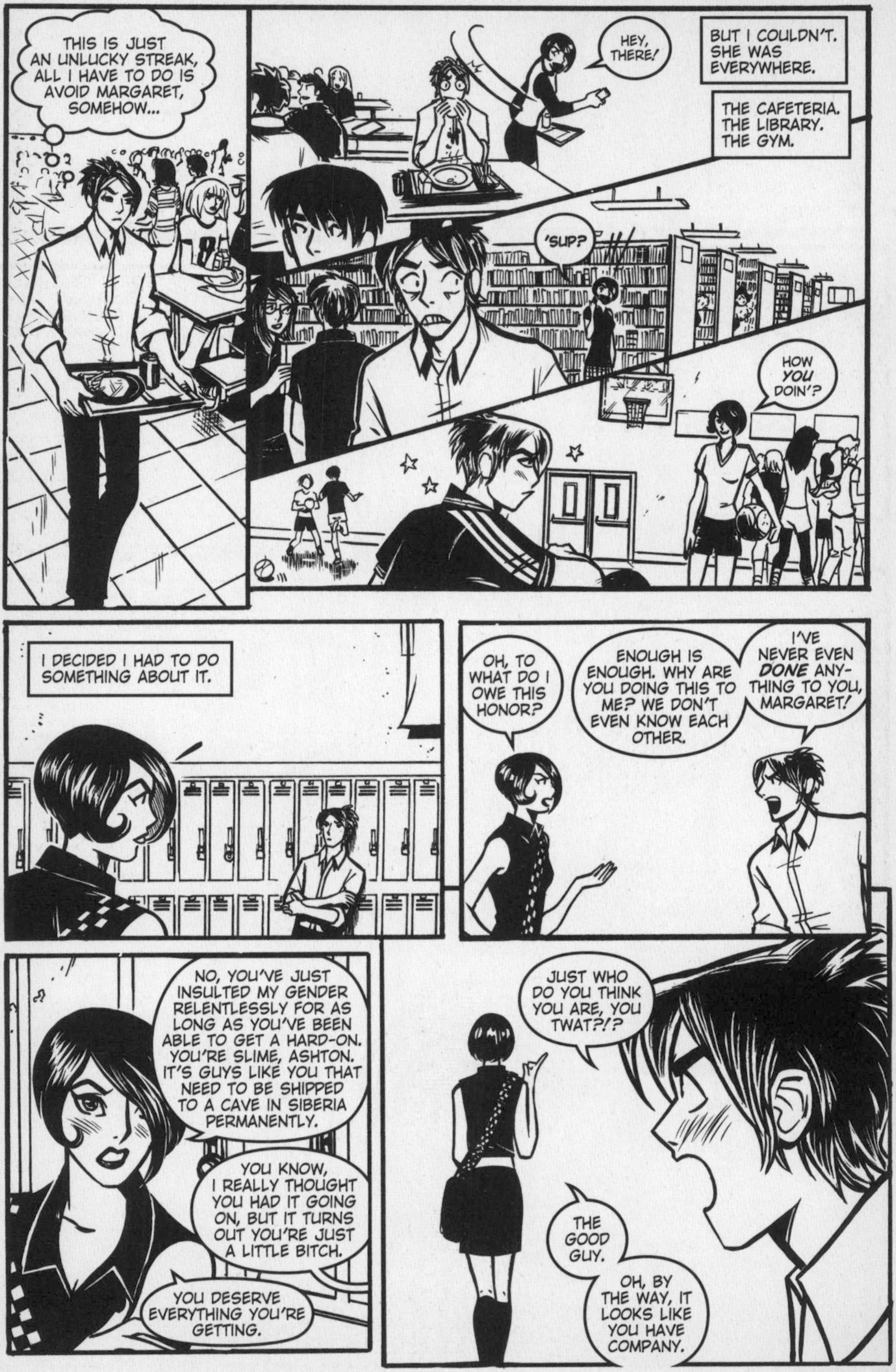
THIS IS JUST AN UNLUCKY STREAK, ALL I HAVE TO DO IS AVOID MARGARET, SOMEHOW...
BUT I COULDN'T. SHE WAS EVERYWHERE.
THE CAFETERIA. THE LIBRARY. THE GYM.
HEY, THERE!
'SUP?
HOW *YOU* DOIN'?
I DECIDED I HAD TO DO SOMETHING ABOUT IT.
OH, TO WHAT DO I OWE THIS HONOR?
ENOUGH IS ENOUGH. WHY ARE YOU DOING THIS TO ME? WE DON'T EVEN KNOW EACH OTHER.
I'VE NEVER EVEN *DONE* ANYTHING TO YOU, MARGARET!
NO, YOU'VE JUST INSULTED MY GENDER RELENTLESSLY FOR AS LONG AS YOU'VE BEEN ABLE TO GET A HARD-ON. YOU'RE SLIME, ASHTON. IT'S GUYS LIKE YOU THAT NEED TO BE SHIPPED TO A CAVE IN SIBERIA PERMANENTLY.
YOU KNOW, I REALLY THOUGHT YOU HAD IT GOING ON, BUT IT TURNS OUT YOU'RE JUST A LITTLE BITCH.
YOU DESERVE EVERYTHING YOU'RE GETTING.
JUST WHO DO YOU THINK YOU ARE, YOU TWAT?!?
THE GOOD GUY.
OH, BY THE WAY, IT LOOKS LIKE YOU HAVE COMPANY.

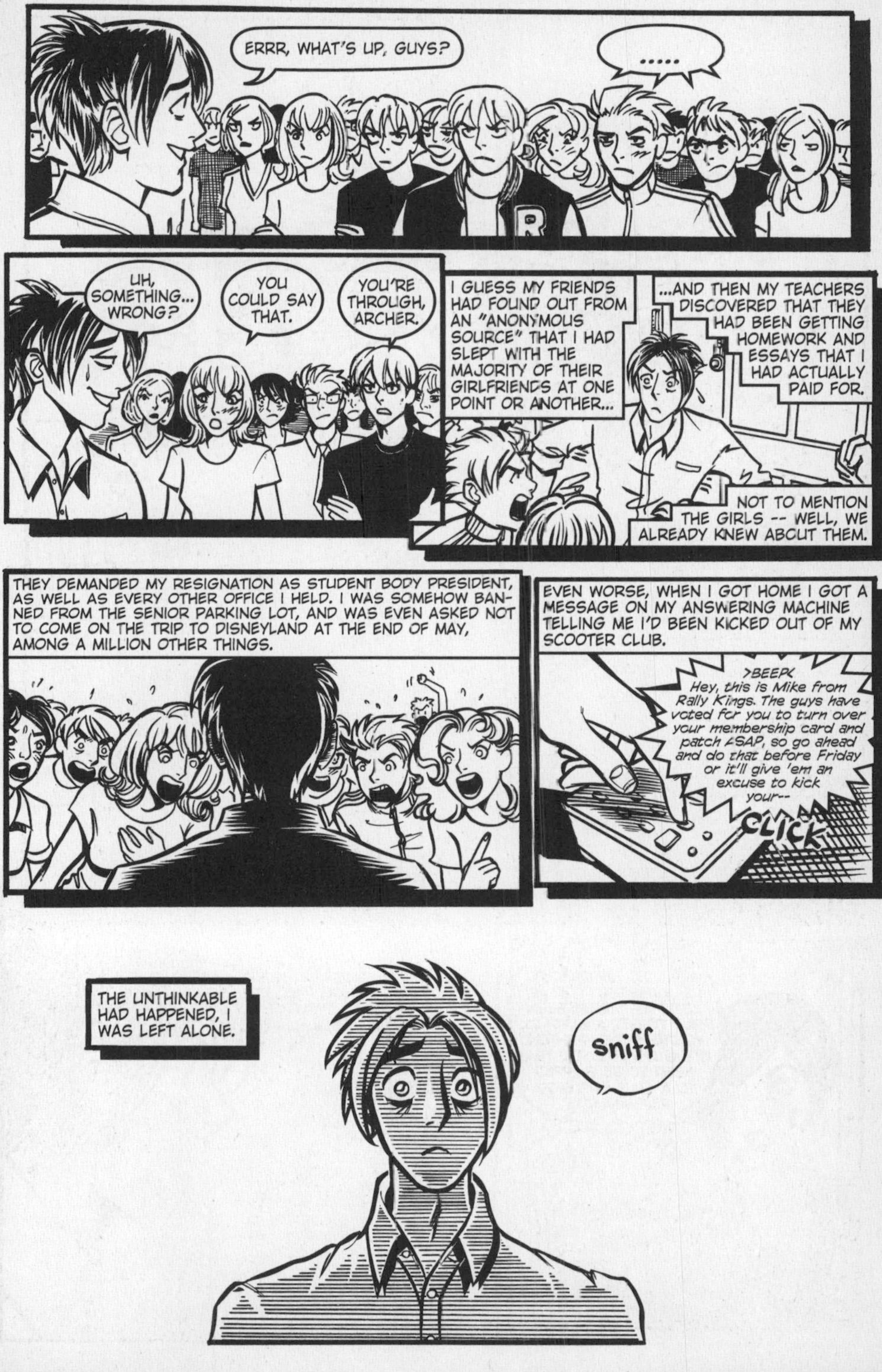
ERRR, WHAT'S UP, GUYS?
.....
UH, SOMETHING... WRONG?
YOU COULD SAY THAT.
YOU'RE THROUGH, ARCHER.
I GUESS MY FRIENDS HAD FOUND OUT FROM AN "ANONYMOUS SOURCE" THAT I HAD SLEPT WITH THE MAJORITY OF THEIR GIRLFRIENDS AT ONE POINT OR ANOTHER...
...AND THEN MY TEACHERS DISCOVERED THAT THEY HAD BEEN GETTING HOMEWORK AND ESSAYS THAT I HAD ACTUALLY PAID FOR.
NOT TO MENTION THE GIRLS -- WELL, WE ALREADY KNEW ABOUT THEM.
THEY DEMANDED MY RESIGNATION AS STUDENT BODY PRESIDENT, AS WELL AS EVERY OTHER OFFICE I HELD. I WAS SOMEHOW BANNED FROM THE SENIOR PARKING LOT, AND WAS EVEN ASKED NOT TO COME ON THE TRIP TO DISNEYLAND AT THE END OF MAY, AMONG A MILLION OTHER THINGS.
EVEN WORSE, WHEN I GOT HOME I GOT A MESSAGE ON MY ANSWERING MACHINE TELLING ME I'D BEEN KICKED OUT OF MY SCOOTER CLUB.
>BEEP< Hey, this is Mike from Rally Kings. The guys have voted for you to turn over your membership card and patch ASAP, so go ahead and do that before Friday or it'll give 'em an excuse to kick your--
CLICK
THE UNTHINKABLE HAD HAPPENED, I WAS LEFT ALONE.
sniff

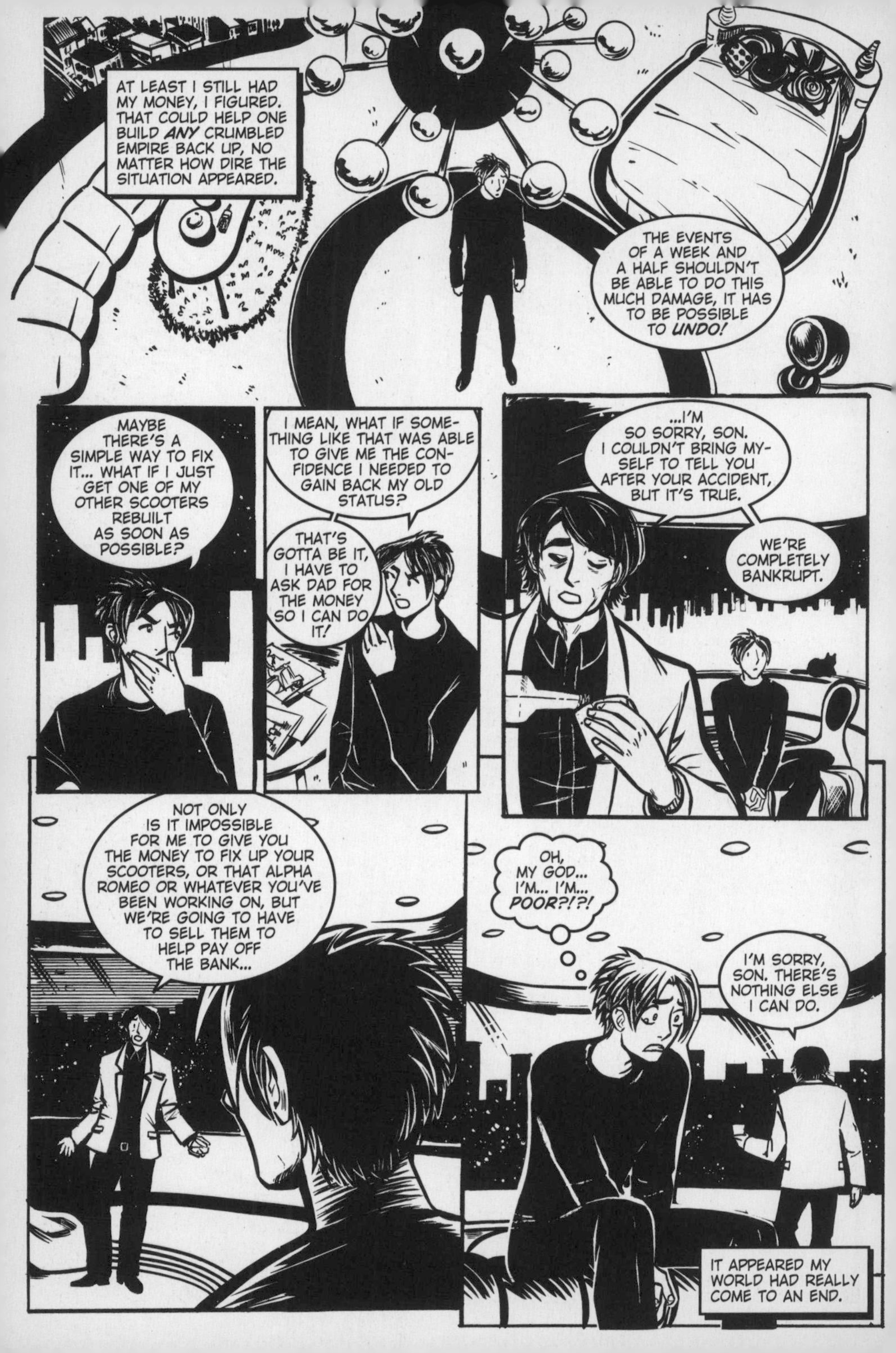
AT LEAST I STILL HAD MY MONEY, I FIGURED. THAT COULD HELP ONE BUILD ANY CRUMBLED EMPIRE BACK UP, NO MATTER HOW DIRE THE SITUATION APPEARED.
THE EVENTS OF A WEEK AND A HALF SHOULDN'T BE ABLE TO DO THIS MUCH DAMAGE, IT HAS TO BE POSSIBLE TO UNDO!
MAYBE THERE'S A SIMPLE WAY TO FIX IT... WHAT IF I JUST GET ONE OF MY OTHER SCOOTERS REBUILT AS SOON AS POSSIBLE?
I MEAN, WHAT IF SOMETHING LIKE THAT WAS ABLE TO GIVE ME THE CONFIDENCE I NEEDED TO GAIN BACK MY OLD STATUS?
THAT'S GOTTA BE IT, I HAVE TO ASK DAD FOR THE MONEY SO I CAN DO IT!
...I'M SO SORRY, SON. I COULDN'T BRING MYSELF TO TELL YOU AFTER YOUR ACCIDENT, BUT IT'S TRUE.
WE'RE COMPLETELY BANKRUPT.
NOT ONLY IS IT IMPOSSIBLE FOR ME TO GIVE YOU THE MONEY TO FIX UP YOUR SCOOTERS, OR THAT ALPHA ROMEO OR WHATEVER YOU'VE BEEN WORKING ON, BUT WE'RE GOING TO HAVE TO SELL THEM TO HELP PAY OFF THE BANK...
OH, MY GOD... I'M... I'M... POOR?!?!
I'M SORRY, SON. THERE'S NOTHING ELSE I CAN DO.
IT APPEARED MY WORLD HAD REALLY COME TO AN END.

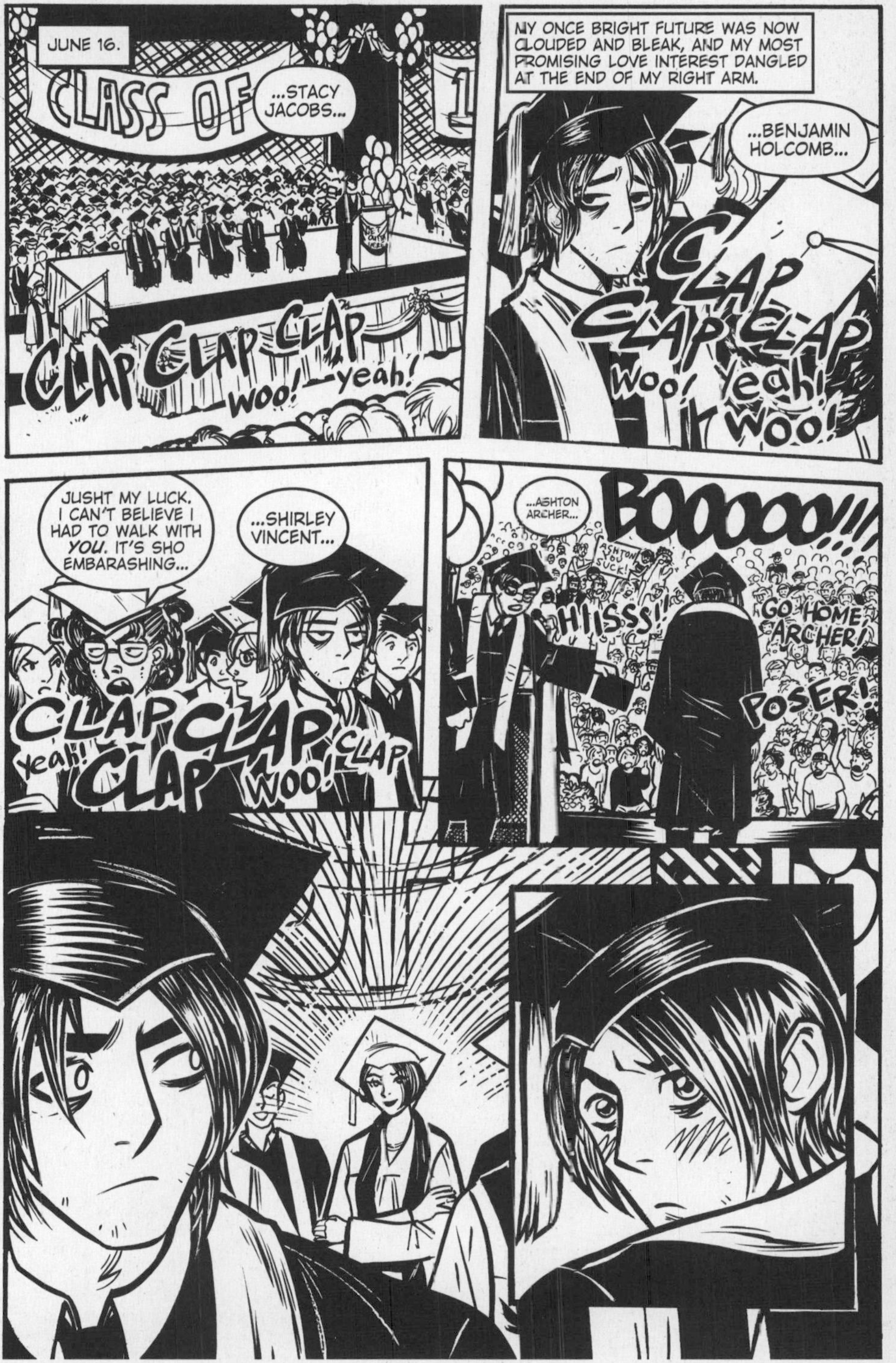

JUNE 16.
CLASS OF
...STACY JACOBS...
CLAP CLAP CLAP
WOO! yeah!
MY ONCE BRIGHT FUTURE WAS NOW CLOUDED AND BLEAK, AND MY MOST PROMISING LOVE INTEREST DANGLED AT THE END OF MY RIGHT ARM.
...BENJAMIN HOLCOMB...
CLAP CLAP CLAP
WOO! yeah! WOO!
JUSHT MY LUCK. I CAN'T BELIEVE I HAD TO WALK WITH *YOU*. IT'S SHO EMBARASHING...
...SHIRLEY VINCENT...
CLAP CLAP CLAP CLAP
yeah! WOO!
...ASHTON ARCHER...
BOOOOO!!!
ASHTON YOU SUCK!
HIISSS!
GO HOME ARCHER!
POSER!

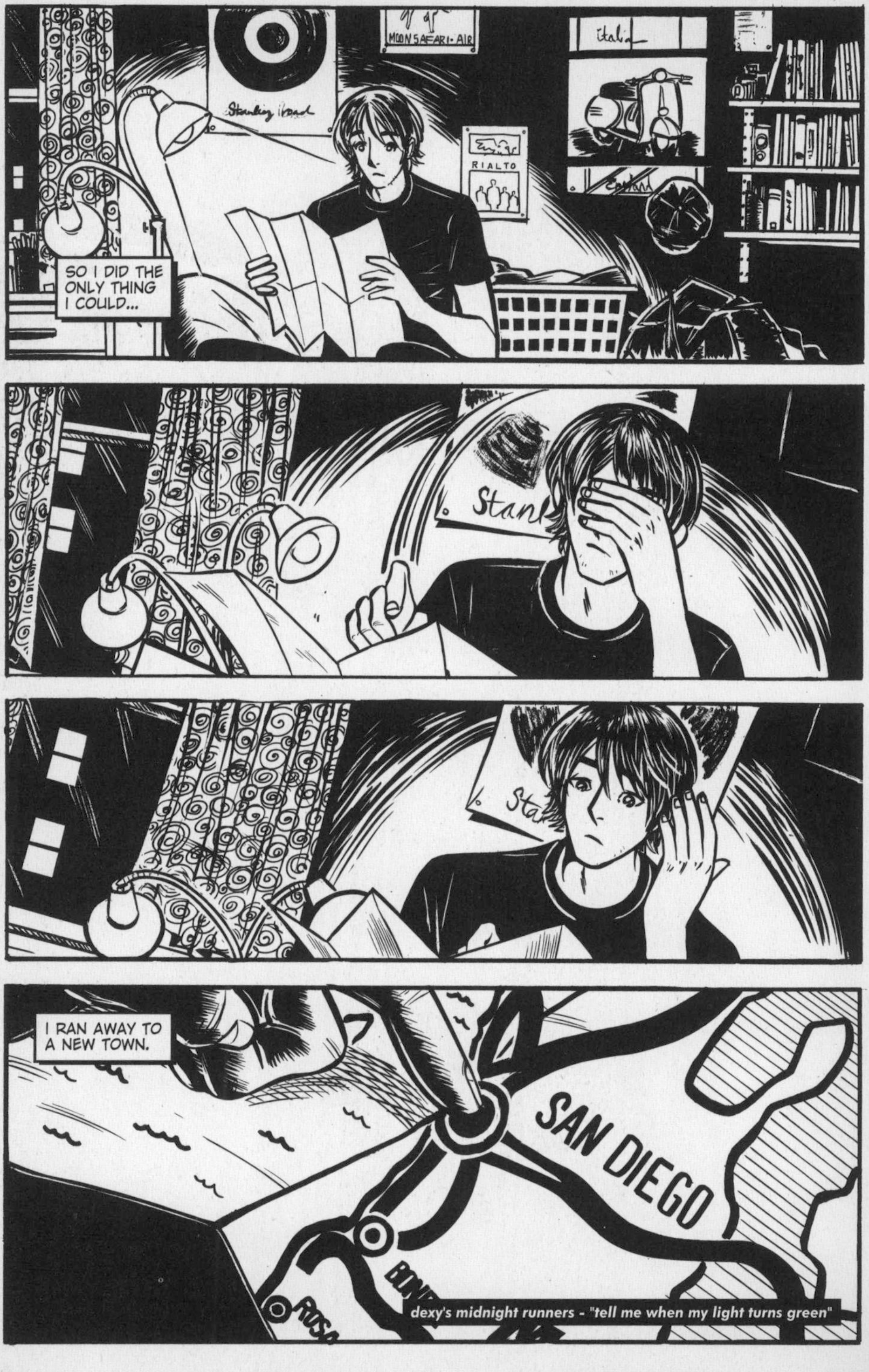
SO I DID THE ONLY THING I COULD...
MOON SAFARI · AIR
italia
RIALTO
I RAN AWAY TO A NEW TOWN.
SAN DIEGO
dexy's midnight runners - "tell me when my light turns green"

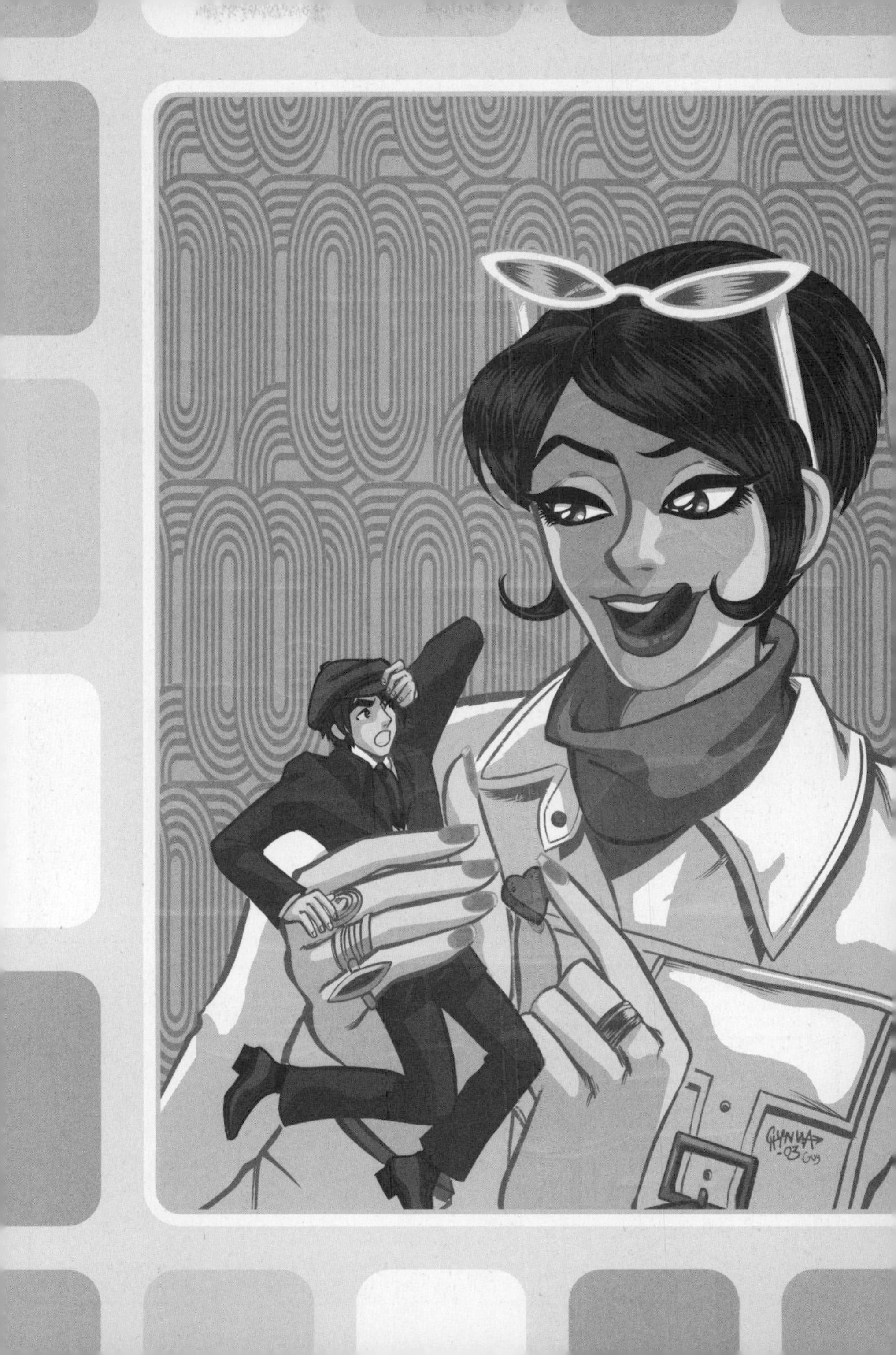

Chapter 2:
"The Bitterest Pill"

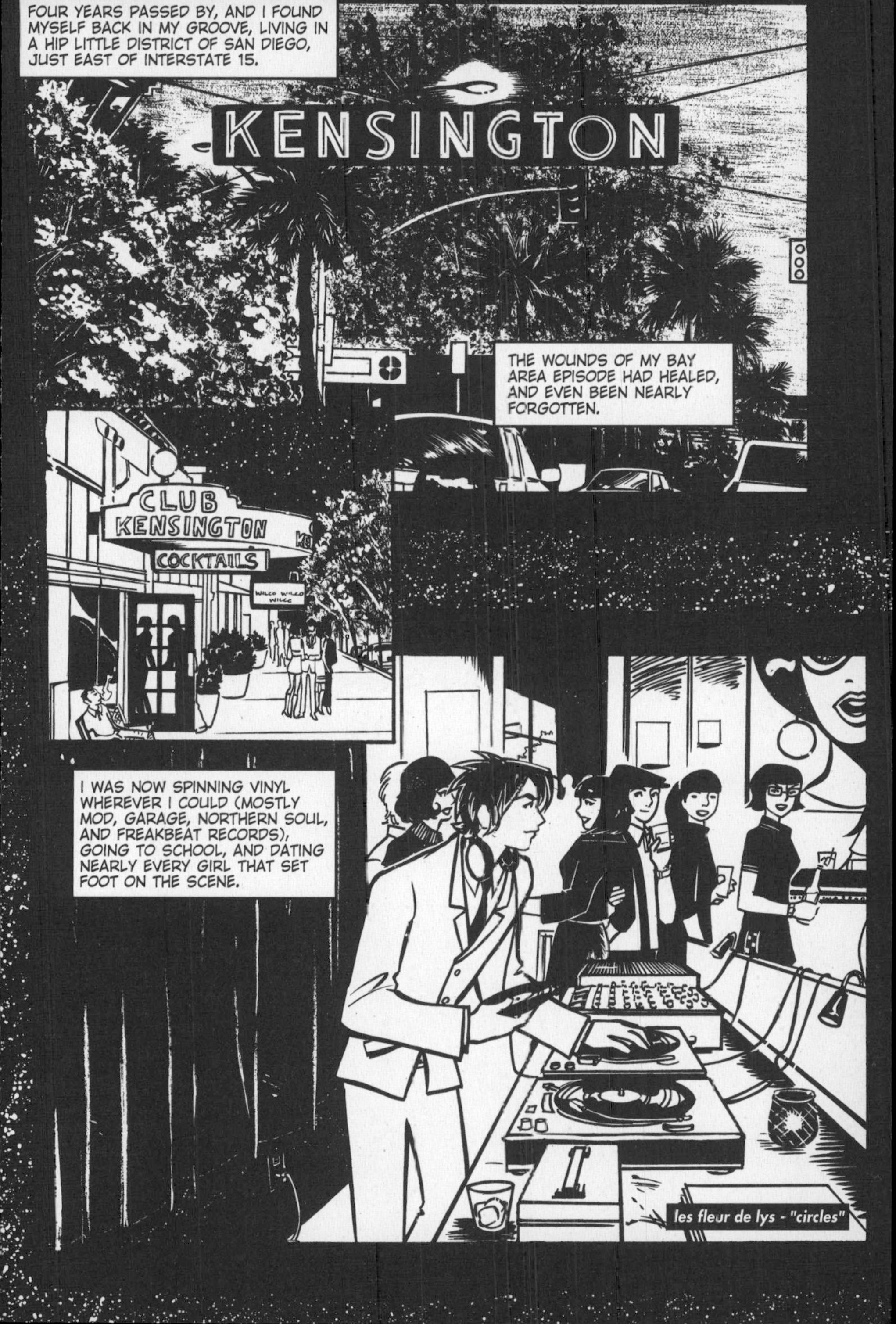
FOUR YEARS PASSED BY, AND I FOUND MYSELF BACK IN MY GROOVE, LIVING IN A HIP LITTLE DISTRICT OF SAN DIEGO, JUST EAST OF INTERSTATE 15.
KENSINGTON
THE WOUNDS OF MY BAY AREA EPISODE HAD HEALED, AND EVEN BEEN NEARLY FORGOTTEN.
CLUB KENSINGTON
COCKTAILS
WILCO WILCO WILCO
I WAS NOW SPINNING VINYL WHEREVER I COULD (MOSTLY MOD, GARAGE, NORTHERN SOUL, AND FREAKBEAT RECORDS), GOING TO SCHOOL, AND DATING NEARLY EVERY GIRL THAT SET FOOT ON THE SCENE.
les fleur de lys - "circles"

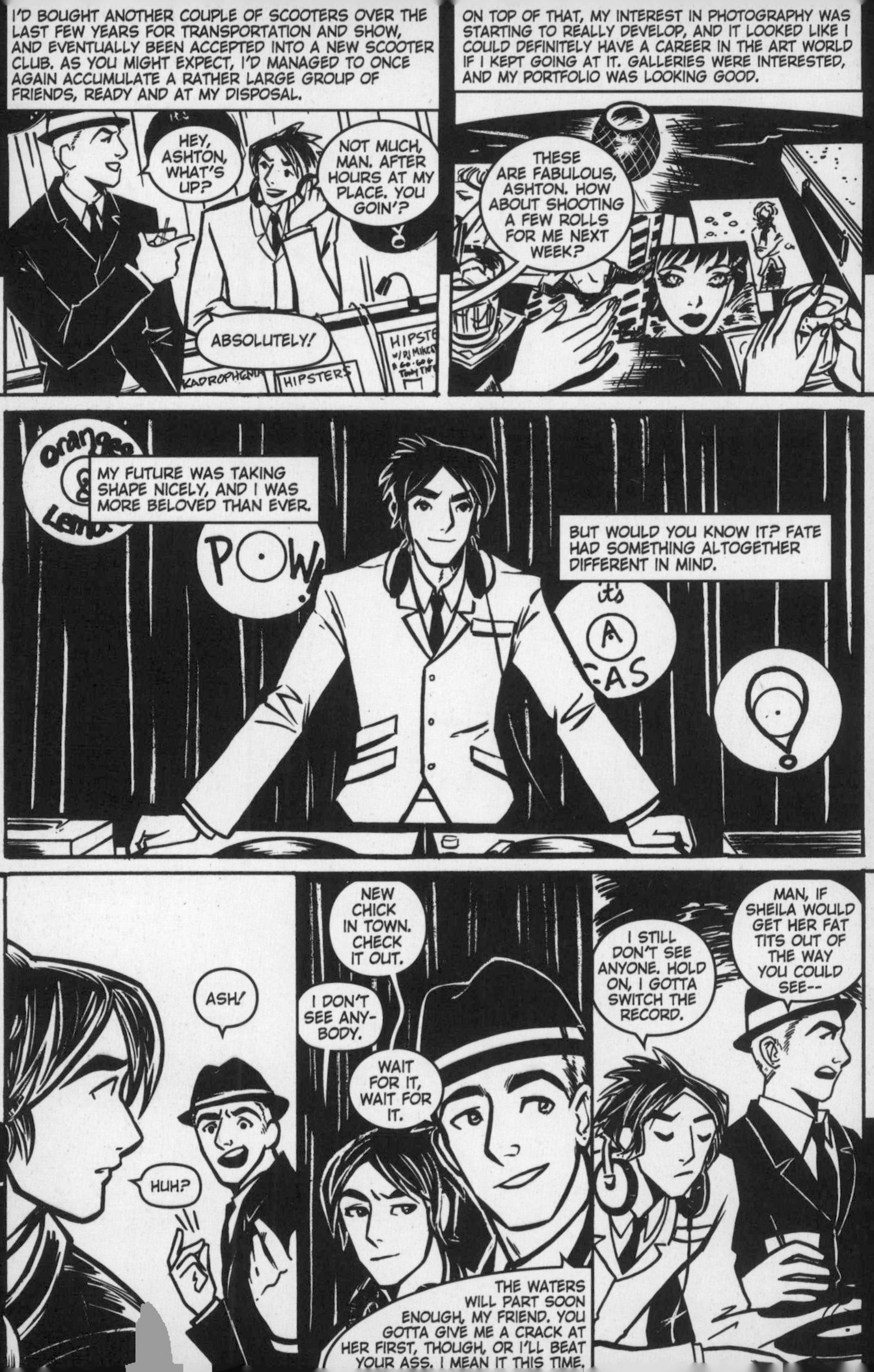

I'D BOUGHT ANOTHER COUPLE OF SCOOTERS OVER THE LAST FEW YEARS FOR TRANSPORTATION AND SHOW, AND EVENTUALLY BEEN ACCEPTED INTO A NEW SCOOTER CLUB. AS YOU MIGHT EXPECT, I'D MANAGED TO ONCE AGAIN ACCUMULATE A RATHER LARGE GROUP OF FRIENDS, READY AND AT MY DISPOSAL.
HEY, ASHTON, WHAT'S UP?
NOT MUCH, MAN. AFTER HOURS AT MY PLACE. YOU GOIN'?
ABSOLUTELY!
HIPSTERS
ON TOP OF THAT, MY INTEREST IN PHOTOGRAPHY WAS STARTING TO REALLY DEVELOP, AND IT LOOKED LIKE I COULD DEFINITELY HAVE A CAREER IN THE ART WORLD IF I KEPT GOING AT IT. GALLERIES WERE INTERESTED, AND MY PORTFOLIO WAS LOOKING GOOD.
THESE ARE FABULOUS, ASHTON. HOW ABOUT SHOOTING A FEW ROLLS FOR ME NEXT WEEK?
MY FUTURE WAS TAKING SHAPE NICELY, AND I WAS MORE BELOVED THAN EVER.
POW!
BUT WOULD YOU KNOW IT? FATE HAD SOMETHING ALTOGETHER DIFFERENT IN MIND.
ASH!
HUH?
NEW CHICK IN TOWN. CHECK IT OUT.
I DON'T SEE ANY-BODY.
WAIT FOR IT, WAIT FOR IT.
I STILL DON'T SEE ANYONE. HOLD ON, I GOTTA SWITCH THE RECORD.
MAN, IF SHEILA WOULD GET HER FAT TITS OUT OF THE WAY YOU COULD SEE--
THE WATERS WILL PART SOON ENOUGH, MY FRIEND. YOU GOTTA GIVE ME A CRACK AT HER FIRST, THOUGH, OR I'LL BEAT YOUR ASS. I MEAN IT THIS TIME.

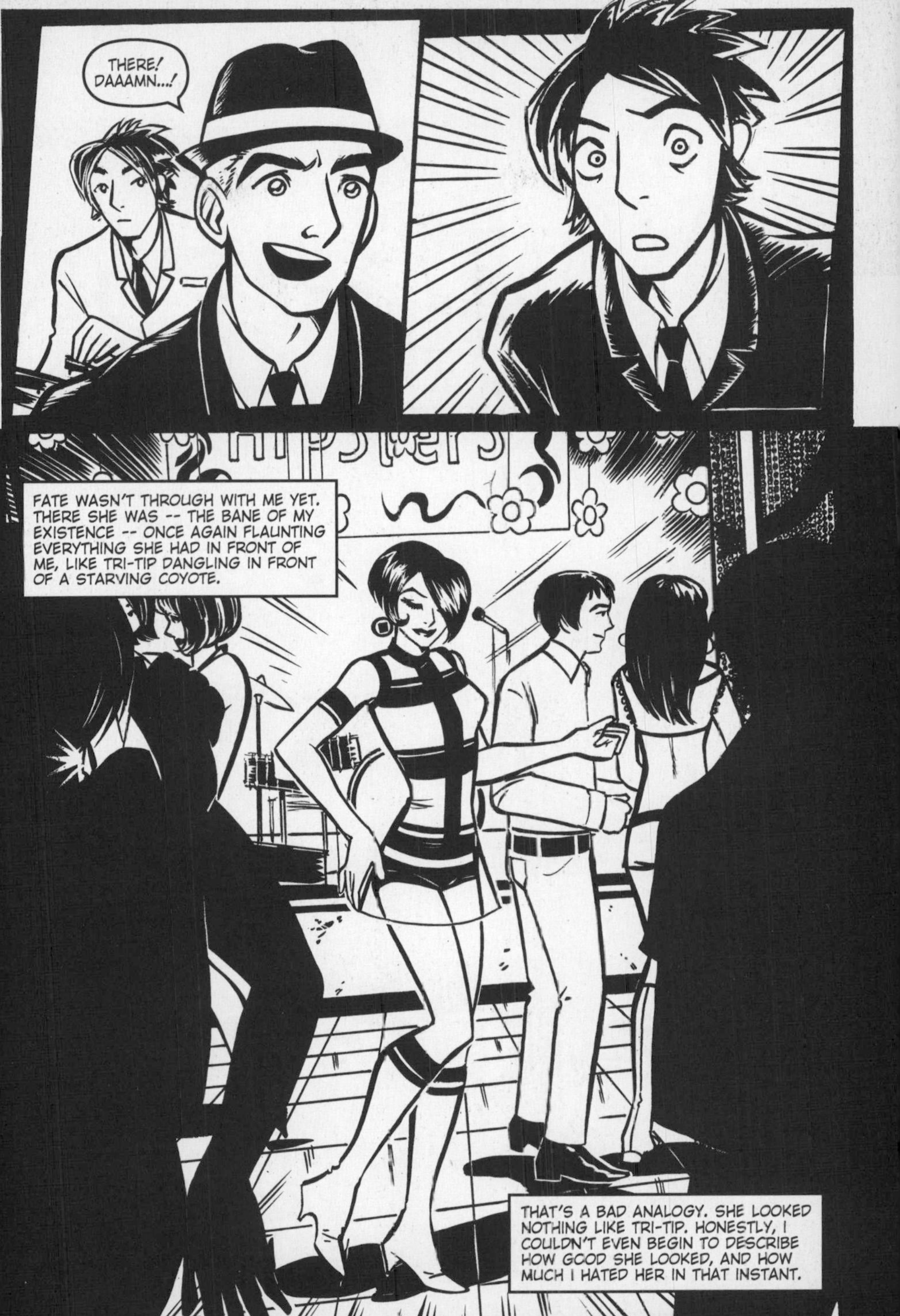
THERE! DAAAMN...!
FATE WASN'T THROUGH WITH ME YET. THERE SHE WAS -- THE BANE OF MY EXISTENCE -- ONCE AGAIN FLAUNTING EVERYTHING SHE HAD IN FRONT OF ME, LIKE TRI-TIP DANGLING IN FRONT OF A STARVING COYOTE.
THAT'S A BAD ANALOGY. SHE LOOKED NOTHING LIKE TRI-TIP. HONESTLY, I COULDN'T EVEN BEGIN TO DESCRIBE HOW GOOD SHE LOOKED, AND HOW MUCH I HATED HER IN THAT INSTANT.

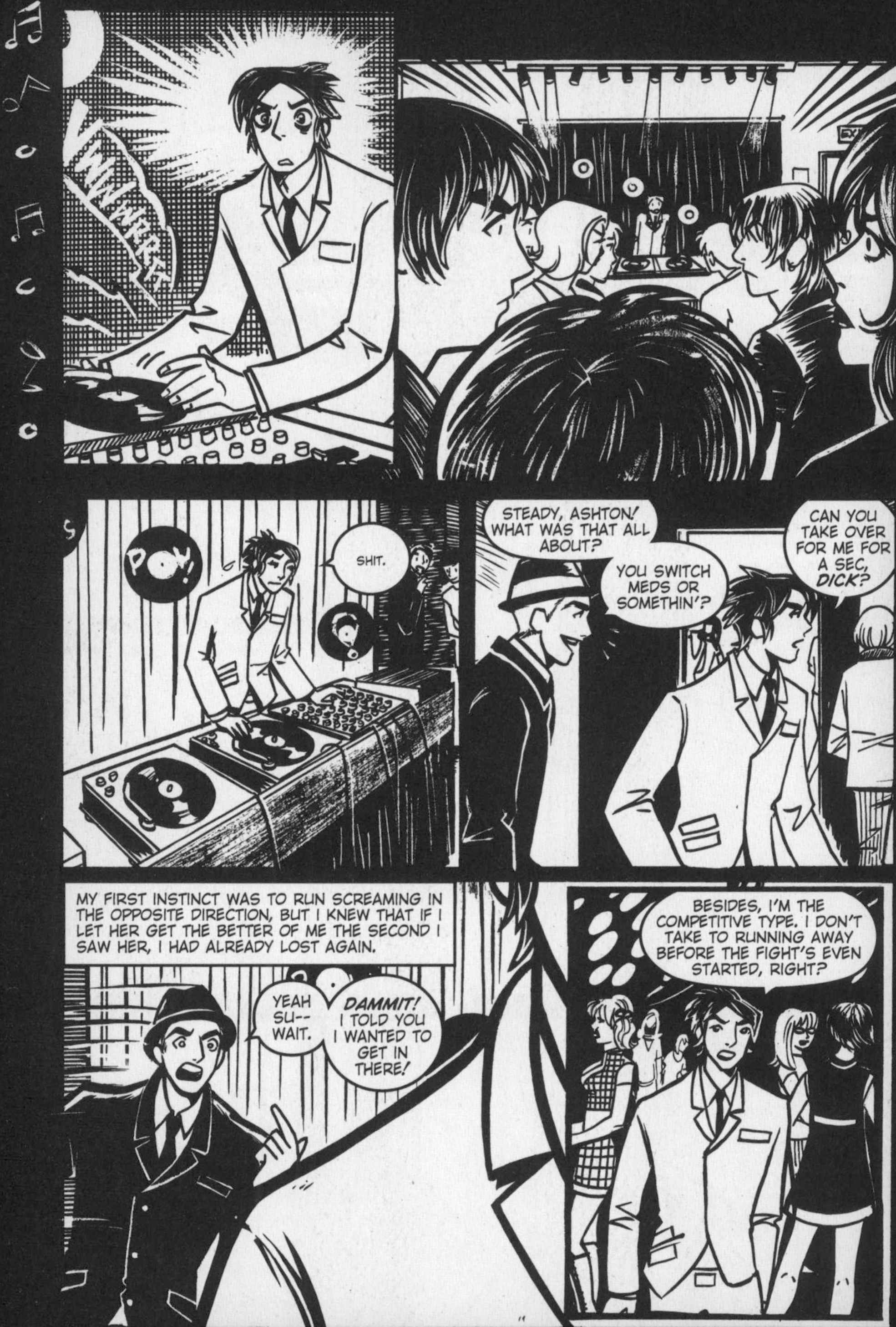
WWWRRRK
POW!
SHIT.
STEADY, ASHTON! WHAT WAS THAT ALL ABOUT?
YOU SWITCH MEDS OR SOMETHIN'?
CAN YOU TAKE OVER FOR ME FOR A SEC, DICK?
MY FIRST INSTINCT WAS TO RUN SCREAMING IN THE OPPOSITE DIRECTION, BUT I KNEW THAT IF I LET HER GET THE BETTER OF ME THE SECOND I SAW HER, I HAD ALREADY LOST AGAIN.
YEAH SU-- WAIT.
DAMMIT! I TOLD YOU I WANTED TO GET IN THERE!
BESIDES, I'M THE COMPETITIVE TYPE. I DON'T TAKE TO RUNNING AWAY BEFORE THE FIGHT'S EVEN STARTED, RIGHT?

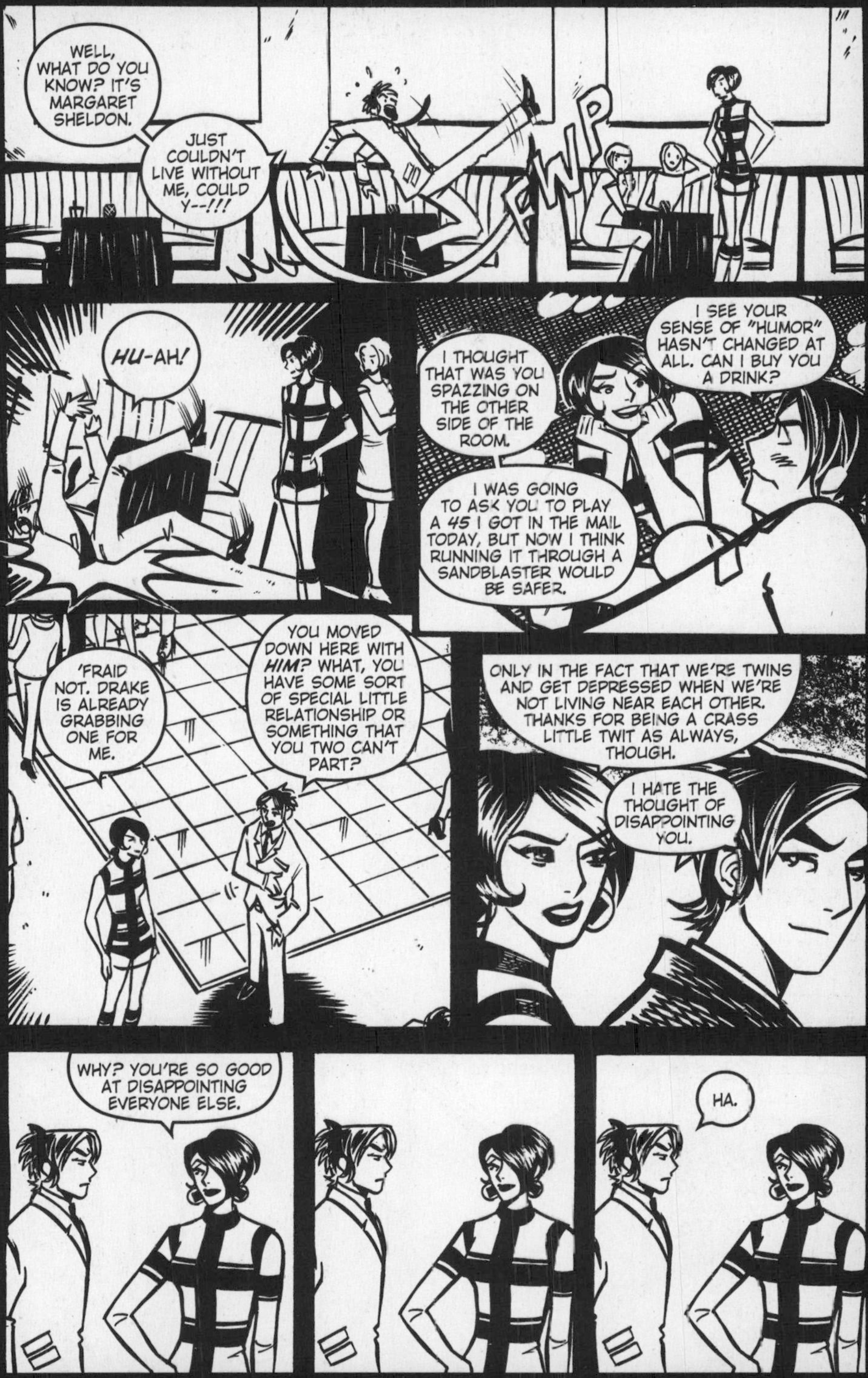
WELL, WHAT DO YOU KNOW? IT'S MARGARET SHELDON.
JUST COULDN'T LIVE WITHOUT ME, COULD Y--!!!
FWP
HU-AH!
I SEE YOUR SENSE OF "HUMOR" HASN'T CHANGED AT ALL. CAN I BUY YOU A DRINK?
I THOUGHT THAT WAS YOU SPAZZING ON THE OTHER SIDE OF THE ROOM.
I WAS GOING TO ASK YOU TO PLAY A 45 I GOT IN THE MAIL TODAY, BUT NOW I THINK RUNNING IT THROUGH A SANDBLASTER WOULD BE SAFER.
'FRAID NOT. DRAKE IS ALREADY GRABBING ONE FOR ME.
YOU MOVED DOWN HERE WITH HIM? WHAT, YOU HAVE SOME SORT OF SPECIAL LITTLE RELATIONSHIP OR SOMETHING THAT YOU TWO CAN'T PART?
ONLY IN THE FACT THAT WE'RE TWINS AND GET DEPRESSED WHEN WE'RE NOT LIVING NEAR EACH OTHER. THANKS FOR BEING A CRASS LITTLE TWIT AS ALWAYS, THOUGH.
I HATE THE THOUGHT OF DISAPPOINTING YOU.
WHY? YOU'RE SO GOOD AT DISAPPOINTING EVERYONE ELSE.
HA.

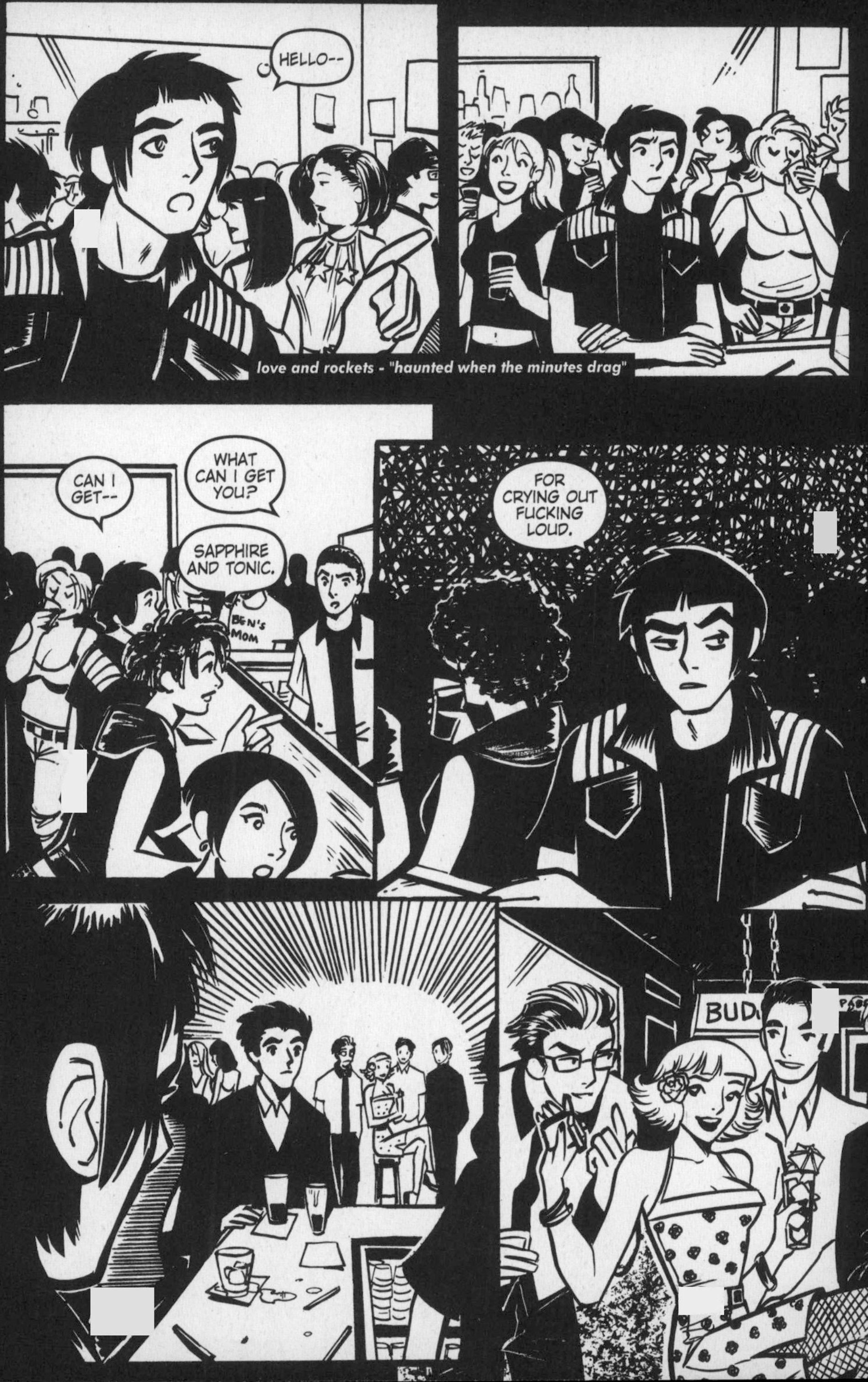
HELLO--
love and rockets - "haunted when the minutes drag"
CAN I GET--
WHAT CAN I GET YOU?
SAPPHIRE AND TONIC.
BEN'S MOM
FOR CRYING OUT FUCKING LOUD.
BUD

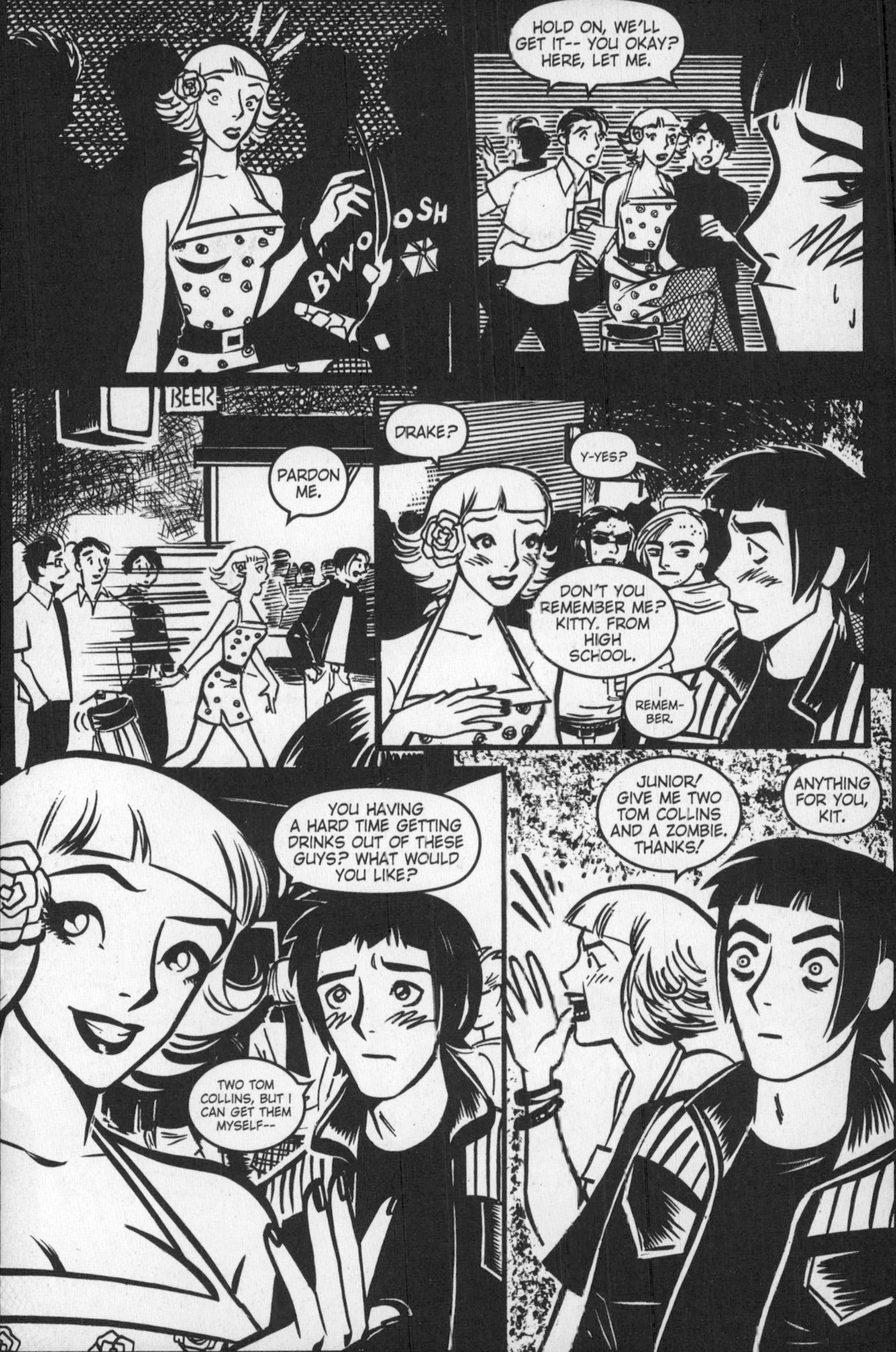
BWOOSH
HOLD ON, WE'LL GET IT-- YOU OKAY? HERE, LET ME.
BEER
PARDON ME.
DRAKE?
Y-YES?
DON'T YOU REMEMBER ME? KITTY. FROM HIGH SCHOOL.
I REMEMBER.
YOU HAVING A HARD TIME GETTING DRINKS OUT OF THESE GUYS? WHAT WOULD YOU LIKE?
TWO TOM COLLINS, BUT I CAN GET THEM MYSELF--
JUNIOR! GIVE ME TWO TOM COLLINS AND A ZOMBIE. THANKS!
ANYTHING FOR YOU, KIT.

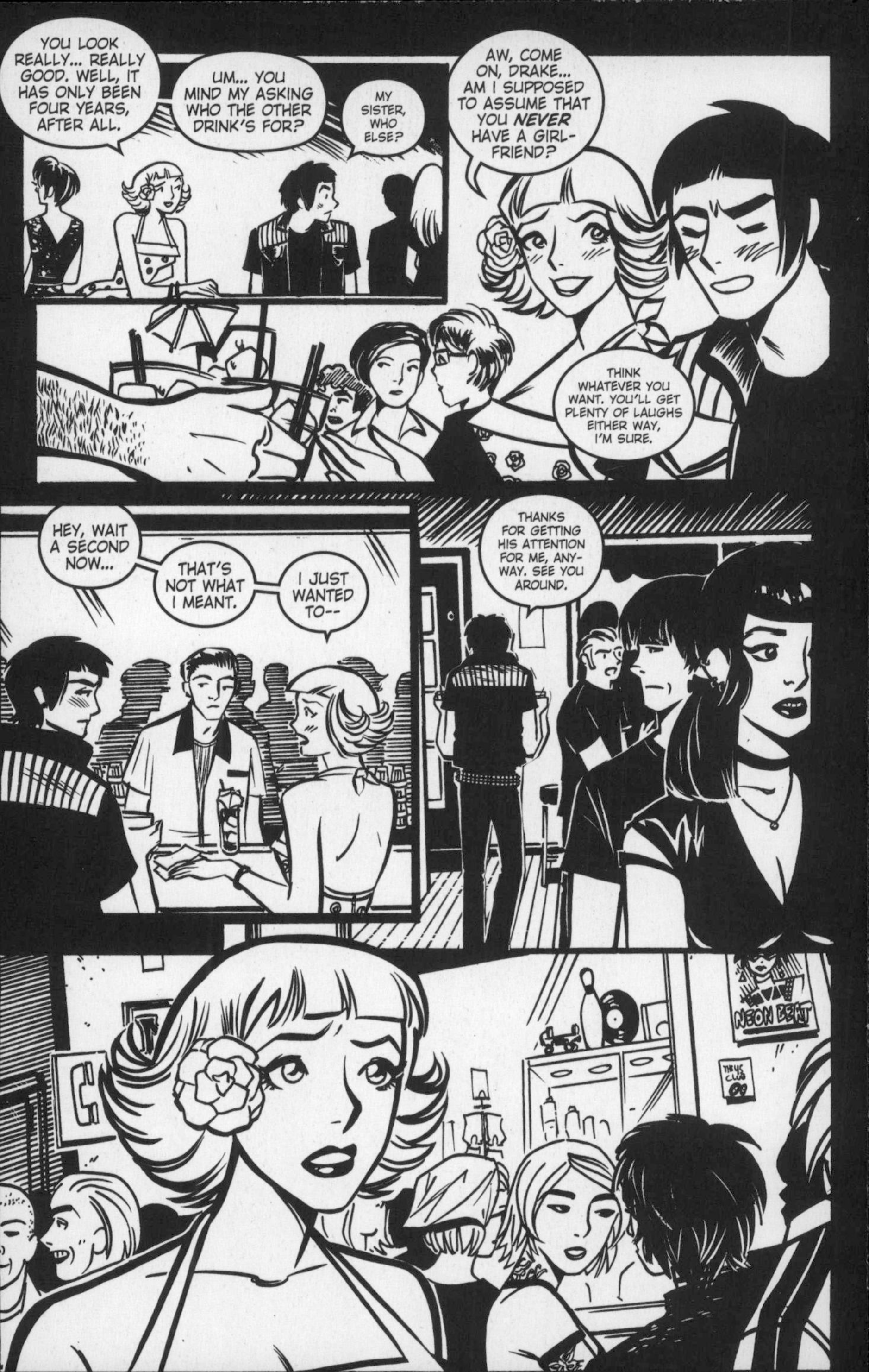
YOU LOOK REALLY... REALLY GOOD. WELL, IT HAS ONLY BEEN FOUR YEARS, AFTER ALL.
UM... YOU MIND MY ASKING WHO THE OTHER DRINK'S FOR?
MY SISTER, WHO ELSE?
AW, COME ON, DRAKE... AM I SUPPOSED TO ASSUME THAT YOU NEVER HAVE A GIRL-FRIEND?
THINK WHATEVER YOU WANT. YOU'LL GET PLENTY OF LAUGHS EITHER WAY, I'M SURE.
HEY, WAIT A SECOND NOW...
THAT'S NOT WHAT I MEANT.
I JUST WANTED TO--
THANKS FOR GETTING HIS ATTENTION FOR ME, ANYWAY. SEE YOU AROUND.
NEON BEAT

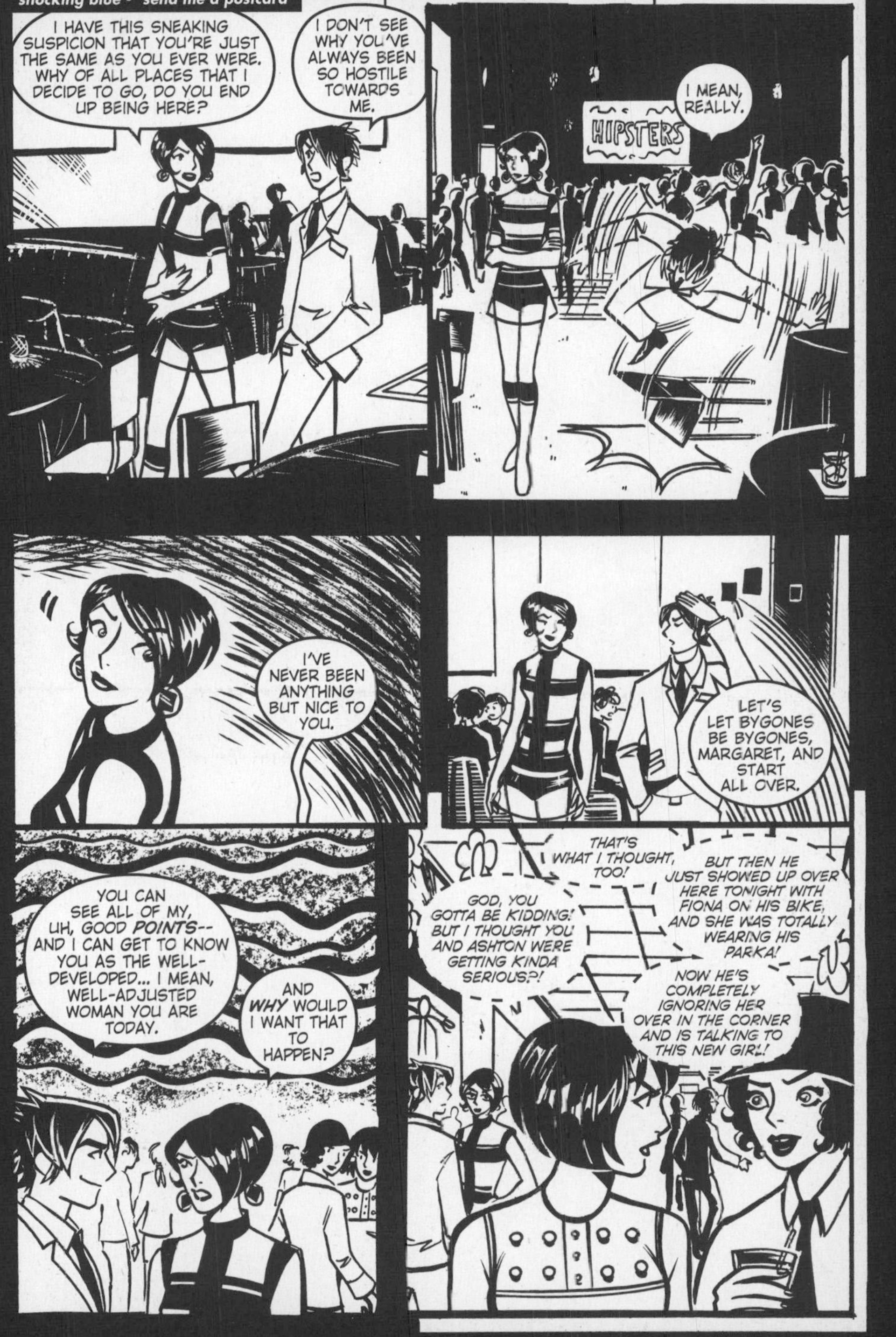
I HAVE THIS SNEAKING SUSPICION THAT YOU'RE JUST THE SAME AS YOU EVER WERE. WHY OF ALL PLACES THAT I DECIDE TO GO, DO YOU END UP BEING HERE?
I DON'T SEE WHY YOU'VE ALWAYS BEEN SO HOSTILE TOWARDS ME.
I MEAN, REALLY.
HIPSTERS
I'VE NEVER BEEN ANYTHING BUT NICE TO YOU.
LET'S LET BYGONES BE BYGONES, MARGARET, AND START ALL OVER.
YOU CAN SEE ALL OF MY, UH, GOOD *POINTS*-- AND I CAN GET TO KNOW YOU AS THE WELL-DEVELOPED... I MEAN, WELL-ADJUSTED WOMAN YOU ARE TODAY.
AND *WHY* WOULD I WANT THAT TO HAPPEN?
GOD, YOU GOTTA BE KIDDING! BUT I THOUGHT YOU AND ASHTON WERE GETTING KINDA SERIOUS?!
THAT'S WHAT I THOUGHT, TOO!
BUT THEN HE JUST SHOWED UP OVER HERE TONIGHT WITH FIONA ON HIS BIKE, AND SHE WAS TOTALLY WEARING HIS PARKA!
NOW HE'S COMPLETELY IGNORING HER OVER IN THE CORNER AND IS TALKING TO THIS NEW GIRL!

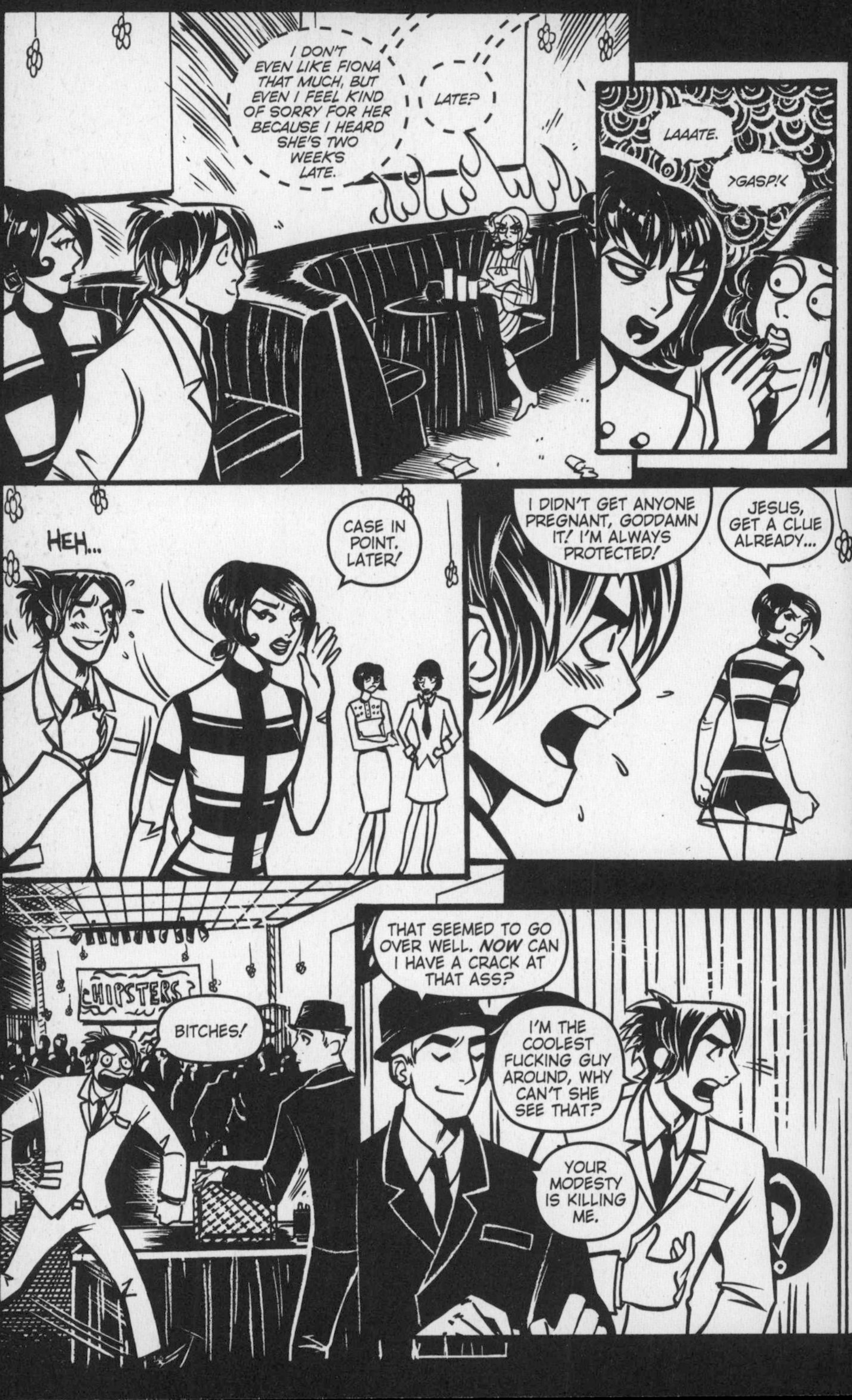
I DON'T EVEN LIKE FIONA THAT MUCH, BUT EVEN I FEEL KIND OF SORRY FOR HER BECAUSE I HEARD SHE'S TWO WEEKS LATE.
LATE?
LAAATE.
>GASP!<
HEH...
CASE IN POINT. LATER!
I DIDN'T GET ANYONE PREGNANT, GODDAMN IT! I'M ALWAYS PROTECTED!
JESUS, GET A CLUE ALREADY...
CHIPSTERS
BITCHES!
THAT SEEMED TO GO OVER WELL. NOW CAN I HAVE A CRACK AT THAT ASS?
I'M THE COOLEST FUCKING GUY AROUND, WHY CAN'T SHE SEE THAT?
YOUR MODESTY IS KILLING ME.

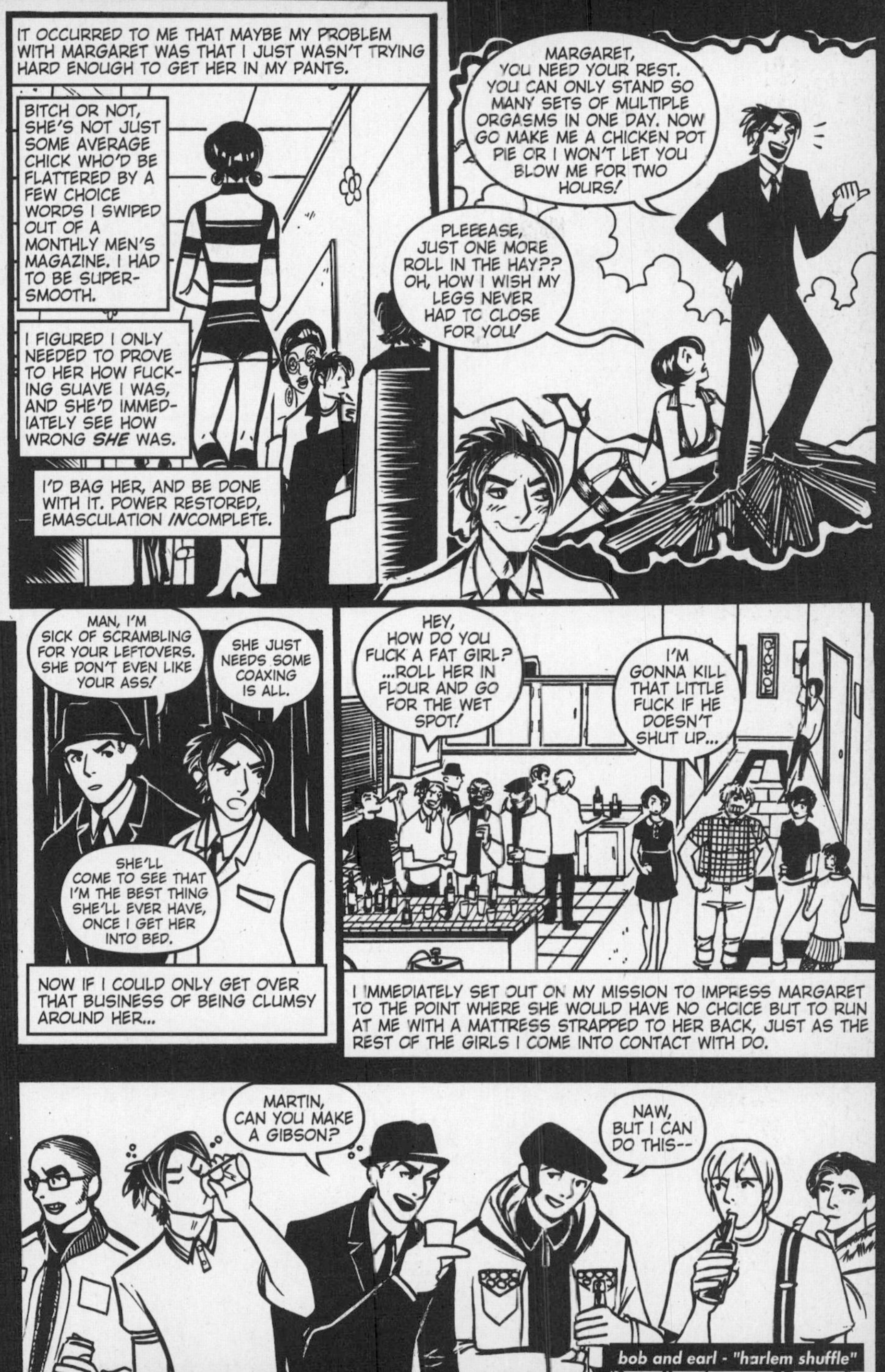
IT OCCURRED TO ME THAT MAYBE MY PROBLEM WITH MARGARET WAS THAT I JUST WASN'T TRYING HARD ENOUGH TO GET HER IN MY PANTS.
BITCH OR NOT, SHE'S NOT JUST SOME AVERAGE CHICK WHO'D BE FLATTERED BY A FEW CHOICE WORDS I SWIPED OUT OF A MONTHLY MEN'S MAGAZINE. I HAD TO BE SUPER-SMOOTH.
I FIGURED I ONLY NEEDED TO PROVE TO HER HOW FUCKING SUAVE I WAS, AND SHE'D IMMEDIATELY SEE HOW WRONG *SHE* WAS.
I'D BAG HER, AND BE DONE WITH IT. POWER RESTORED, EMASCULATION *IN*COMPLETE.
MARGARET, YOU NEED YOUR REST. YOU CAN ONLY STAND SO MANY SETS OF MULTIPLE ORGASMS IN ONE DAY. NOW GO MAKE ME A CHICKEN POT PIE OR I WON'T LET YOU BLOW ME FOR TWO HOURS!
PLEEEASE, JUST ONE MORE ROLL IN THE HAY?? OH, HOW I WISH MY LEGS NEVER HAD TO CLOSE FOR YOU!
MAN, I'M SICK OF SCRAMBLING FOR YOUR LEFTOVERS. SHE DON'T EVEN LIKE YOUR ASS!
SHE JUST NEEDS SOME COAXING IS ALL.
SHE'LL COME TO SEE THAT I'M THE BEST THING SHE'LL EVER HAVE, ONCE I GET HER INTO BED.
NOW IF I COULD ONLY GET OVER THAT BUSINESS OF BEING CLUMSY AROUND HER...
HEY, HOW DO YOU FUCK A FAT GIRL? ...ROLL HER IN FLOUR AND GO FOR THE WET SPOT!
I'M GONNA KILL THAT LITTLE FUCK IF HE DOESN'T SHUT UP...
I IMMEDIATELY SET OUT ON MY MISSION TO IMPRESS MARGARET TO THE POINT WHERE SHE WOULD HAVE NO CHOICE BUT TO RUN AT ME WITH A MATTRESS STRAPPED TO HER BACK, JUST AS THE REST OF THE GIRLS I COME INTO CONTACT WITH DO.
MARTIN, CAN YOU MAKE A GIBSON?
NAW, BUT I CAN DO THIS--
bob and earl - "harlem shuffle"

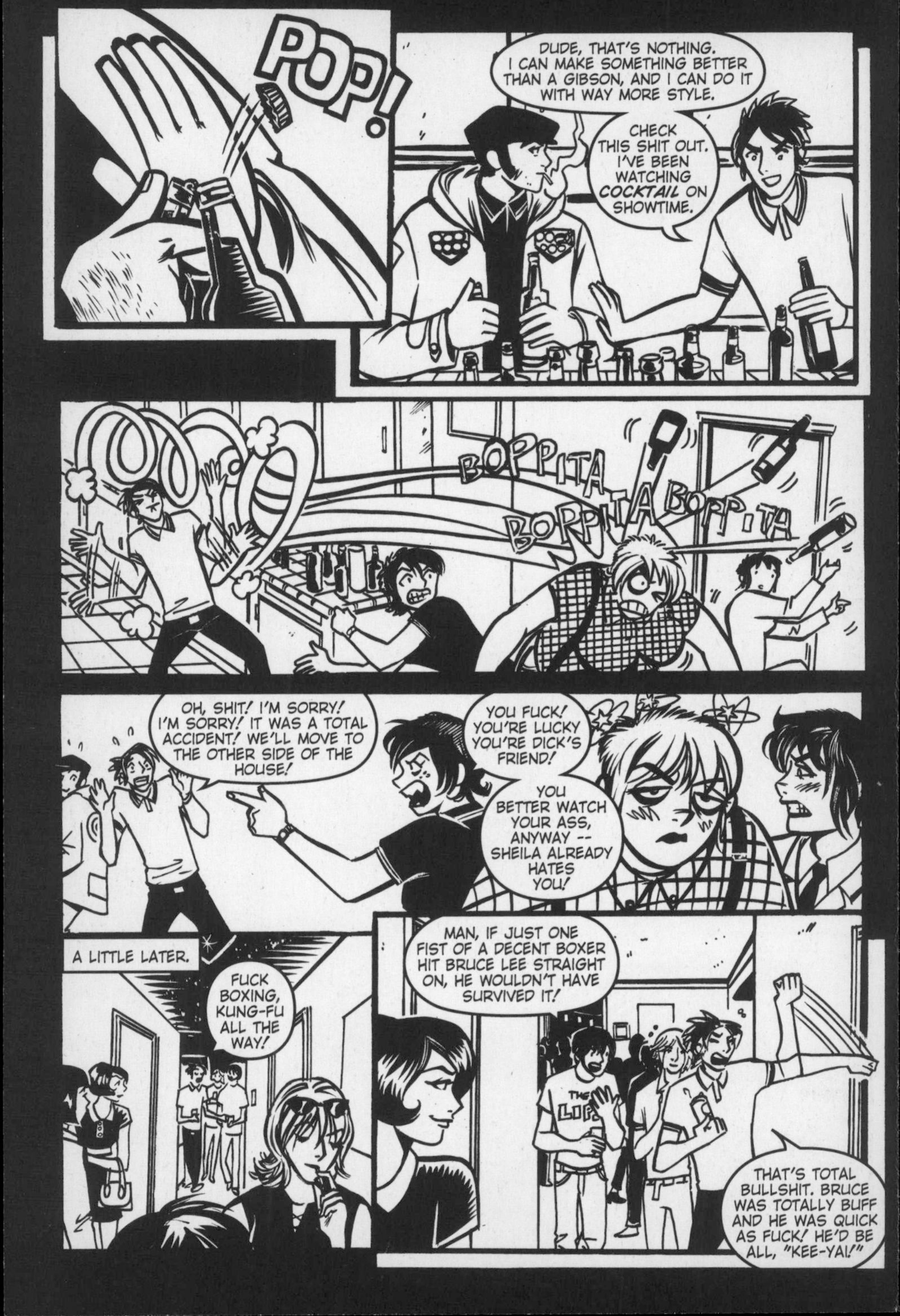
POP!
DUDE, THAT'S NOTHING. I CAN MAKE SOMETHING BETTER THAN A GIBSON, AND I CAN DO IT WITH WAY MORE STYLE.
CHECK THIS SHIT OUT. I'VE BEEN WATCHING *COCKTAIL* ON SHOWTIME.
BOPPITA
BOPPITA BOPPITA
BOPPITA
OH, SHIT! I'M SORRY! I'M SORRY! IT WAS A TOTAL ACCIDENT! WE'LL MOVE TO THE OTHER SIDE OF THE HOUSE!
YOU FUCK! YOU'RE LUCKY YOU'RE DICK'S FRIEND!
YOU BETTER WATCH YOUR ASS, ANYWAY -- SHEILA ALREADY HATES YOU!
A LITTLE LATER.
FUCK BOXING, KUNG-FU ALL THE WAY!
MAN, IF JUST ONE FIST OF A DECENT BOXER HIT BRUCE LEE STRAIGHT ON, HE WOULDN'T HAVE SURVIVED IT!
THAT'S TOTAL BULLSHIT. BRUCE WAS TOTALLY BUFF AND HE WAS QUICK AS FUCK! HE'D BE ALL, "KEE-YAI!"

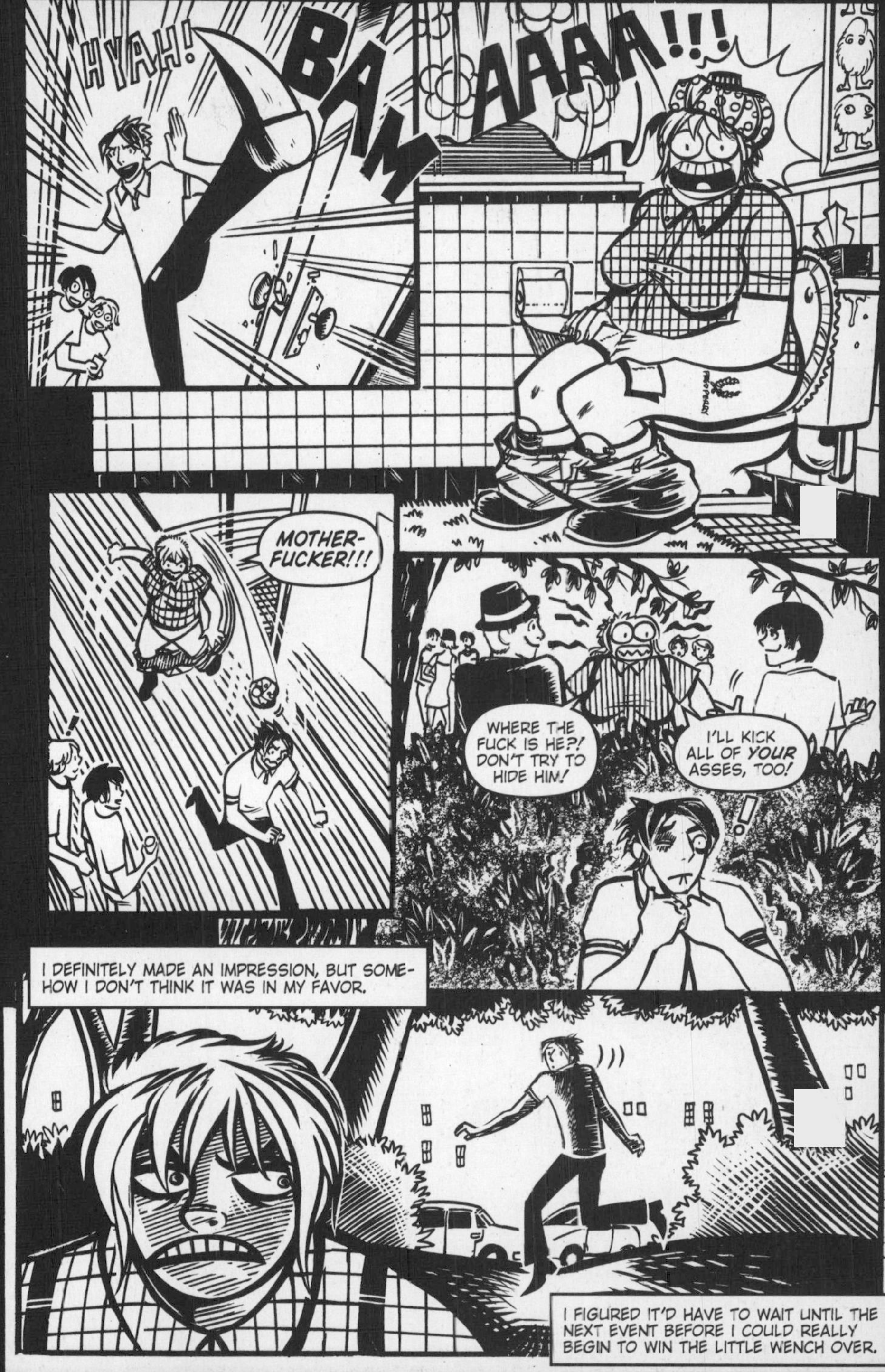
HYAH!
BAM
AAAAA!!!
MOTHER-FUCKER!!!
WHERE THE FUCK IS HE?! DON'T TRY TO HIDE HIM!
I'LL KICK ALL OF YOUR ASSES, TOO!
I DEFINITELY MADE AN IMPRESSION, BUT SOMEHOW I DON'T THINK IT WAS IN MY FAVOR.
I FIGURED IT'D HAVE TO WAIT UNTIL THE NEXT EVENT BEFORE I COULD REALLY BEGIN TO WIN THE LITTLE WENCH OVER.

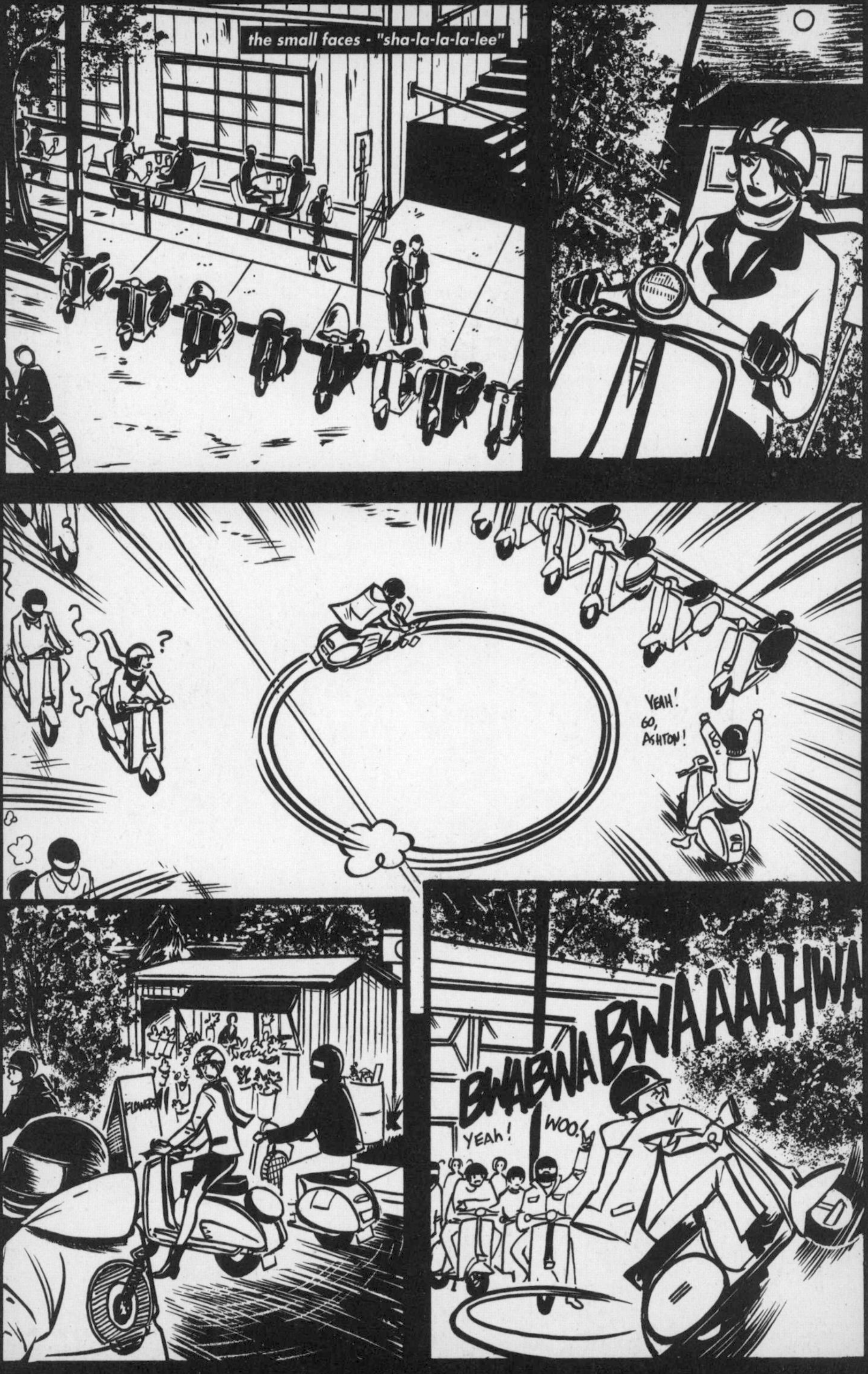

the small faces - "sha-la-la-la-lee"
?
YEAH! GO, ASHTON!
FLOWERS
BWABWA BWAAAAHWA
YEAH!
WOO!

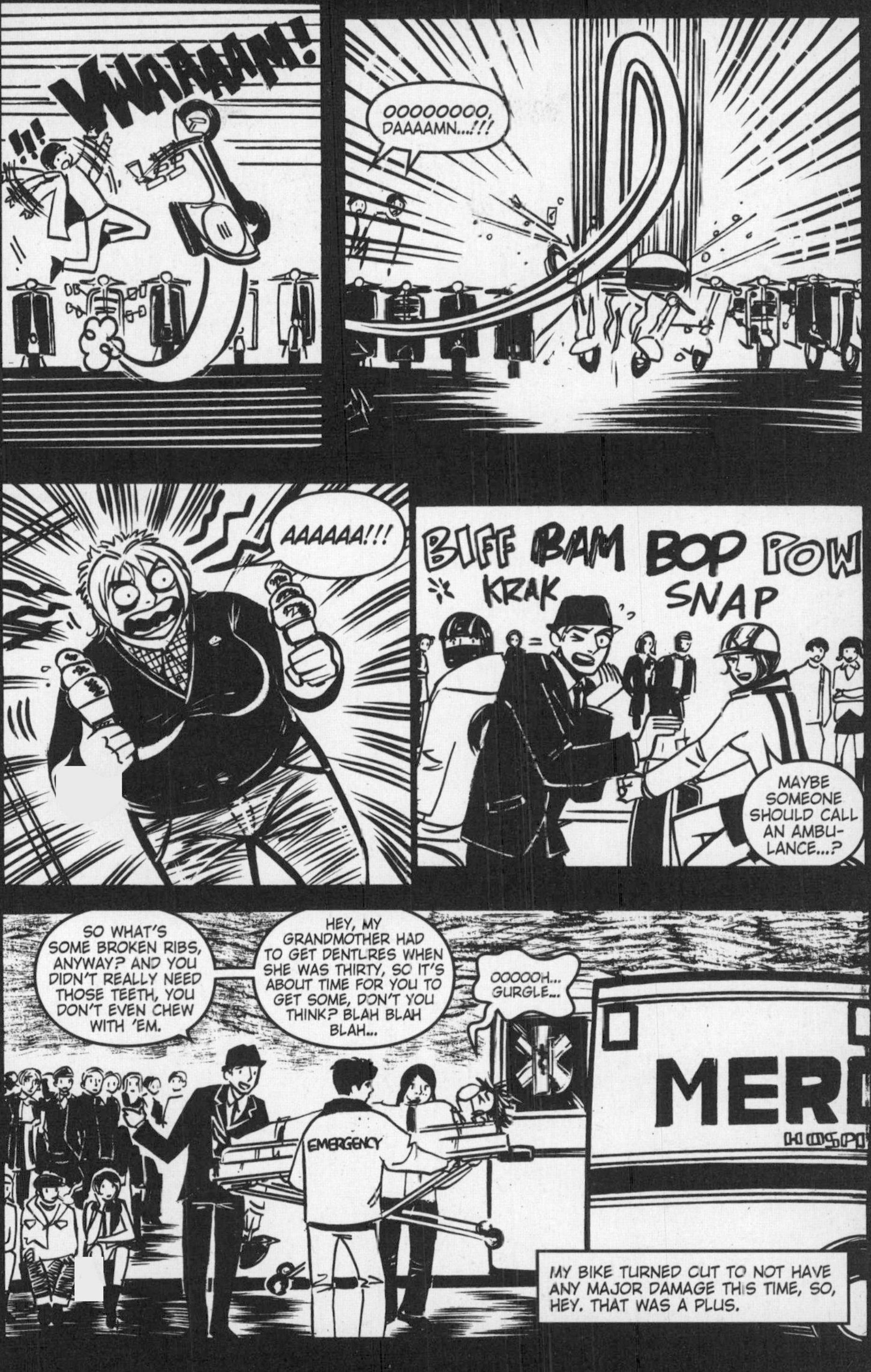
VWAAAAM!
OOOOOOOO, DAAAAMN...!!!
AAAAAA!!!
BIFF BAM BOP POW
KRAK
SNAP
MAYBE SOMEONE SHOULD CALL AN AMBU-LANCE...?
SO WHAT'S SOME BROKEN RIBS, ANYWAY? AND YOU DIDN'T REALLY NEED THOSE TEETH, YOU DON'T EVEN CHEW WITH 'EM.
HEY, MY GRANDMOTHER HAD TO GET DENTURES WHEN SHE WAS THIRTY, SO IT'S ABOUT TIME FOR YOU TO GET SOME, DON'T YOU THINK? BLAH BLAH BLAH...
OOOOOH... GURGLE...
EMERGENCY
MERC
MY BIKE TURNED OUT TO NOT HAVE ANY MAJOR DAMAGE THIS TIME, SO, HEY. THAT WAS A PLUS.

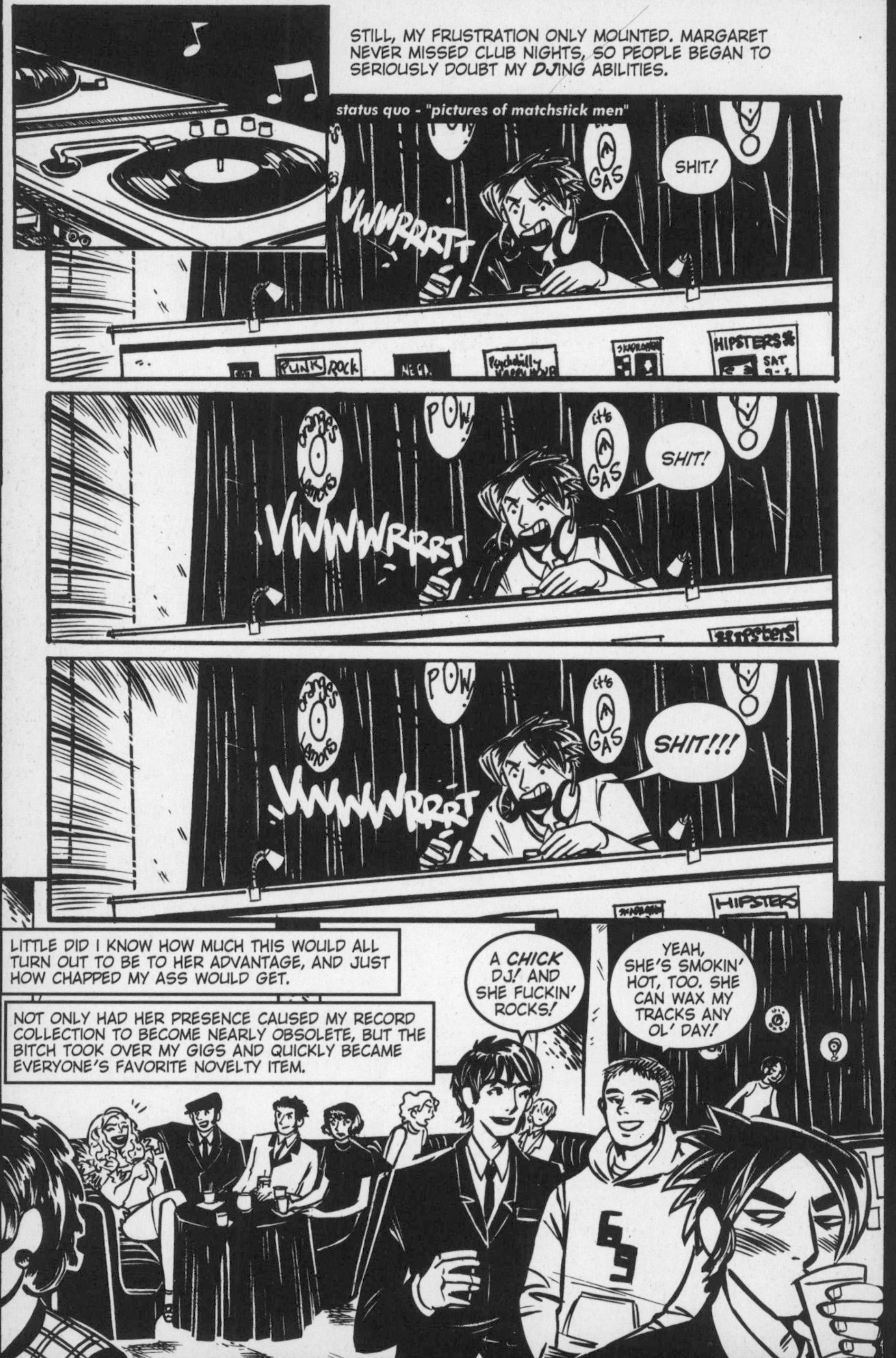
STILL, MY FRUSTRATION ONLY MOUNTED. MARGARET NEVER MISSED CLUB NIGHTS, SO PEOPLE BEGAN TO SERIOUSLY DOUBT MY DJING ABILITIES.
status quo - "pictures of matchstick men"
VWWRRRT
SHIT!
PUNK ROCK
HIPSTERS
VWWWRRRT
SHIT!
VWWWWRRRT
SHIT!!!
HIPSTERS
LITTLE DID I KNOW HOW MUCH THIS WOULD ALL TURN OUT TO BE TO HER ADVANTAGE, AND JUST HOW CHAPPED MY ASS WOULD GET.
NOT ONLY HAD HER PRESENCE CAUSED MY RECORD COLLECTION TO BECOME NEARLY OBSOLETE, BUT THE BITCH TOOK OVER MY GIGS AND QUICKLY BECAME EVERYONE'S FAVORITE NOVELTY ITEM.
A CHICK DJ! AND SHE FUCKIN' ROCKS!
YEAH, SHE'S SMOKIN' HOT, TOO. SHE CAN WAX MY TRACKS ANY OL' DAY!

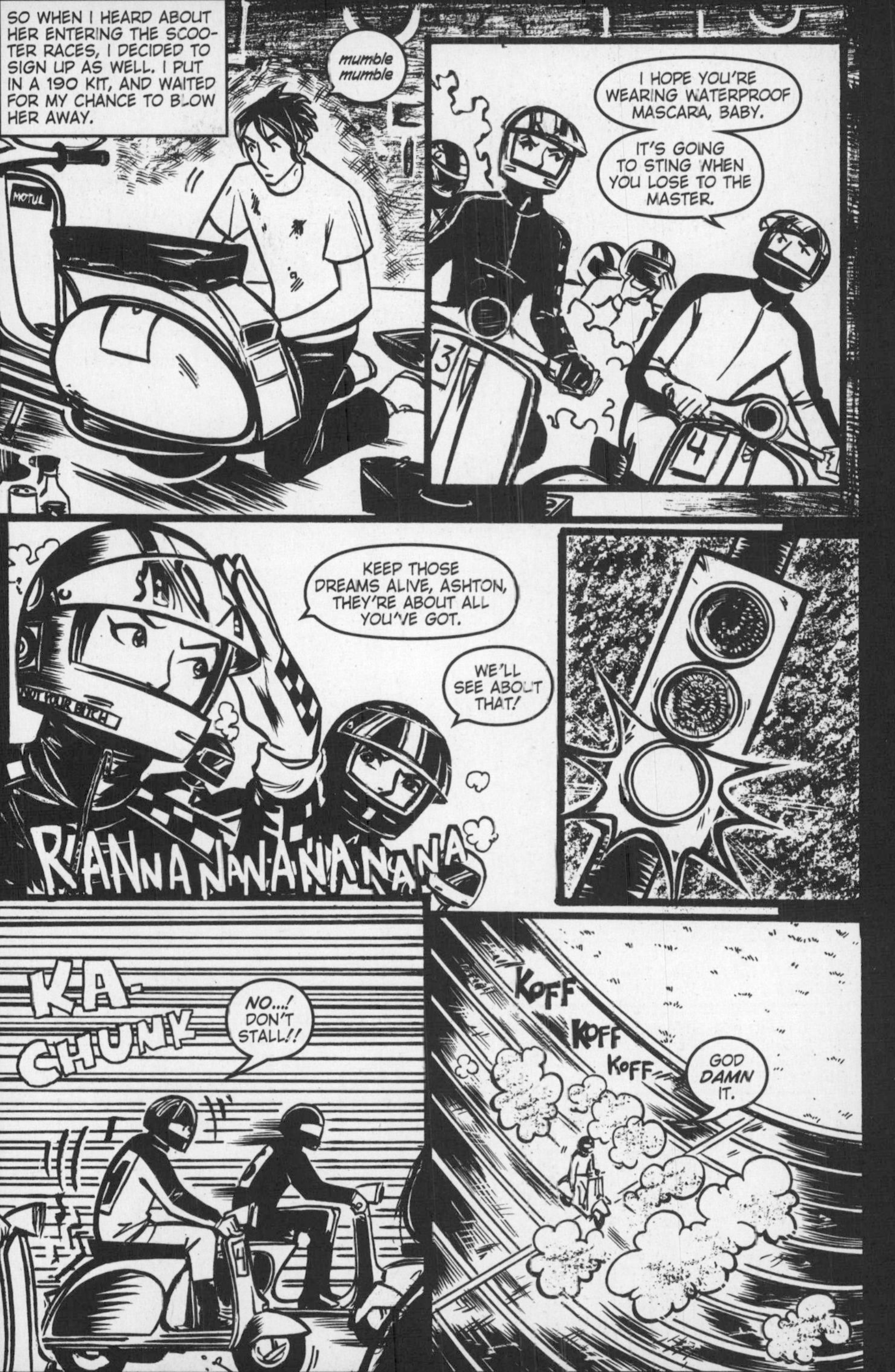

SO WHEN I HEARD ABOUT HER ENTERING THE SCOOTER RACES, I DECIDED TO SIGN UP AS WELL. I PUT IN A 190 KIT, AND WAITED FOR MY CHANCE TO BLOW HER AWAY.
mumble mumble
MOTUL
I HOPE YOU'RE WEARING WATERPROOF MASCARA, BABY.
IT'S GOING TO STING WHEN YOU LOSE TO THE MASTER.
KEEP THOSE DREAMS ALIVE, ASHTON, THEY'RE ABOUT ALL YOU'VE GOT.
WE'LL SEE ABOUT THAT!
RIANNANANANANANA
KA-CHUNK
NO...! DON'T STALL!!
KOFF
KOFF
KOFF
GOD DAMN IT.

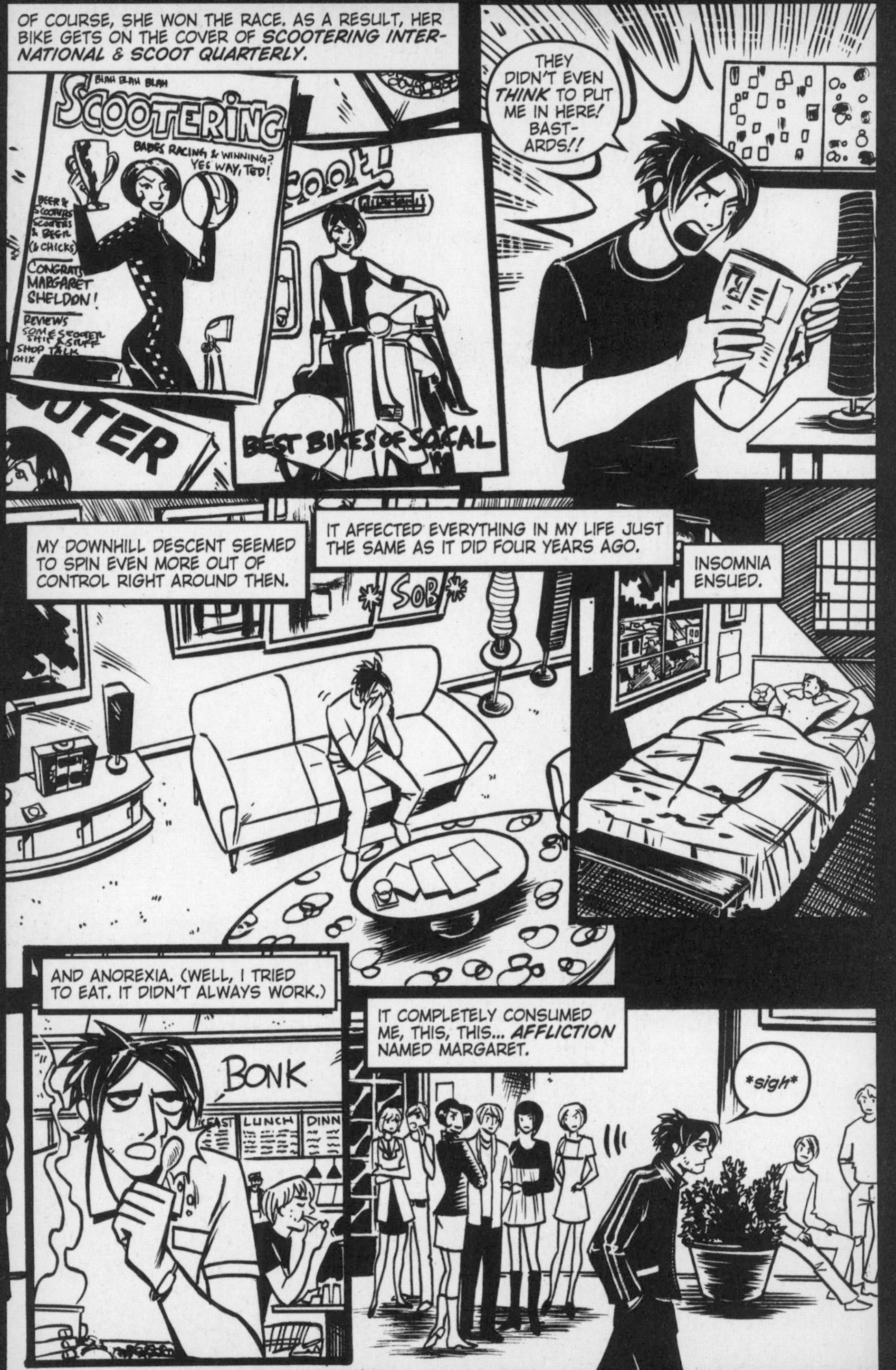

OF COURSE, SHE WON THE RACE. AS A RESULT, HER BIKE GETS ON THE COVER OF *SCOOTERING INTERNATIONAL & SCOOT QUARTERLY*.
BLAH BLAH BLAH
SCOOTERING
BABES RACING & WINNING? YES WAY, TED!
BEER & SCOOTERS
SCOOTERS & BEER (& CHICKS)
CONGRATS MARGARET SHELDON!
REVIEWS
SHOP TALK
SCOOT!
QUARTERLY
BEST BIKES OF SOCAL
THEY DIDN'T EVEN *THINK* TO PUT ME IN HERE! BASTARDS!!
MY DOWNHILL DESCENT SEEMED TO SPIN EVEN MORE OUT OF CONTROL RIGHT AROUND THEN.
IT AFFECTED EVERYTHING IN MY LIFE JUST THE SAME AS IT DID FOUR YEARS AGO.
SOB
INSOMNIA ENSUED.
AND ANOREXIA. (WELL, I TRIED TO EAT. IT DIDN'T ALWAYS WORK.)
BONK
LUNCH
IT COMPLETELY CONSUMED ME, THIS, THIS... *AFFLICTION* NAMED MARGARET.
sigh

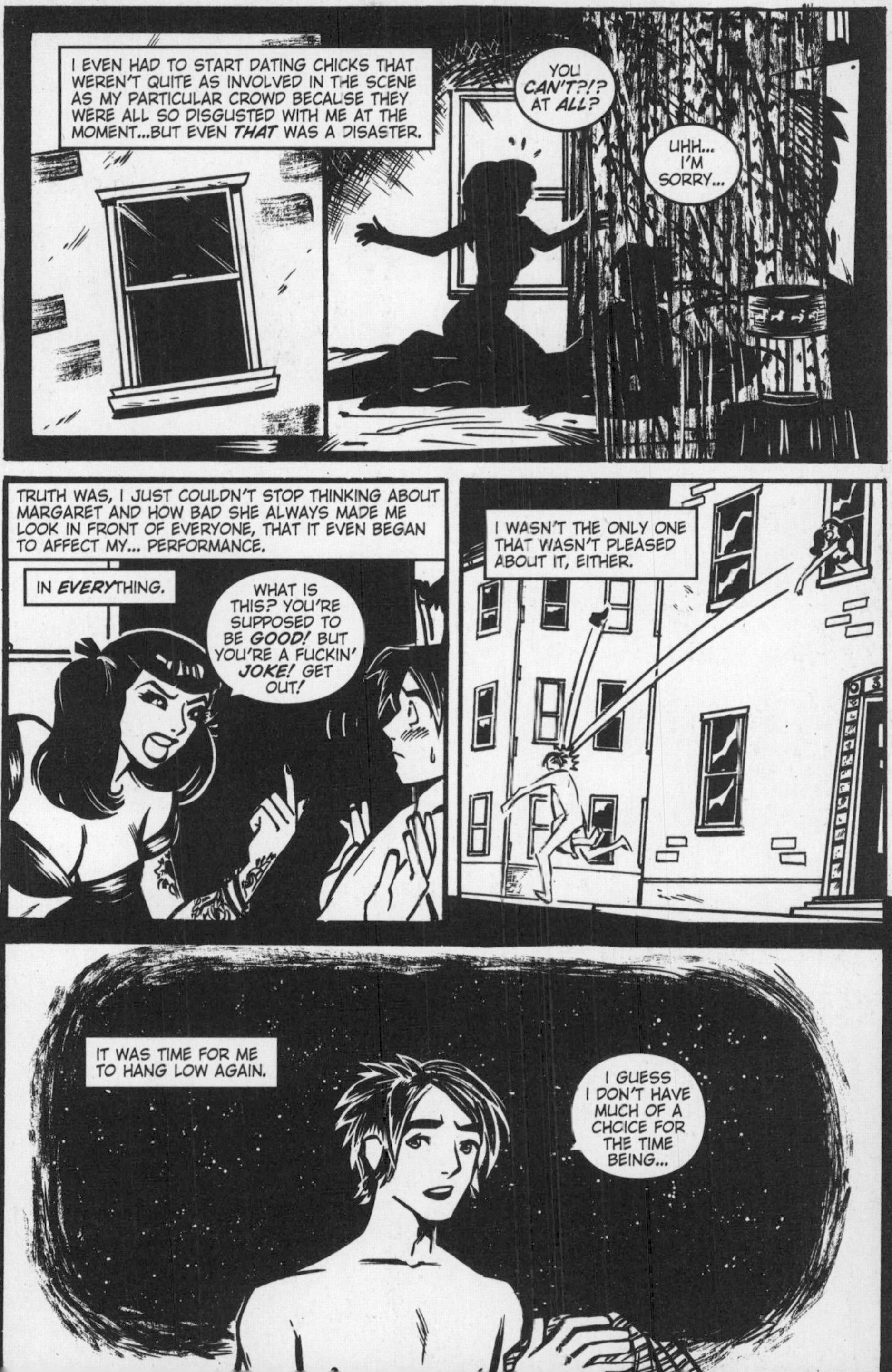
I EVEN HAD TO START DATING CHICKS THAT WEREN'T QUITE AS INVOLVED IN THE SCENE AS MY PARTICULAR CROWD BECAUSE THEY WERE ALL SO DISGUSTED WITH ME AT THE MOMENT...BUT EVEN *THAT* WAS A DISASTER.
YOU *CAN'T?!?* AT *ALL?*
UHH... I'M SORRY...
TRUTH WAS, I JUST COULDN'T STOP THINKING ABOUT MARGARET AND HOW BAD SHE ALWAYS MADE ME LOOK IN FRONT OF EVERYONE, THAT IT EVEN BEGAN TO AFFECT MY... PERFORMANCE.
IN *EVERY*THING.
WHAT IS THIS? YOU'RE SUPPOSED TO BE *GOOD!* BUT YOU'RE A FUCKIN' *JOKE!* GET OUT!
I WASN'T THE ONLY ONE THAT WASN'T PLEASED ABOUT IT, EITHER.
IT WAS TIME FOR ME TO HANG LOW AGAIN.
I GUESS I DON'T HAVE MUCH OF A CHCICE FOR THE TIME BEING...

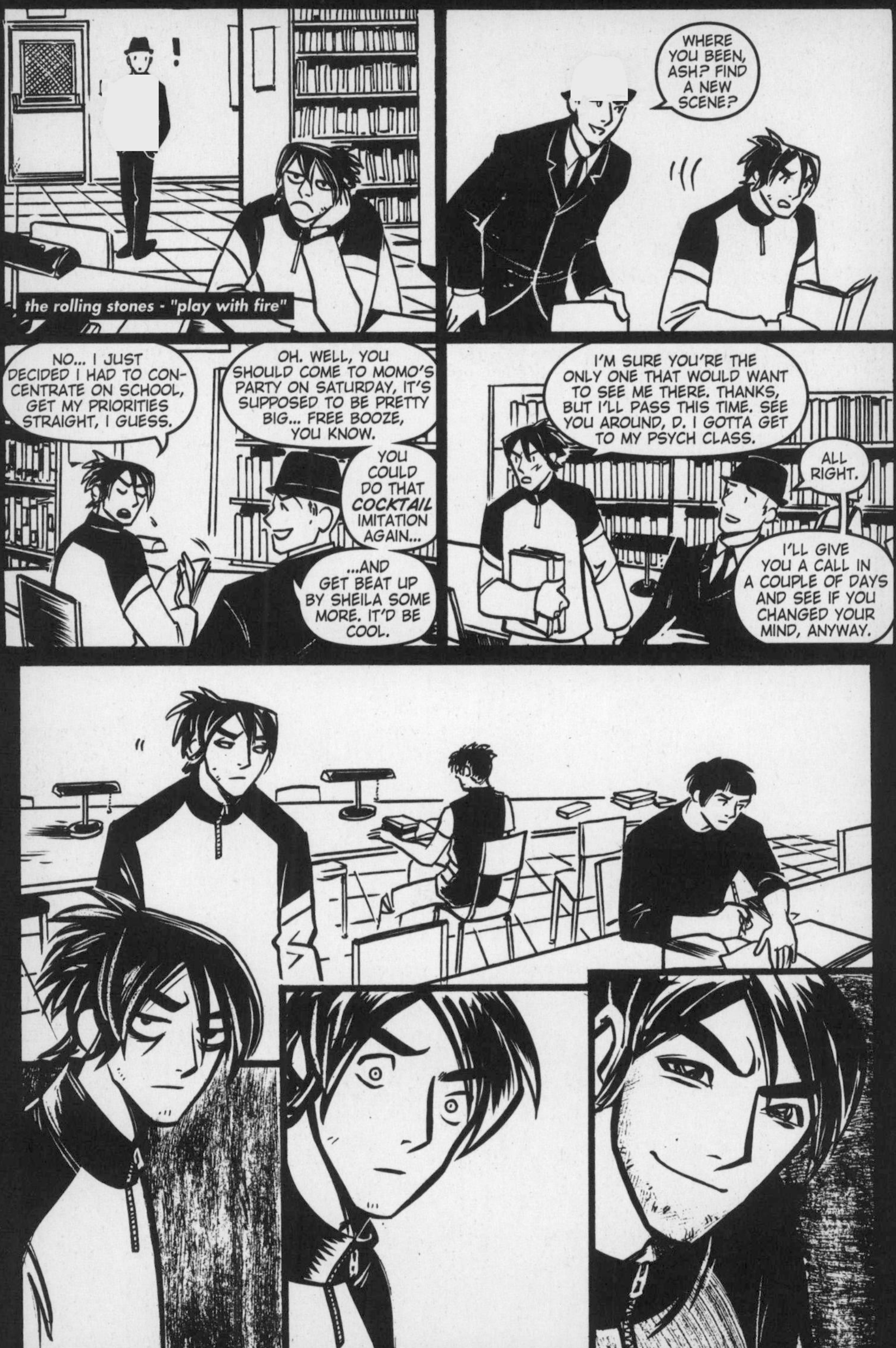

!
the rolling stones - "play with fire"
WHERE YOU BEEN, ASH? FIND A NEW SCENE?
NO... I JUST DECIDED I HAD TO CON-CENTRATE ON SCHOOL, GET MY PRIORITIES STRAIGHT, I GUESS.
OH. WELL, YOU SHOULD COME TO MOMO'S PARTY ON SATURDAY, IT'S SUPPOSED TO BE PRETTY BIG... FREE BOOZE, YOU KNOW.
YOU COULD DO THAT COCKTAIL IMITATION AGAIN...
...AND GET BEAT UP BY SHEILA SOME MORE. IT'D BE COOL.
I'M SURE YOU'RE THE ONLY ONE THAT WOULD WANT TO SEE ME THERE. THANKS, BUT I'LL PASS THIS TIME. SEE YOU AROUND, D. I GOTTA GET TO MY PSYCH CLASS.
ALL RIGHT.
I'LL GIVE YOU A CALL IN A COUPLE OF DAYS AND SEE IF YOU CHANGED YOUR MIND, ANYWAY.

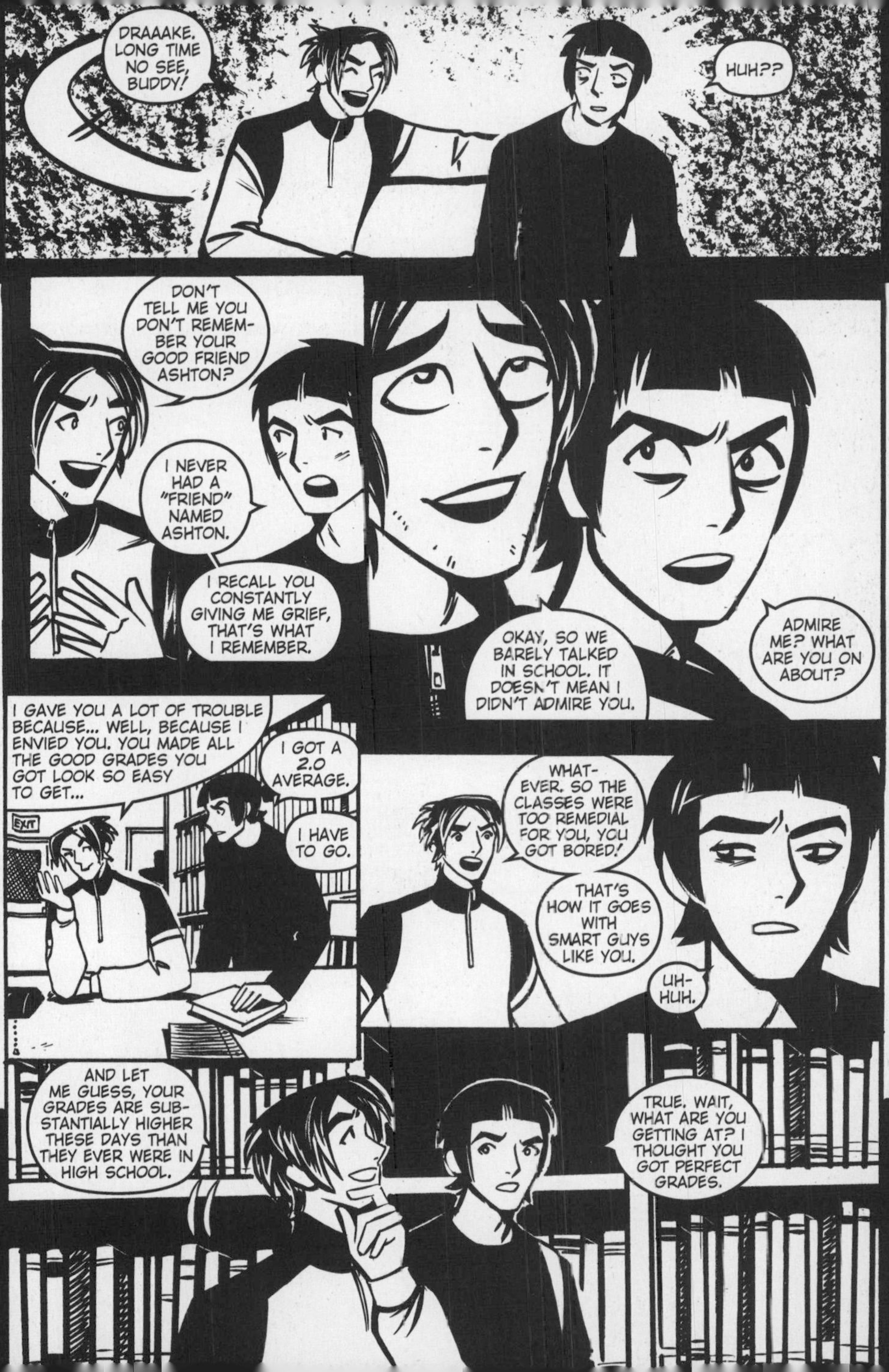
DRAAAKE. LONG TIME NO SEE, BUDDY!
HUH??
DON'T TELL ME YOU DON'T REMEMBER YOUR GOOD FRIEND ASHTON?
I NEVER HAD A "FRIEND" NAMED ASHTON.
I RECALL YOU CONSTANTLY GIVING ME GRIEF, THAT'S WHAT I REMEMBER.
OKAY, SO WE BARELY TALKED IN SCHOOL. IT DOESN'T MEAN I DIDN'T ADMIRE YOU.
ADMIRE ME? WHAT ARE YOU ON ABOUT?
I GAVE YOU A LOT OF TROUBLE BECAUSE... WELL, BECAUSE I ENVIED YOU. YOU MADE ALL THE GOOD GRADES YOU GOT LOOK SO EASY TO GET...
I GOT A 2.0 AVERAGE.
I HAVE TO GO.
EXIT
WHATEVER. SO THE CLASSES WERE TOO REMEDIAL FOR YOU, YOU GOT BORED!
THAT'S HOW IT GOES WITH SMART GUYS LIKE YOU.
UH-HUH.
AND LET ME GUESS, YOUR GRADES ARE SUBSTANTIALLY HIGHER THESE DAYS THAN THEY EVER WERE IN HIGH SCHOOL.
TRUE. WAIT, WHAT ARE YOU GETTING AT? I THOUGHT YOU GOT PERFECT GRADES.

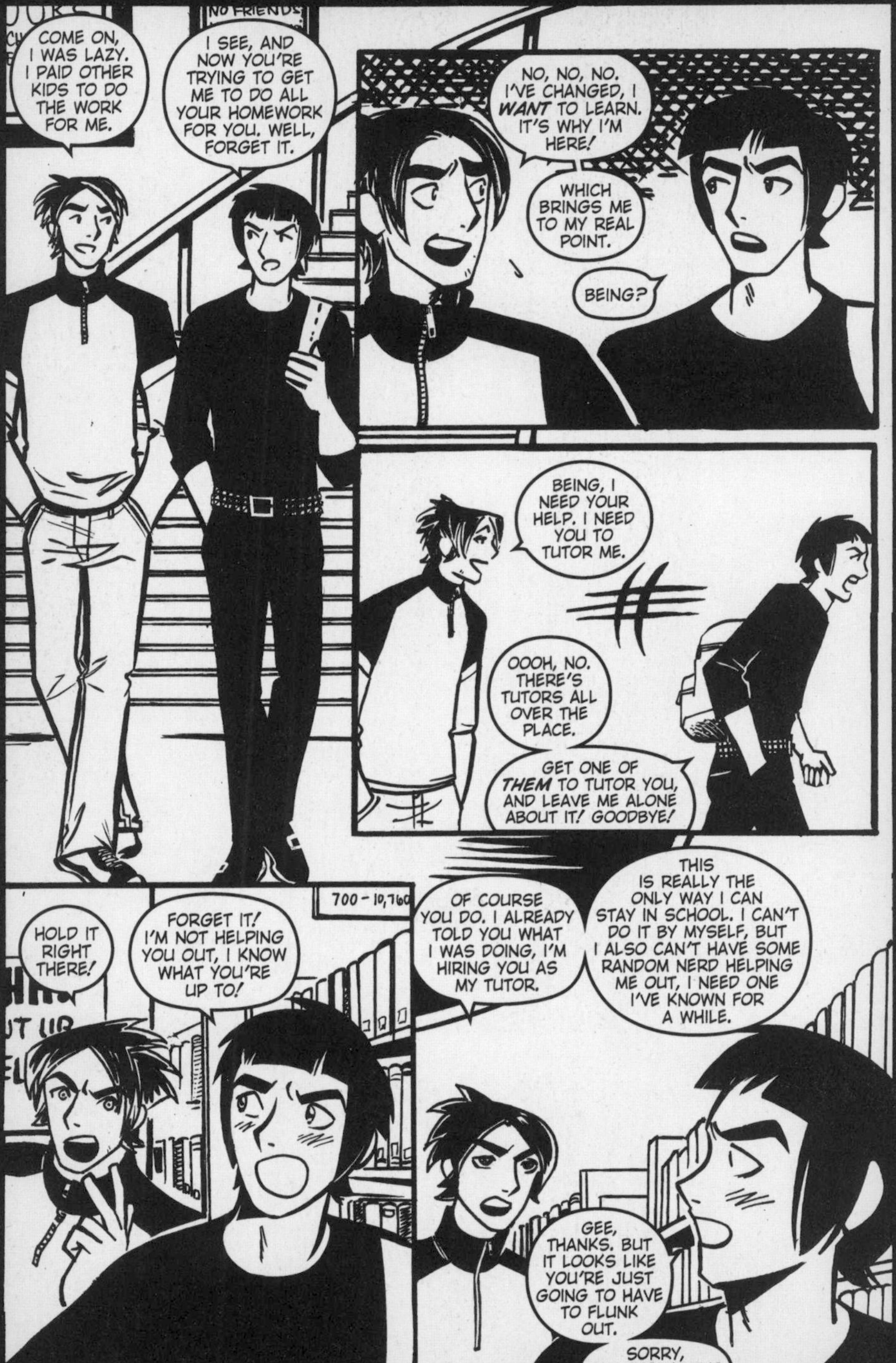
NO FRIENDS
COME ON, I WAS LAZY. I PAID OTHER KIDS TO DO THE WORK FOR ME.
I SEE, AND NOW YOU'RE TRYING TO GET ME TO DO ALL YOUR HOMEWORK FOR YOU. WELL, FORGET IT.
NO, NO, NO. I'VE CHANGED, I *WANT* TO LEARN. IT'S WHY I'M HERE!
WHICH BRINGS ME TO MY REAL POINT.
BEING?
BEING, I NEED YOUR HELP. I NEED YOU TO TUTOR ME.
OOOH, NO. THERE'S TUTORS ALL OVER THE PLACE.
GET ONE OF *THEM* TO TUTOR YOU, AND LEAVE ME ALONE ABOUT IT! GOODBYE!
700 - 10,760
HOLD IT RIGHT THERE!
FORGET IT! I'M NOT HELPING YOU OUT, I KNOW WHAT YOU'RE UP TO!
OF COURSE YOU DO. I ALREADY TOLD YOU WHAT I WAS DOING, I'M HIRING YOU AS MY TUTOR.
THIS IS REALLY THE ONLY WAY I CAN STAY IN SCHOOL. I CAN'T DO IT BY MYSELF, BUT I ALSO CAN'T HAVE SOME RANDOM NERD HELPING ME OUT, I NEED ONE I'VE KNOWN FOR A WHILE.
GEE, THANKS. BUT IT LOOKS LIKE YOU'RE JUST GOING TO HAVE TO FLUNK OUT.
SORRY, BUT THEM'S THE BREAKS.

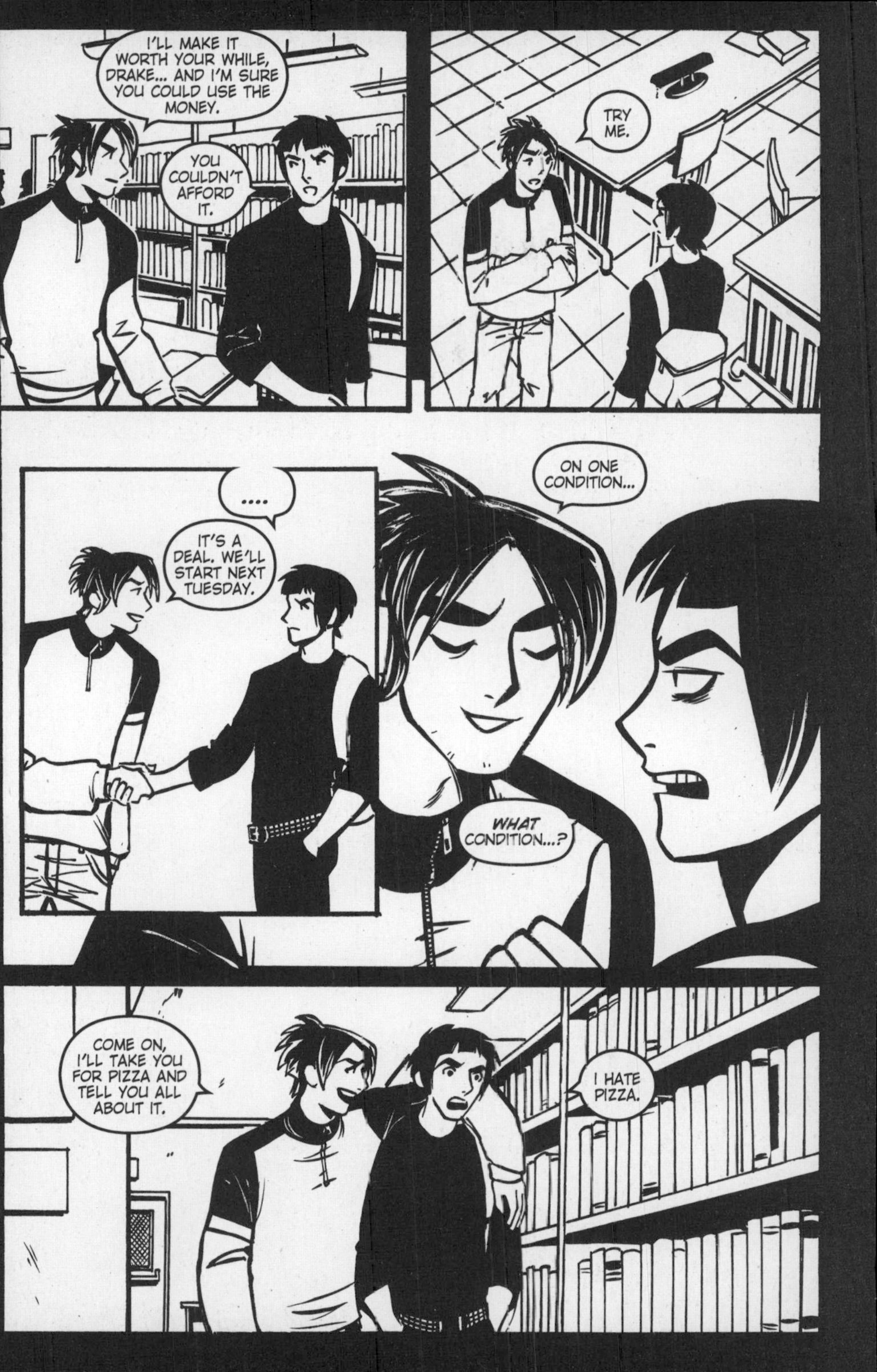
I'LL MAKE IT WORTH YOUR WHILE, DRAKE... AND I'M SURE YOU COULD USE THE MONEY.
YOU COULDN'T AFFORD IT.
TRY ME.
....
IT'S A DEAL. WE'LL START NEXT TUESDAY.
ON ONE CONDITION...
WHAT CONDITION...?
COME ON, I'LL TAKE YOU FOR PIZZA AND TELL YOU ALL ABOUT IT.
I HATE PIZZA.

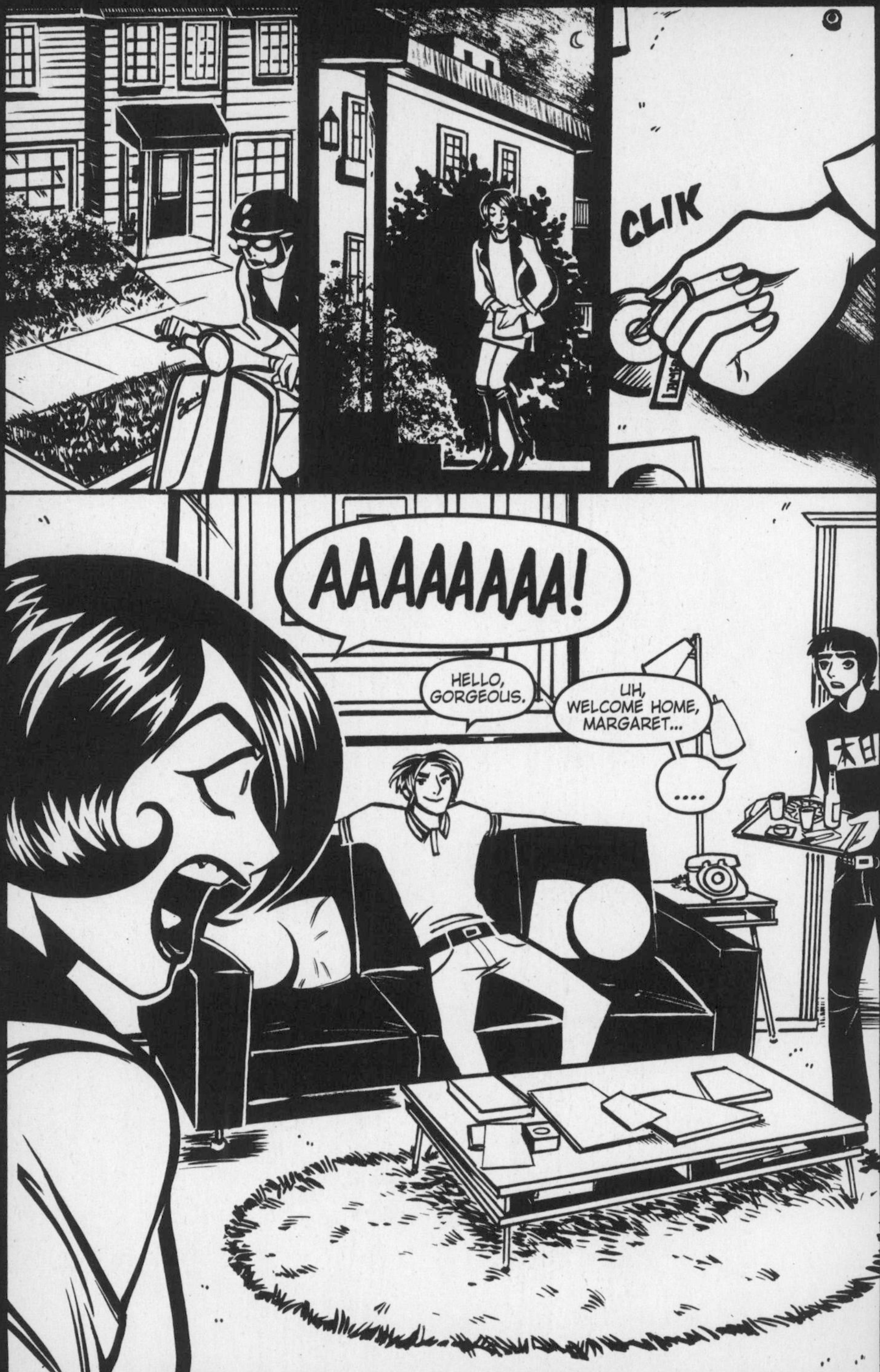
CLIK
AAAAAAAA!
HELLO, GORGEOUS.
UH, WELCOME HOME, MARGARET...
.....

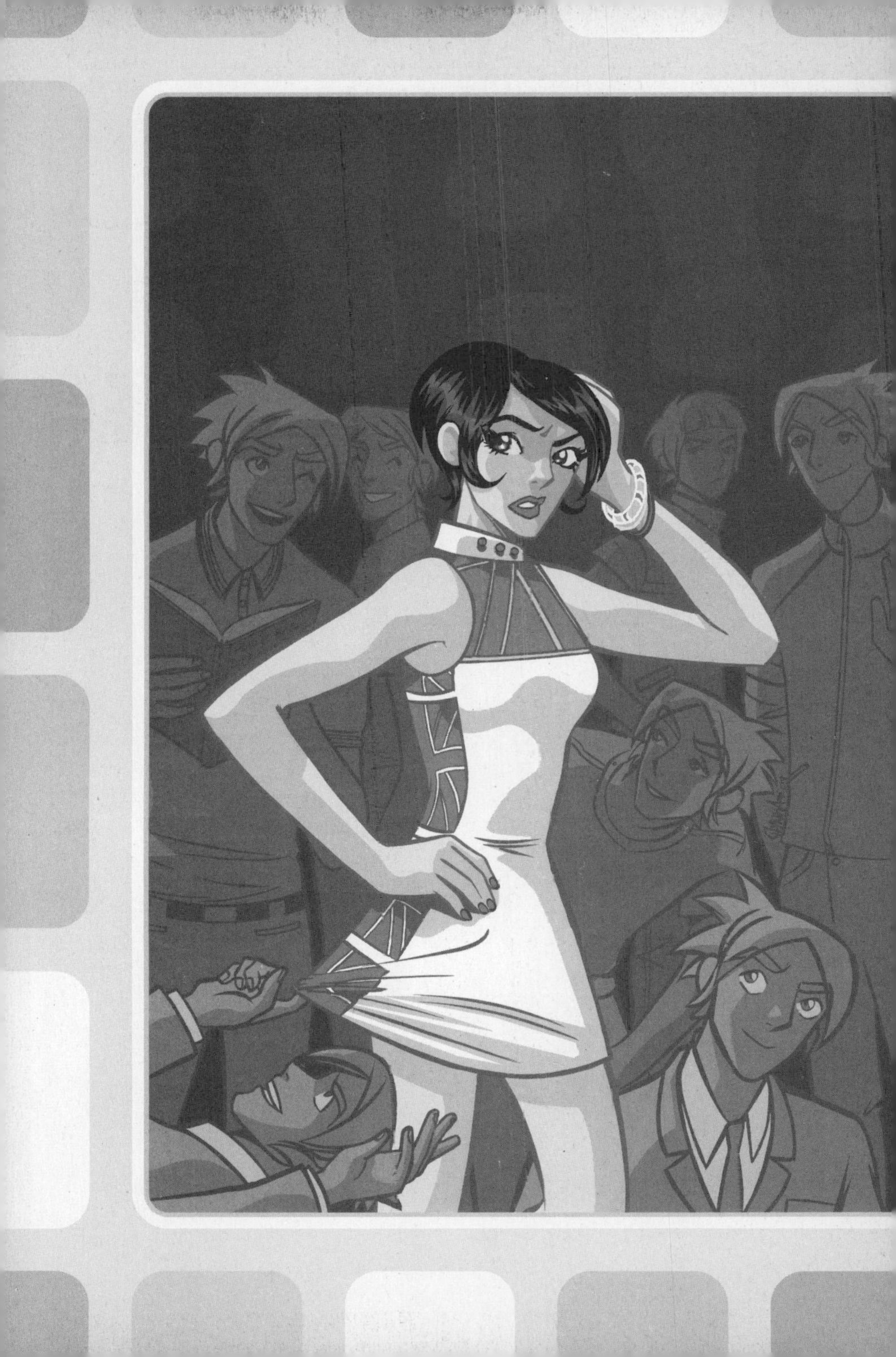

Chapter 3:
"Yesterday, Today, & Tomorrow"

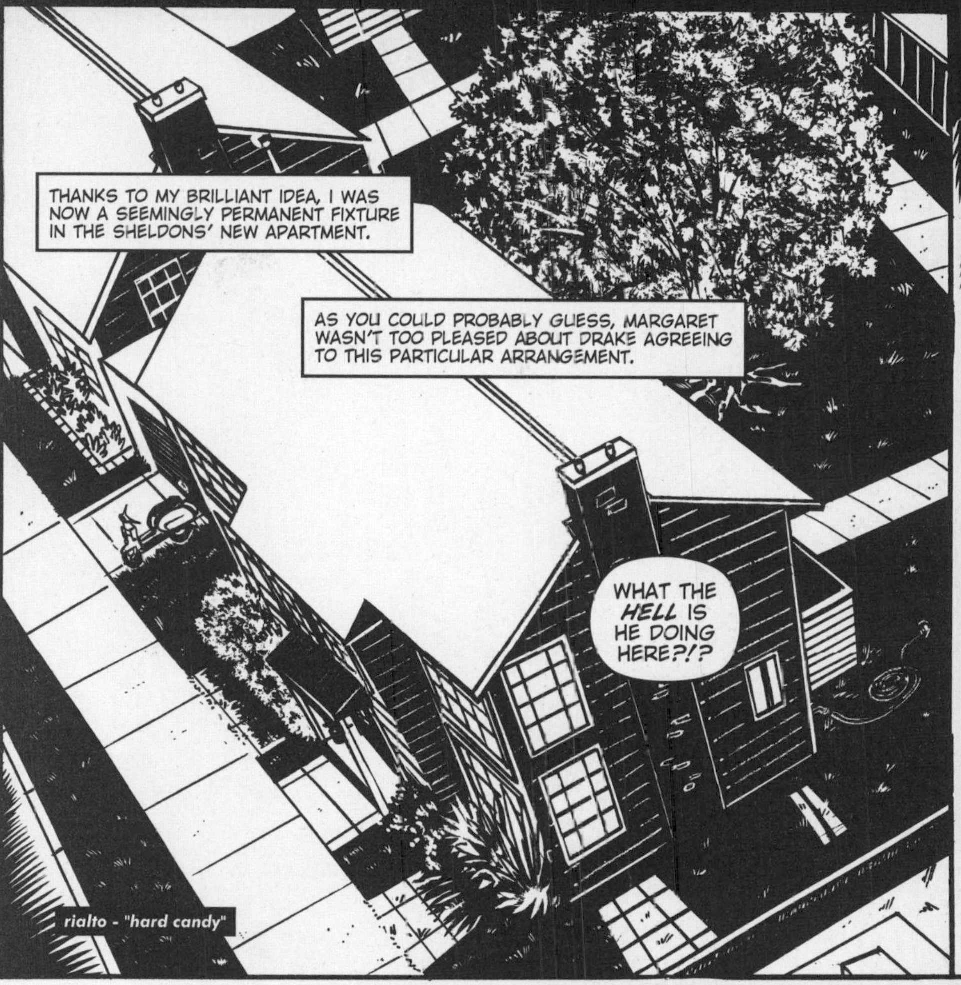
THANKS TO MY BRILLIANT IDEA, I WAS NOW A SEEMINGLY PERMANENT FIXTURE IN THE SHELDONS' NEW APARTMENT.
AS YOU COULD PROBABLY GUESS, MARGARET WASN'T TOO PLEASED ABOUT DRAKE AGREEING TO THIS PARTICULAR ARRANGEMENT.
WHAT THE *HELL* IS HE DOING HERE?!?
rialto - "hard candy"

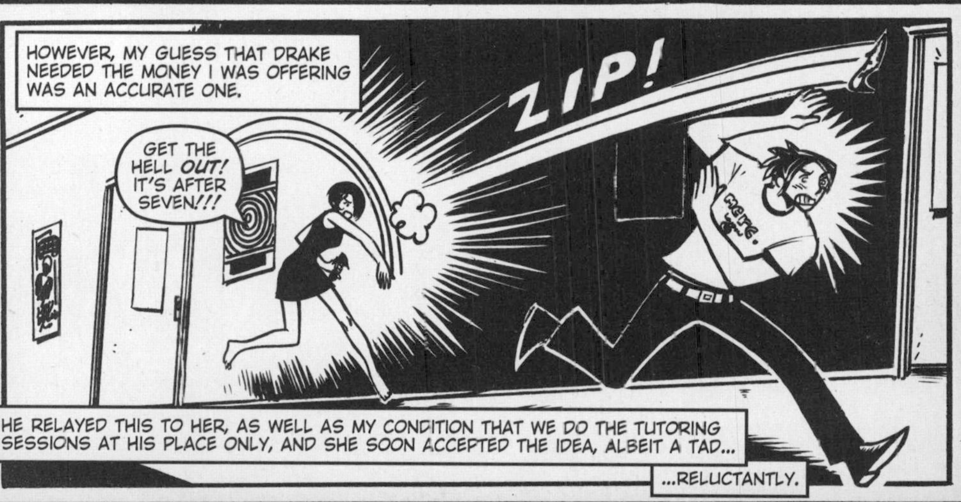
HOWEVER, MY GUESS THAT DRAKE NEEDED THE MONEY I WAS OFFERING WAS AN ACCURATE ONE.
ZIP!
GET THE HELL *OUT!* IT'S AFTER SEVEN!!!
HE RELAYED THIS TO HER, AS WELL AS MY CONDITION THAT WE DO THE TUTORING SESSIONS AT HIS PLACE ONLY, AND SHE SOON ACCEPTED THE IDEA, ALBEIT A TAD...
...RELUCTANTLY.

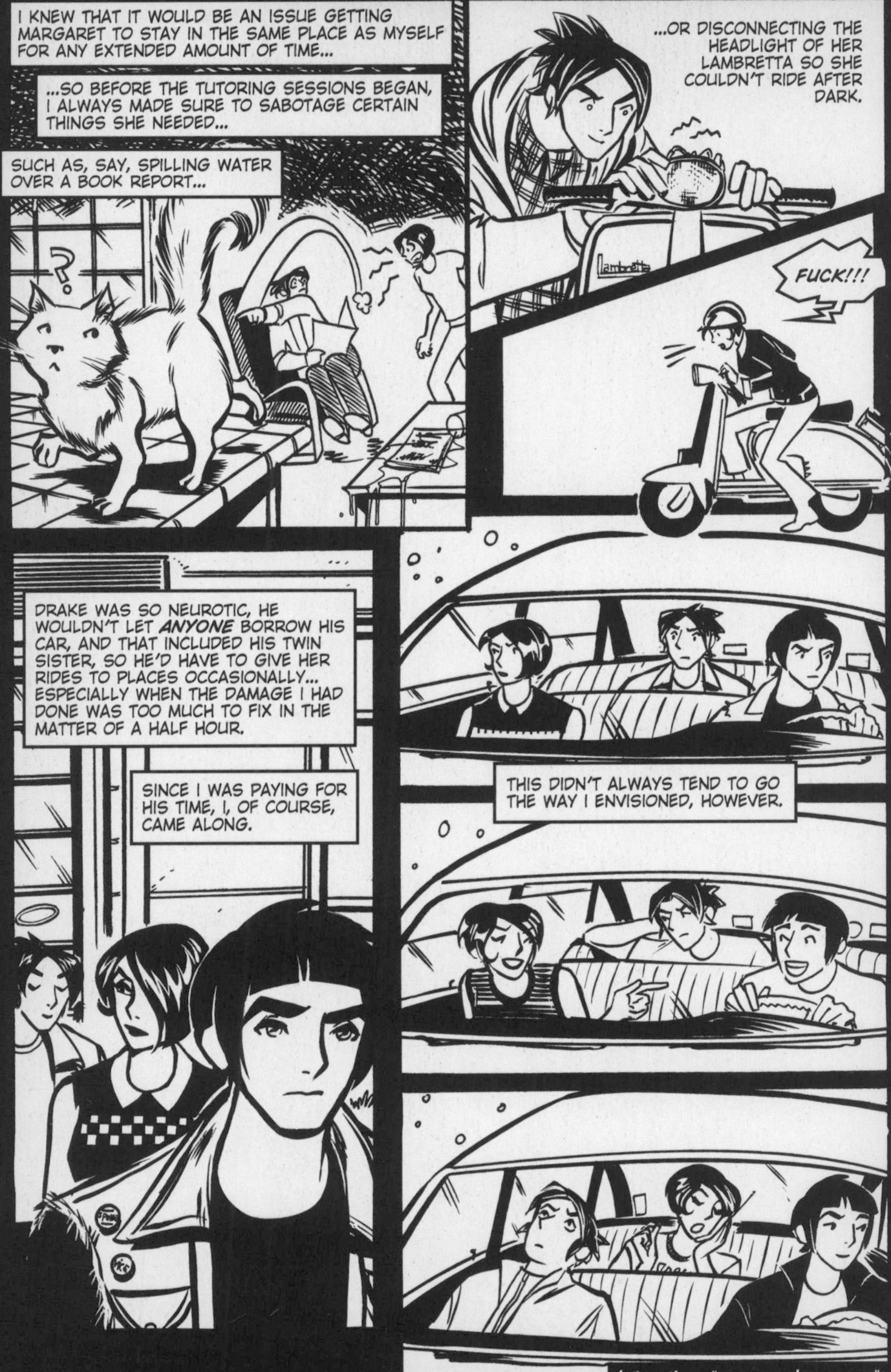
I KNEW THAT IT WOULD BE AN ISSUE GETTING MARGARET TO STAY IN THE SAME PLACE AS MYSELF FOR ANY EXTENDED AMOUNT OF TIME...
...SO BEFORE THE TUTORING SESSIONS BEGAN, I ALWAYS MADE SURE TO SABOTAGE CERTAIN THINGS SHE NEEDED...
SUCH AS, SAY, SPILLING WATER OVER A BOOK REPORT...
?
...OR DISCONNECTING THE HEADLIGHT OF HER LAMBRETTA SO SHE COULDN'T RIDE AFTER DARK.
Lambretta
FUCK!!!
DRAKE WAS SO NEUROTIC, HE WOULDN'T LET *ANYONE* BORROW HIS CAR, AND THAT INCLUDED HIS TWIN SISTER, SO HE'D HAVE TO GIVE HER RIDES TO PLACES OCCASIONALLY... ESPECIALLY WHEN THE DAMAGE I HAD DONE WAS TOO MUCH TO FIX IN THE MATTER OF A HALF HOUR.
SINCE I WAS PAYING FOR HIS TIME, I, OF COURSE, CAME ALONG.
THIS DIDN'T ALWAYS TEND TO GO THE WAY I ENVISIONED, HOWEVER.

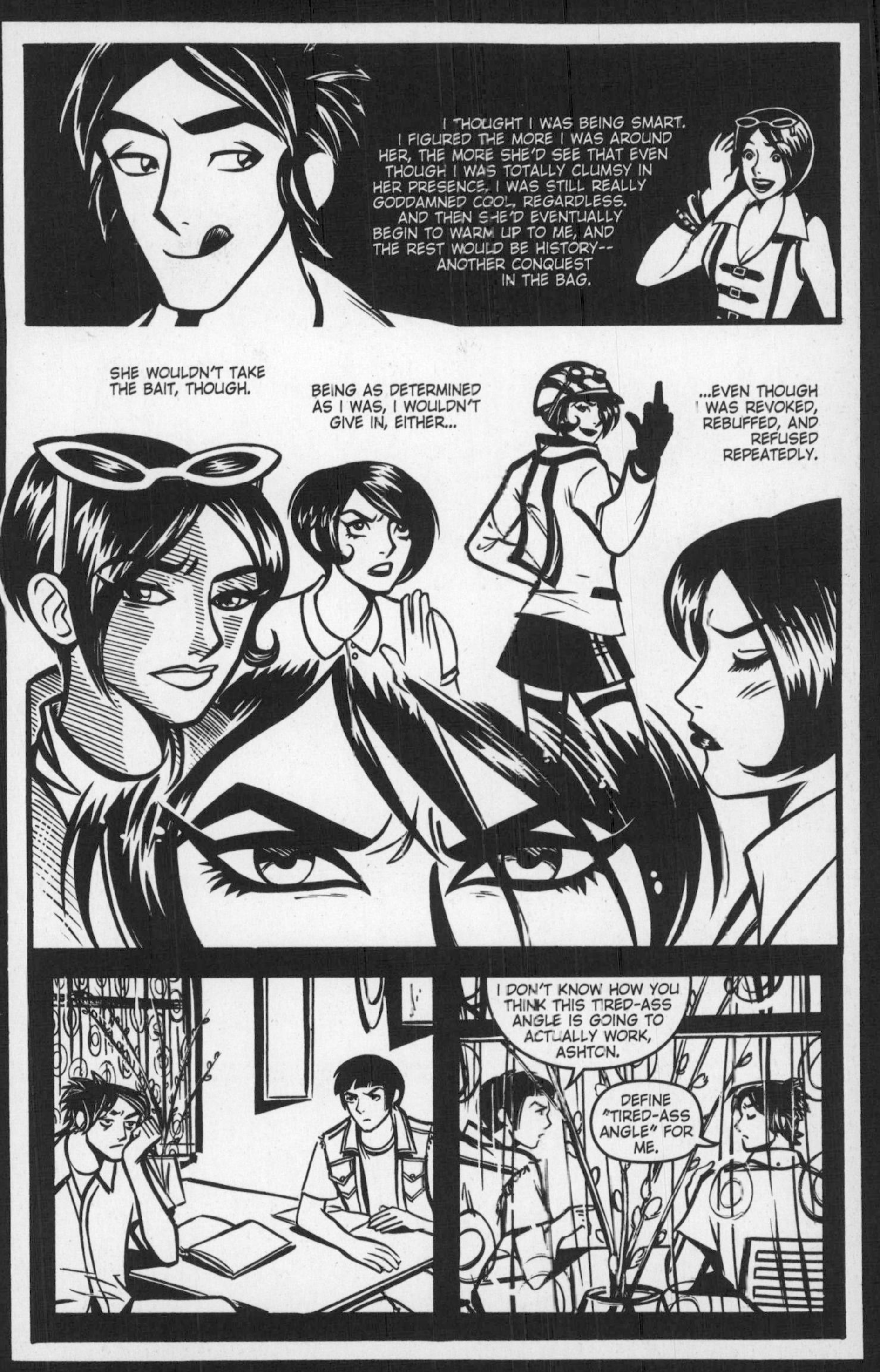
I THOUGHT I WAS BEING SMART. I FIGURED THE MORE I WAS AROUND HER, THE MORE SHE'D SEE THAT EVEN THOUGH I WAS TOTALLY CLUMSY IN HER PRESENCE, I WAS STILL REALLY GODDAMNED COOL, REGARDLESS. AND THEN SHE'D EVENTUALLY BEGIN TO WARM UP TO ME, AND THE REST WOULD BE HISTORY-- ANOTHER CONQUEST IN THE BAG.
SHE WOULDN'T TAKE THE BAIT, THOUGH.
BEING AS DETERMINED AS I WAS, I WOULDN'T GIVE IN, EITHER...
...EVEN THOUGH I WAS REVOKED, REBUFFED, AND REFUSED REPEATEDLY.
I DON'T KNOW HOW YOU THINK THIS TIRED-ASS ANGLE IS GOING TO ACTUALLY WORK, ASHTON.
DEFINE "TIRED-ASS ANGLE" FOR ME.

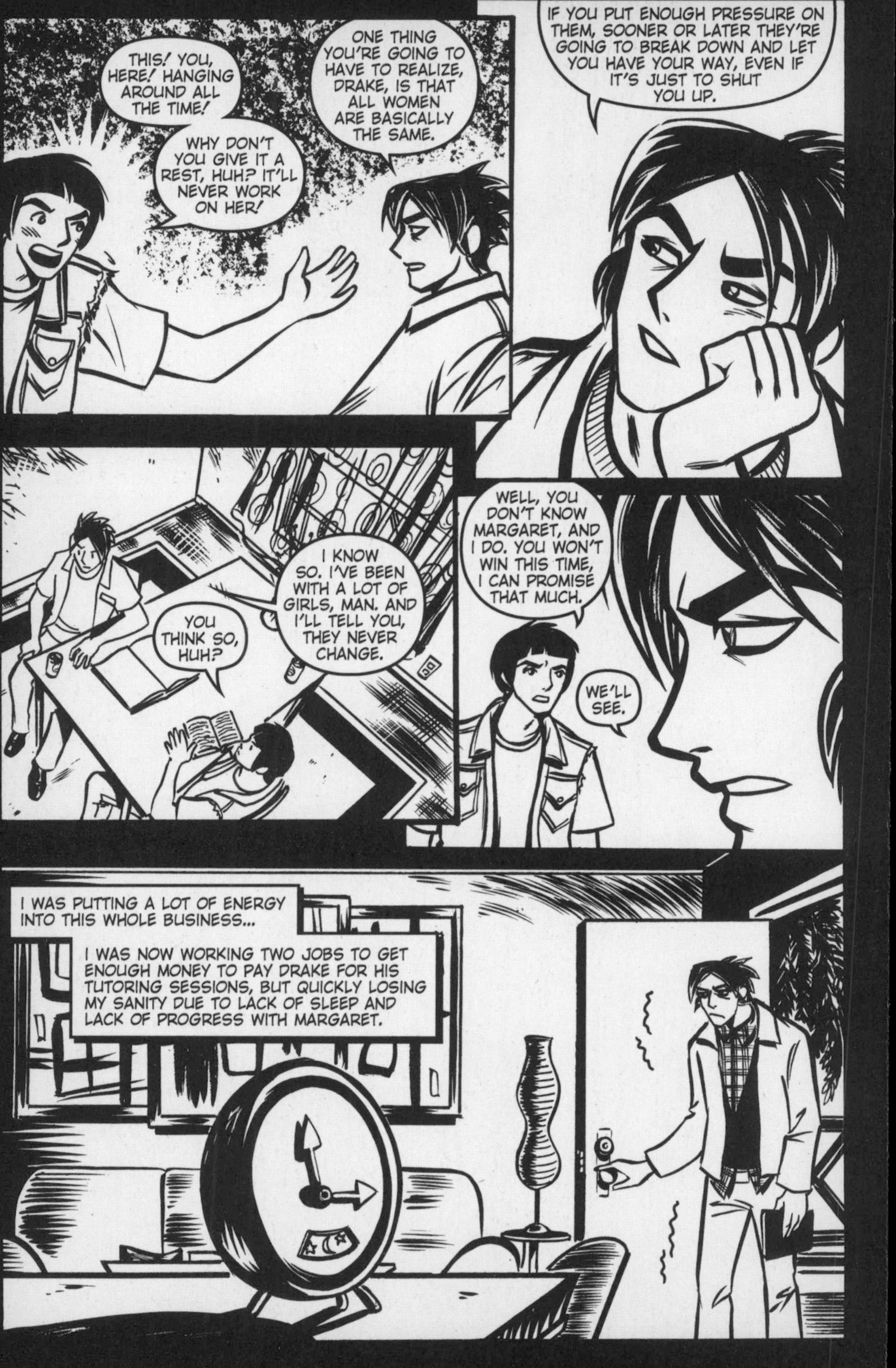
THIS! YOU, HERE! HANGING AROUND ALL THE TIME!
WHY DON'T YOU GIVE IT A REST, HUH? IT'LL NEVER WORK ON HER!
ONE THING YOU'RE GOING TO HAVE TO REALIZE, DRAKE, IS THAT ALL WOMEN ARE BASICALLY THE SAME.
IF YOU PUT ENOUGH PRESSURE ON THEM, SOONER OR LATER THEY'RE GOING TO BREAK DOWN AND LET YOU HAVE YOUR WAY, EVEN IF IT'S JUST TO SHUT YOU UP.
YOU THINK SO, HUH?
I KNOW SO. I'VE BEEN WITH A LOT OF GIRLS, MAN. AND I'LL TELL YOU, THEY NEVER CHANGE.
WELL, YOU DON'T KNOW MARGARET, AND I DO. YOU WON'T WIN THIS TIME, I CAN PROMISE THAT MUCH.
WE'LL SEE.
I WAS PUTTING A LOT OF ENERGY INTO THIS WHOLE BUSINESS...
I WAS NOW WORKING TWO JOBS TO GET ENOUGH MONEY TO PAY DRAKE FOR HIS TUTORING SESSIONS, BUT QUICKLY LOSING MY SANITY DUE TO LACK OF SLEEP AND LACK OF PROGRESS WITH MARGARET.

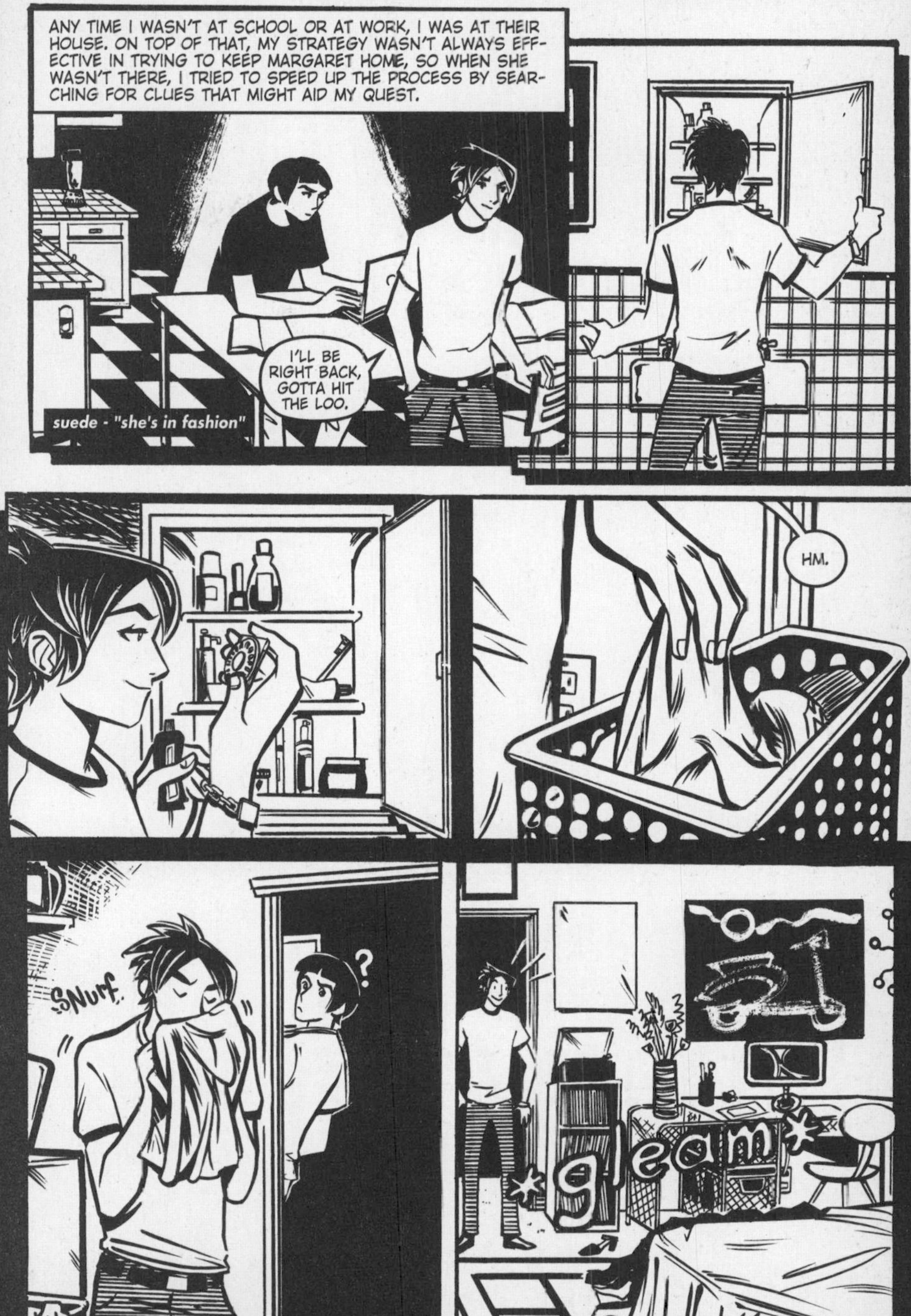
ANY TIME I WASN'T AT SCHOOL OR AT WORK, I WAS AT THEIR HOUSE. ON TOP OF THAT, MY STRATEGY WASN'T ALWAYS EFFECTIVE IN TRYING TO KEEP MARGARET HOME, SO WHEN SHE WASN'T THERE, I TRIED TO SPEED UP THE PROCESS BY SEARCHING FOR CLUES THAT MIGHT AID MY QUEST.
I'LL BE RIGHT BACK, GOTTA HIT THE LOO.
suede - "she's in fashion"
HM.
SNURF
?
gleam

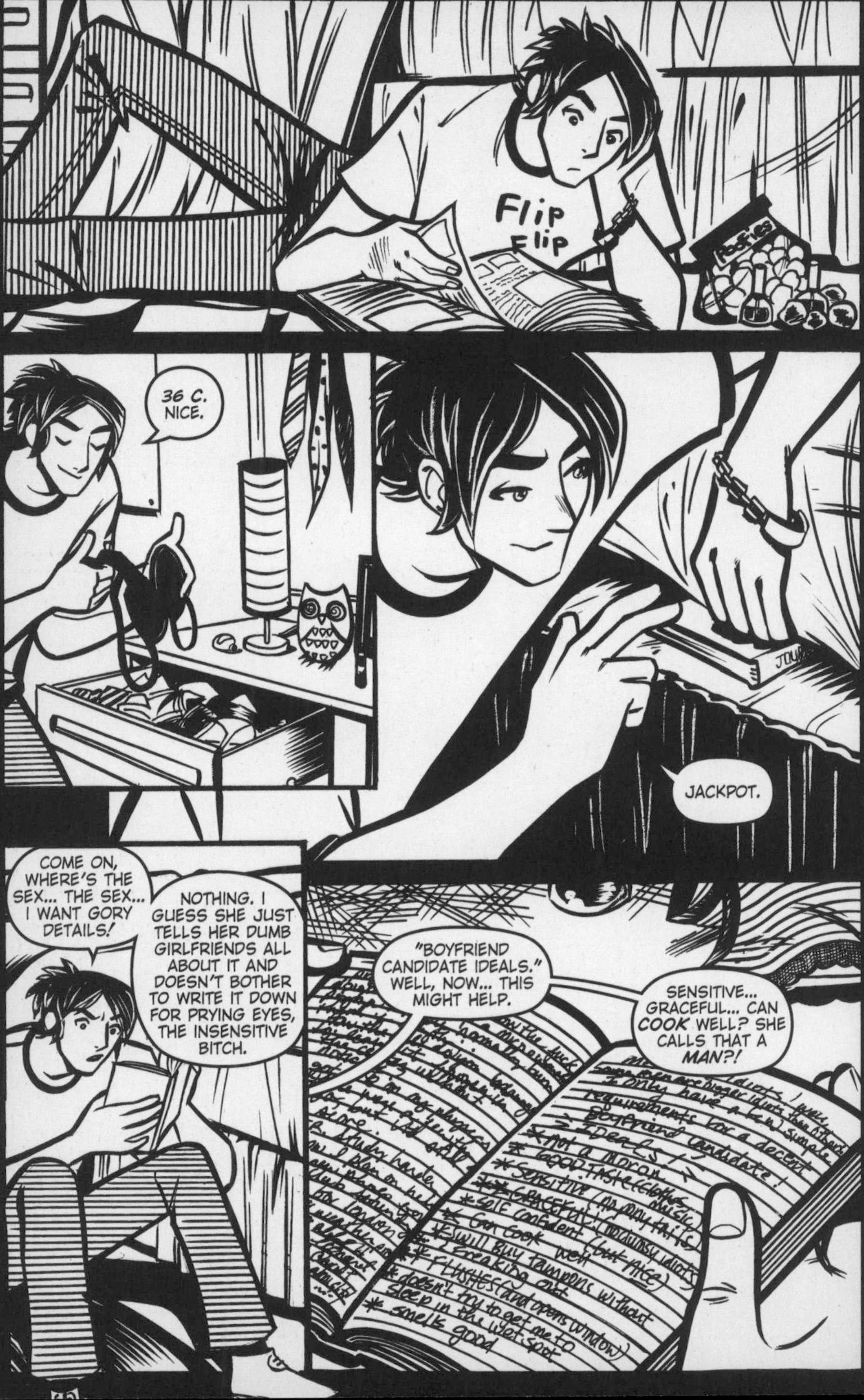
Flip
Flip
36 C. NICE.
JACKPOT.
COME ON, WHERE'S THE SEX... THE SEX... I WANT GORY DETAILS!
NOTHING. I GUESS SHE JUST TELLS HER DUMB GIRLFRIENDS ALL ABOUT IT AND DOESN'T BOTHER TO WRITE IT DOWN FOR PRYING EYES, THE INSENSITIVE BITCH.
"BOYFRIEND CANDIDATE IDEALS." WELL, NOW... THIS MIGHT HELP.
SENSITIVE... GRACEFUL... CAN COOK WELL? SHE CALLS THAT A MAN?!
requirements for a decent
Boyfriend Candidate!
*Not a moron
*Good Taste (clothes, music)
*Sensitive (no pony tails)
*Graceful (no clumsy idiots)
*self confident (but nice)
*can cook well
*will buy tampons without freaking out
*Flushes (and opens window)
*doesn't try to get me to sleep in the wet spot
*smells good

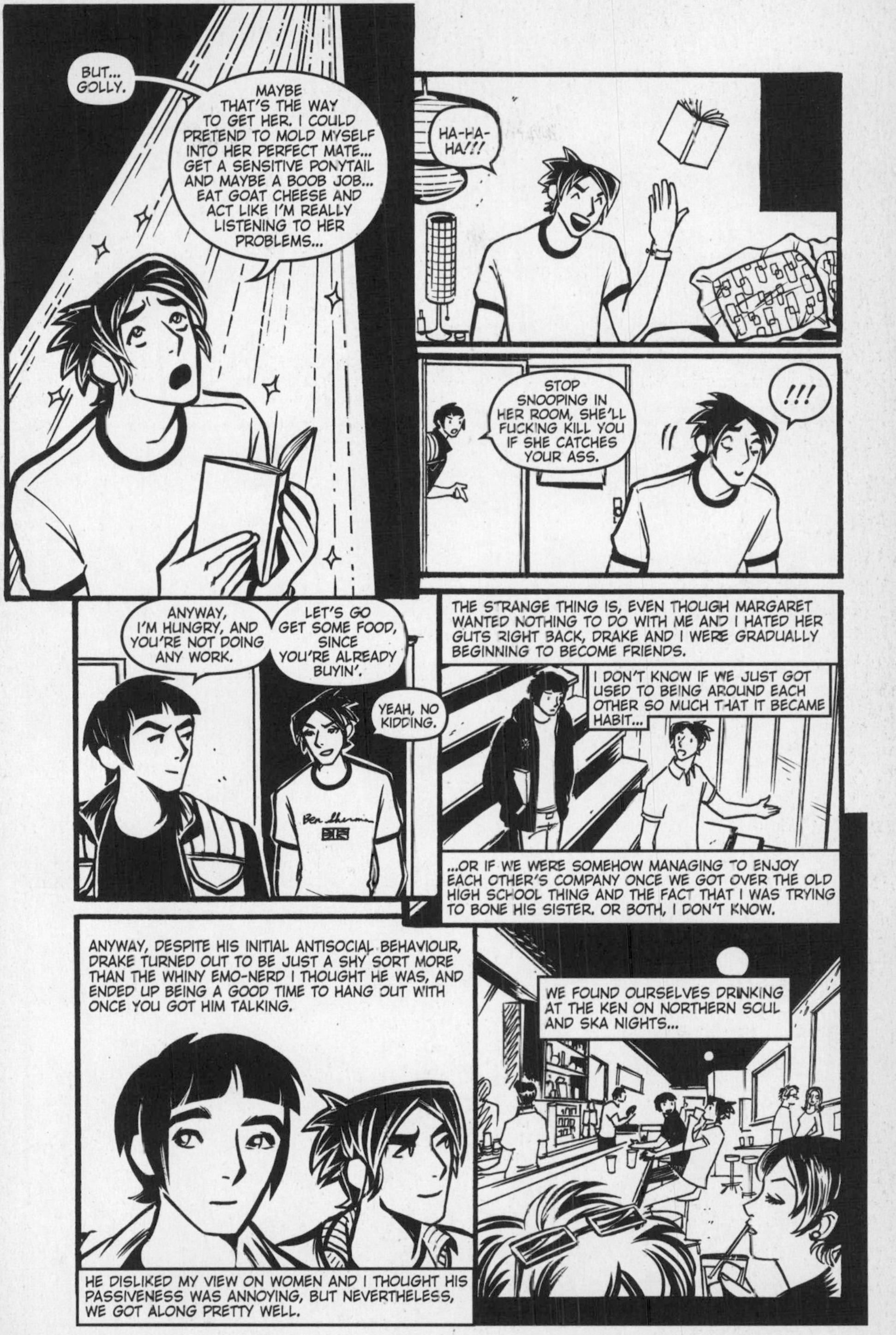

BUT... GOLLY.
MAYBE THAT'S THE WAY TO GET HER. I COULD PRETEND TO MOLD MYSELF INTO HER PERFECT MATE... GET A SENSITIVE PONYTAIL AND MAYBE A BOOB JOB... EAT GOAT CHEESE AND ACT LIKE I'M REALLY LISTENING TO HER PROBLEMS...
HA-HA-HA!!!
STOP SNOOPING IN HER ROOM, SHE'LL FUCKING KILL YOU IF SHE CATCHES YOUR ASS.
!!!
ANYWAY, I'M HUNGRY, AND YOU'RE NOT DOING ANY WORK.
LET'S GO GET SOME FOOD, SINCE YOU'RE ALREADY BUYIN'.
YEAH, NO KIDDING.
Ben Sherman
THE STRANGE THING IS, EVEN THOUGH MARGARET WANTED NOTHING TO DO WITH ME AND I HATED HER GUTS RIGHT BACK, DRAKE AND I WERE GRADUALLY BEGINNING TO BECOME FRIENDS.
I DON'T KNOW IF WE JUST GOT USED TO BEING AROUND EACH OTHER SO MUCH THAT IT BECAME HABIT...
...OR IF WE WERE SOMEHOW MANAGING TO ENJOY EACH OTHER'S COMPANY ONCE WE GOT OVER THE OLD HIGH SCHOOL THING AND THE FACT THAT I WAS TRYING TO BONE HIS SISTER. OR BOTH, I DON'T KNOW.
ANYWAY, DESPITE HIS INITIAL ANTISOCIAL BEHAVIOUR, DRAKE TURNED OUT TO BE JUST A SHY SORT MORE THAN THE WHINY EMO-NERD I THOUGHT HE WAS, AND ENDED UP BEING A GOOD TIME TO HANG OUT WITH ONCE YOU GOT HIM TALKING.
HE DISLIKED MY VIEW ON WOMEN AND I THOUGHT HIS PASSIVENESS WAS ANNOYING, BUT NEVERTHELESS, WE GOT ALONG PRETTY WELL.
WE FOUND OURSELVES DRINKING AT THE KEN ON NORTHERN SOUL AND SKA NIGHTS...

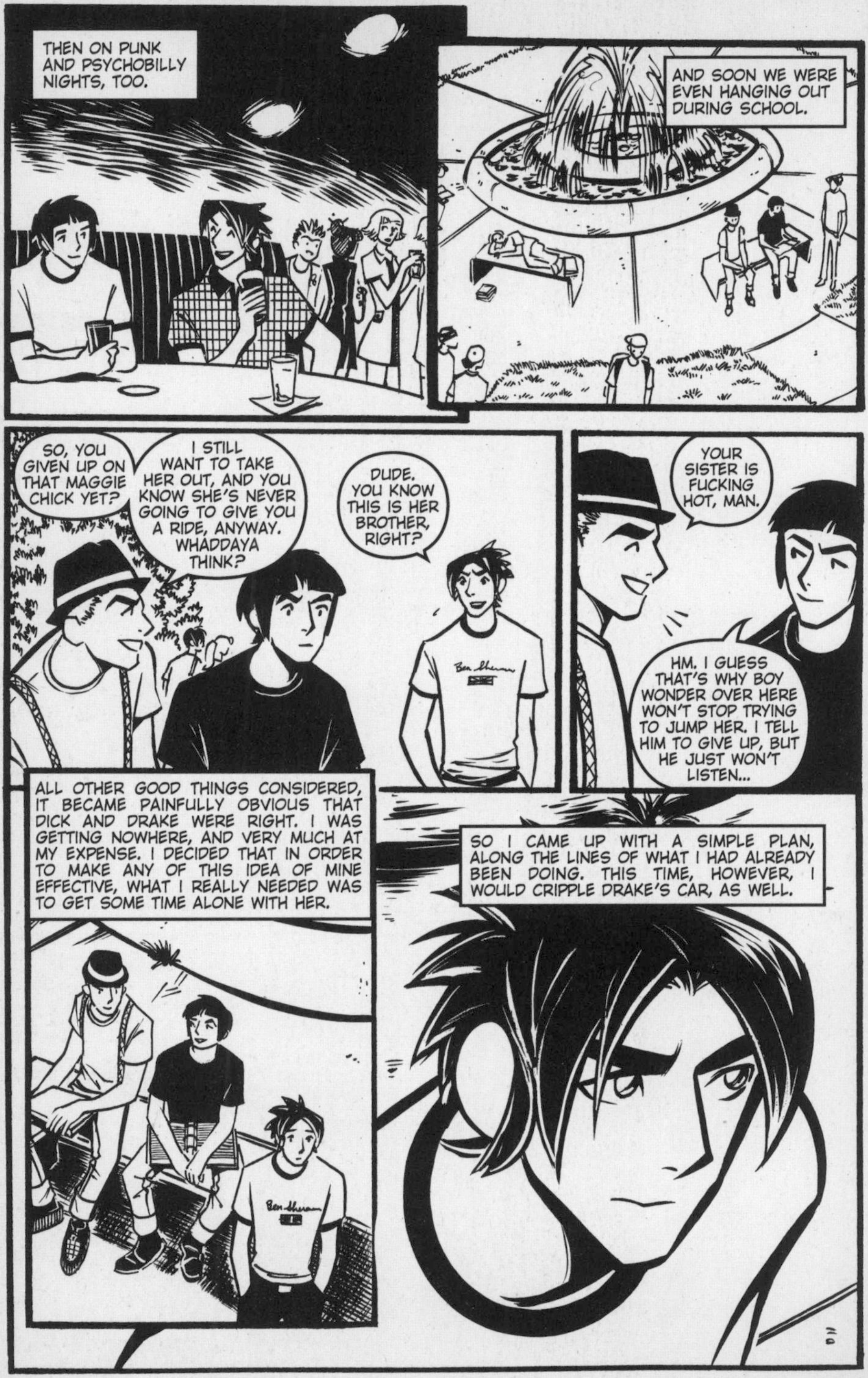
THEN ON PUNK AND PSYCHOBILLY NIGHTS, TOO.
AND SOON WE WERE EVEN HANGING OUT DURING SCHOOL.
SO, YOU GIVEN UP ON THAT MAGGIE CHICK YET?
I STILL WANT TO TAKE HER OUT, AND YOU KNOW SHE'S NEVER GOING TO GIVE YOU A RIDE, ANYWAY. WHADDAYA THINK?
DUDE. YOU KNOW THIS IS HER BROTHER, RIGHT?
YOUR SISTER IS FUCKING HOT, MAN.
HM. I GUESS THAT'S WHY BOY WONDER OVER HERE WON'T STOP TRYING TO JUMP HER. I TELL HIM TO GIVE UP, BUT HE JUST WON'T LISTEN...
ALL OTHER GOOD THINGS CONSIDERED, IT BECAME PAINFULLY OBVIOUS THAT DICK AND DRAKE WERE RIGHT. I WAS GETTING NOWHERE, AND VERY MUCH AT MY EXPENSE. I DECIDED THAT IN ORDER TO MAKE ANY OF THIS IDEA OF MINE EFFECTIVE, WHAT I REALLY NEEDED WAS TO GET SOME TIME ALONE WITH HER.
SO I CAME UP WITH A SIMPLE PLAN, ALONG THE LINES OF WHAT I HAD ALREADY BEEN DOING. THIS TIME, HOWEVER, I WOULD CRIPPLE DRAKE'S CAR, AS WELL.

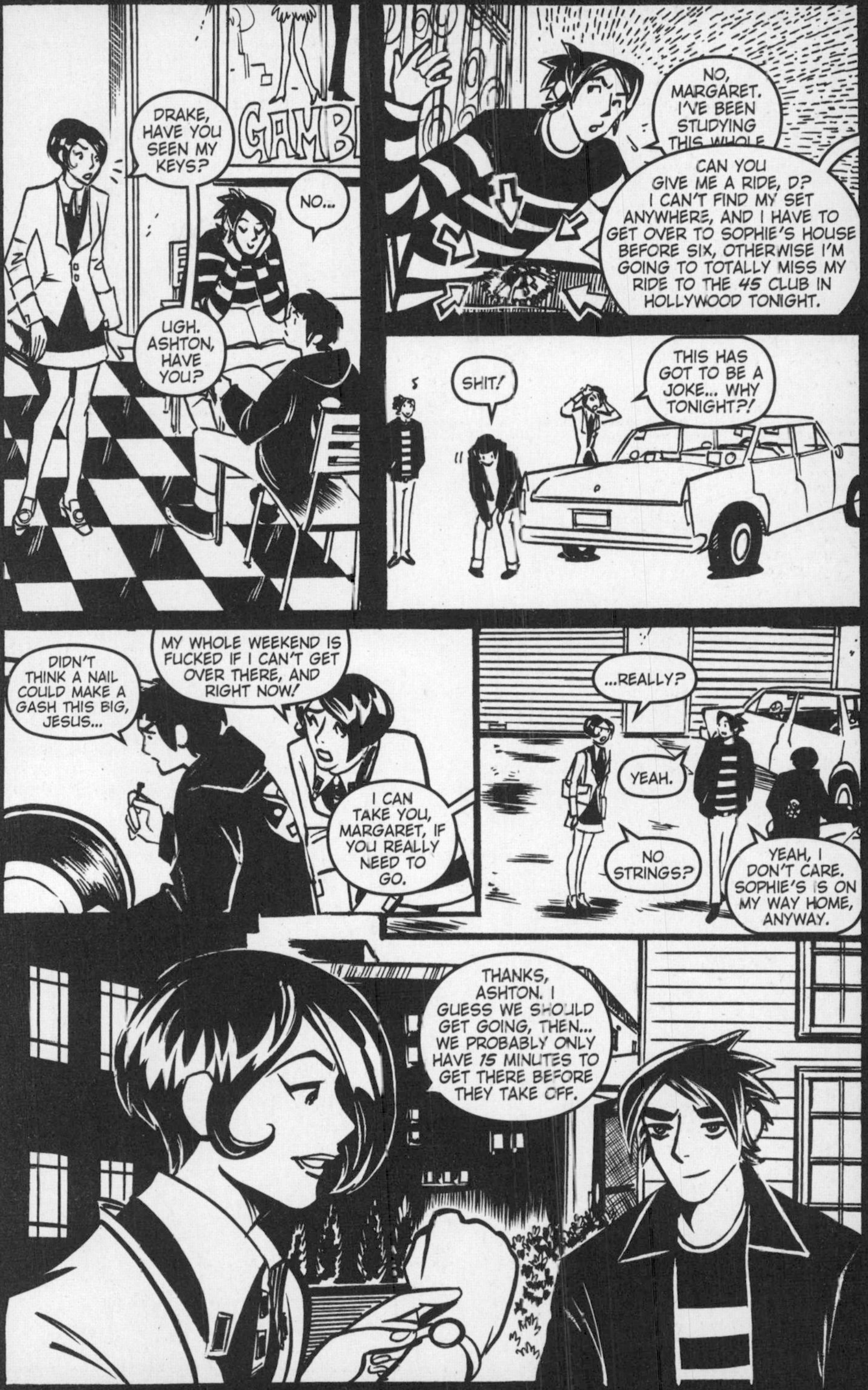

DRAKE, HAVE YOU SEEN MY KEYS?
NO...
UGH. ASHTON, HAVE YOU?
NO, MARGARET. I'VE BEEN STUDYING THIS WHOLE
CAN YOU GIVE ME A RIDE, D? I CAN'T FIND MY SET ANYWHERE, AND I HAVE TO GET OVER TO SOPHIE'S HOUSE BEFORE SIX, OTHERWISE I'M GOING TO TOTALLY MISS MY RIDE TO THE 45 CLUB IN HOLLYWOOD TONIGHT.
SHIT!
THIS HAS GOT TO BE A JOKE... WHY TONIGHT?!
DIDN'T THINK A NAIL COULD MAKE A GASH THIS BIG, JESUS...
MY WHOLE WEEKEND IS FUCKED IF I CAN'T GET OVER THERE, AND RIGHT NOW!
I CAN TAKE YOU, MARGARET, IF YOU REALLY NEED TO GO.
...REALLY?
YEAH.
NO STRINGS?
YEAH, I DON'T CARE. SOPHIE'S IS ON MY WAY HOME, ANYWAY.
THANKS, ASHTON. I GUESS WE SHOULD GET GOING, THEN... WE PROBABLY ONLY HAVE 15 MINUTES TO GET THERE BEFORE THEY TAKE OFF.

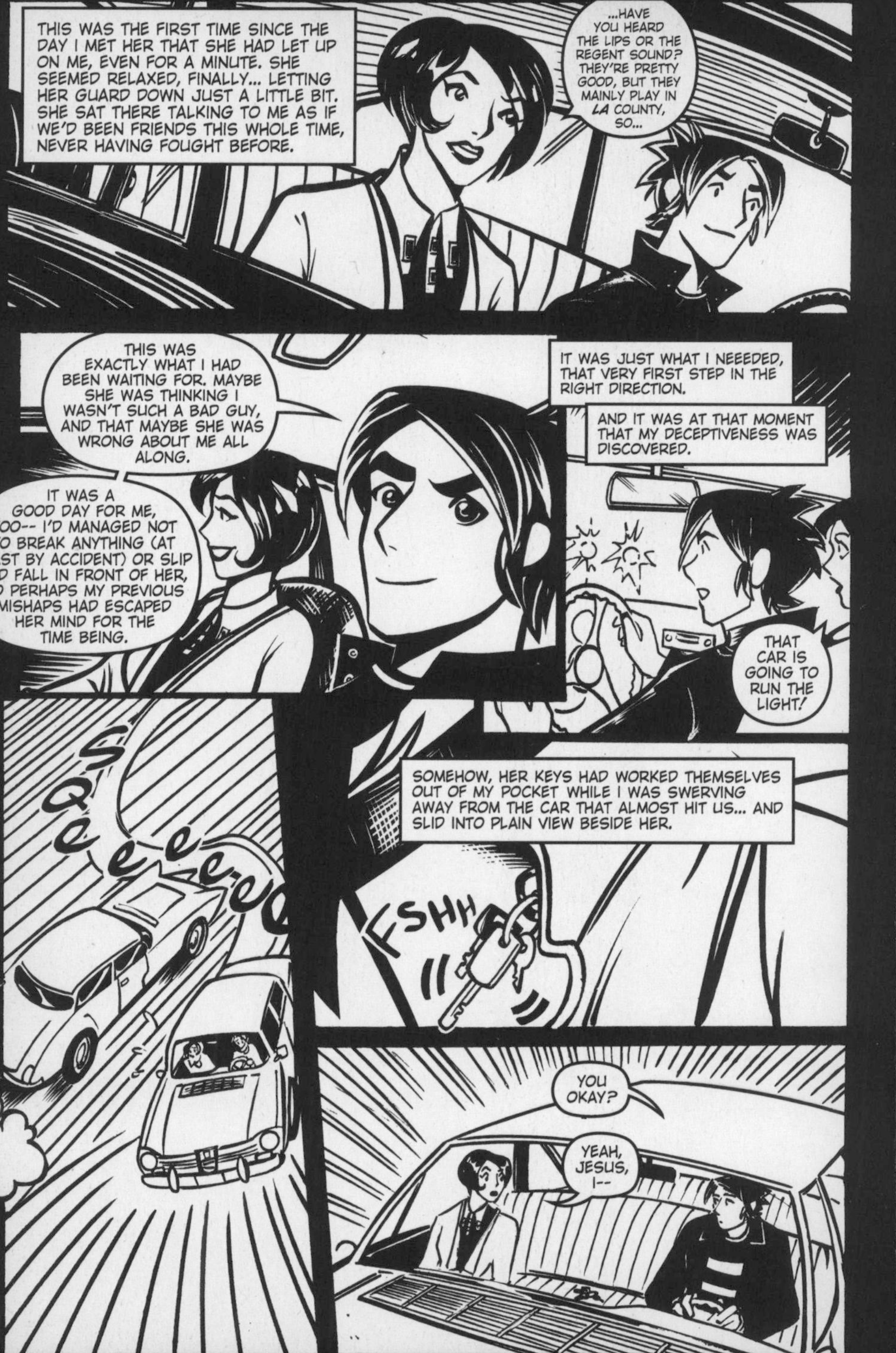
THIS WAS THE FIRST TIME SINCE THE DAY I MET HER THAT SHE HAD LET UP ON ME, EVEN FOR A MINUTE. SHE SEEMED RELAXED, FINALLY... LETTING HER GUARD DOWN JUST A LITTLE BIT. SHE SAT THERE TALKING TO ME AS IF WE'D BEEN FRIENDS THIS WHOLE TIME, NEVER HAVING FOUGHT BEFORE.
...HAVE YOU HEARD THE LIPS OR THE REGENT SOUND? THEY'RE PRETTY GOOD, BUT THEY MAINLY PLAY IN LA COUNTY, SO...
THIS WAS EXACTLY WHAT I HAD BEEN WAITING FOR. MAYBE SHE WAS THINKING I WASN'T SUCH A BAD GUY, AND THAT MAYBE SHE WAS WRONG ABOUT ME ALL ALONG.
IT WAS A GOOD DAY FOR ME, TOO-- I'D MANAGED NOT TO BREAK ANYTHING (AT LEAST BY ACCIDENT) OR SLIP AND FALL IN FRONT OF HER, SO PERHAPS MY PREVIOUS MISHAPS HAD ESCAPED HER MIND FOR THE TIME BEING.
IT WAS JUST WHAT I NEEEDED, THAT VERY FIRST STEP IN THE RIGHT DIRECTION.
AND IT WAS AT THAT MOMENT THAT MY DECEPTIVENESS WAS DISCOVERED.
THAT CAR IS GOING TO RUN THE LIGHT!
SQUEEEEEEE
SOMEHOW, HER KEYS HAD WORKED THEMSELVES OUT OF MY POCKET WHILE I WAS SWERVING AWAY FROM THE CAR THAT ALMOST HIT US... AND SLID INTO PLAIN VIEW BESIDE HER.
FSHH
YOU OKAY?
YEAH, JESUS, I--

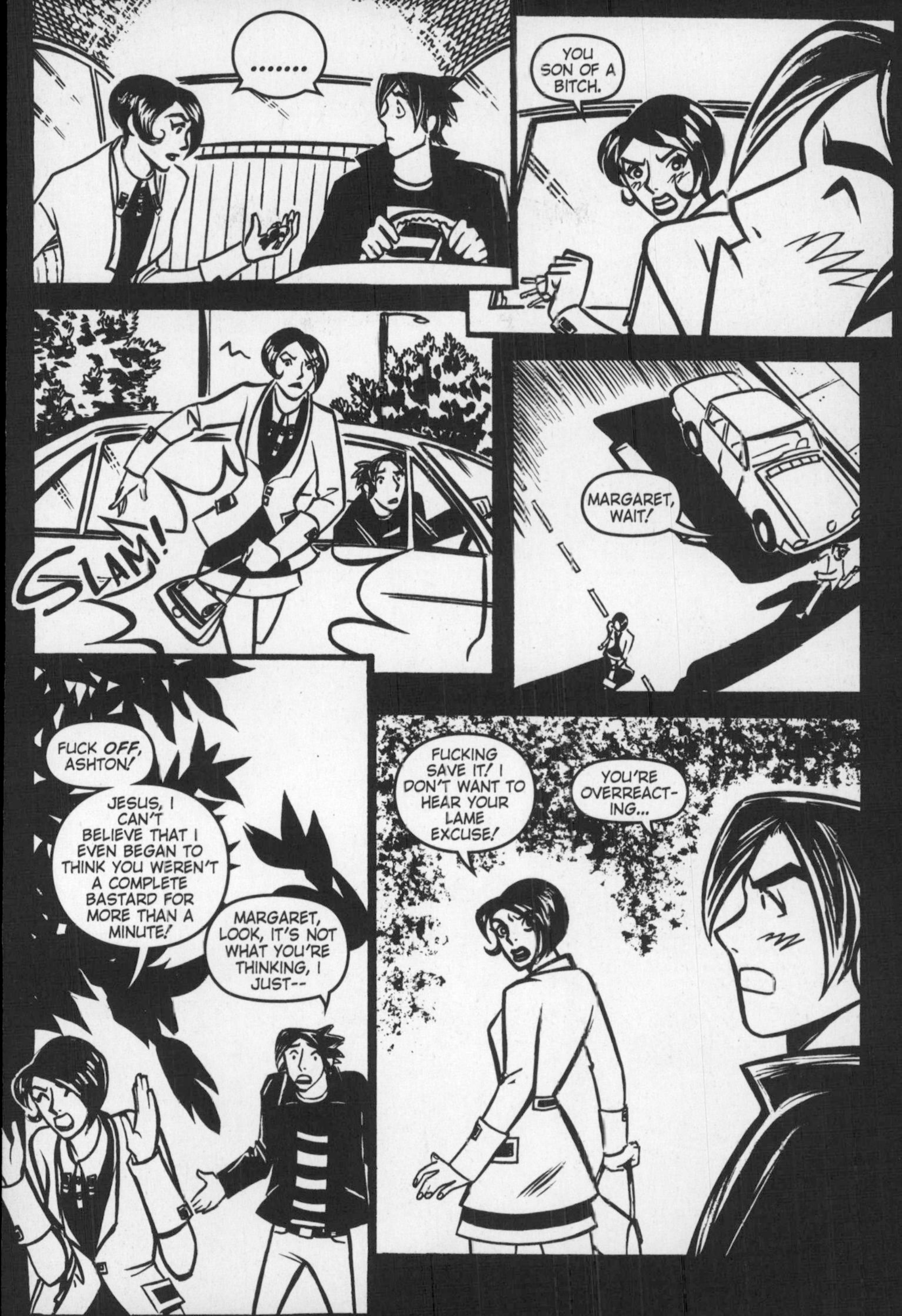
....
YOU SON OF A BITCH.
SLAM!
MARGARET, WAIT!
FUCK OFF, ASHTON!
JESUS, I CAN'T BELIEVE THAT I EVEN BEGAN TO THINK YOU WEREN'T A COMPLETE BASTARD FOR MORE THAN A MINUTE!
MARGARET, LOOK, IT'S NOT WHAT YOU'RE THINKING, I JUST--
YOU'RE OVERREACT-ING...
FUCKING SAVE IT! I DON'T WANT TO HEAR YOUR LAME EXCUSE!

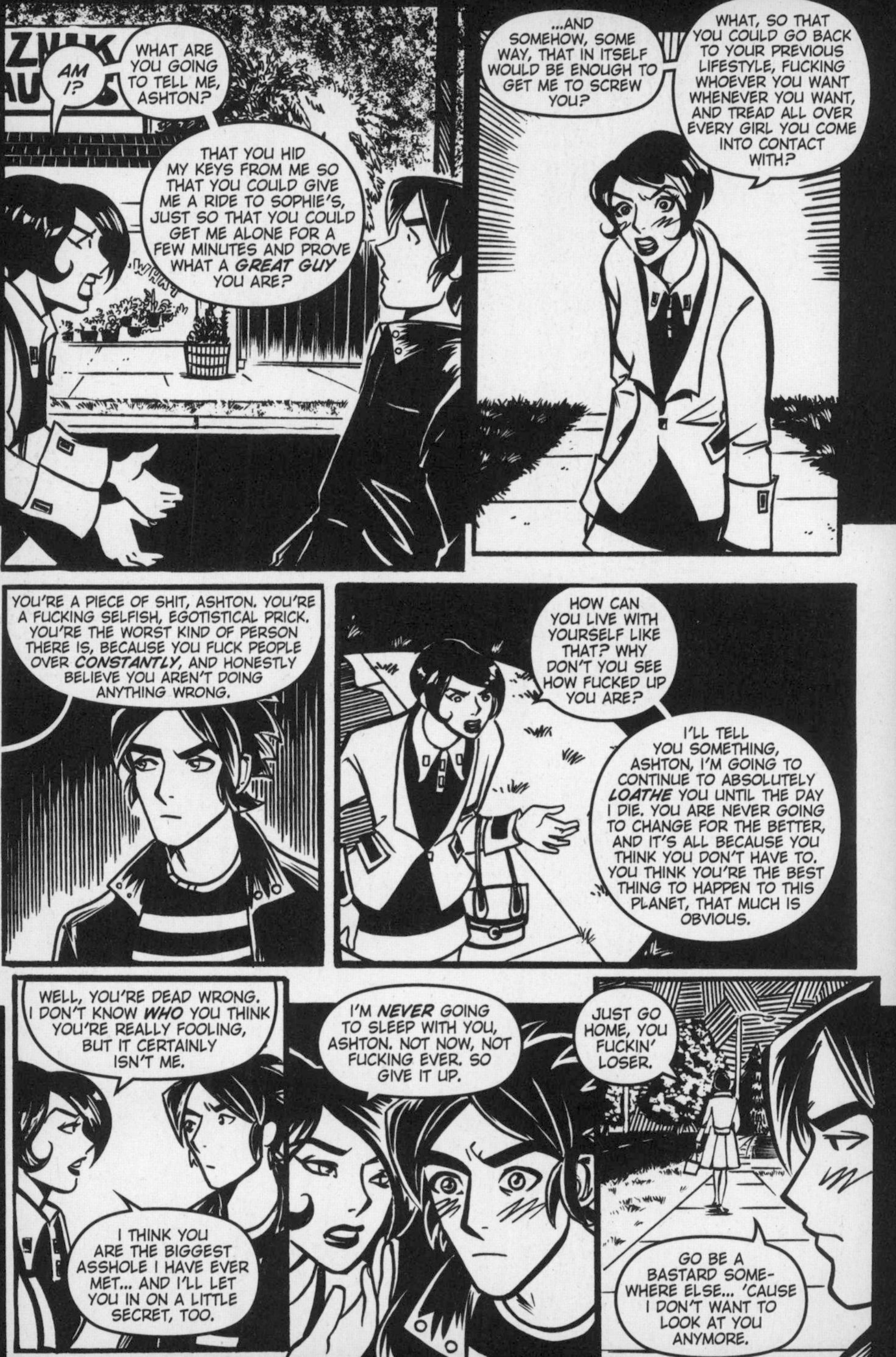
AM I?
WHAT ARE YOU GOING TO TELL ME, ASHTON?
THAT YOU HID MY KEYS FROM ME SO THAT YOU COULD GIVE ME A RIDE TO SOPHIE'S, JUST SO THAT YOU COULD GET ME ALONE FOR A FEW MINUTES AND PROVE WHAT A GREAT GUY YOU ARE?
...AND SOMEHOW, SOME WAY, THAT IN ITSELF WOULD BE ENOUGH TO GET ME TO SCREW YOU?
WHAT, SO THAT YOU COULD GO BACK TO YOUR PREVIOUS LIFESTYLE, FUCKING WHOEVER YOU WANT WHENEVER YOU WANT, AND TREAD ALL OVER EVERY GIRL YOU COME INTO CONTACT WITH?
YOU'RE A PIECE OF SHIT, ASHTON. YOU'RE A FUCKING SELFISH, EGOTISTICAL PRICK. YOU'RE THE WORST KIND OF PERSON THERE IS, BECAUSE YOU FUCK PEOPLE OVER CONSTANTLY, AND HONESTLY BELIEVE YOU AREN'T DOING ANYTHING WRONG.
HOW CAN YOU LIVE WITH YOURSELF LIKE THAT? WHY DON'T YOU SEE HOW FUCKED UP YOU ARE?
I'LL TELL YOU SOMETHING, ASHTON, I'M GOING TO CONTINUE TO ABSOLUTELY LOATHE YOU UNTIL THE DAY I DIE. YOU ARE NEVER GOING TO CHANGE FOR THE BETTER, AND IT'S ALL BECAUSE YOU THINK YOU DON'T HAVE TO. YOU THINK YOU'RE THE BEST THING TO HAPPEN TO THIS PLANET, THAT MUCH IS OBVIOUS.
WELL, YOU'RE DEAD WRONG. I DON'T KNOW WHO YOU THINK YOU'RE REALLY FOOLING, BUT IT CERTAINLY ISN'T ME.
I THINK YOU ARE THE BIGGEST ASSHOLE I HAVE EVER MET... AND I'LL LET YOU IN ON A LITTLE SECRET, TOO.
I'M NEVER GOING TO SLEEP WITH YOU, ASHTON. NOT NOW, NOT FUCKING EVER. SO GIVE IT UP.
JUST GO HOME, YOU FUCKIN' LOSER.
GO BE A BASTARD SOME-WHERE ELSE... 'CAUSE I DON'T WANT TO LOOK AT YOU ANYMORE.

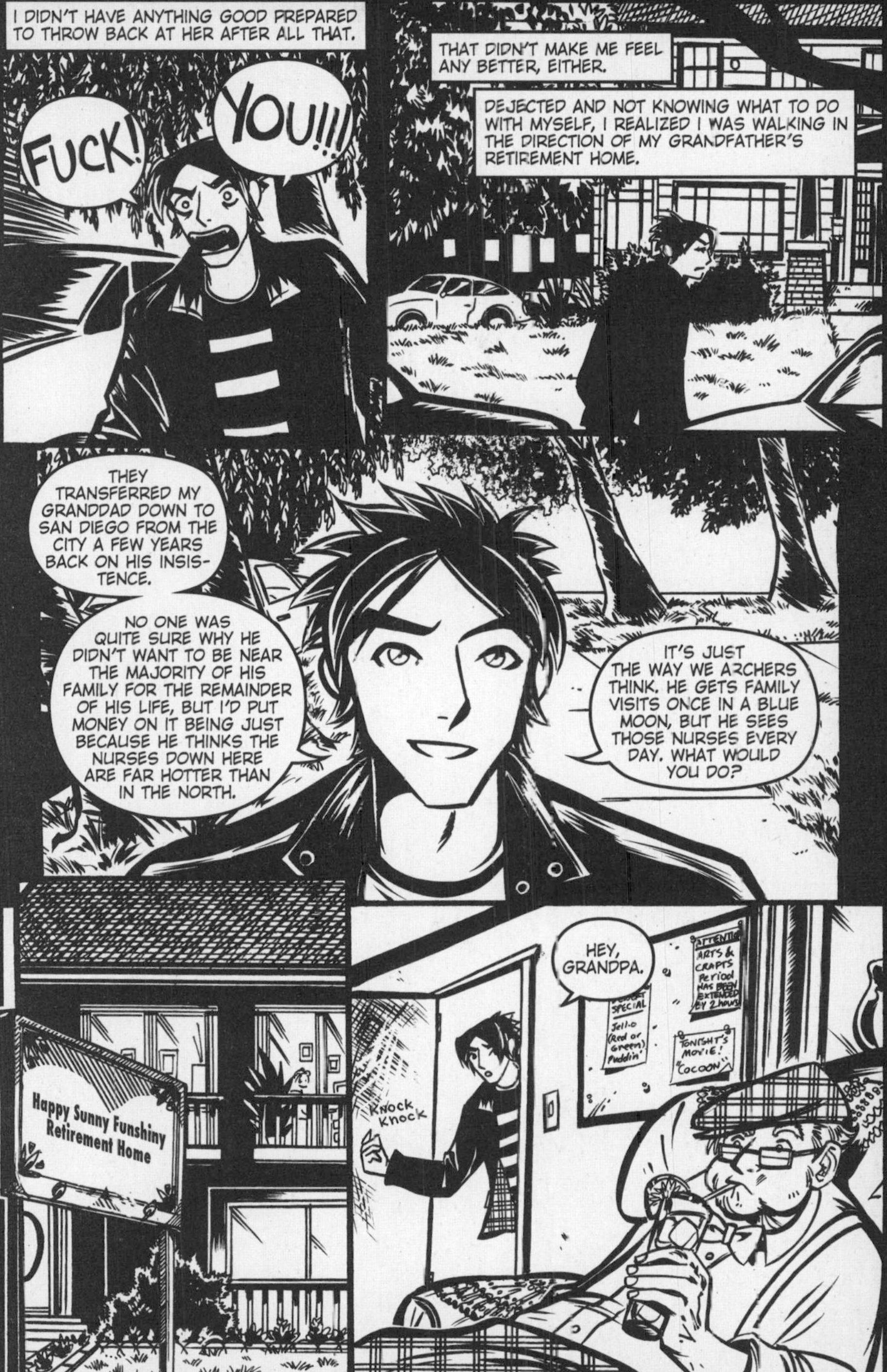
I DIDN'T HAVE ANYTHING GOOD PREPARED TO THROW BACK AT HER AFTER ALL THAT.
FUCK!
YOU!!!!
THAT DIDN'T MAKE ME FEEL ANY BETTER, EITHER.
DEJECTED AND NOT KNOWING WHAT TO DO WITH MYSELF, I REALIZED I WAS WALKING IN THE DIRECTION OF MY GRANDFATHER'S RETIREMENT HOME.
THEY TRANSFERRED MY GRANDDAD DOWN TO SAN DIEGO FROM THE CITY A FEW YEARS BACK ON HIS INSISTENCE.
NO ONE WAS QUITE SURE WHY HE DIDN'T WANT TO BE NEAR THE MAJORITY OF HIS FAMILY FOR THE REMAINDER OF HIS LIFE, BUT I'D PUT MONEY ON IT BEING JUST BECAUSE HE THINKS THE NURSES DOWN HERE ARE FAR HOTTER THAN IN THE NORTH.
IT'S JUST THE WAY WE ARCHERS THINK. HE GETS FAMILY VISITS ONCE IN A BLUE MOON, BUT HE SEES THOSE NURSES EVERY DAY. WHAT WOULD YOU DO?
Happy Sunny Funshiny Retirement Home
Knock Knock
HEY, GRANDPA.
SPECIAL Jell-o (Red or Green) Puddin'
ARTS & CRAPTS Period HAS BEEN EXTENDED BY 2 hours
TONIGHT'S MOVIE! "COCOON"

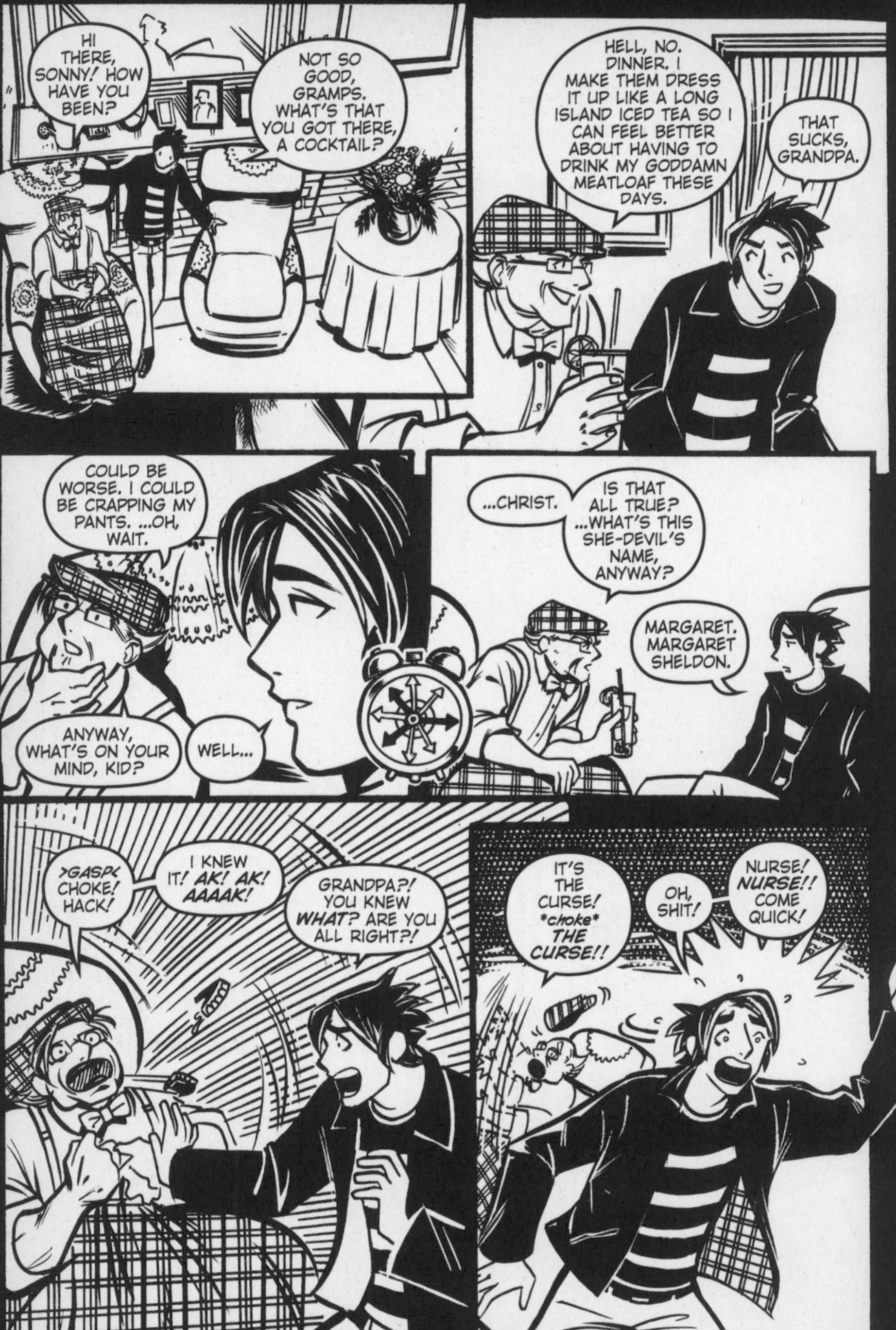
HI THERE, SONNY! HOW HAVE YOU BEEN?
NOT SO GOOD, GRAMPS. WHAT'S THAT YOU GOT THERE, A COCKTAIL?
HELL, NO. DINNER. I MAKE THEM DRESS IT UP LIKE A LONG ISLAND ICED TEA SO I CAN FEEL BETTER ABOUT HAVING TO DRINK MY GODDAMN MEATLOAF THESE DAYS.
THAT SUCKS, GRANDPA.
COULD BE WORSE. I COULD BE CRAPPING MY PANTS. ...OH, WAIT.
ANYWAY, WHAT'S ON YOUR MIND, KID?
WELL...
...CHRIST.
IS THAT ALL TRUE? ...WHAT'S THIS SHE-DEVIL'S NAME, ANYWAY?
MARGARET. MARGARET SHELDON.
>GASP< CHOKE! HACK!
I KNEW IT! AK! AK! AAAAK!
GRANDPA?! YOU KNEW WHAT? ARE YOU ALL RIGHT?!
IT'S THE CURSE! *choke* THE CURSE!!
OH, SHIT!
NURSE! NURSE!! COME QUICK!

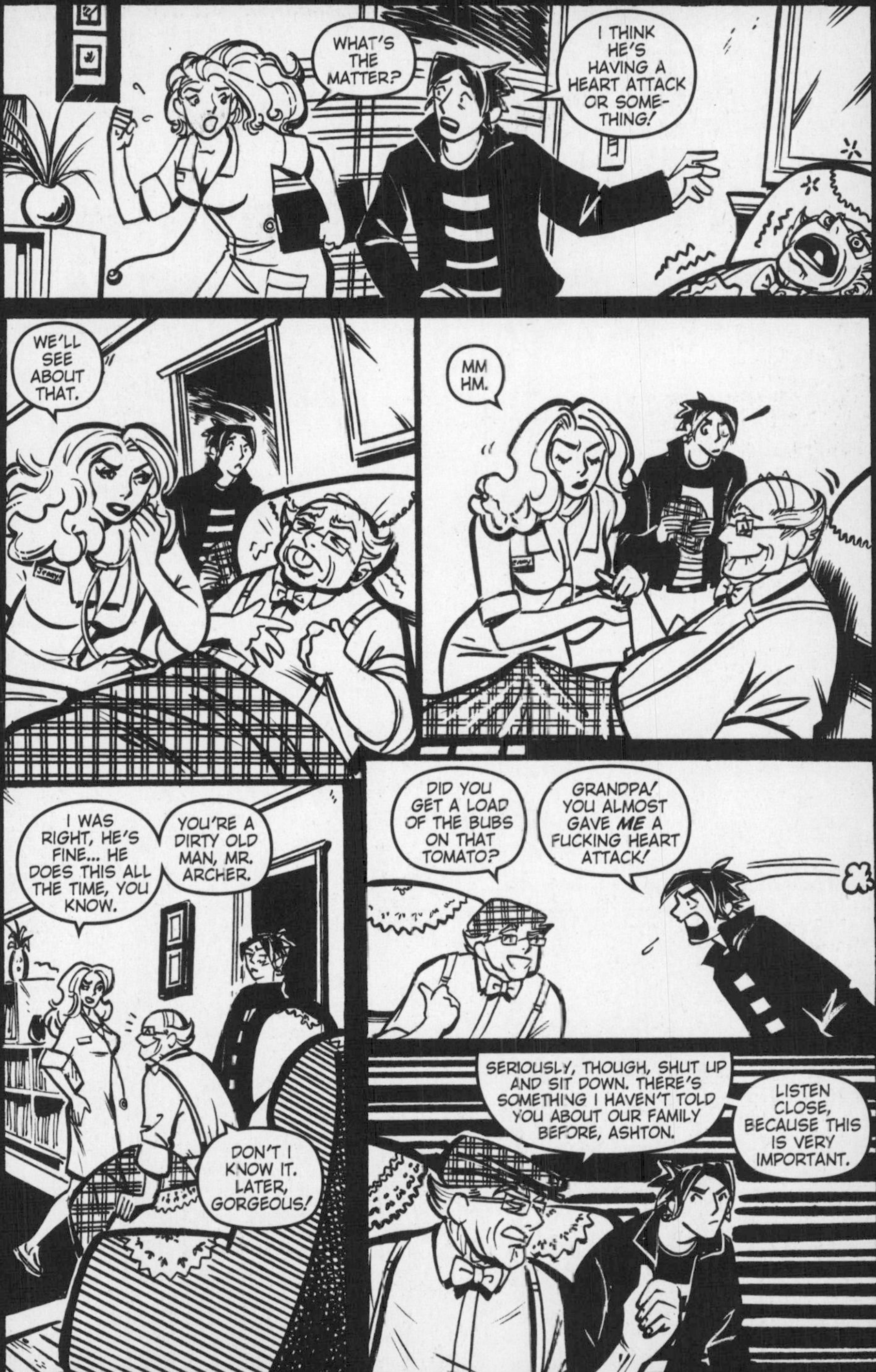
WHAT'S THE MATTER?
I THINK HE'S HAVING A HEART ATTACK OR SOME-THING!
WE'LL SEE ABOUT THAT.
MM HM.
I WAS RIGHT, HE'S FINE... HE DOES THIS ALL THE TIME, YOU KNOW.
YOU'RE A DIRTY OLD MAN, MR. ARCHER.
DON'T I KNOW IT. LATER, GORGEOUS!
DID YOU GET A LOAD OF THE BUBS ON THAT TOMATO?
GRANDPA! YOU ALMOST GAVE ME A FUCKING HEART ATTACK!
SERIOUSLY, THOUGH, SHUT UP AND SIT DOWN. THERE'S SOMETHING I HAVEN'T TOLD YOU ABOUT OUR FAMILY BEFORE, ASHTON.
LISTEN CLOSE, BECAUSE THIS IS VERY IMPORTANT.

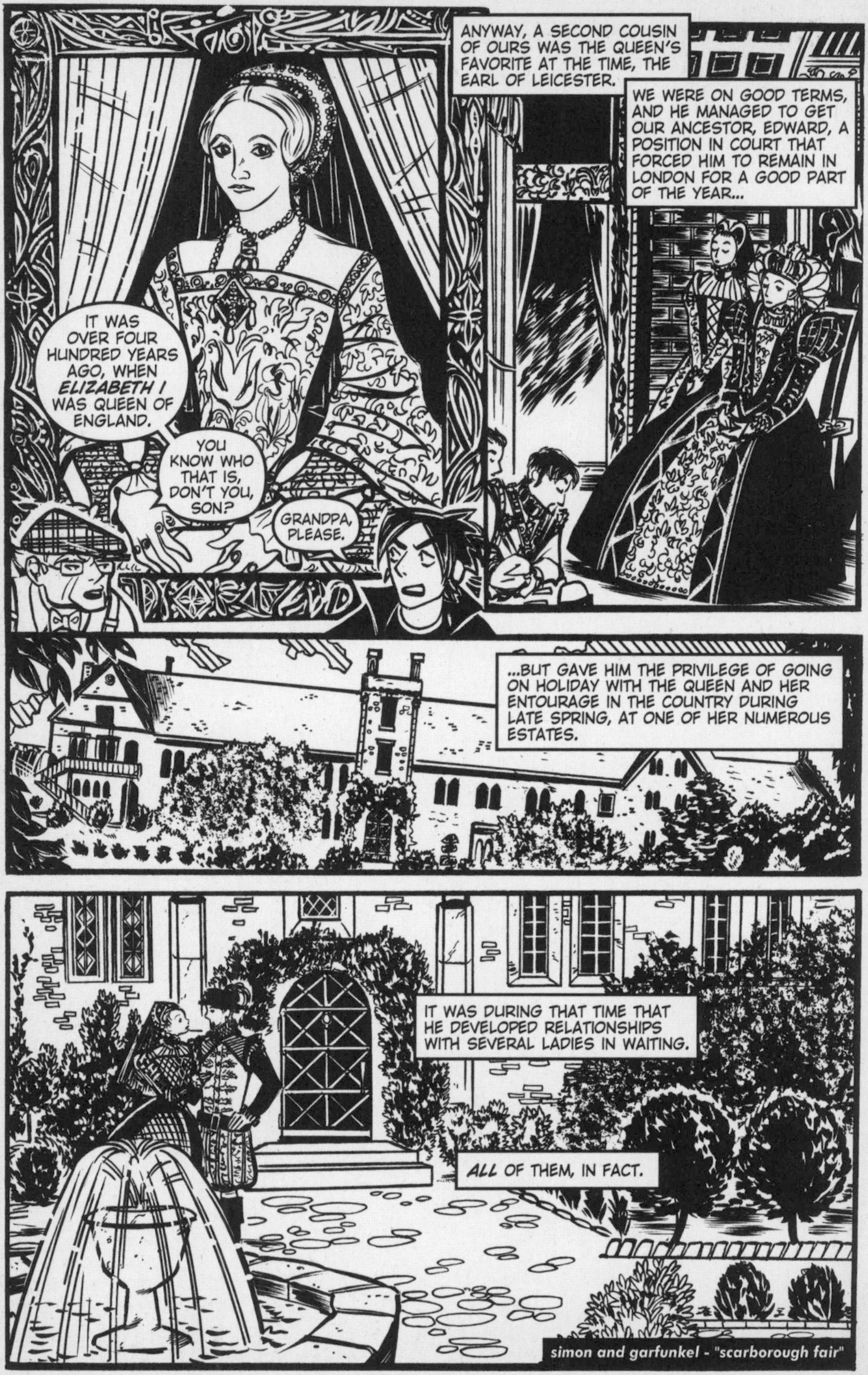

IT WAS OVER FOUR HUNDRED YEARS AGO, WHEN ***ELIZABETH I*** WAS QUEEN OF ENGLAND.
YOU KNOW WHO THAT IS, DON'T YOU, SON?
GRANDPA, PLEASE.
ANYWAY, A SECOND COUSIN OF OURS WAS THE QUEEN'S FAVORITE AT THE TIME, THE EARL OF LEICESTER.
WE WERE ON GOOD TERMS, AND HE MANAGED TO GET OUR ANCESTOR, EDWARD, A POSITION IN COURT THAT FORCED HIM TO REMAIN IN LONDON FOR A GOOD PART OF THE YEAR...
...BUT GAVE HIM THE PRIVILEGE OF GOING ON HOLIDAY WITH THE QUEEN AND HER ENTOURAGE IN THE COUNTRY DURING LATE SPRING, AT ONE OF HER NUMEROUS ESTATES.
IT WAS DURING THAT TIME THAT HE DEVELOPED RELATIONSHIPS WITH SEVERAL LADIES IN WAITING.
ALL OF THEM, IN FACT.
simon and garfunkel - "scarborough fair"

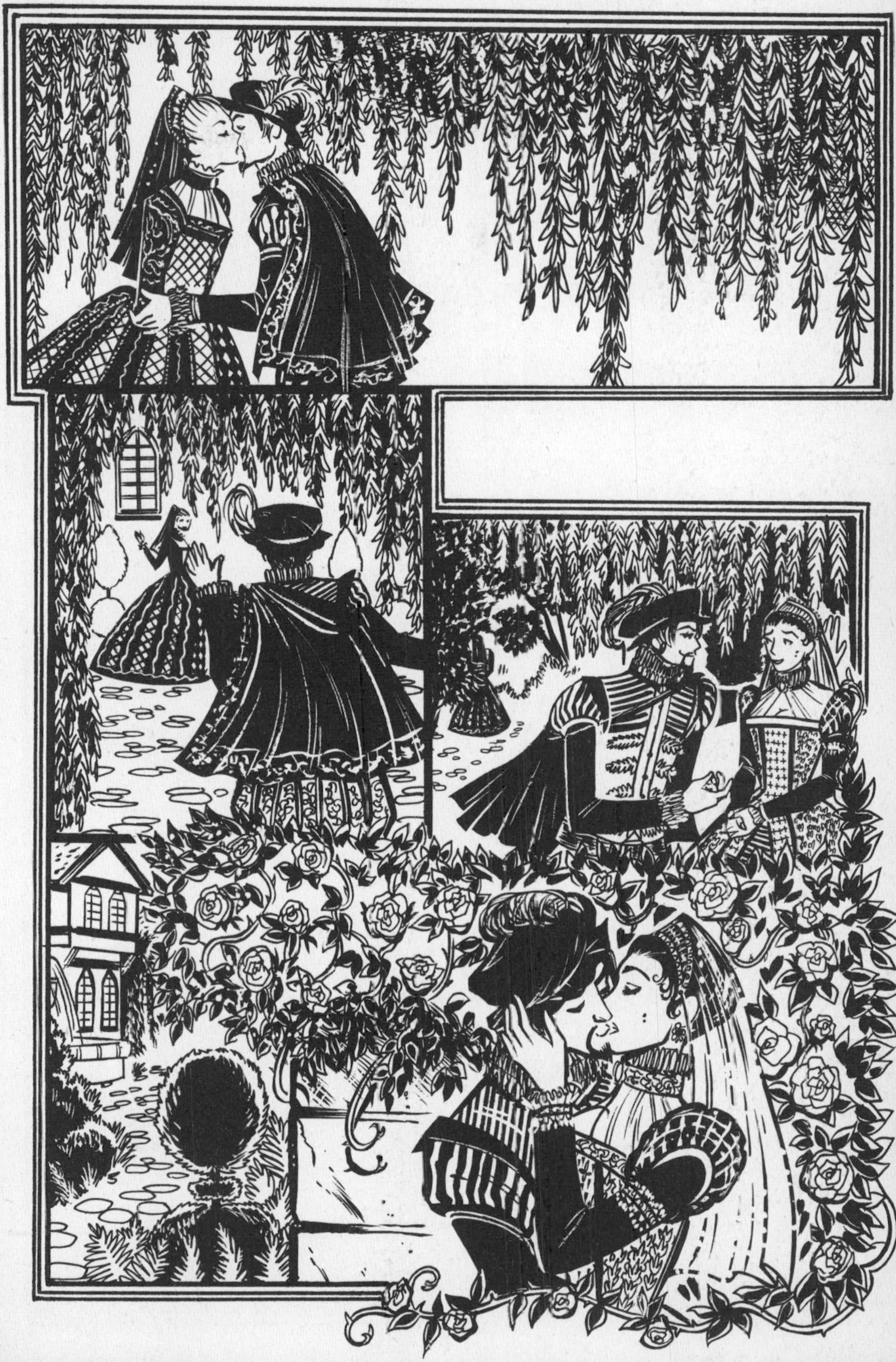

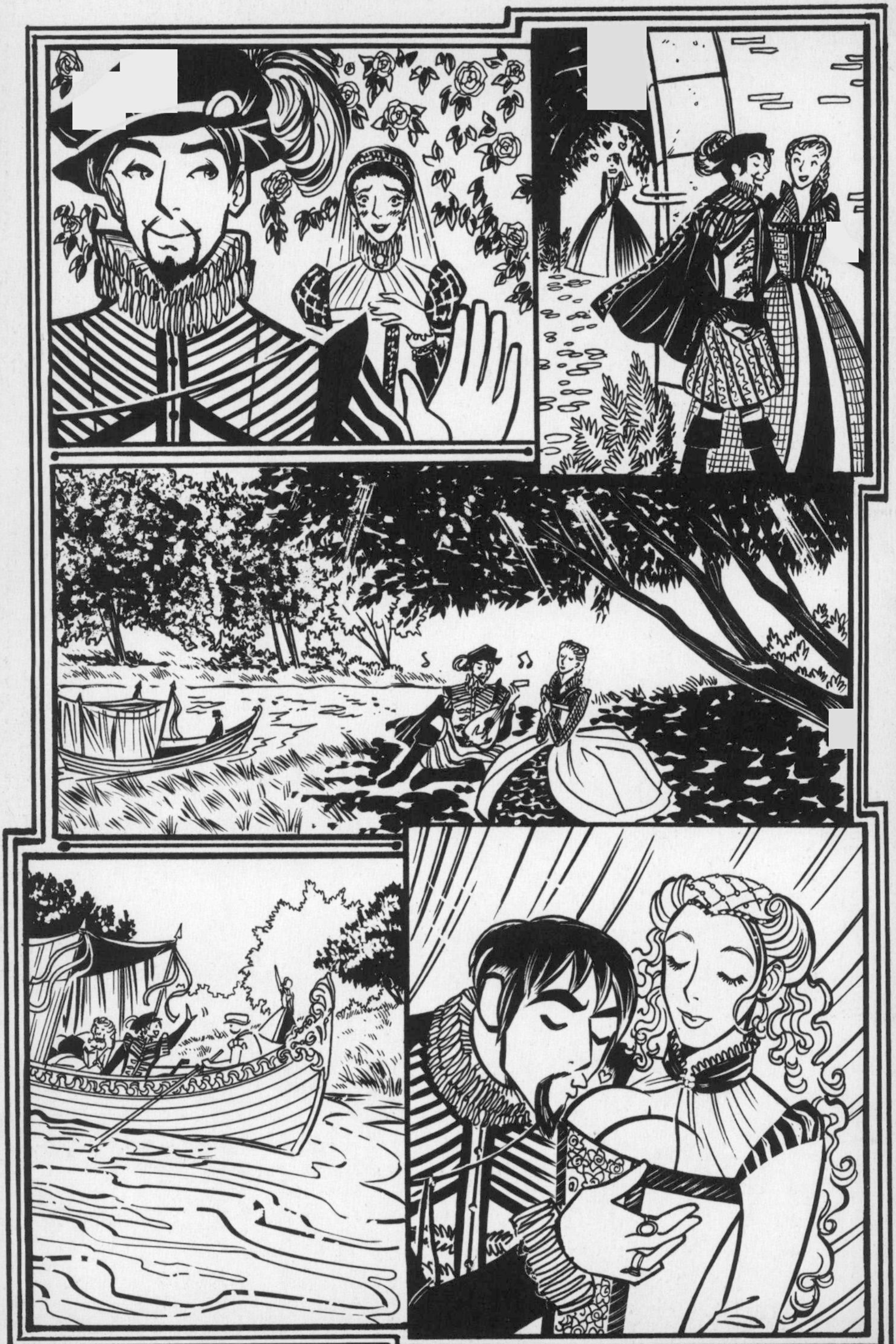

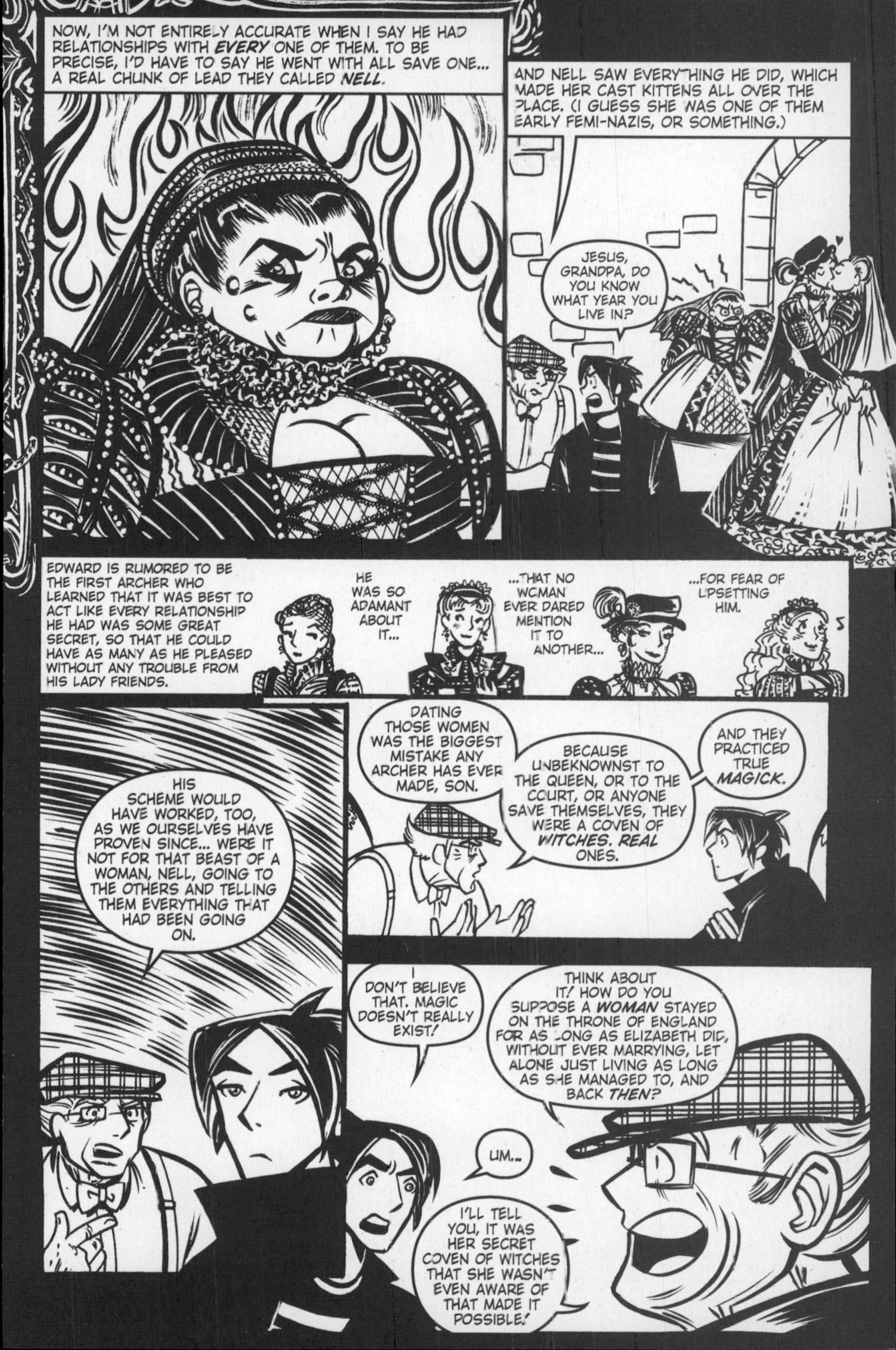
NOW, I'M NOT ENTIRELY ACCURATE WHEN I SAY HE HAD RELATIONSHIPS WITH *EVERY* ONE OF THEM. TO BE PRECISE, I'D HAVE TO SAY HE WENT WITH ALL SAVE ONE... A REAL CHUNK OF LEAD THEY CALLED *NELL*.
AND NELL SAW EVERYTHING HE DID, WHICH MADE HER CAST KITTENS ALL OVER THE PLACE. (I GUESS SHE WAS ONE OF THEM EARLY FEMI-NAZIS, OR SOMETHING.)
JESUS, GRANDPA, DO YOU KNOW WHAT YEAR YOU LIVE IN?
EDWARD IS RUMORED TO BE THE FIRST ARCHER WHO LEARNED THAT IT WAS BEST TO ACT LIKE EVERY RELATIONSHIP HE HAD WAS SOME GREAT SECRET, SO THAT HE COULD HAVE AS MANY AS HE PLEASED WITHOUT ANY TROUBLE FROM HIS LADY FRIENDS.
HE WAS SO ADAMANT ABOUT IT...
...THAT NO WOMAN EVER DARED MENTION IT TO ANOTHER...
...FOR FEAR OF UPSETTING HIM.
HIS SCHEME WOULD HAVE WORKED, TOO, AS WE OURSELVES HAVE PROVEN SINCE... WERE IT NOT FOR THAT BEAST OF A WOMAN, NELL, GOING TO THE OTHERS AND TELLING THEM EVERYTHING THAT HAD BEEN GOING ON.
DATING THOSE WOMEN WAS THE BIGGEST MISTAKE ANY ARCHER HAS EVER MADE, SON.
BECAUSE UNBEKNOWNST TO THE QUEEN, OR TO THE COURT, OR ANYONE SAVE THEMSELVES, THEY WERE A COVEN OF *WITCHES. REAL* ONES.
AND THEY PRACTICED TRUE *MAGICK*.
I DON'T BELIEVE THAT. MAGIC DOESN'T REALLY EXIST!
THINK ABOUT IT! HOW DO YOU SUPPOSE A *WOMAN* STAYED ON THE THRONE OF ENGLAND FOR AS LONG AS ELIZABETH DID, WITHOUT EVER MARRYING, LET ALONE JUST LIVING AS LONG AS SHE MANAGED TO, AND BACK *THEN*?
UM...
I'LL TELL YOU, IT WAS HER SECRET COVEN OF WITCHES THAT SHE WASN'T EVEN AWARE OF THAT MADE IT POSSIBLE!

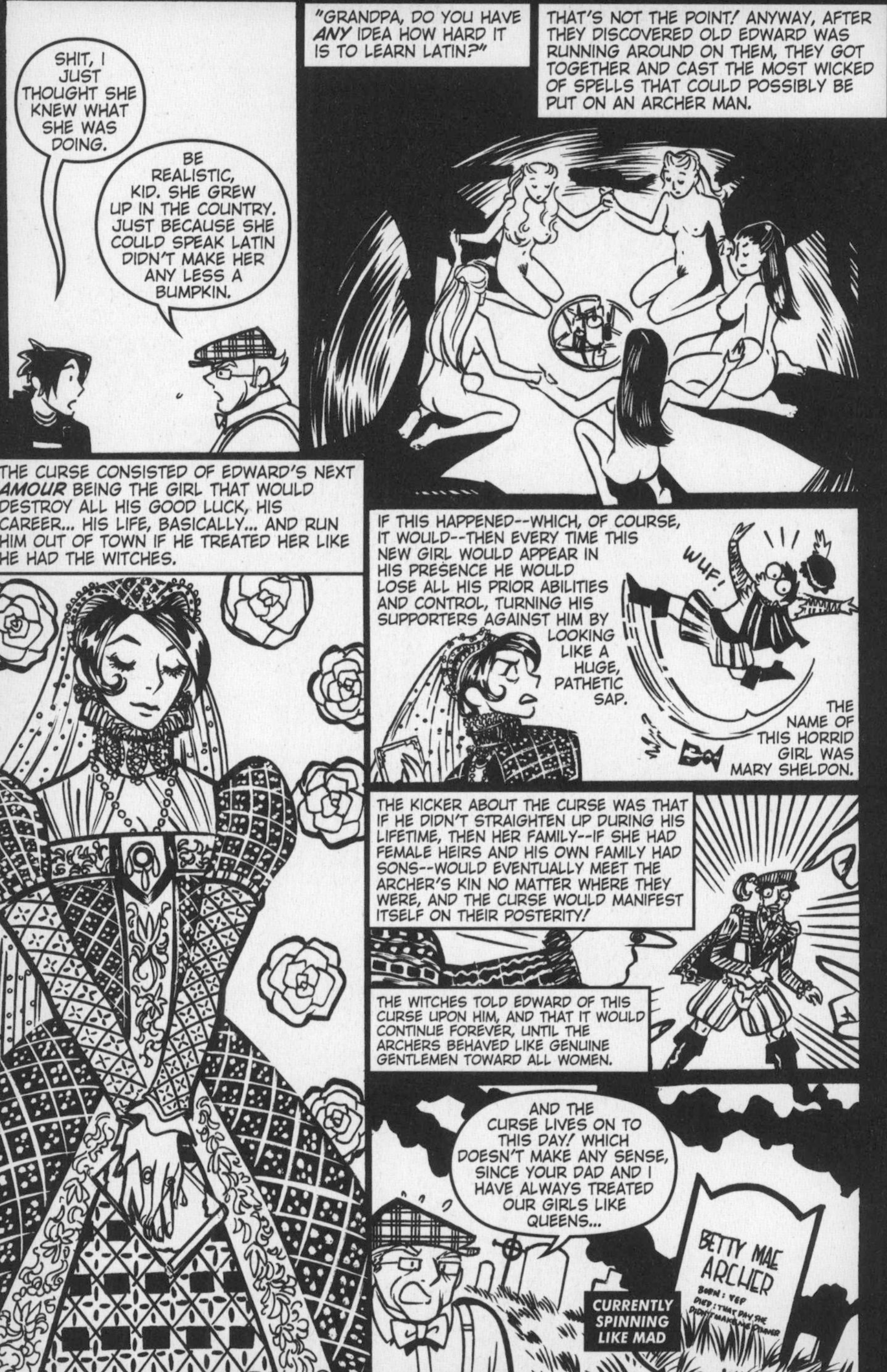
SHIT, I JUST THOUGHT SHE KNEW WHAT SHE WAS DOING.
BE REALISTIC, KID. SHE GREW UP IN THE COUNTRY. JUST BECAUSE SHE COULD SPEAK LATIN DIDN'T MAKE HER ANY LESS A BUMPKIN.
"GRANDPA, DO YOU HAVE ANY IDEA HOW HARD IT IS TO LEARN LATIN?"
THAT'S NOT THE POINT! ANYWAY, AFTER THEY DISCOVERED OLD EDWARD WAS RUNNING AROUND ON THEM, THEY GOT TOGETHER AND CAST THE MOST WICKED OF SPELLS THAT COULD POSSIBLY BE PUT ON AN ARCHER MAN.
THE CURSE CONSISTED OF EDWARD'S NEXT AMOUR BEING THE GIRL THAT WOULD DESTROY ALL HIS GOOD LUCK, HIS CAREER... HIS LIFE, BASICALLY... AND RUN HIM OUT OF TOWN IF HE TREATED HER LIKE HE HAD THE WITCHES.
IF THIS HAPPENED--WHICH, OF COURSE, IT WOULD--THEN EVERY TIME THIS NEW GIRL WOULD APPEAR IN HIS PRESENCE HE WOULD LOSE ALL HIS PRIOR ABILITIES AND CONTROL, TURNING HIS SUPPORTERS AGAINST HIM BY LOOKING LIKE A HUGE, PATHETIC SAP.
WHF!
THE NAME OF THIS HORRID GIRL WAS MARY SHELDON.
THE KICKER ABOUT THE CURSE WAS THAT IF HE DIDN'T STRAIGHTEN UP DURING HIS LIFETIME, THEN HER FAMILY--IF SHE HAD FEMALE HEIRS AND HIS OWN FAMILY HAD SONS--WOULD EVENTUALLY MEET THE ARCHER'S KIN NO MATTER WHERE THEY WERE, AND THE CURSE WOULD MANIFEST ITSELF ON THEIR POSTERITY!
THE WITCHES TOLD EDWARD OF THIS CURSE UPON HIM, AND THAT IT WOULD CONTINUE FOREVER, UNTIL THE ARCHERS BEHAVED LIKE GENUINE GENTLEMEN TOWARD ALL WOMEN.
AND THE CURSE LIVES ON TO THIS DAY! WHICH DOESN'T MAKE ANY SENSE, SINCE YOUR DAD AND I HAVE ALWAYS TREATED OUR GIRLS LIKE QUEENS...
BETTY MAE ARCHER
BORN: YEP
DIED: THAT DAY SHE DIDN'T MAKE ME DINNER
CURRENTLY SPINNING LIKE MAD

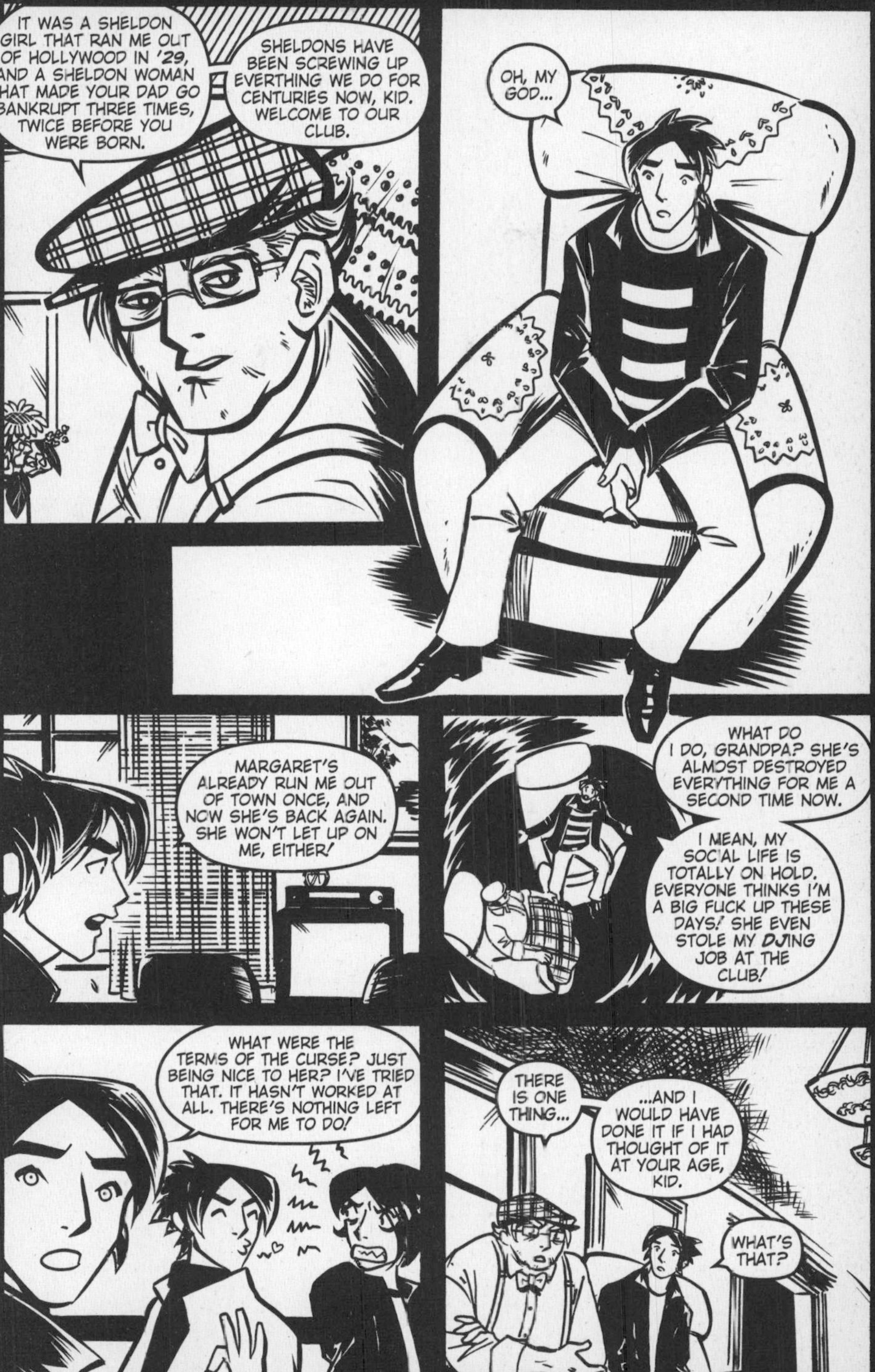
IT WAS A SHELDON GIRL THAT RAN ME OUT OF HOLLYWOOD IN '29, AND A SHELDON WOMAN THAT MADE YOUR DAD GO BANKRUPT THREE TIMES, TWICE BEFORE YOU WERE BORN.
SHELDONS HAVE BEEN SCREWING UP EVERTHING WE DO FOR CENTURIES NOW, KID. WELCOME TO OUR CLUB.
OH, MY GOD...
MARGARET'S ALREADY RUN ME OUT OF TOWN ONCE, AND NOW SHE'S BACK AGAIN. SHE WON'T LET UP ON ME, EITHER!
WHAT DO I DO, GRANDPA? SHE'S ALMOST DESTROYED EVERYTHING FOR ME A SECOND TIME NOW.
I MEAN, MY SOCIAL LIFE IS TOTALLY ON HOLD. EVERYONE THINKS I'M A BIG FUCK UP THESE DAYS! SHE EVEN STOLE MY DJING JOB AT THE CLUB!
WHAT WERE THE TERMS OF THE CURSE? JUST BEING NICE TO HER? I'VE TRIED THAT. IT HASN'T WORKED AT ALL. THERE'S NOTHING LEFT FOR ME TO DO!
THERE IS ONE THING...
...AND I WOULD HAVE DONE IT IF I HAD THOUGHT OF IT AT YOUR AGE, KID.
WHAT'S THAT?

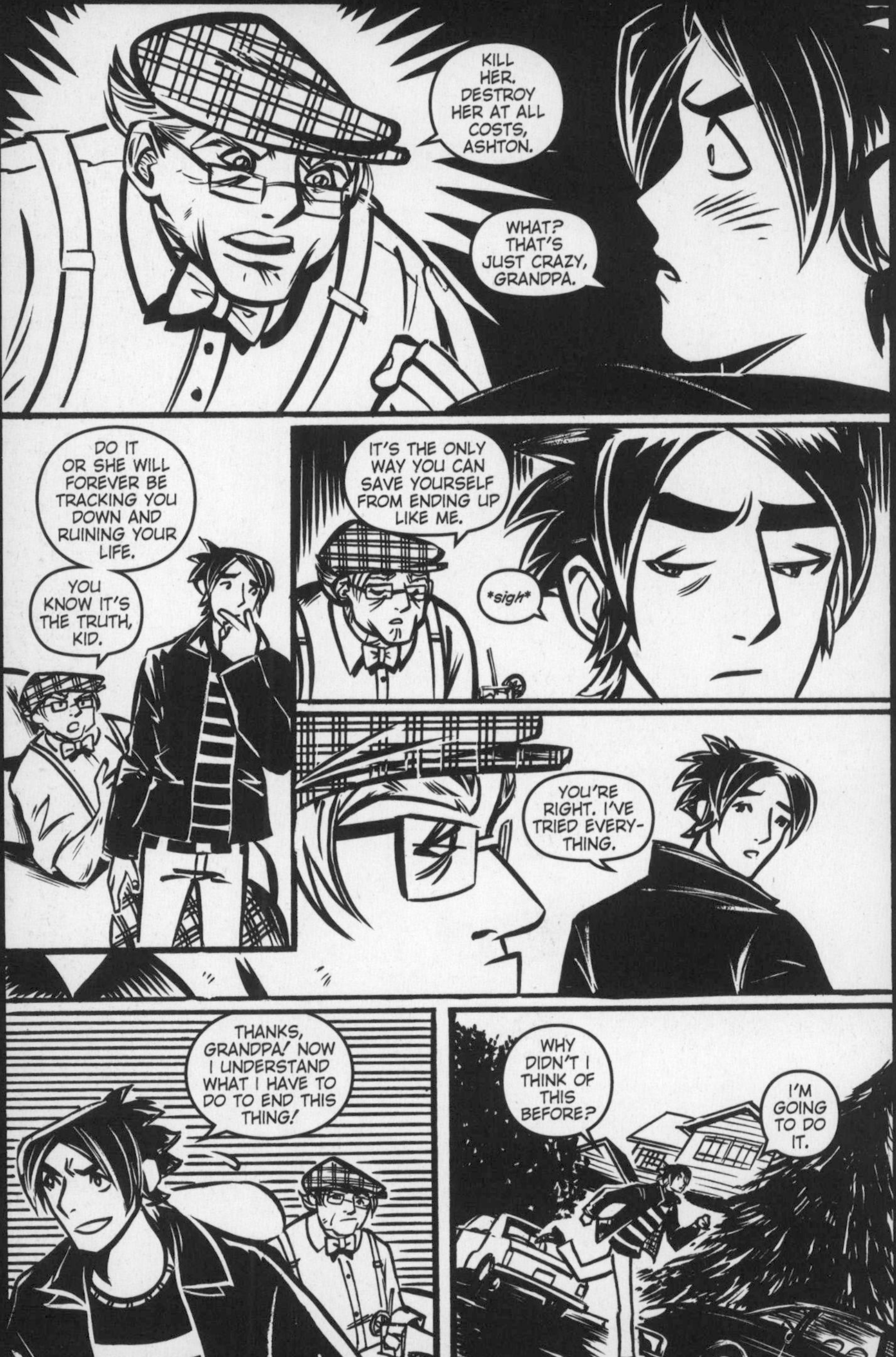
KILL HER. DESTROY HER AT ALL COSTS, ASHTON.
WHAT? THAT'S JUST CRAZY, GRANDPA.
DO IT OR SHE WILL FOREVER BE TRACKING YOU DOWN AND RUINING YOUR LIFE.
YOU KNOW IT'S THE TRUTH, KID.
IT'S THE ONLY WAY YOU CAN SAVE YOURSELF FROM ENDING UP LIKE ME.
sigh
YOU'RE RIGHT. I'VE TRIED EVERY-THING.
THANKS, GRANDPA! NOW I UNDERSTAND WHAT I HAVE TO DO TO END THIS THING!
WHY DIDN'T I THINK OF THIS BEFORE?
I'M GOING TO DO IT.

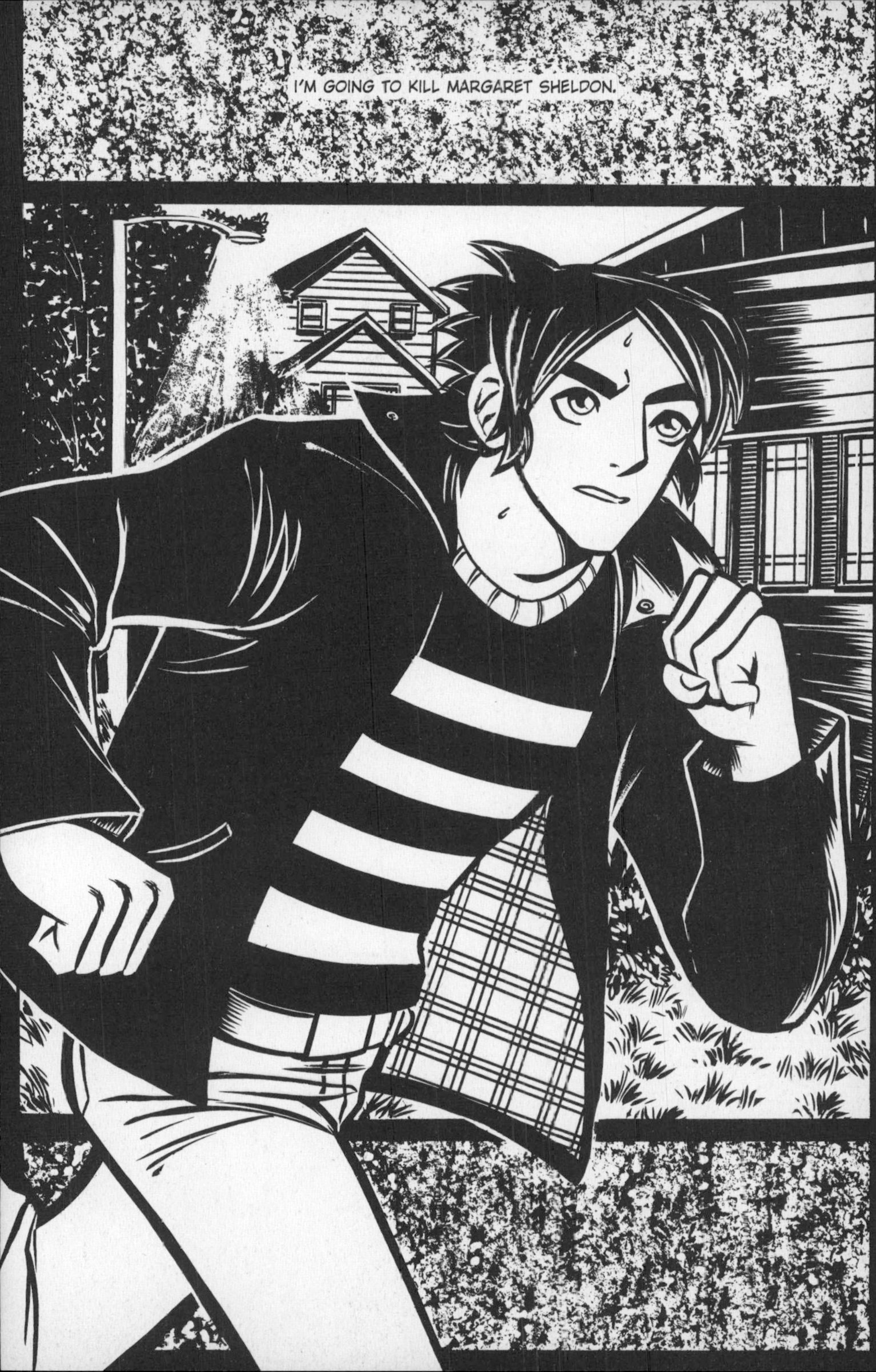
I'M GOING TO KILL MARGARET SHELDON.

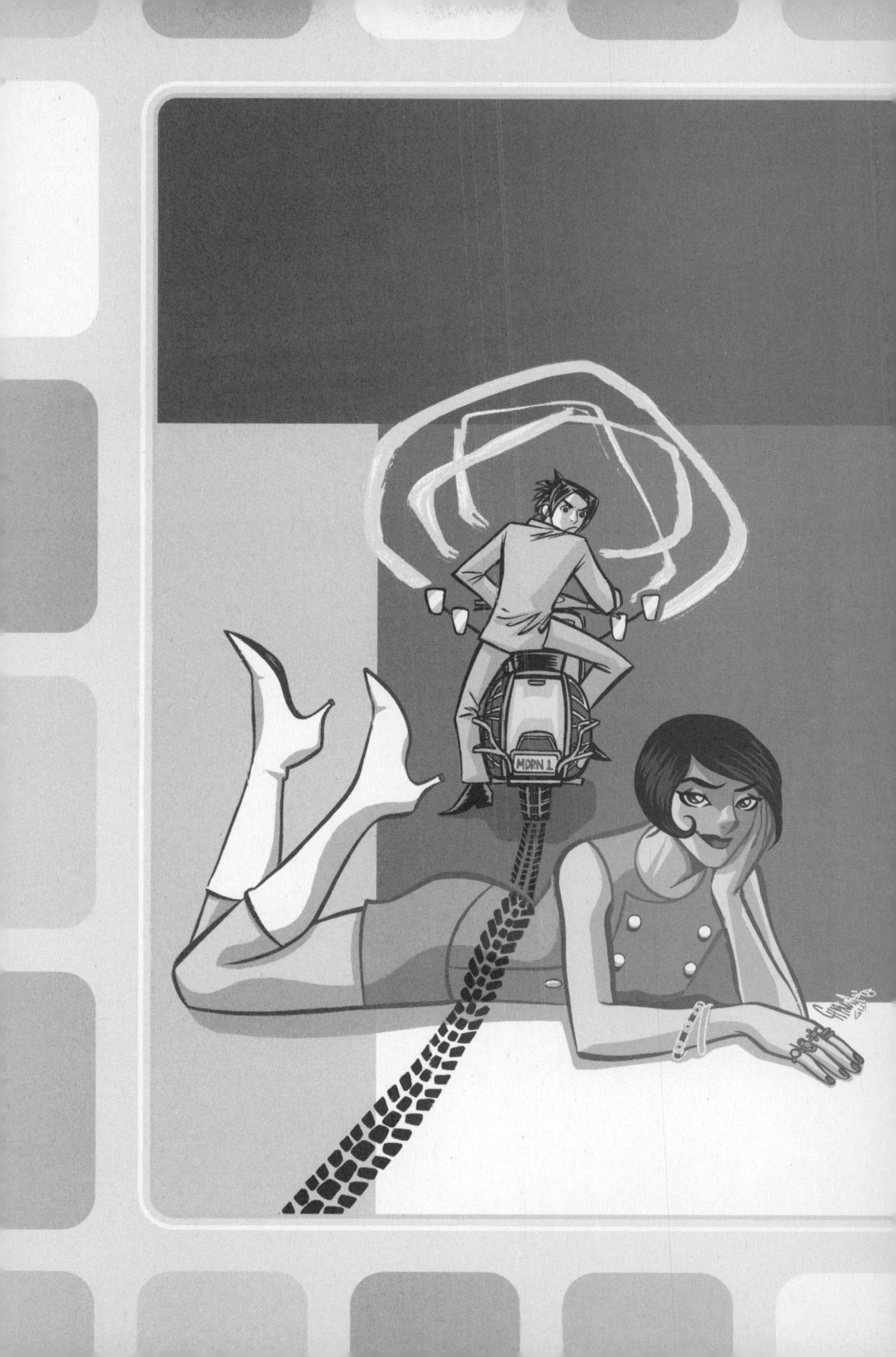
MDRN 1

Chapter 4:
"The Changing Man"

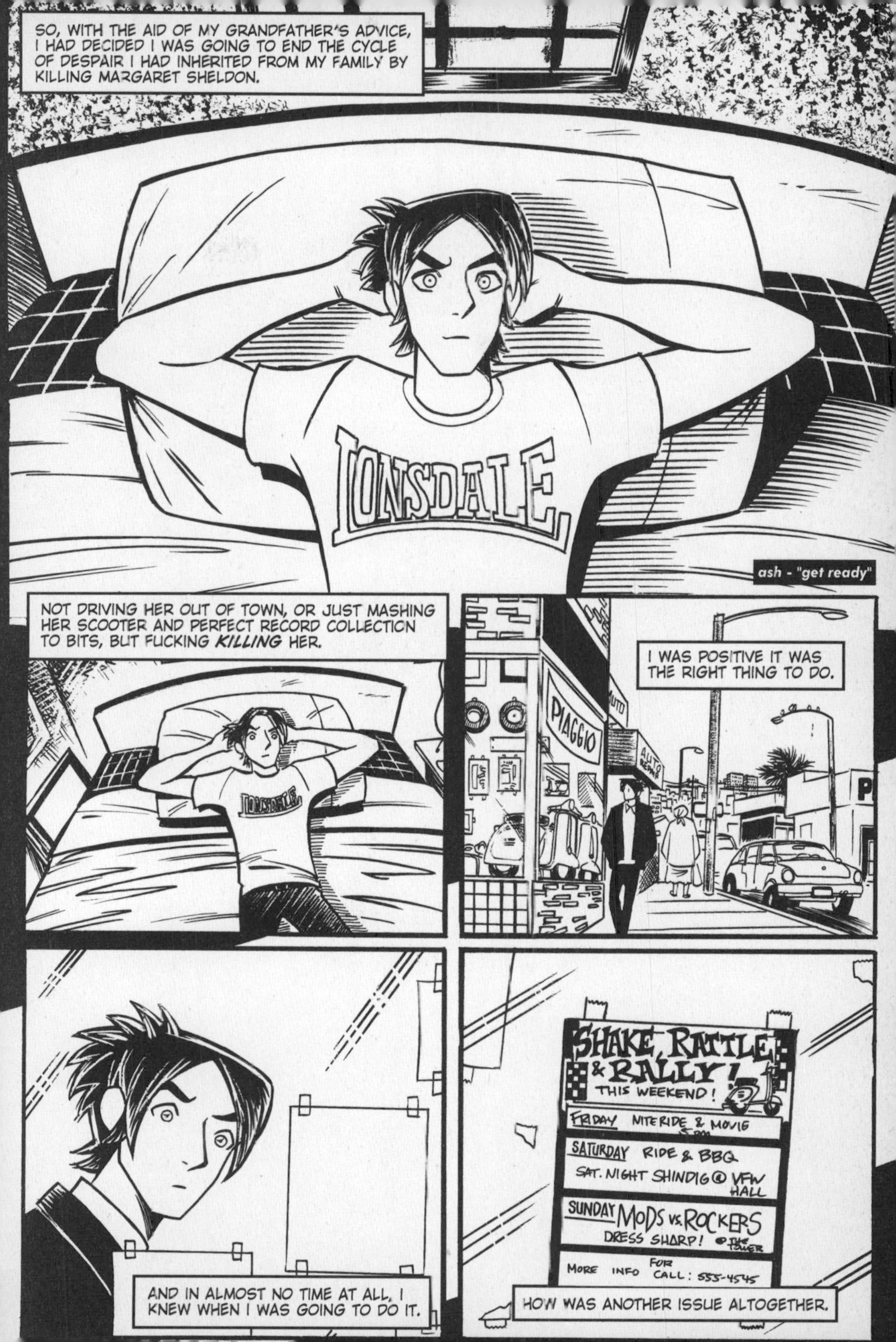
SO, WITH THE AID OF MY GRANDFATHER'S ADVICE, I HAD DECIDED I WAS GOING TO END THE CYCLE OF DESPAIR I HAD INHERITED FROM MY FAMILY BY KILLING MARGARET SHELDON.
LONSDALE
ash - "get ready"
NOT DRIVING HER OUT OF TOWN, OR JUST MASHING HER SCOOTER AND PERFECT RECORD COLLECTION TO BITS, BUT FUCKING *KILLING* HER.
LONSDALE
I WAS POSITIVE IT WAS THE RIGHT THING TO DO.
PIAGGIO
AUTO REPAIR
AND IN ALMOST NO TIME AT ALL, I KNEW WHEN I WAS GOING TO DO IT.
SHAKE, RATTLE & RALLY!
THIS WEEKEND!
FRIDAY NITE RIDE & MOVIE
SATURDAY RIDE & BBQ
SAT. NIGHT SHINDIG @ VFW HALL
SUNDAY MODS vs. ROCKERS
DRESS SHARP!
MORE INFO CALL: 555-4545
HOW WAS ANOTHER ISSUE ALTOGETHER.

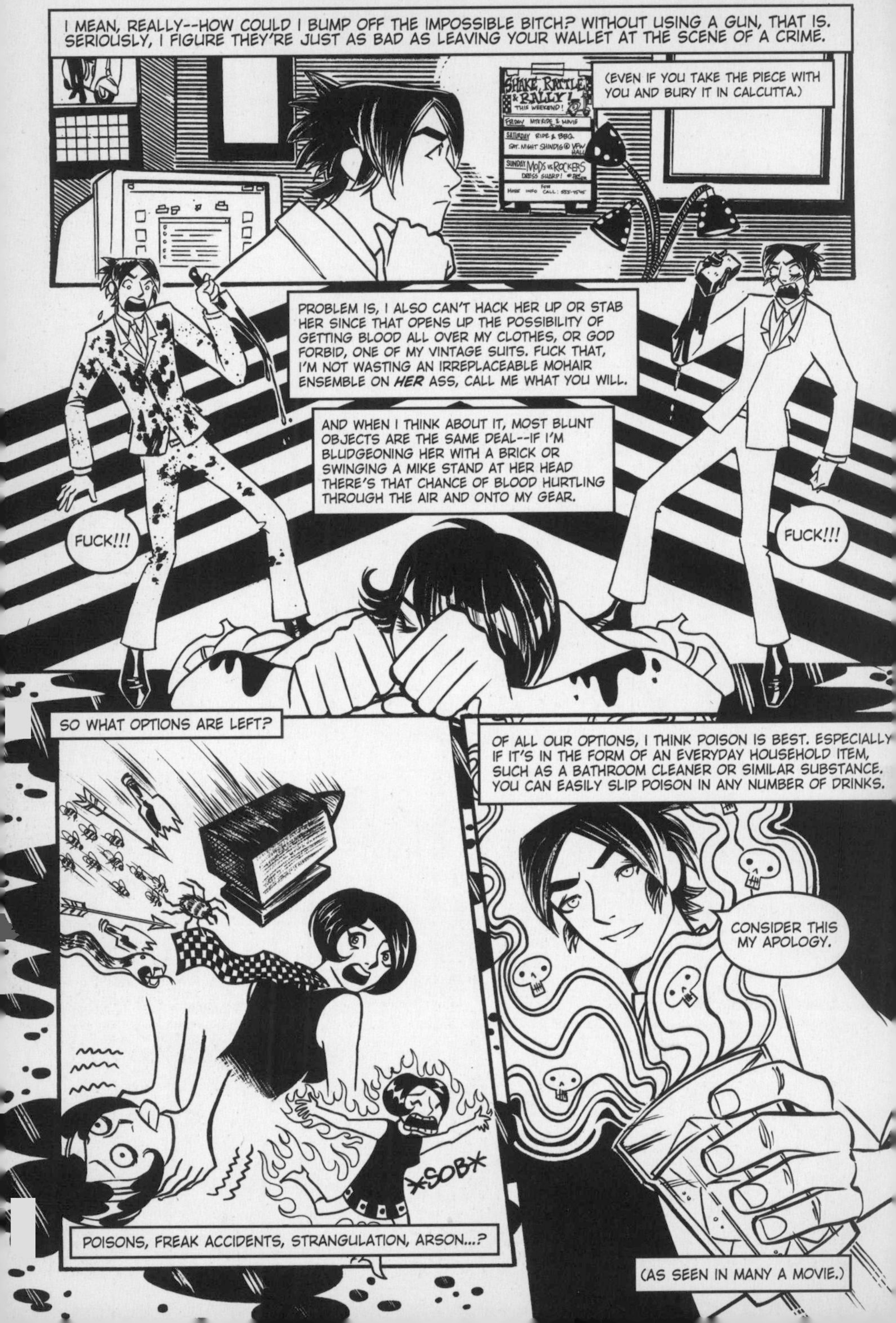
I MEAN, REALLY--HOW COULD I BUMP OFF THE IMPOSSIBLE BITCH? WITHOUT USING A GUN, THAT IS. SERIOUSLY, I FIGURE THEY'RE JUST AS BAD AS LEAVING YOUR WALLET AT THE SCENE OF A CRIME.
SHAKE, RATTLE & RALLY! THIS WEEKEND!
FRIDAY NITE RIDE & MOVIE
SATURDAY RIDE & BBQ
SAT. NIGHT SHINDIG @ VFW HALL
SUNDAY MODS vs. ROCKERS DRESS SHARP!
FOR MORE INFO CALL: 555-4545
(EVEN IF YOU TAKE THE PIECE WITH YOU AND BURY IT IN CALCUTTA.)
PROBLEM IS, I ALSO CAN'T HACK HER UP OR STAB HER SINCE THAT OPENS UP THE POSSIBILITY OF GETTING BLOOD ALL OVER MY CLOTHES, OR GOD FORBID, ONE OF MY VINTAGE SUITS. FUCK THAT, I'M NOT WASTING AN IRREPLACEABLE MOHAIR ENSEMBLE ON ***HER*** ASS, CALL ME WHAT YOU WILL.
AND WHEN I THINK ABOUT IT, MOST BLUNT OBJECTS ARE THE SAME DEAL--IF I'M BLUDGEONING HER WITH A BRICK OR SWINGING A MIKE STAND AT HER HEAD THERE'S THAT CHANCE OF BLOOD HURTLING THROUGH THE AIR AND ONTO MY GEAR.
FUCK!!!
FUCK!!!
SO WHAT OPTIONS ARE LEFT?
SOB
POISONS, FREAK ACCIDENTS, STRANGULATION, ARSON...?
OF ALL OUR OPTIONS, I THINK POISON IS BEST. ESPECIALLY IF IT'S IN THE FORM OF AN EVERYDAY HOUSEHOLD ITEM, SUCH AS A BATHROOM CLEANER OR SIMILAR SUBSTANCE. YOU CAN EASILY SLIP POISON IN ANY NUMBER OF DRINKS.
CONSIDER THIS MY APOLOGY.
(AS SEEN IN MANY A MOVIE.)

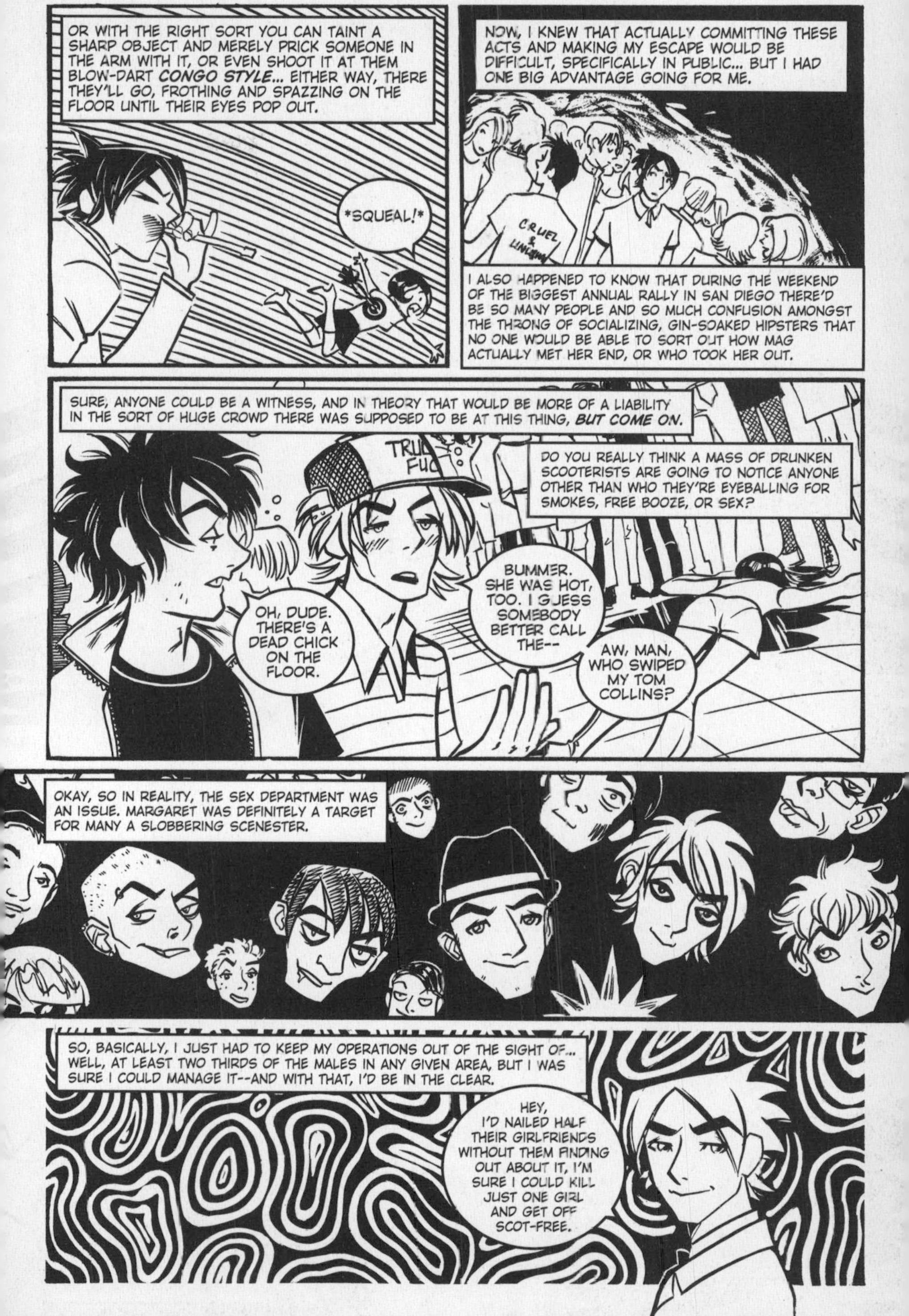
OR WITH THE RIGHT SORT YOU CAN TAINT A SHARP OBJECT AND MERELY PRICK SOMEONE IN THE ARM WITH IT, OR EVEN SHOOT IT AT THEM BLOW-DART **CONGO STYLE**... EITHER WAY, THERE THEY'LL GO, FROTHING AND SPAZZING ON THE FLOOR UNTIL THEIR EYES POP OUT.
SQUEAL!
NOW, I KNEW THAT ACTUALLY COMMITTING THESE ACTS AND MAKING MY ESCAPE WOULD BE DIFFICULT, SPECIFICALLY IN PUBLIC... BUT I HAD ONE BIG ADVANTAGE GOING FOR ME.
CRUEL & UNUSUAL
I ALSO HAPPENED TO KNOW THAT DURING THE WEEKEND OF THE BIGGEST ANNUAL RALLY IN SAN DIEGO THERE'D BE SO MANY PEOPLE AND SO MUCH CONFUSION AMONGST THE THRONG OF SOCIALIZING, GIN-SOAKED HIPSTERS THAT NO ONE WOULD BE ABLE TO SORT OUT HOW MAG ACTUALLY MET HER END, OR WHO TOOK HER OUT.
SURE, ANYONE COULD BE A WITNESS, AND IN THEORY THAT WOULD BE MORE OF A LIABILITY IN THE SORT OF HUGE CROWD THERE WAS SUPPOSED TO BE AT THIS THING, ***BUT COME ON.***
DO YOU REALLY THINK A MASS OF DRUNKEN SCOOTERISTS ARE GOING TO NOTICE ANYONE OTHER THAN WHO THEY'RE EYEBALLING FOR SMOKES, FREE BOOZE, OR SEX?
OH, DUDE. THERE'S A DEAD CHICK ON THE FLOOR.
BUMMER. SHE WAS HOT, TOO. I GUESS SOMEBODY BETTER CALL THE--
AW, MAN, WHO SWIPED MY TOM COLLINS?
OKAY, SO IN REALITY, THE SEX DEPARTMENT WAS AN ISSUE. MARGARET WAS DEFINITELY A TARGET FOR MANY A SLOBBERING SCENESTER.
SO, BASICALLY, I JUST HAD TO KEEP MY OPERATIONS OUT OF THE SIGHT OF... WELL, AT LEAST TWO THIRDS OF THE MALES IN ANY GIVEN AREA, BUT I WAS SURE I COULD MANAGE IT--AND WITH THAT, I'D BE IN THE CLEAR.
HEY, I'D NAILED HALF THEIR GIRLFRIENDS WITHOUT THEM FINDING OUT ABOUT IT, I'M SURE I COULD KILL JUST ONE GIRL AND GET OFF SCOT-FREE.

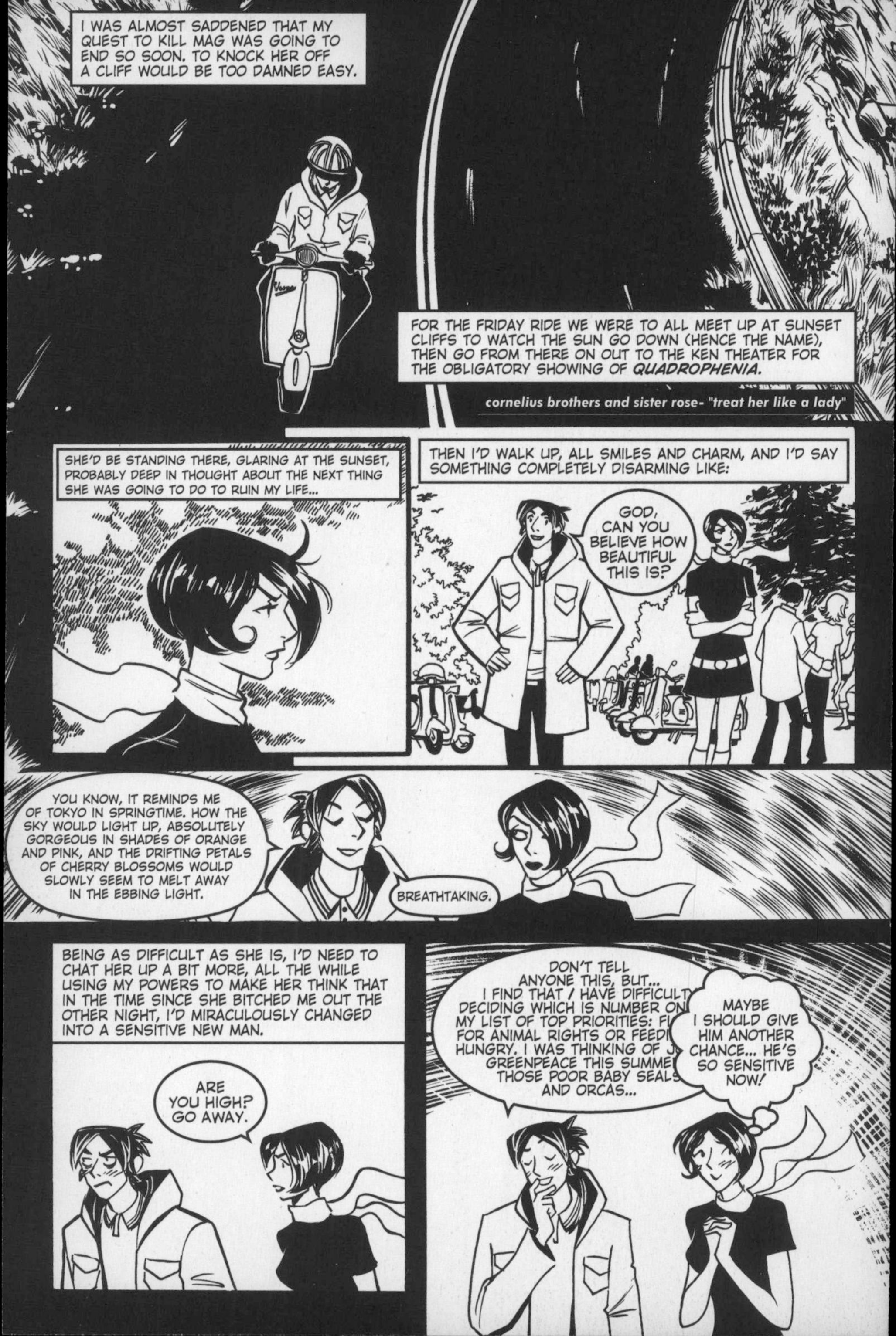

I WAS ALMOST SADDENED THAT MY QUEST TO KILL MAG WAS GOING TO END SO SOON. TO KNOCK HER OFF A CLIFF WOULD BE TOO DAMNED EASY.
FOR THE FRIDAY RIDE WE WERE TO ALL MEET UP AT SUNSET CLIFFS TO WATCH THE SUN GO DOWN (HENCE THE NAME), THEN GO FROM THERE ON OUT TO THE KEN THEATER FOR THE OBLIGATORY SHOWING OF QUADROPHENIA.
cornelius brothers and sister rose- "treat her like a lady"
SHE'D BE STANDING THERE, GLARING AT THE SUNSET, PROBABLY DEEP IN THOUGHT ABOUT THE NEXT THING SHE WAS GOING TO DO TO RUIN MY LIFE...
THEN I'D WALK UP, ALL SMILES AND CHARM, AND I'D SAY SOMETHING COMPLETELY DISARMING LIKE:
GOD, CAN YOU BELIEVE HOW BEAUTIFUL THIS IS?
YOU KNOW, IT REMINDS ME OF TOKYO IN SPRINGTIME. HOW THE SKY WOULD LIGHT UP, ABSOLUTELY GORGEOUS IN SHADES OF ORANGE AND PINK, AND THE DRIFTING PETALS OF CHERRY BLOSSOMS WOULD SLOWLY SEEM TO MELT AWAY IN THE EBBING LIGHT.
BREATHTAKING.
BEING AS DIFFICULT AS SHE IS, I'D NEED TO CHAT HER UP A BIT MORE, ALL THE WHILE USING MY POWERS TO MAKE HER THINK THAT IN THE TIME SINCE SHE BITCHED ME OUT THE OTHER NIGHT, I'D MIRACULOUSLY CHANGED INTO A SENSITIVE NEW MAN.
ARE YOU HIGH? GO AWAY.
DON'T TELL ANYONE THIS, BUT... I FIND THAT I HAVE DIFFICULT DECIDING WHICH IS NUMBER ON MY LIST OF TOP PRIORITIES: FI FOR ANIMAL RIGHTS OR FEEDI HUNGRY. I WAS THINKING OF J GREENPEACE THIS SUMME THOSE POOR BABY SEALS AND ORCAS...
MAYBE I SHOULD GIVE HIM ANOTHER CHANCE... HE'S SO SENSITIVE NOW!

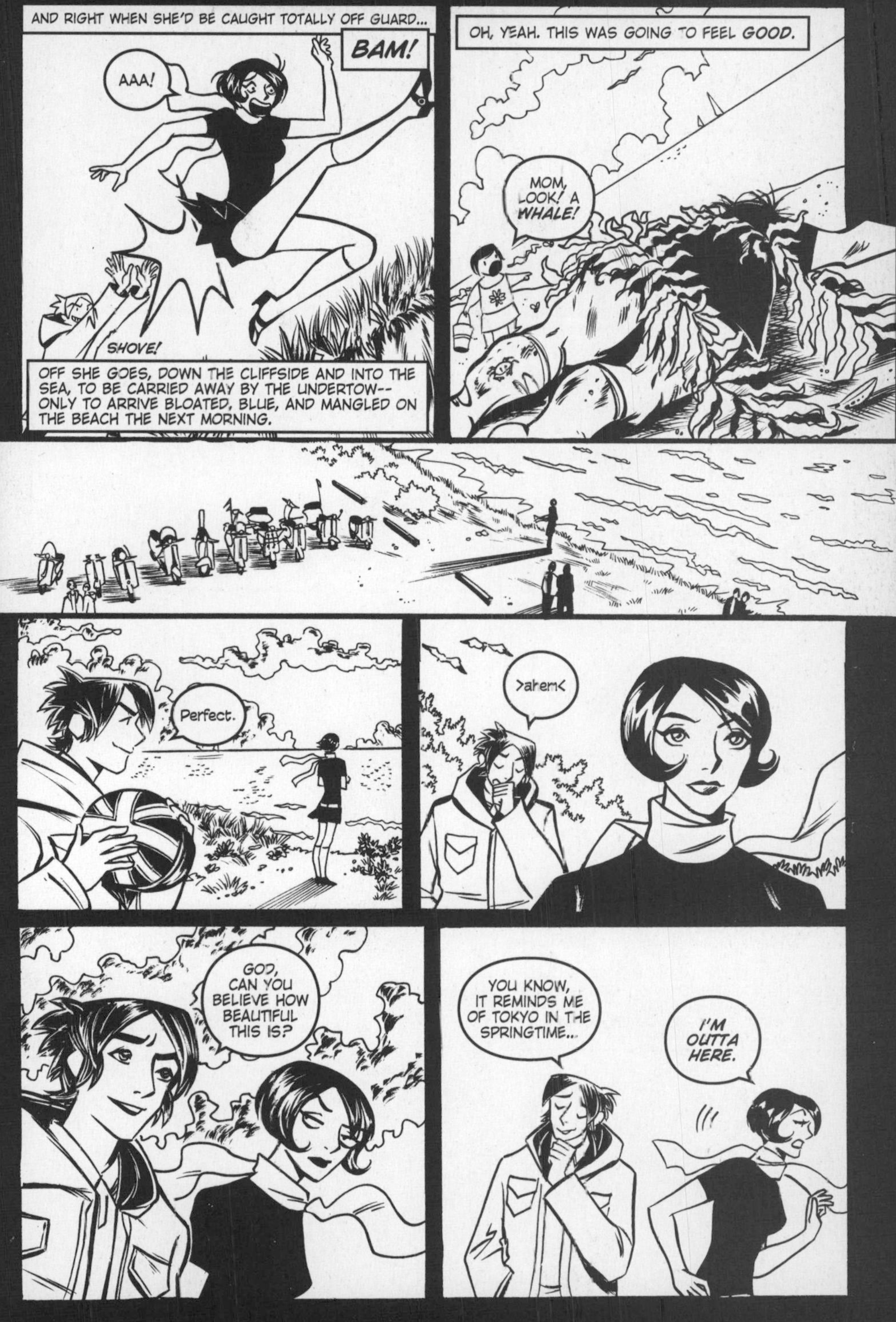
AND RIGHT WHEN SHE'D BE CAUGHT TOTALLY OFF GUARD...
BAM!
AAA!
SHOVE!
OFF SHE GOES, DOWN THE CLIFFSIDE AND INTO THE SEA, TO BE CARRIED AWAY BY THE UNDERTOW-- ONLY TO ARRIVE BLOATED, BLUE, AND MANGLED ON THE BEACH THE NEXT MORNING.
OH, YEAH. THIS WAS GOING TO FEEL GOOD.
MOM, LOOK! A WHALE!
Perfect.
>ahem<
GOD, CAN YOU BELIEVE HOW BEAUTIFUL THIS IS?
YOU KNOW, IT REMINDS ME OF TOKYO IN THE SPRINGTIME...
I'M OUTTA HERE.

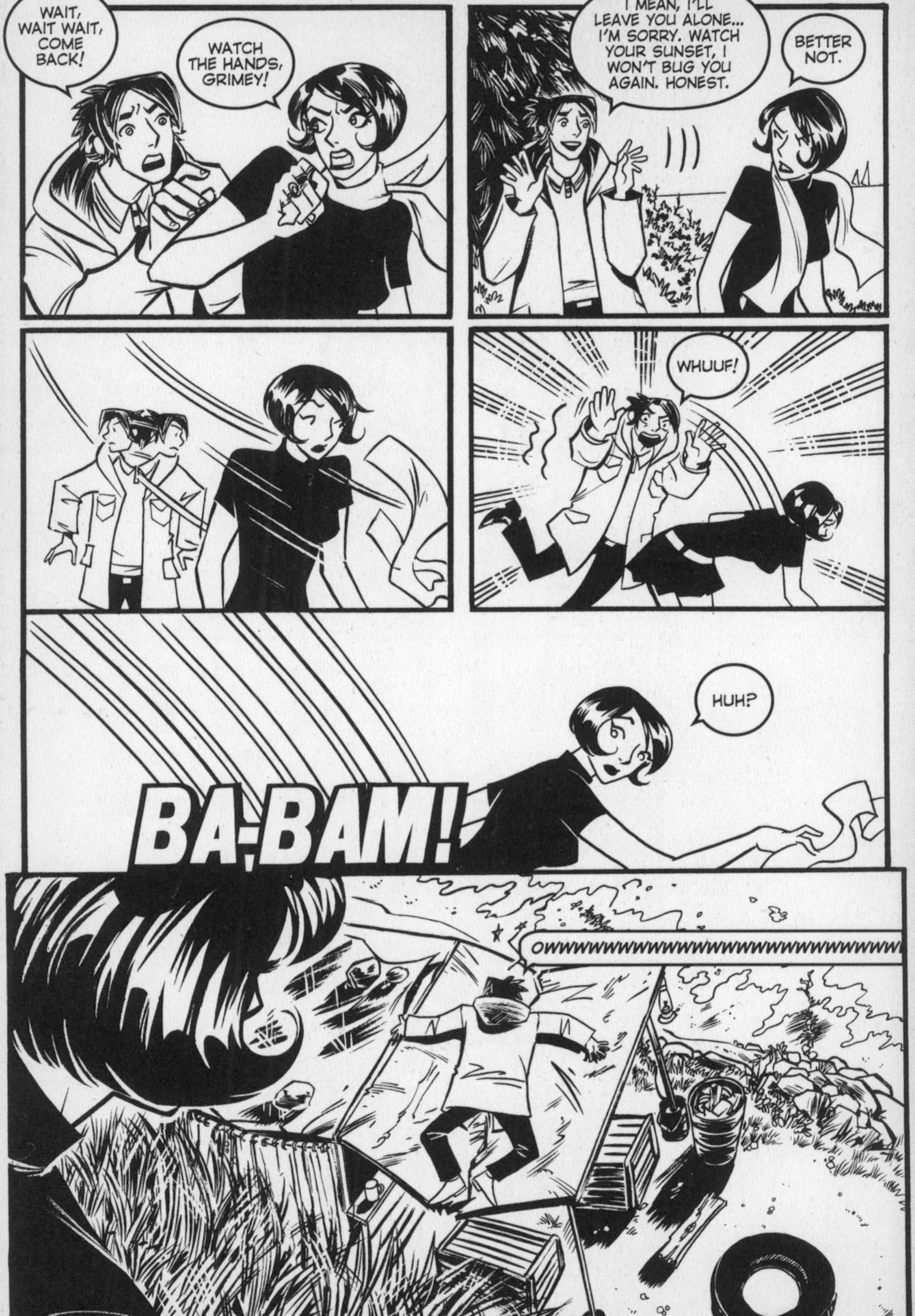
WAIT, WAIT WAIT, COME BACK!
WATCH THE HANDS, GRIMEY!
I MEAN, I'LL LEAVE YOU ALONE... I'M SORRY. WATCH YOUR SUNSET, I WON'T BUG YOU AGAIN. HONEST.
BETTER NOT.
WHUUF!
HUH?
BA-BAM!
OWWWWWWWWWWWWWWWWWWWWWWWWWWW

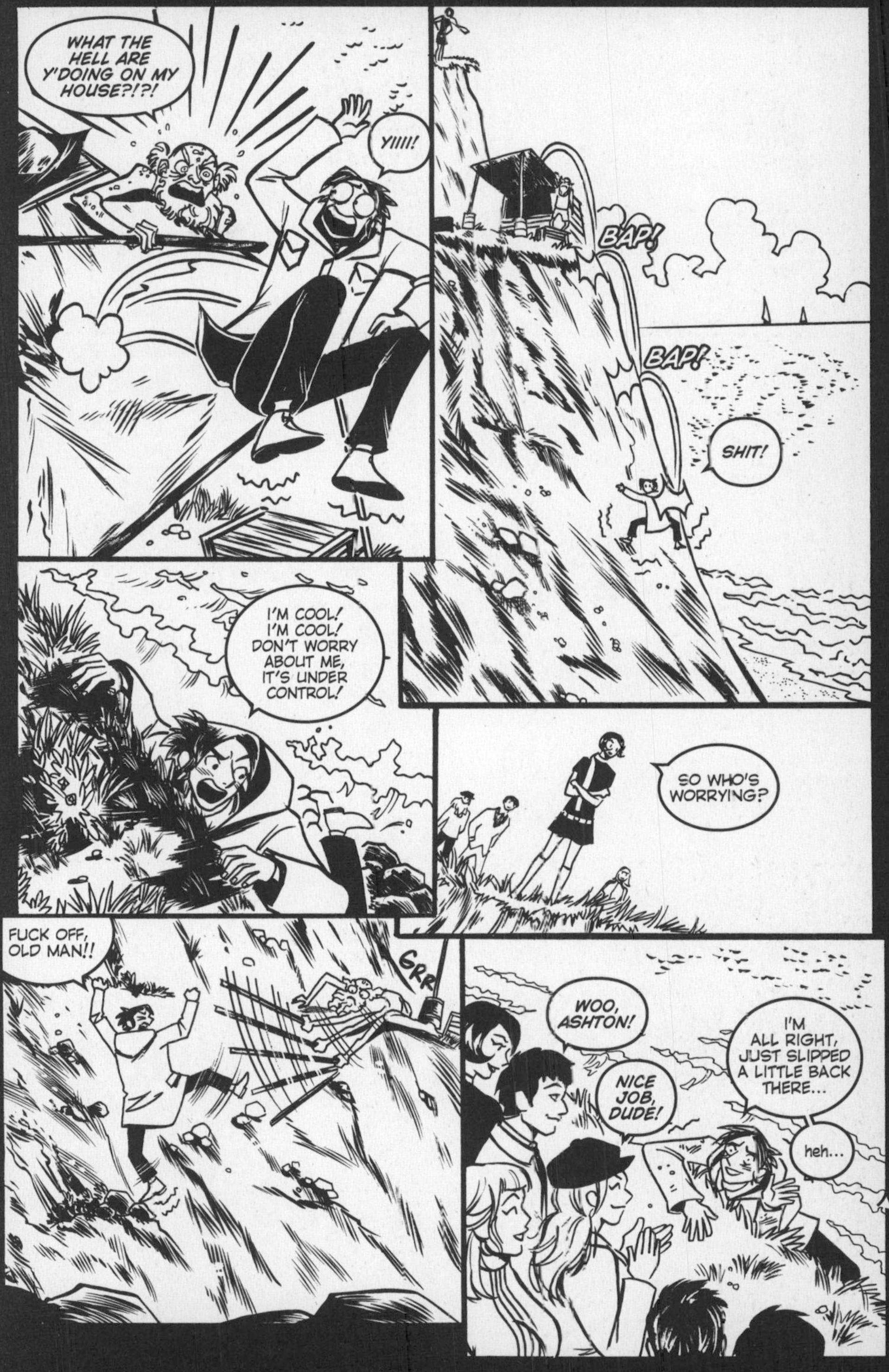
WHAT THE HELL ARE Y'DOING ON MY HOUSE?!?!
YIIII!
BAP!
BAP!
SHIT!
I'M COOL! I'M COOL! DON'T WORRY ABOUT ME, IT'S UNDER CONTROL!
SO WHO'S WORRYING?
FUCK OFF, OLD MAN!!
GRR
WOO, ASHTON!
NICE JOB, DUDE!
I'M ALL RIGHT, JUST SLIPPED A LITTLE BACK THERE...
heh...

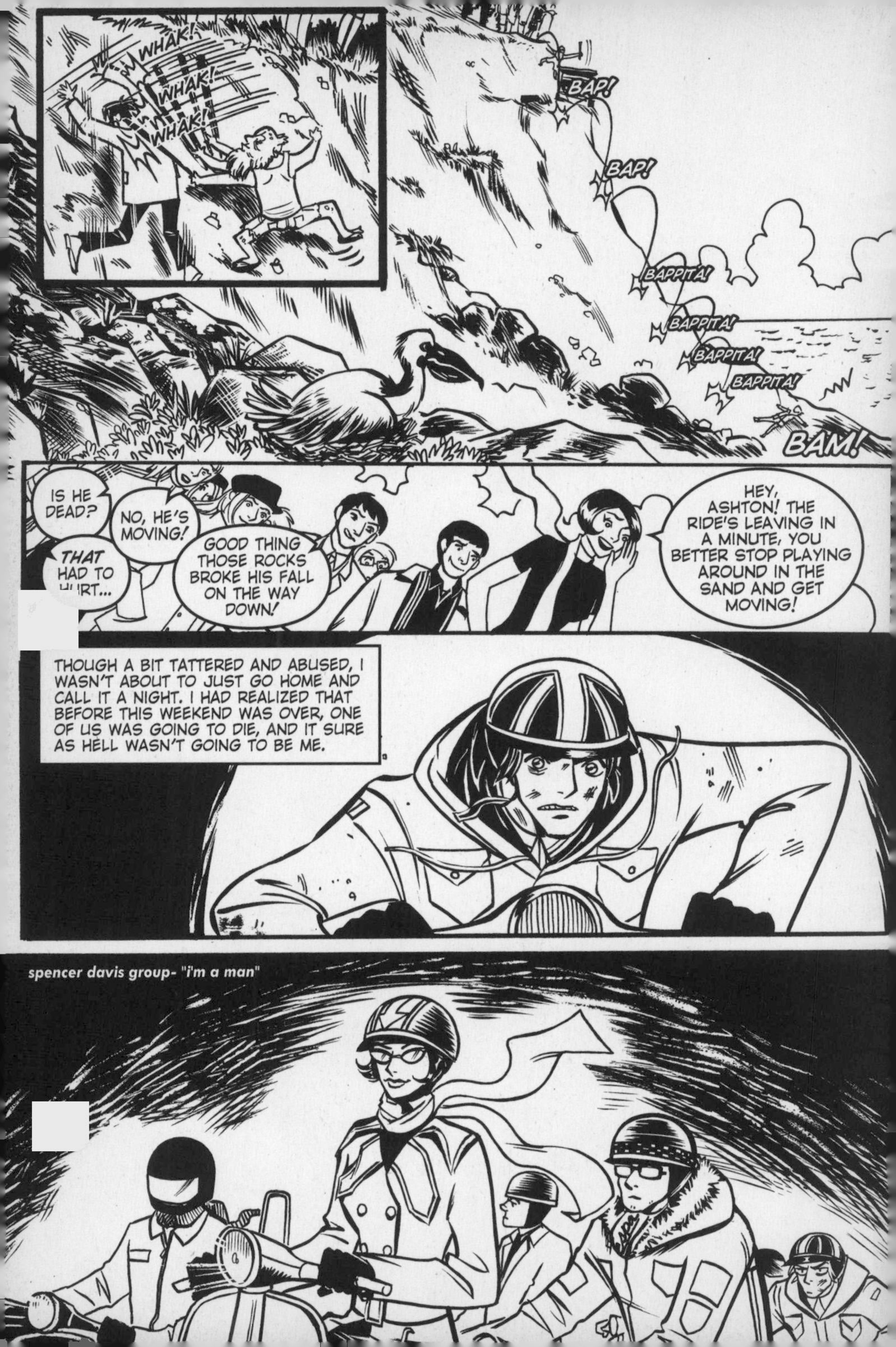
WHAK!
WHAK!
WHAK!
BAP!
BAP!
BAPPITA!
BAPPITA!
BAPPITA!
BAPPITA!
BAM!
IS HE DEAD?
NO, HE'S MOVING!
THAT HAD TO HURT...
GOOD THING THOSE ROCKS BROKE HIS FALL ON THE WAY DOWN!
HEY, ASHTON! THE RIDE'S LEAVING IN A MINUTE, YOU BETTER STOP PLAYING AROUND IN THE SAND AND GET MOVING!
THOUGH A BIT TATTERED AND ABUSED, I WASN'T ABOUT TO JUST GO HOME AND CALL IT A NIGHT. I HAD REALIZED THAT BEFORE THIS WEEKEND WAS OVER, ONE OF US WAS GOING TO DIE, AND IT SURE AS HELL WASN'T GOING TO BE ME.
spencer davis group- "i'm a man"

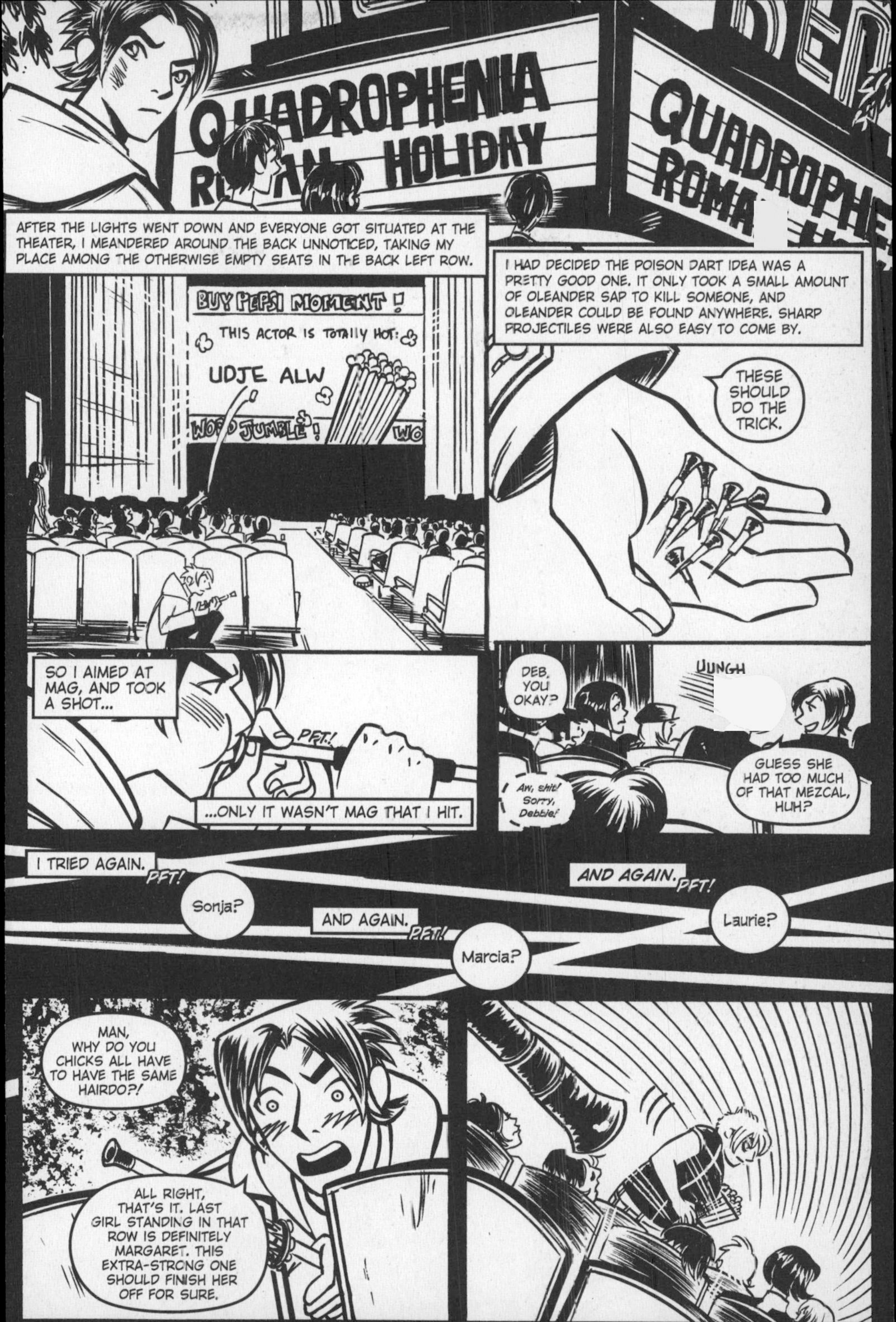
QUADROPHENIA
HOLIDAY
QUADROPHE
AFTER THE LIGHTS WENT DOWN AND EVERYONE GOT SITUATED AT THE THEATER, I MEANDERED AROUND THE BACK UNNOTICED, TAKING MY PLACE AMONG THE OTHERWISE EMPTY SEATS IN THE BACK LEFT ROW.
I HAD DECIDED THE POISON DART IDEA WAS A PRETTY GOOD ONE. IT ONLY TOOK A SMALL AMOUNT OF OLEANDER SAP TO KILL SOMEONE, AND OLEANDER COULD BE FOUND ANYWHERE. SHARP PROJECTILES WERE ALSO EASY TO COME BY.
BUY PEPSI MOMENT!
THIS ACTOR IS TOTALLY HOT:
UDJE ALW
JUMBLE!
THESE SHOULD DO THE TRICK.
SO I AIMED AT MAG, AND TOOK A SHOT...
PFT!
...ONLY IT WASN'T MAG THAT I HIT.
DEB, YOU OKAY?
UUNGH
Aw, shit! Sorry, Debbie!
GUESS SHE HAD TOO MUCH OF THAT MEZCAL, HUH?
I TRIED AGAIN.
PFT!
Sonja?
AND AGAIN.
PFT!
Marcia?
AND AGAIN.
PFT!
Laurie?
MAN, WHY DO YOU CHICKS ALL HAVE TO HAVE THE SAME HAIRDO?!
ALL RIGHT, THAT'S IT. LAST GIRL STANDING IN THAT ROW IS DEFINITELY MARGARET. THIS EXTRA-STRONG ONE SHOULD FINISH HER OFF FOR SURE.

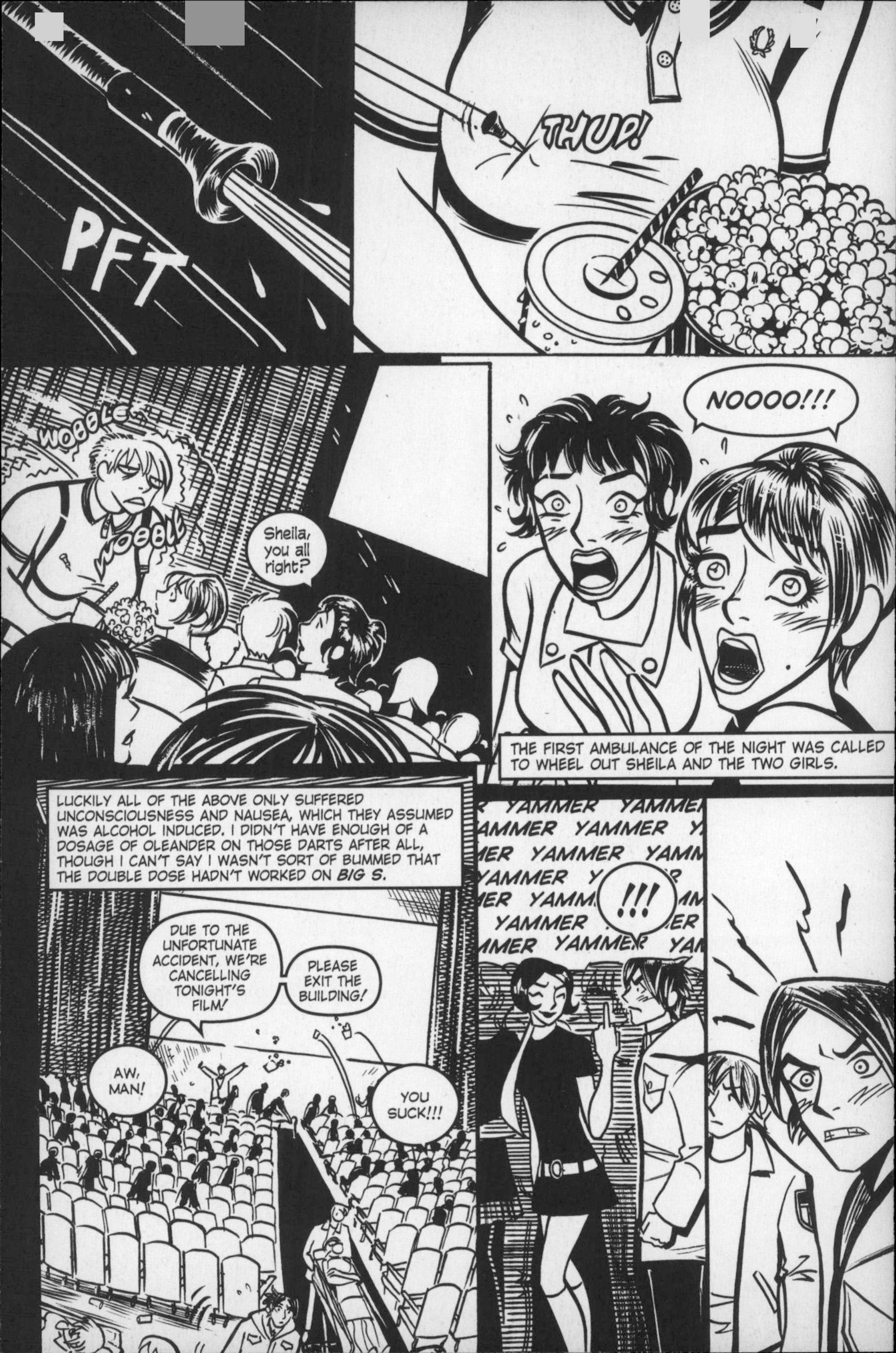
PFT
THUP!
WOBBLE
WOBBLE
Sheila, you all right?
NOOOO!!!
THE FIRST AMBULANCE OF THE NIGHT WAS CALLED TO WHEEL OUT SHEILA AND THE TWO GIRLS.
LUCKILY ALL OF THE ABOVE ONLY SUFFERED UNCONSCIOUSNESS AND NAUSEA, WHICH THEY ASSUMED WAS ALCOHOL INDUCED. I DIDN'T HAVE ENOUGH OF A DOSAGE OF OLEANDER ON THOSE DARTS AFTER ALL, THOUGH I CAN'T SAY I WASN'T SORT OF BUMMED THAT THE DOUBLE DOSE HADN'T WORKED ON *BIG S*.
DUE TO THE UNFORTUNATE ACCIDENT, WE'RE CANCELLING TONIGHT'S FILM!
PLEASE EXIT THE BUILDING!
AW, MAN!
YOU SUCK!!!
YAMMER YAMMER
!!!

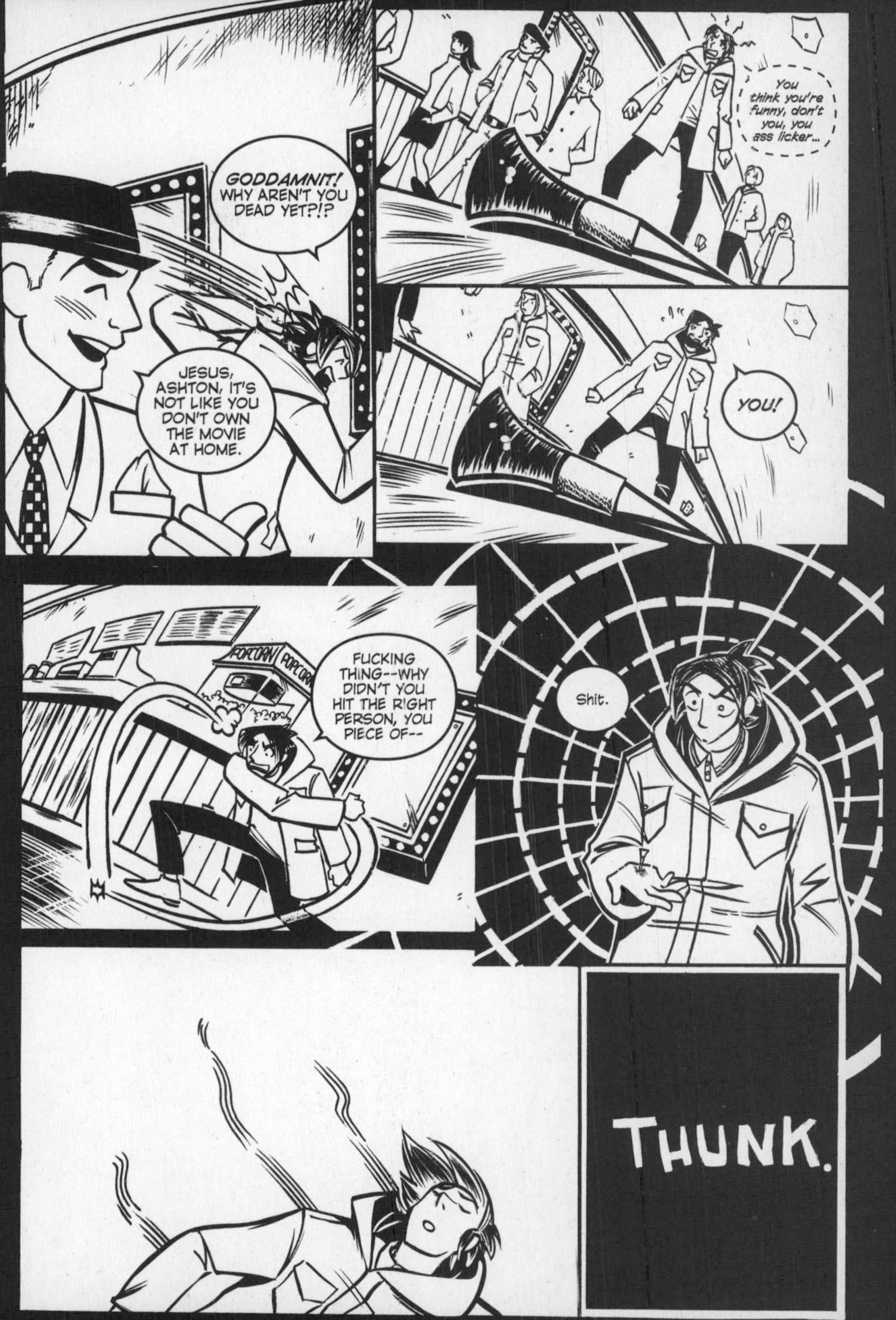
GODDAMNIT! WHY AREN'T YOU DEAD YET?!?
JESUS, ASHTON, IT'S NOT LIKE YOU DON'T OWN THE MOVIE AT HOME.
You think you're funny, don't you, you ass licker...
YOU!
POPCORN
POPCORN
FUCKING THING--WHY DIDN'T YOU HIT THE RIGHT PERSON, YOU PIECE OF--
Shit.
THUNK.

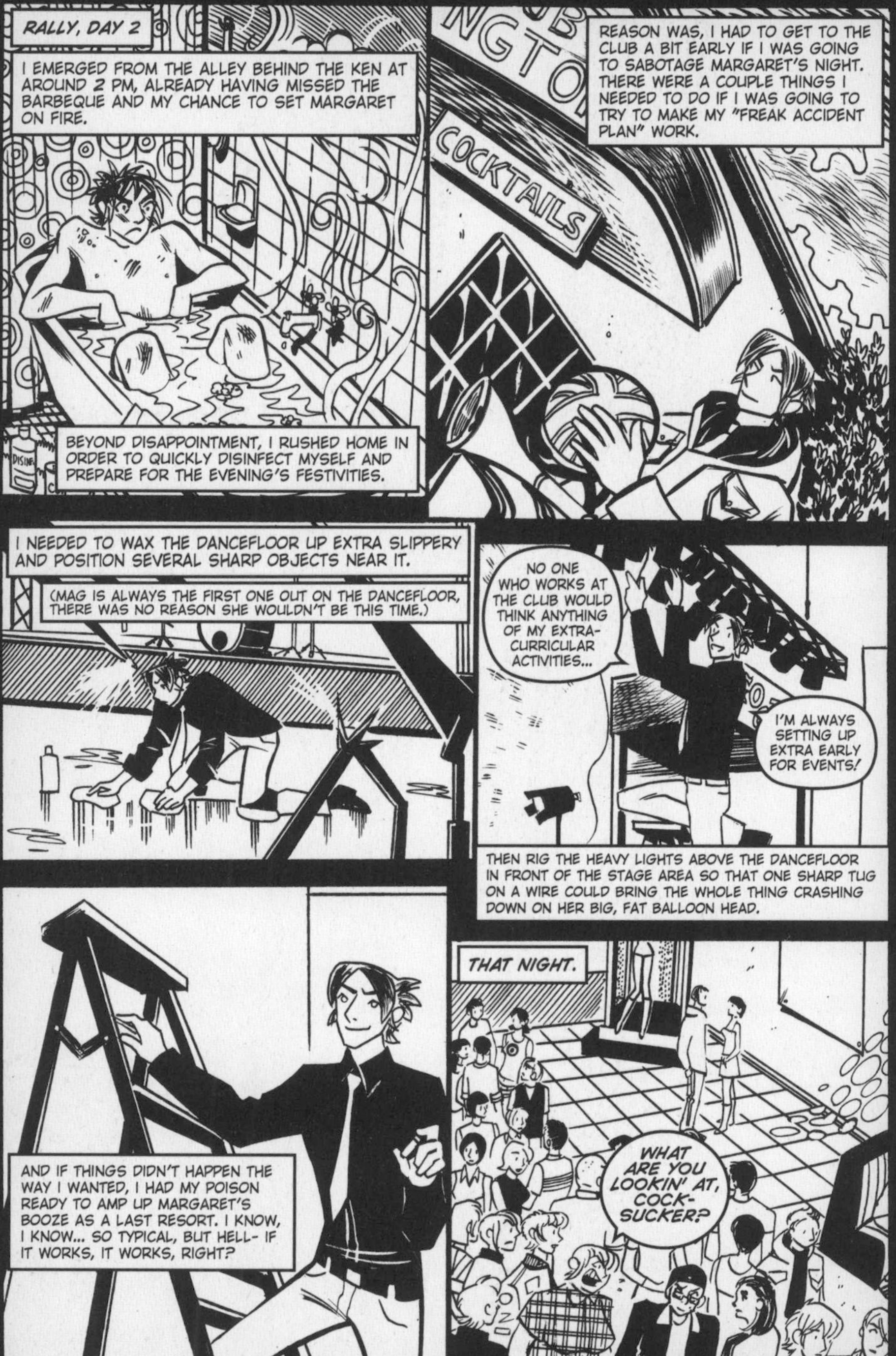
RALLY, DAY 2
I EMERGED FROM THE ALLEY BEHIND THE KEN AT AROUND 2 PM, ALREADY HAVING MISSED THE BARBEQUE AND MY CHANCE TO SET MARGARET ON FIRE.
BEYOND DISAPPOINTMENT, I RUSHED HOME IN ORDER TO QUICKLY DISINFECT MYSELF AND PREPARE FOR THE EVENING'S FESTIVITIES.
REASON WAS, I HAD TO GET TO THE CLUB A BIT EARLY IF I WAS GOING TO SABOTAGE MARGARET'S NIGHT. THERE WERE A COUPLE THINGS I NEEDED TO DO IF I WAS GOING TO TRY TO MAKE MY "FREAK ACCIDENT PLAN" WORK.
COCKTAILS
I NEEDED TO WAX THE DANCEFLOOR UP EXTRA SLIPPERY AND POSITION SEVERAL SHARP OBJECTS NEAR IT.
(MAG IS ALWAYS THE FIRST ONE OUT ON THE DANCEFLOOR, THERE WAS NO REASON SHE WOULDN'T BE THIS TIME.)
NO ONE WHO WORKS AT THE CLUB WOULD THINK ANYTHING OF MY EXTRA-CURRICULAR ACTIVITIES...
I'M ALWAYS SETTING UP EXTRA EARLY FOR EVENTS!
THEN RIG THE HEAVY LIGHTS ABOVE THE DANCEFLOOR IN FRONT OF THE STAGE AREA SO THAT ONE SHARP TUG ON A WIRE COULD BRING THE WHOLE THING CRASHING DOWN ON HER BIG, FAT BALLOON HEAD.
AND IF THINGS DIDN'T HAPPEN THE WAY I WANTED, I HAD MY POISON READY TO AMP UP MARGARET'S BOOZE AS A LAST RESORT. I KNOW, I KNOW... SO TYPICAL, BUT HELL- IF IT WORKS, IT WORKS, RIGHT?
THAT NIGHT.
WHAT ARE YOU LOOKIN' AT, COCK-SUCKER?

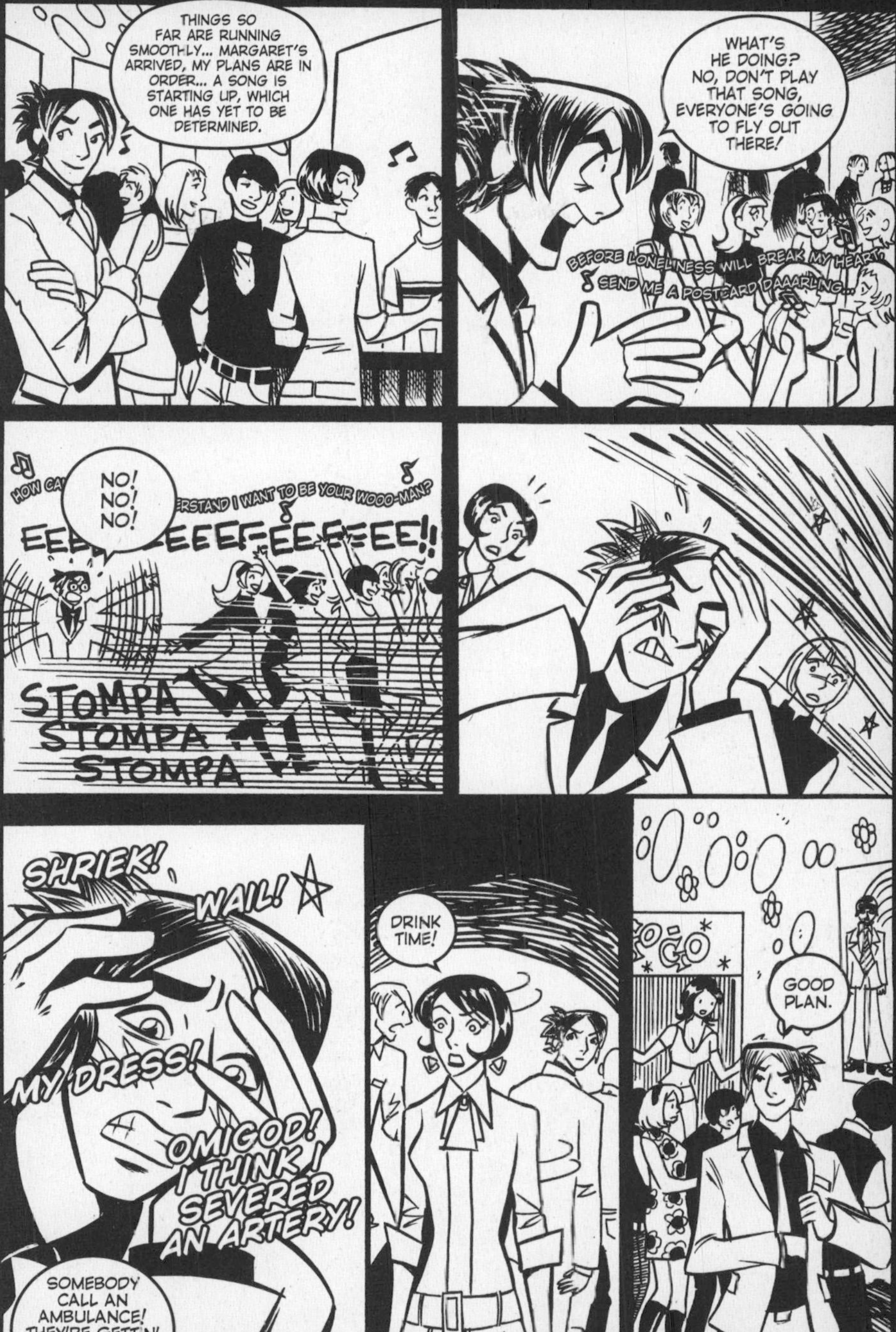

THINGS SO FAR ARE RUNNING SMOOTHLY... MARGARET'S ARRIVED, MY PLANS ARE IN ORDER... A SONG IS STARTING UP, WHICH ONE HAS YET TO BE DETERMINED.
WHAT'S HE DOING? NO, DON'T PLAY THAT SONG, EVERYONE'S GOING TO FLY OUT THERE!
BEFORE LONELINESS WILL BREAK MY HEART
SEND ME A POSTCARD DAAARLING...
NO! NO! NO!
ERSTAND I WANT TO BE YOUR WOOO-MAN?
EEEEE-EE-EEEE!!
STOMPA
STOMPA
STOMPA
SHRIEK!
WAIL!
MY DRESS!
OMIGOD! I THINK I SEVERED AN ARTERY!
SOMEBODY CALL AN AMBULANCE! THEY'RE GETTIN' BLOOD ALL OVER THE PLACE!
DRINK TIME!
GO-GO
GOOD PLAN.

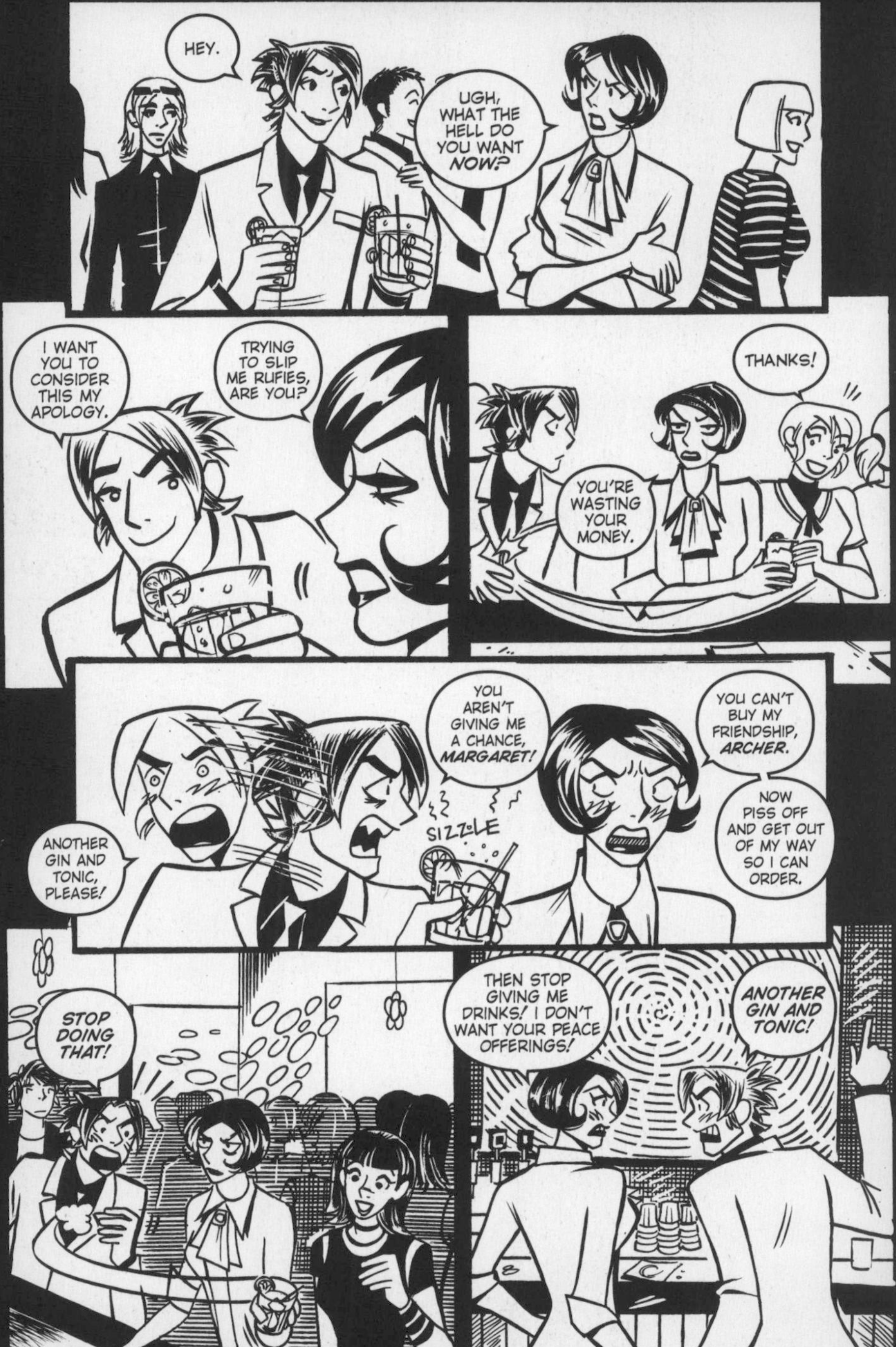
HEY.
UGH, WHAT THE HELL DO YOU WANT *NOW?*
I WANT YOU TO CONSIDER THIS MY APOLOGY.
TRYING TO SLIP ME RUFIES, ARE YOU?
THANKS!
YOU'RE WASTING YOUR MONEY.
YOU AREN'T GIVING ME A CHANCE, *MARGARET!*
YOU CAN'T BUY MY FRIENDSHIP, *ARCHER.*
NOW PISS OFF AND GET OUT OF MY WAY SO I CAN ORDER.
ANOTHER GIN AND TONIC, PLEASE!
SIZZLE
STOP DOING THAT!
THEN STOP GIVING ME DRINKS! I DON'T WANT YOUR PEACE OFFERINGS!
ANOTHER GIN AND TONIC!

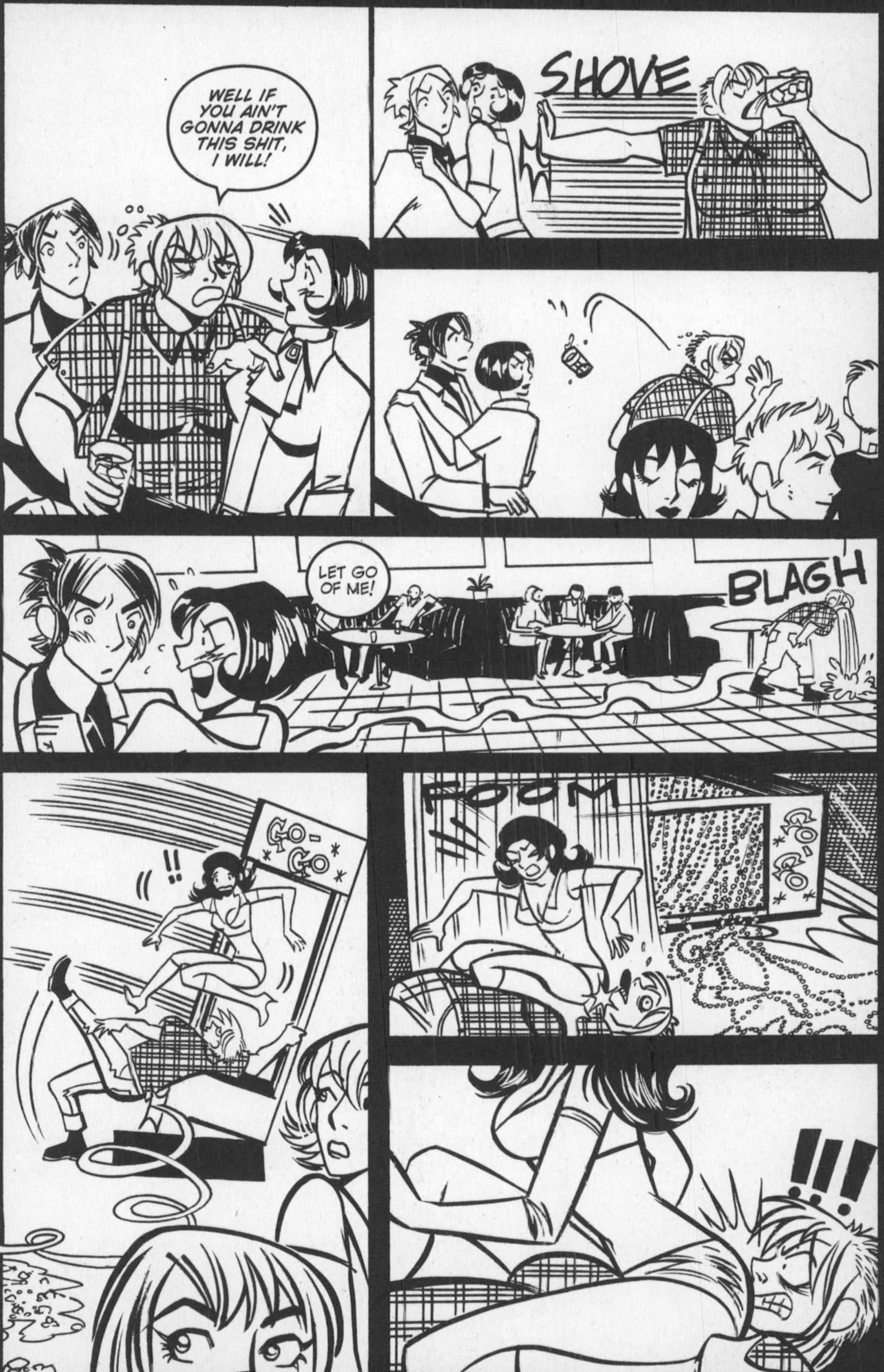

WELL IF YOU AIN'T GONNA DRINK THIS SHIT, I WILL!
SHOVE
LET GO OF ME!
BLAGH
GO-GO
FOOM
!!!

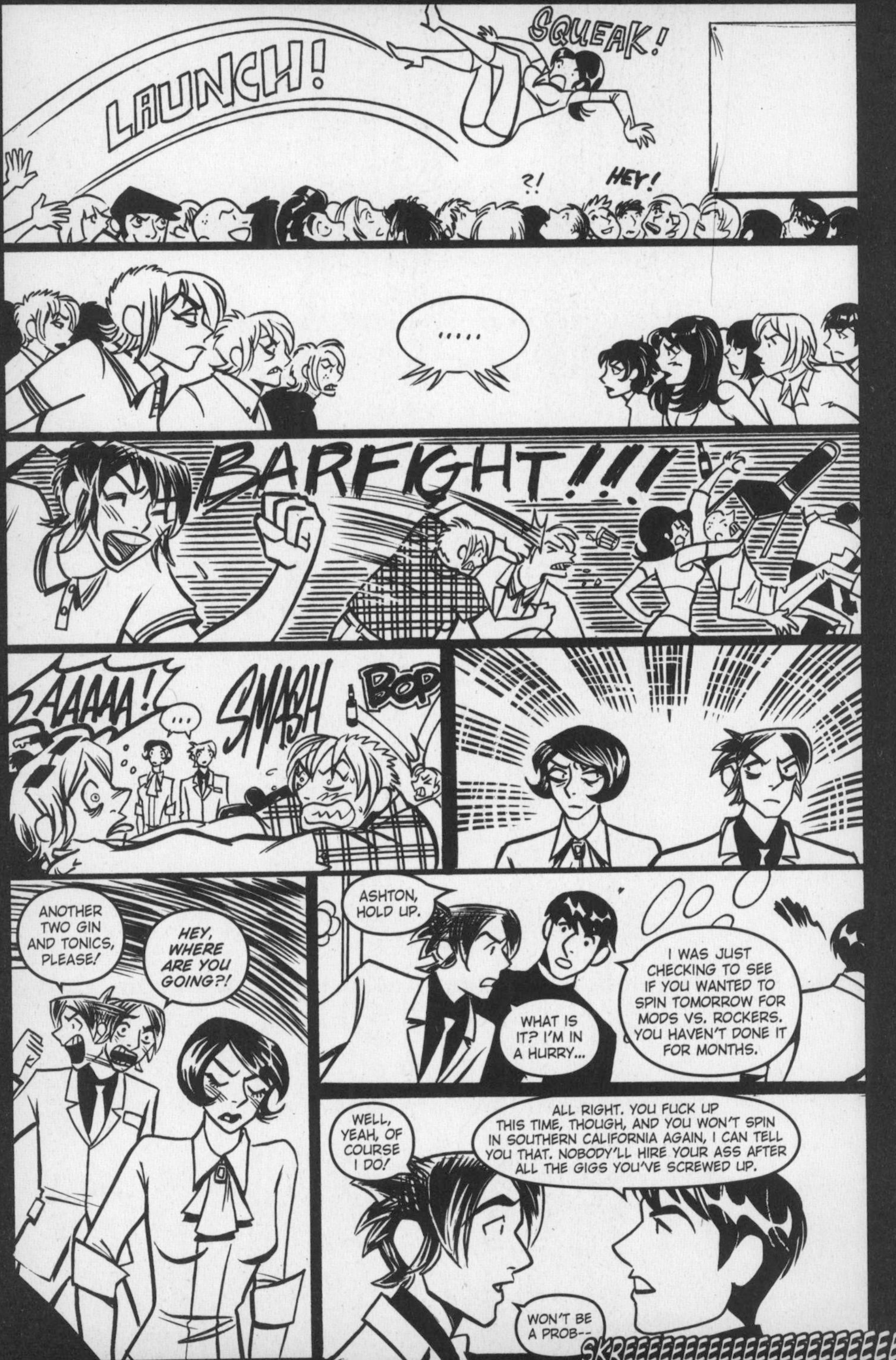

LAUNCH!
SQUEAK!
?!
HEY!
.....
BARFIGHT!!!!
AAAAA!
...
SMASH
BOP
ANOTHER TWO GIN AND TONICS, PLEASE!
HEY, WHERE ARE YOU GOING?!
ASHTON, HOLD UP.
WHAT IS IT? I'M IN A HURRY...
I WAS JUST CHECKING TO SEE IF YOU WANTED TO SPIN TOMORROW FOR MODS VS. ROCKERS. YOU HAVEN'T DONE IT FOR MONTHS.
WELL, YEAH, OF COURSE I DO!
ALL RIGHT. YOU FUCK UP THIS TIME, THOUGH, AND YOU WON'T SPIN IN SOUTHERN CALIFORNIA AGAIN, I CAN TELL YOU THAT. NOBODY'LL HIRE YOUR ASS AFTER ALL THE GIGS YOU'VE SCREWED UP.
WON'T BE A PROB--
SKREEEEEEEEEEEEEEEEEEEEEEEE

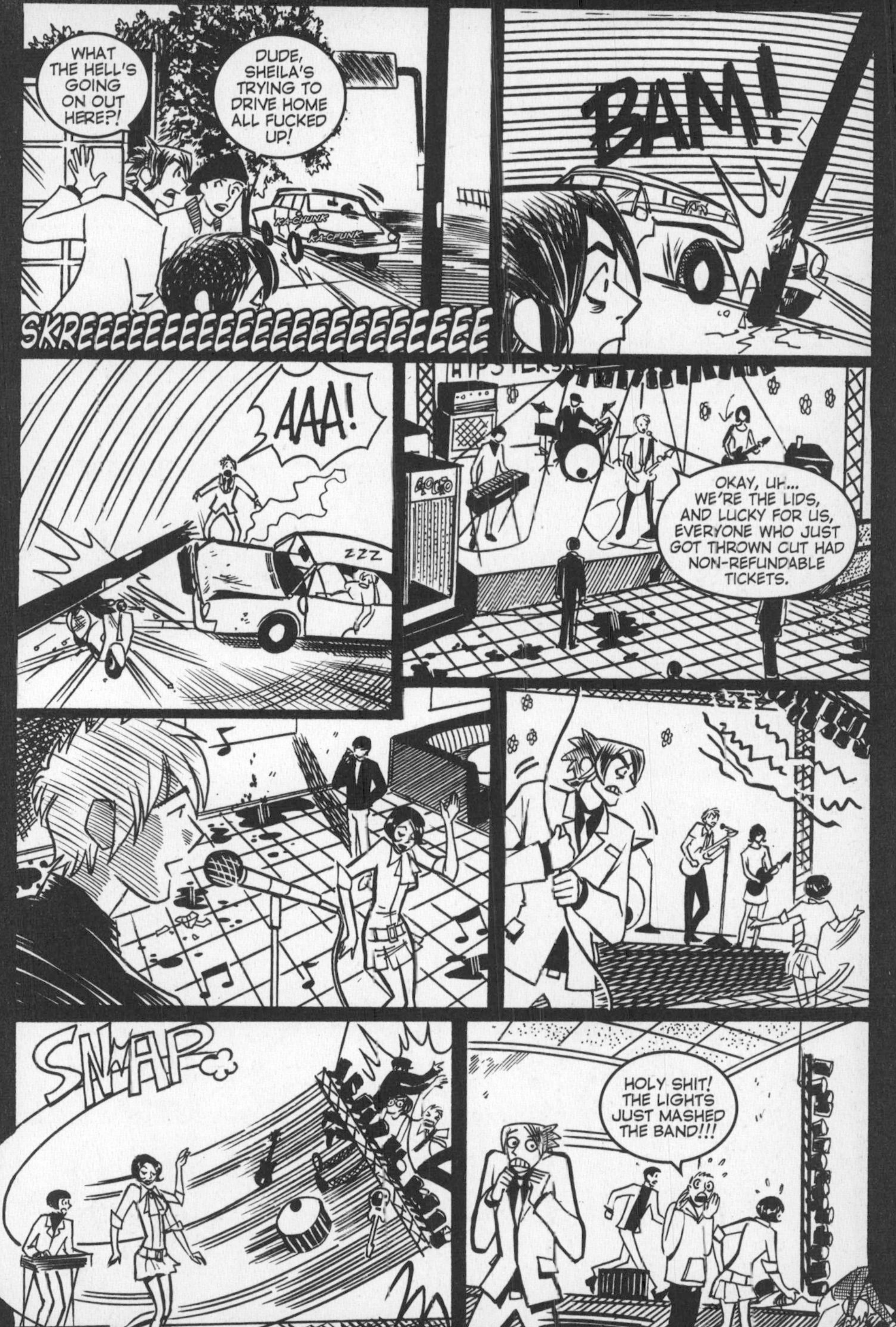
WHAT THE HELL'S GOING ON OUT HERE?!
DUDE, SHEILA'S TRYING TO DRIVE HOME ALL FUCKED UP!
KA-CHUNK
KA-CHUNK
SKREEEEEEEEEEEEEEEEEEEEEEEEE
BAM!
AAA!
ZZZ
OKAY, UH... WE'RE THE LIDS, AND LUCKY FOR US, EVERYONE WHO JUST GOT THROWN OUT HAD NON-REFUNDABLE TICKETS.
SNAP
HOLY SHIT! THE LIGHTS JUST MASHED THE BAND!!!

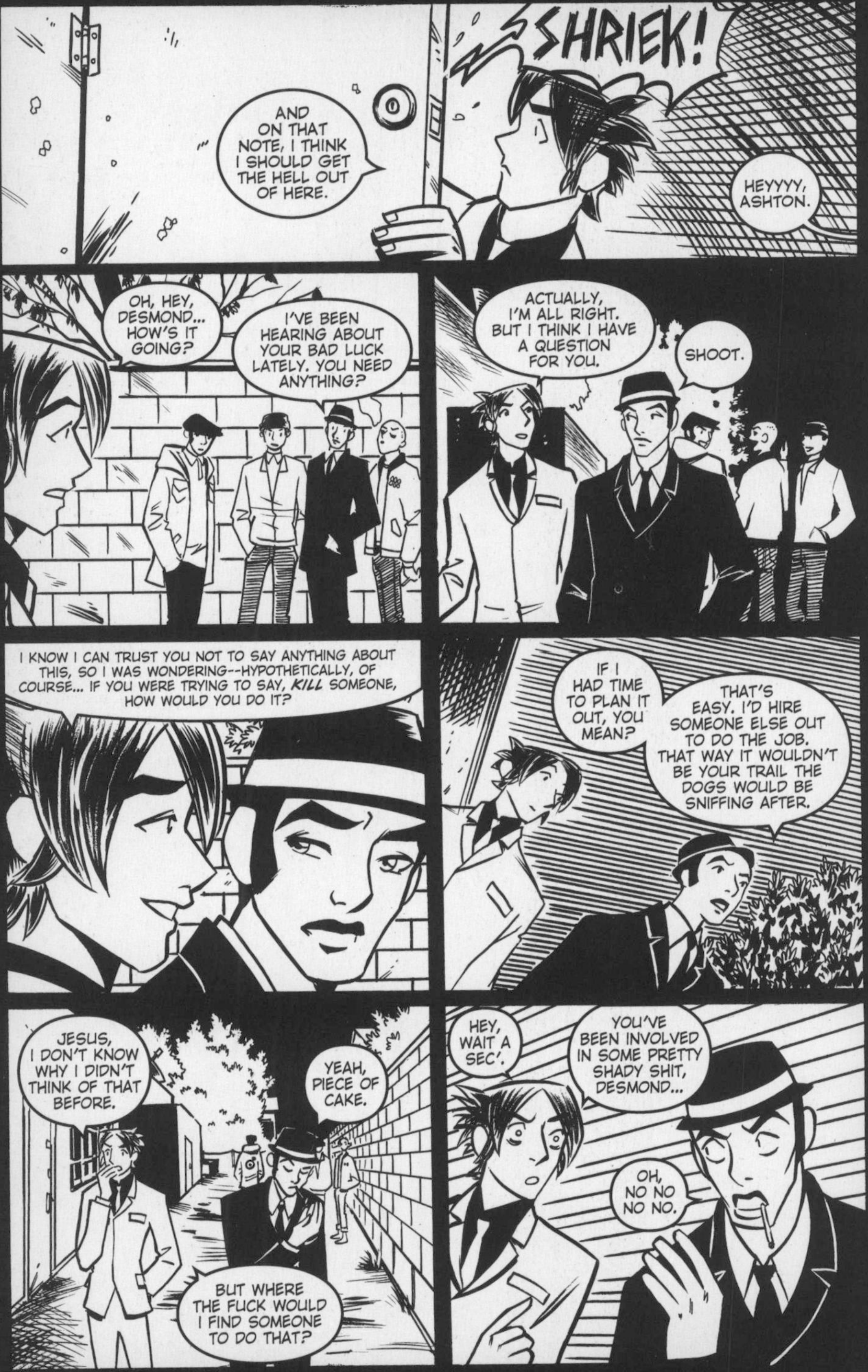
AND ON THAT NOTE, I THINK I SHOULD GET THE HELL OUT OF HERE.
SHRIEK!
HEYYYY, ASHTON.
OH, HEY, DESMOND... HOW'S IT GOING?
I'VE BEEN HEARING ABOUT YOUR BAD LUCK LATELY. YOU NEED ANYTHING?
ACTUALLY, I'M ALL RIGHT. BUT I THINK I HAVE A QUESTION FOR YOU.
SHOOT.
I KNOW I CAN TRUST YOU NOT TO SAY ANYTHING ABOUT THIS, SO I WAS WONDERING--HYPOTHETICALLY, OF COURSE... IF YOU WERE TRYING TO SAY, KILL SOMEONE, HOW WOULD YOU DO IT?
IF I HAD TIME TO PLAN IT OUT, YOU MEAN?
THAT'S EASY. I'D HIRE SOMEONE ELSE OUT TO DO THE JOB. THAT WAY IT WOULDN'T BE YOUR TRAIL THE DOGS WOULD BE SNIFFING AFTER.
JESUS, I DON'T KNOW WHY I DIDN'T THINK OF THAT BEFORE.
YEAH, PIECE OF CAKE.
BUT WHERE THE FUCK WOULD I FIND SOMEONE TO DO THAT?
HEY, WAIT A SEC'.
YOU'VE BEEN INVOLVED IN SOME PRETTY SHADY SHIT, DESMOND...
OH, NO NO NO NO.

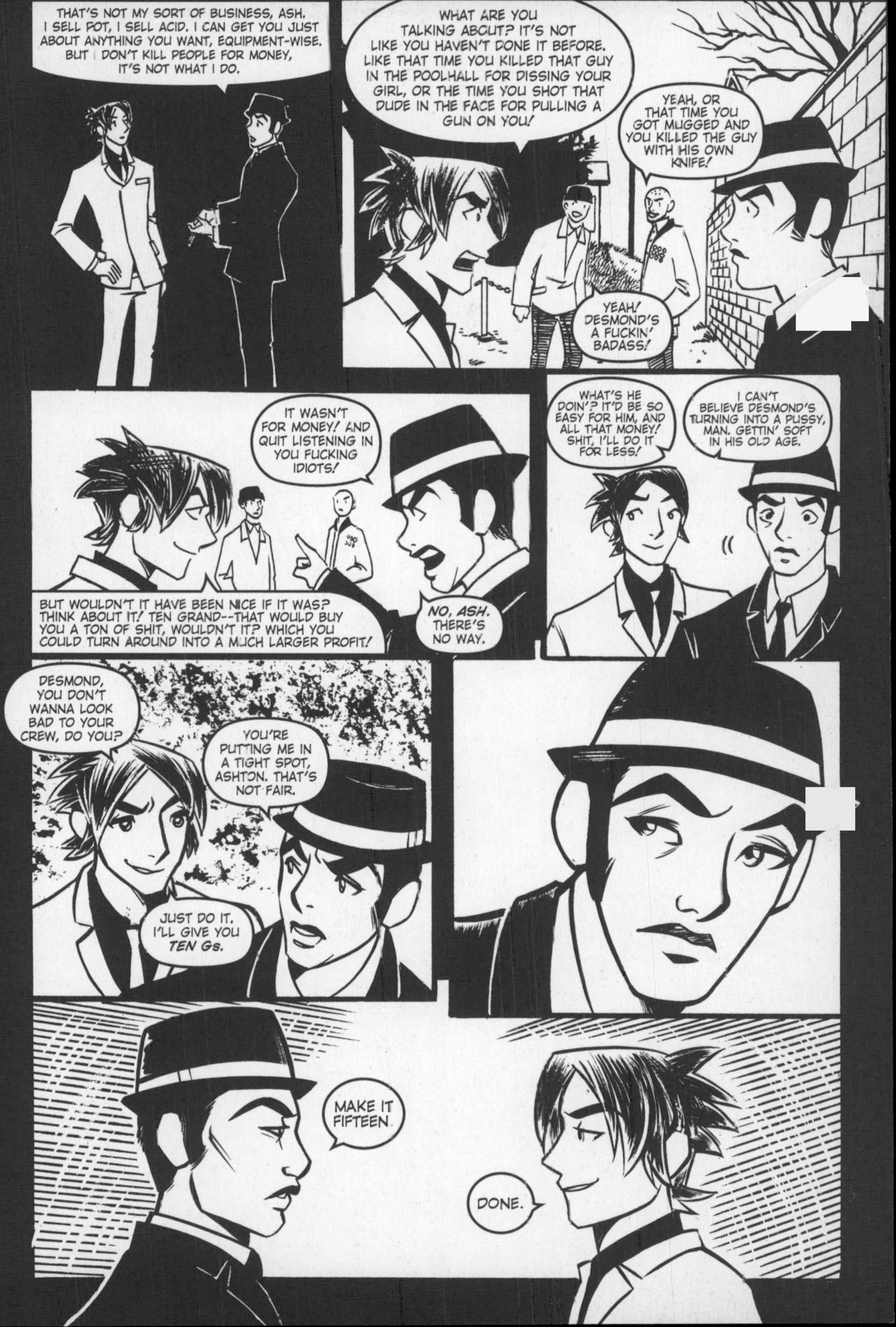
THAT'S NOT MY SORT OF BUSINESS, ASH. I SELL POT, I SELL ACID. I CAN GET YOU JUST ABOUT ANYTHING YOU WANT, EQUIPMENT-WISE. BUT I DON'T KILL PEOPLE FOR MONEY, IT'S NOT WHAT I DO.
WHAT ARE YOU TALKING ABOUT? IT'S NOT LIKE YOU HAVEN'T DONE IT BEFORE. LIKE THAT TIME YOU KILLED THAT GUY IN THE POOLHALL FOR DISSING YOUR GIRL, OR THE TIME YOU SHOT THAT DUDE IN THE FACE FOR PULLING A GUN ON YOU!
YEAH, OR THAT TIME YOU GOT MUGGED AND YOU KILLED THE GUY WITH HIS OWN KNIFE!
YEAH! DESMOND'S A FUCKIN' BADASS!
IT WASN'T FOR MONEY! AND QUIT LISTENING IN YOU FUCKING IDIOTS!
BUT WOULDN'T IT HAVE BEEN NICE IF IT WAS? THINK ABOUT IT! TEN GRAND--THAT WOULD BUY YOU A TON OF SHIT, WOULDN'T IT? WHICH YOU COULD TURN AROUND INTO A MUCH LARGER PROFIT!
NO, ASH. THERE'S NO WAY.
WHAT'S HE DOIN'? IT'D BE SO EASY FOR HIM, AND ALL THAT MONEY! SHIT, I'LL DO IT FOR LESS!
I CAN'T BELIEVE DESMOND'S TURNING INTO A PUSSY, MAN. GETTIN' SOFT IN HIS OLD AGE.
DESMOND, YOU DON'T WANNA LOOK BAD TO YOUR CREW, DO YOU?
YOU'RE PUTTING ME IN A TIGHT SPOT, ASHTON. THAT'S NOT FAIR.
JUST DO IT. I'LL GIVE YOU TEN Gs.
MAKE IT FIFTEEN.
DONE.

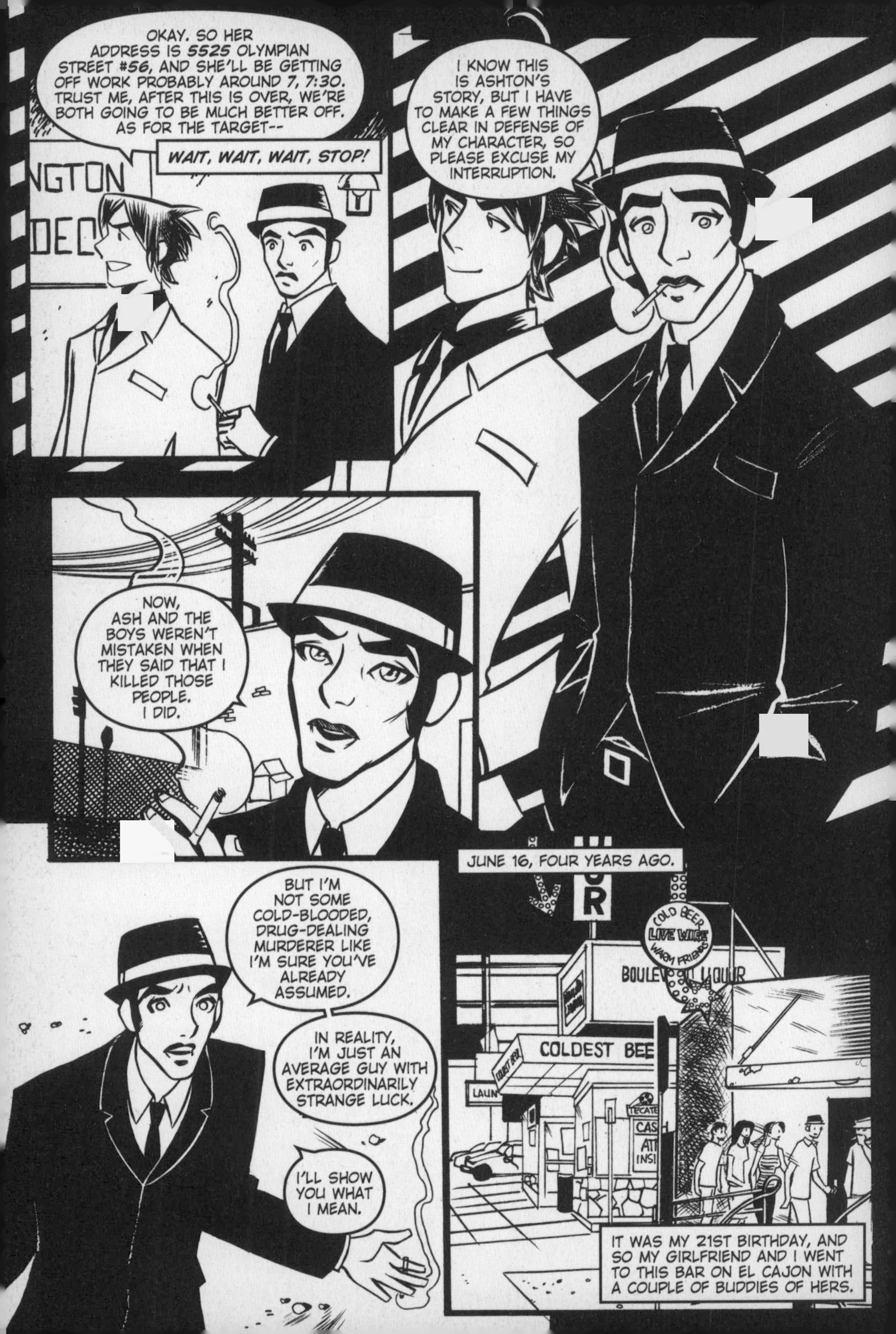
OKAY. SO HER ADDRESS IS 5525 OLYMPIAN STREET #56, AND SHE'LL BE GETTING OFF WORK PROBABLY AROUND 7, 7:30. TRUST ME, AFTER THIS IS OVER, WE'RE BOTH GOING TO BE MUCH BETTER OFF. AS FOR THE TARGET--
WAIT, WAIT, WAIT, STOP!
NGTON
DEC
I KNOW THIS IS ASHTON'S STORY, BUT I HAVE TO MAKE A FEW THINGS CLEAR IN DEFENSE OF MY CHARACTER, SO PLEASE EXCUSE MY INTERRUPTION.
NOW, ASH AND THE BOYS WEREN'T MISTAKEN WHEN THEY SAID THAT I KILLED THOSE PEOPLE. I DID.
BUT I'M NOT SOME COLD-BLOODED, DRUG-DEALING MURDERER LIKE I'M SURE YOU'VE ALREADY ASSUMED.
IN REALITY, I'M JUST AN AVERAGE GUY WITH EXTRAORDINARILY STRANGE LUCK.
I'LL SHOW YOU WHAT I MEAN.
JUNE 16, FOUR YEARS AGO.
COLD BEER
LIVE WIRE
WARM FRIENDS
COLDEST BEE
IT WAS MY 21ST BIRTHDAY, AND SO MY GIRLFRIEND AND I WENT TO THIS BAR ON EL CAJON WITH A COUPLE OF BUDDIES OF HERS.

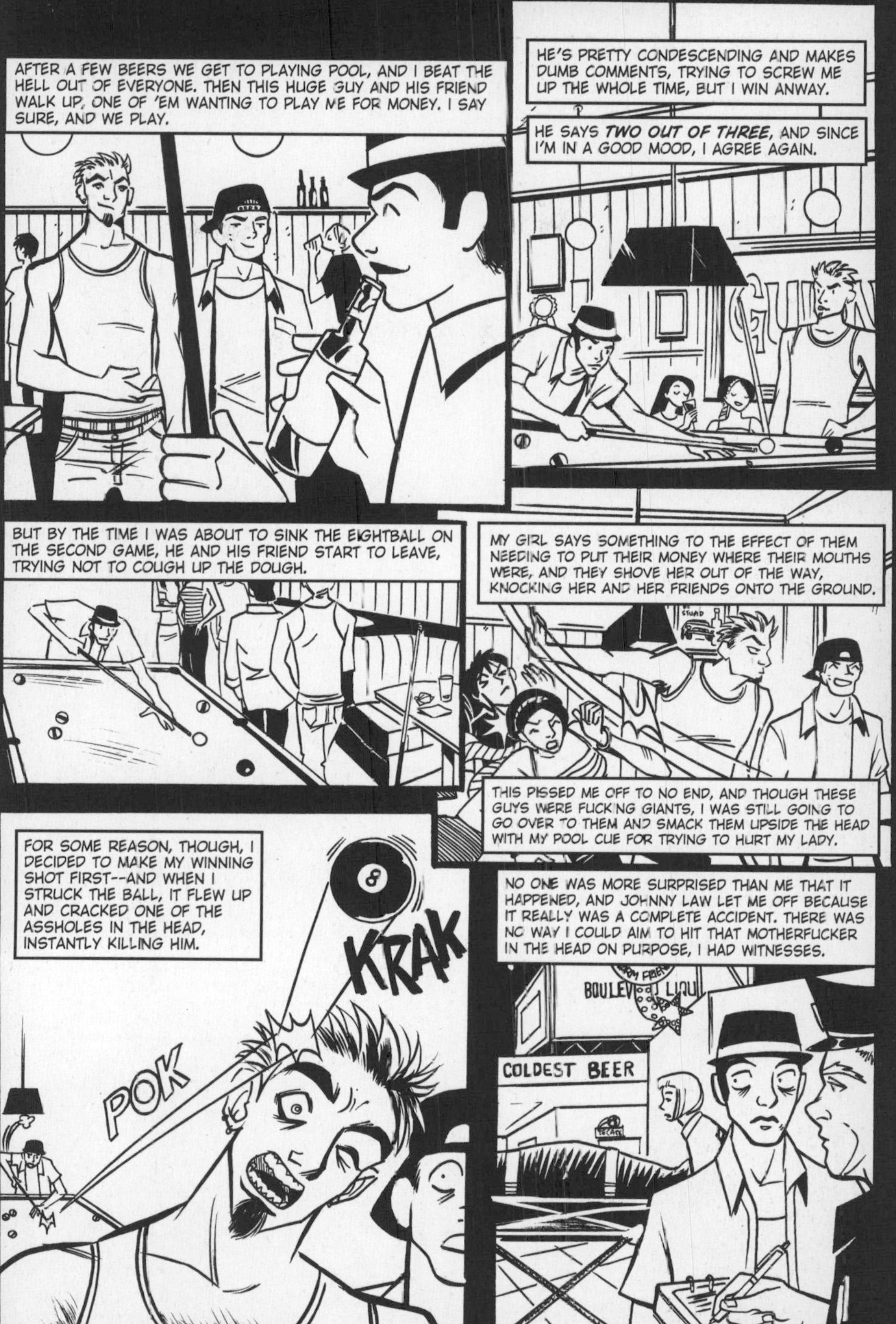
AFTER A FEW BEERS WE GET TO PLAYING POOL, AND I BEAT THE HELL OUT OF EVERYONE. THEN THIS HUGE GUY AND HIS FRIEND WALK UP, ONE OF 'EM WANTING TO PLAY ME FOR MONEY. I SAY SURE, AND WE PLAY.
HE'S PRETTY CONDESCENDING AND MAKES DUMB COMMENTS, TRYING TO SCREW ME UP THE WHOLE TIME, BUT I WIN ANWAY.
HE SAYS *TWO OUT OF THREE*, AND SINCE I'M IN A GOOD MOOD, I AGREE AGAIN.
BUT BY THE TIME I WAS ABOUT TO SINK THE EIGHTBALL ON THE SECOND GAME, HE AND HIS FRIEND START TO LEAVE, TRYING NOT TO COUGH UP THE DOUGH.
MY GIRL SAYS SOMETHING TO THE EFFECT OF THEM NEEDING TO PUT THEIR MONEY WHERE THEIR MOUTHS WERE, AND THEY SHOVE HER OUT OF THE WAY, KNOCKING HER AND HER FRIENDS ONTO THE GROUND.
THIS PISSED ME OFF TO NO END, AND THOUGH THESE GUYS WERE FUCKING GIANTS, I WAS STILL GOING TO GO OVER TO THEM AND SMACK THEM UPSIDE THE HEAD WITH MY POOL CUE FOR TRYING TO HURT MY LADY.
FOR SOME REASON, THOUGH, I DECIDED TO MAKE MY WINNING SHOT FIRST--AND WHEN I STRUCK THE BALL, IT FLEW UP AND CRACKED ONE OF THE ASSHOLES IN THE HEAD, INSTANTLY KILLING HIM.
8
KRAK
POK
NO ONE WAS MORE SURPRISED THAN ME THAT IT HAPPENED, AND JOHNNY LAW LET ME OFF BECAUSE IT REALLY WAS A COMPLETE ACCIDENT. THERE WAS NO WAY I COULD AIM TO HIT THAT MOTHERFUCKER IN THE HEAD ON PURPOSE, I HAD WITNESSES.
COLDEST BEER
OF COURSE, NO ONE WILL PLAY ME POOL ANYMORE.

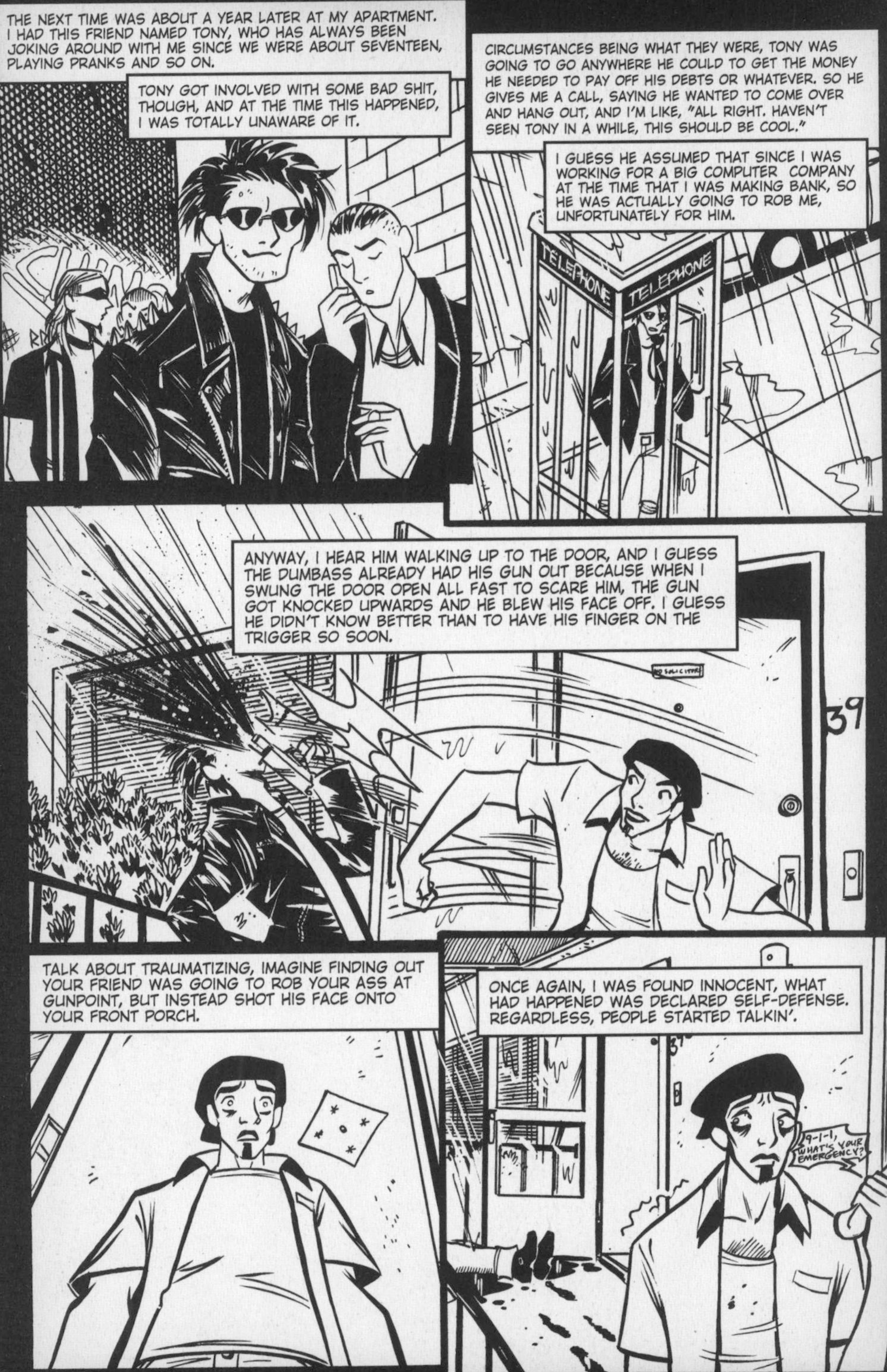
THE NEXT TIME WAS ABOUT A YEAR LATER AT MY APARTMENT. I HAD THIS FRIEND NAMED TONY, WHO HAS ALWAYS BEEN JOKING AROUND WITH ME SINCE WE WERE ABOUT SEVENTEEN, PLAYING PRANKS AND SO ON.
TONY GOT INVOLVED WITH SOME BAD SHIT, THOUGH, AND AT THE TIME THIS HAPPENED, I WAS TOTALLY UNAWARE OF IT.
CIRCUMSTANCES BEING WHAT THEY WERE, TONY WAS GOING TO GO ANYWHERE HE COULD TO GET THE MONEY HE NEEDED TO PAY OFF HIS DEBTS OR WHATEVER. SO HE GIVES ME A CALL, SAYING HE WANTED TO COME OVER AND HANG OUT, AND I'M LIKE, "ALL RIGHT. HAVEN'T SEEN TONY IN A WHILE, THIS SHOULD BE COOL."
I GUESS HE ASSUMED THAT SINCE I WAS WORKING FOR A BIG COMPUTER COMPANY AT THE TIME THAT I WAS MAKING BANK, SO HE WAS ACTUALLY GOING TO ROB ME, UNFORTUNATELY FOR HIM.
TELEPHONE
TELEPHONE
ANYWAY, I HEAR HIM WALKING UP TO THE DOOR, AND I GUESS THE DUMBASS ALREADY HAD HIS GUN OUT BECAUSE WHEN I SWUNG THE DOOR OPEN ALL FAST TO SCARE HIM, THE GUN GOT KNOCKED UPWARDS AND HE BLEW HIS FACE OFF. I GUESS HE DIDN'T KNOW BETTER THAN TO HAVE HIS FINGER ON THE TRIGGER SO SOON.
39
TALK ABOUT TRAUMATIZING, IMAGINE FINDING OUT YOUR FRIEND WAS GOING TO ROB YOUR ASS AT GUNPOINT, BUT INSTEAD SHOT HIS FACE ONTO YOUR FRONT PORCH.
ONCE AGAIN, I WAS FOUND INNOCENT, WHAT HAD HAPPENED WAS DECLARED SELF-DEFENSE. REGARDLESS, PEOPLE STARTED TALKIN'.
9-1-1, WHAT'S YOUR EMERGENCY?

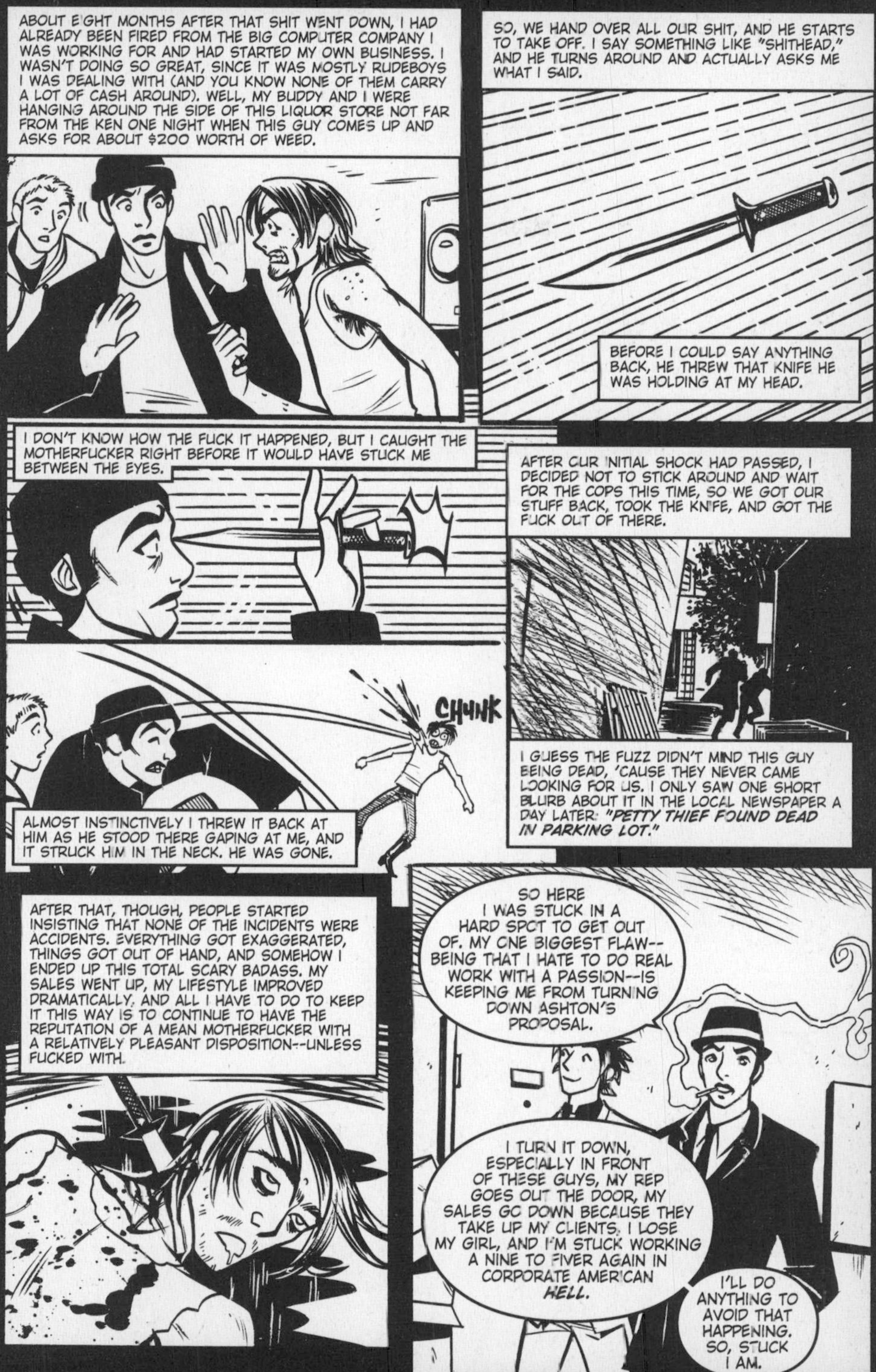
ABOUT EIGHT MONTHS AFTER THAT SHIT WENT DOWN, I HAD ALREADY BEEN FIRED FROM THE BIG COMPUTER COMPANY I WAS WORKING FOR AND HAD STARTED MY OWN BUSINESS. I WASN'T DOING SO GREAT, SINCE IT WAS MOSTLY RUDEBOYS I WAS DEALING WITH (AND YOU KNOW NONE OF THEM CARRY A LOT OF CASH AROUND). WELL, MY BUDDY AND I WERE HANGING AROUND THE SIDE OF THIS LIQUOR STORE NOT FAR FROM THE KEN ONE NIGHT WHEN THIS GUY COMES UP AND ASKS FOR ABOUT $200 WORTH OF WEED.
SO, WE HAND OVER ALL OUR SHIT, AND HE STARTS TO TAKE OFF. I SAY SOMETHING LIKE "SHITHEAD," AND HE TURNS AROUND AND ACTUALLY ASKS ME WHAT I SAID.
BEFORE I COULD SAY ANYTHING BACK, HE THREW THAT KNIFE HE WAS HOLDING AT MY HEAD.
I DON'T KNOW HOW THE FUCK IT HAPPENED, BUT I CAUGHT THE MOTHERFUCKER RIGHT BEFORE IT WOULD HAVE STUCK ME BETWEEN THE EYES.
CHUNK
ALMOST INSTINCTIVELY I THREW IT BACK AT HIM AS HE STOOD THERE GAPING AT ME, AND IT STRUCK HIM IN THE NECK. HE WAS GONE.
AFTER OUR INITIAL SHOCK HAD PASSED, I DECIDED NOT TO STICK AROUND AND WAIT FOR THE COPS THIS TIME, SO WE GOT OUR STUFF BACK, TOOK THE KNIFE, AND GOT THE FUCK OUT OF THERE.
I GUESS THE FUZZ DIDN'T MIND THIS GUY BEING DEAD, 'CAUSE THEY NEVER CAME LOOKING FOR US. I ONLY SAW ONE SHORT BLURB ABOUT IT IN THE LOCAL NEWSPAPER A DAY LATER: "PETTY THIEF FOUND DEAD IN PARKING LOT."
AFTER THAT, THOUGH, PEOPLE STARTED INSISTING THAT NONE OF THE INCIDENTS WERE ACCIDENTS. EVERYTHING GOT EXAGGERATED, THINGS GOT OUT OF HAND, AND SOMEHOW I ENDED UP THIS TOTAL SCARY BADASS. MY SALES WENT UP, MY LIFESTYLE IMPROVED DRAMATICALLY, AND ALL I HAVE TO DO TO KEEP IT THIS WAY IS TO CONTINUE TO HAVE THE REPUTATION OF A MEAN MOTHERFUCKER WITH A RELATIVELY PLEASANT DISPOSITION--UNLESS FUCKED WITH.
SO HERE I WAS STUCK IN A HARD SPOT TO GET OUT OF. MY ONE BIGGEST FLAW--BEING THAT I HATE TO DO REAL WORK WITH A PASSION--IS KEEPING ME FROM TURNING DOWN ASHTON'S PROPOSAL.
I TURN IT DOWN, ESPECIALLY IN FRONT OF THESE GUYS, MY REP GOES OUT THE DOOR, MY SALES GO DOWN BECAUSE THEY TAKE UP MY CLIENTS, I LOSE MY GIRL, AND I'M STUCK WORKING A NINE TO FIVER AGAIN IN CORPORATE AMERICAN HELL.
I'LL DO ANYTHING TO AVOID THAT HAPPENING. SO, STUCK I AM.

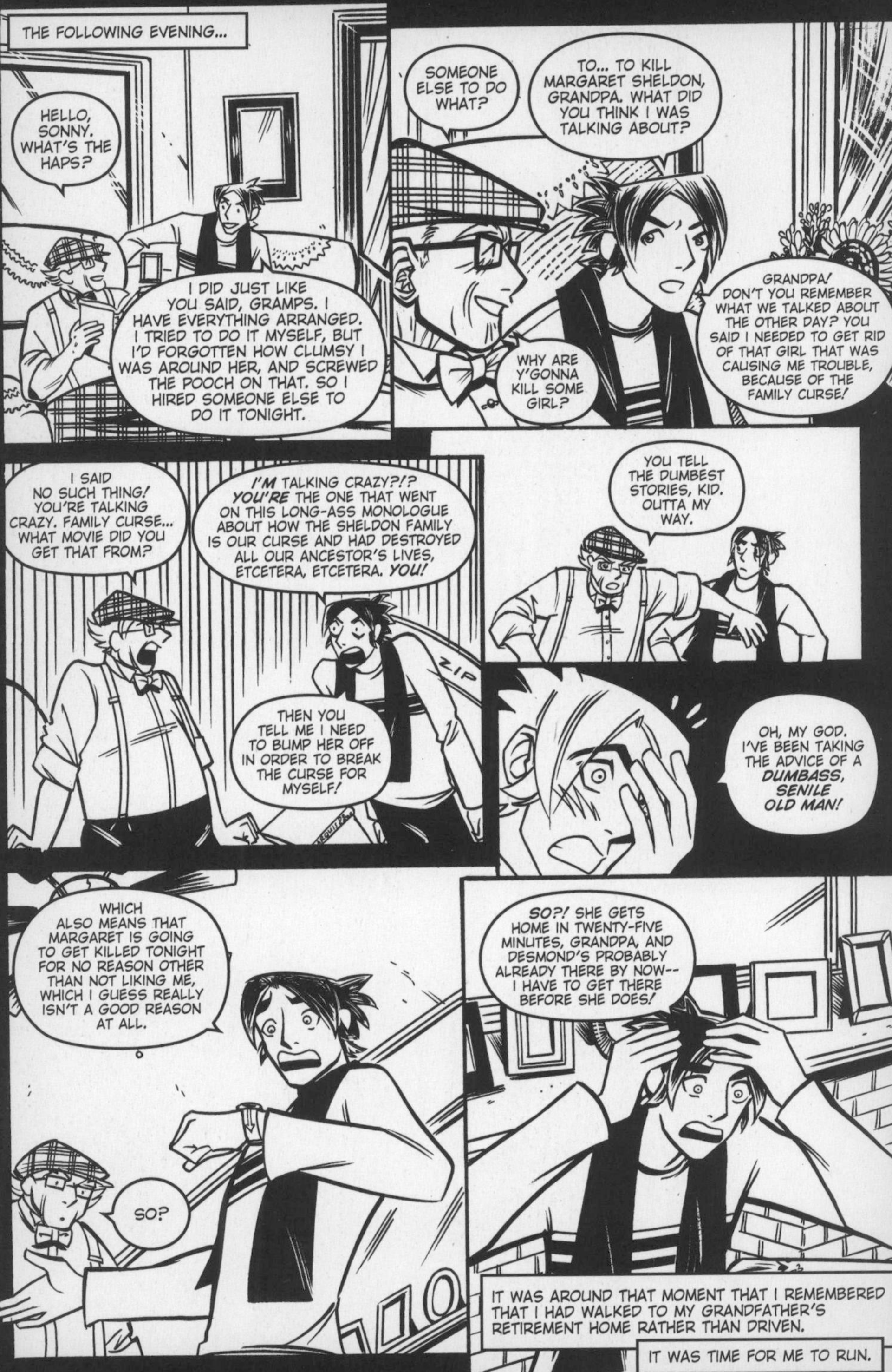
THE FOLLOWING EVENING...
HELLO, SONNY. WHAT'S THE HAPS?
I DID JUST LIKE YOU SAID, GRAMPS. I HAVE EVERYTHING ARRANGED. I TRIED TO DO IT MYSELF, BUT I'D FORGOTTEN HOW CLUMSY I WAS AROUND HER, AND SCREWED THE POOCH ON THAT. SO I HIRED SOMEONE ELSE TO DO IT TONIGHT.
SOMEONE ELSE TO DO WHAT?
TO... TO KILL MARGARET SHELDON, GRANDPA. WHAT DID YOU THINK I WAS TALKING ABOUT?
WHY ARE Y'GONNA KILL SOME GIRL?
GRANDPA! DON'T YOU REMEMBER WHAT WE TALKED ABOUT THE OTHER DAY? YOU SAID I NEEDED TO GET RID OF THAT GIRL THAT WAS CAUSING ME TROUBLE, BECAUSE OF THE FAMILY CURSE!
I SAID NO SUCH THING! YOU'RE TALKING CRAZY. FAMILY CURSE... WHAT MOVIE DID YOU GET THAT FROM?
I'M TALKING CRAZY?!? YOU'RE THE ONE THAT WENT ON THIS LONG-ASS MONOLOGUE ABOUT HOW THE SHELDON FAMILY IS OUR CURSE AND HAD DESTROYED ALL OUR ANCESTOR'S LIVES, ETCETERA, ETCETERA. YOU!
ZIP
THEN YOU TELL ME I NEED TO BUMP HER OFF IN ORDER TO BREAK THE CURSE FOR MYSELF!
YOU TELL THE DUMBEST STORIES, KID. OUTTA MY WAY.
OH, MY GOD. I'VE BEEN TAKING THE ADVICE OF A DUMBASS, SENILE OLD MAN!
WHICH ALSO MEANS THAT MARGARET IS GOING TO GET KILLED TONIGHT FOR NO REASON OTHER THAN NOT LIKING ME, WHICH I GUESS REALLY ISN'T A GOOD REASON AT ALL.
SO?
SO?! SHE GETS HOME IN TWENTY-FIVE MINUTES, GRANDPA, AND DESMOND'S PROBABLY ALREADY THERE BY NOW-- I HAVE TO GET THERE BEFORE SHE DOES!
IT WAS AROUND THAT MOMENT THAT I REMEMBERED THAT I HAD WALKED TO MY GRANDFATHER'S RETIREMENT HOME RATHER THAN DRIVEN.
IT WAS TIME FOR ME TO RUN.

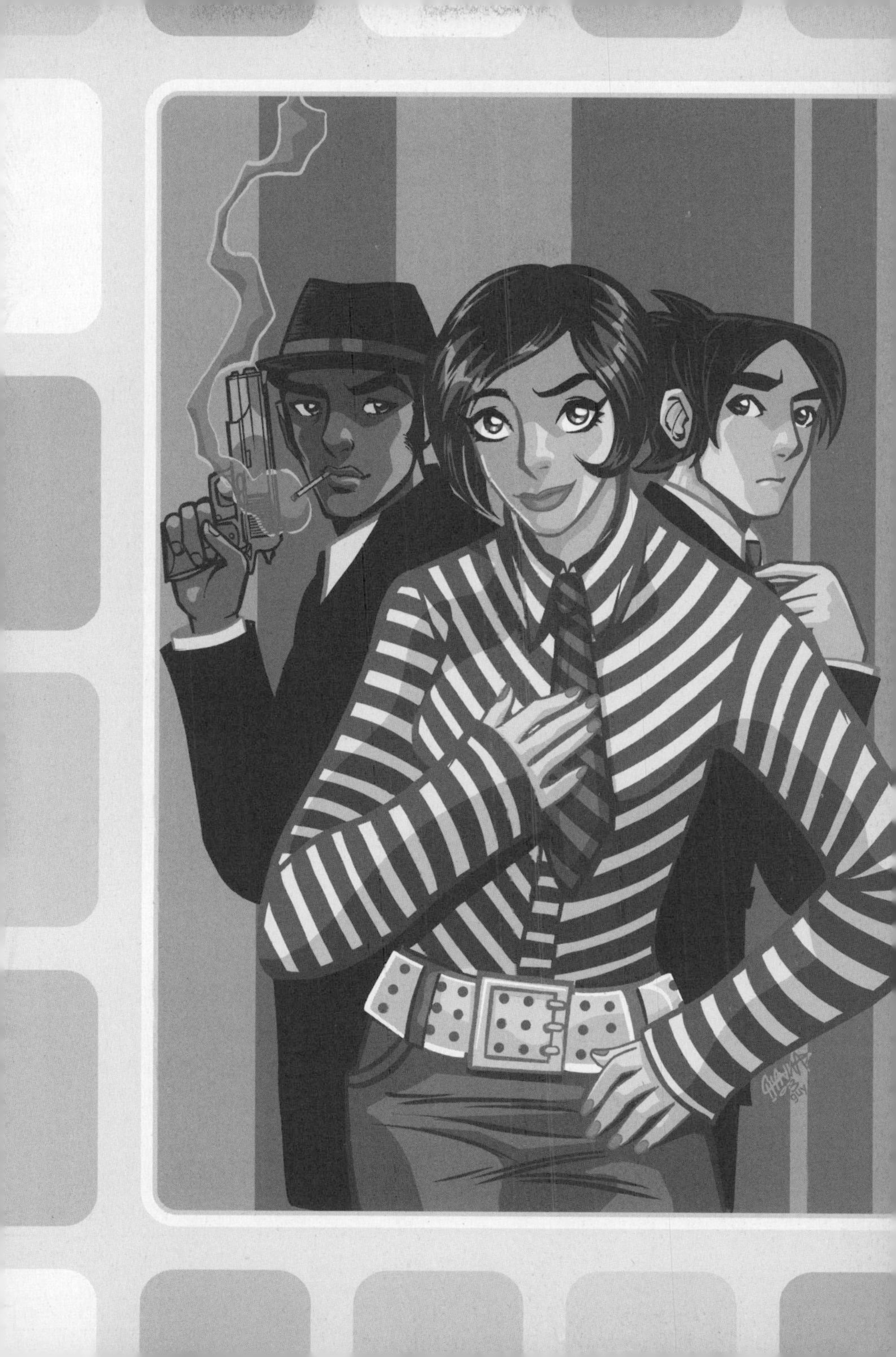

Chapter 5:
"Heart Full of Soul"

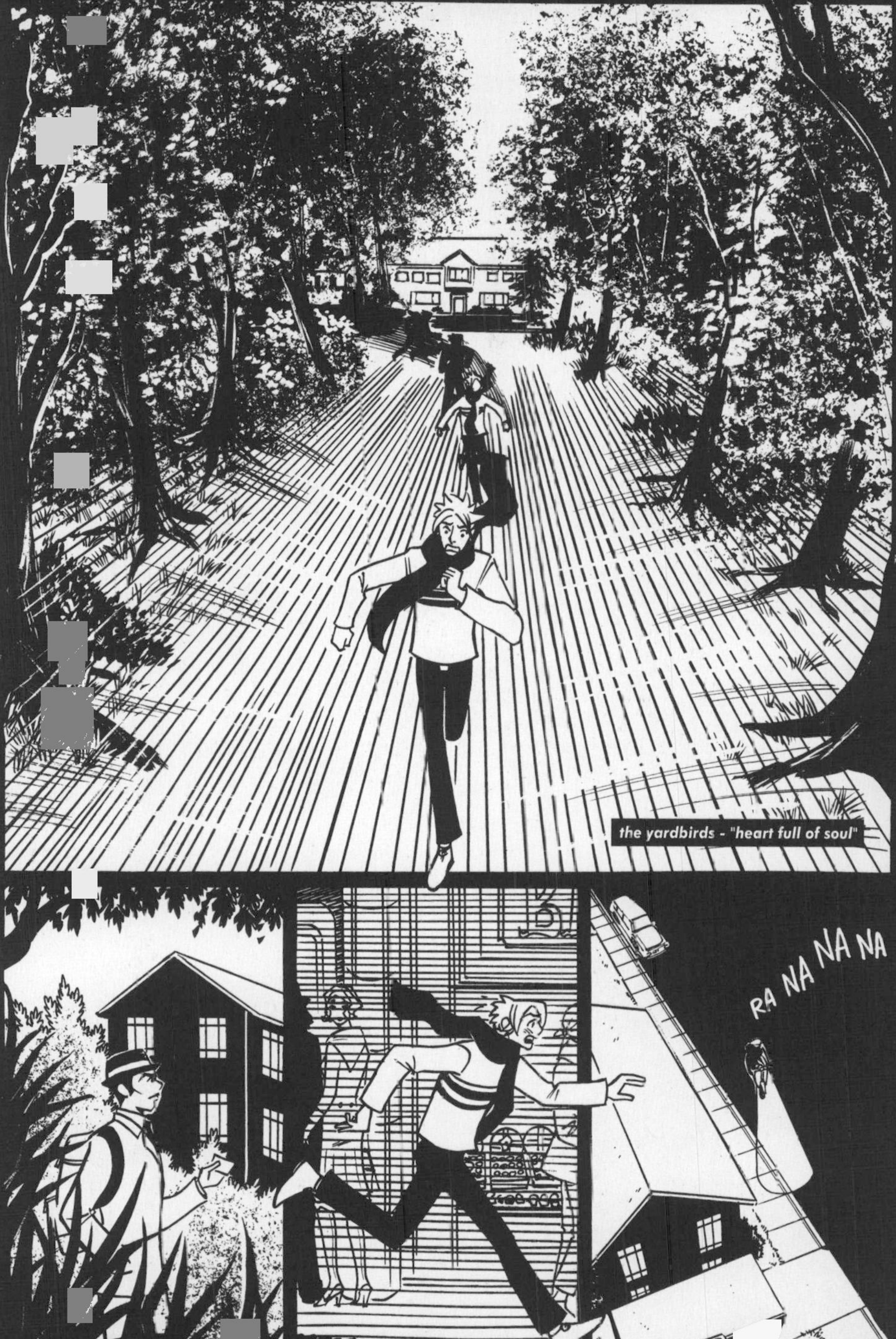
the yardbirds - "heart full of soul"
RA NA NA NA

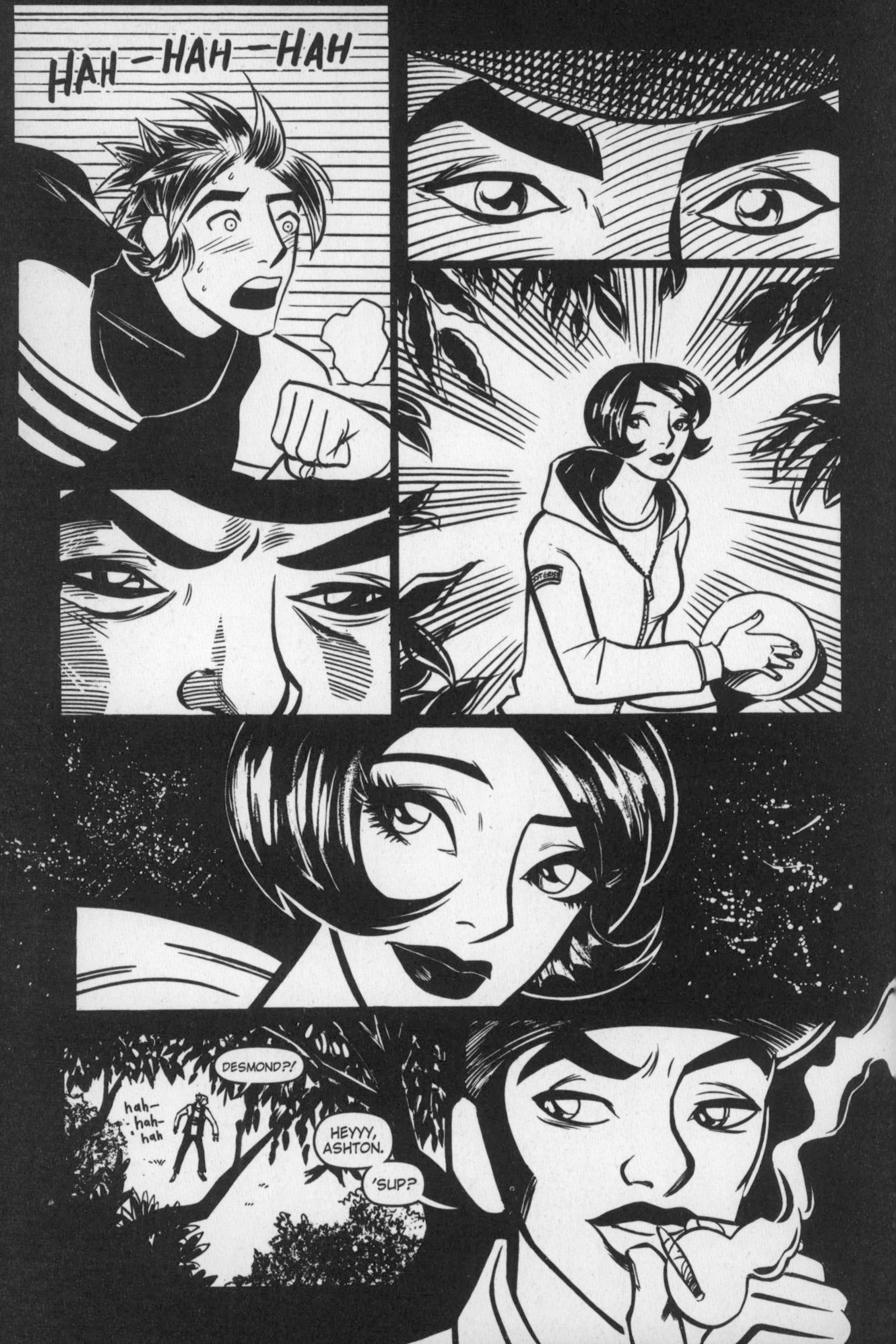
HAH-HAH-HAH
hah-hah-hah
DESMOND?!
HEYYY, ASHTON.
'SUP?

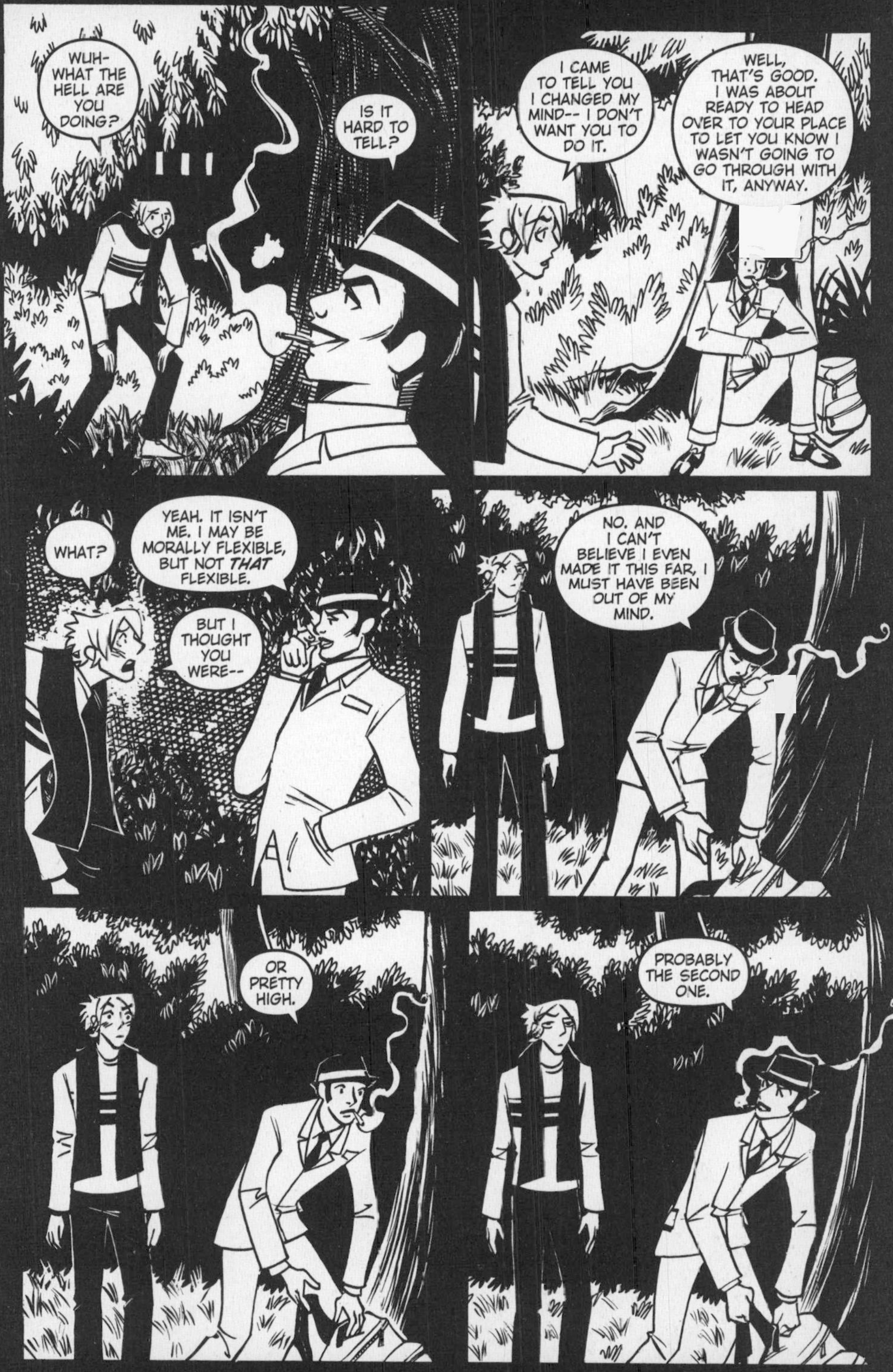
WUH-WHAT THE HELL ARE YOU DOING?
IS IT HARD TO TELL?
I CAME TO TELL YOU I CHANGED MY MIND-- I DON'T WANT YOU TO DO IT.
WELL, THAT'S GOOD. I WAS ABOUT READY TO HEAD OVER TO YOUR PLACE TO LET YOU KNOW I WASN'T GOING TO GO THROUGH WITH IT, ANYWAY.
WHAT?
YEAH. IT ISN'T ME. I MAY BE MORALLY FLEXIBLE, BUT NOT *THAT* FLEXIBLE.
BUT I THOUGHT YOU WERE--
NO. AND I CAN'T BELIEVE I EVEN MADE IT THIS FAR, I MUST HAVE BEEN OUT OF MY MIND.
OR PRETTY HIGH.
PROBABLY THE SECOND ONE.

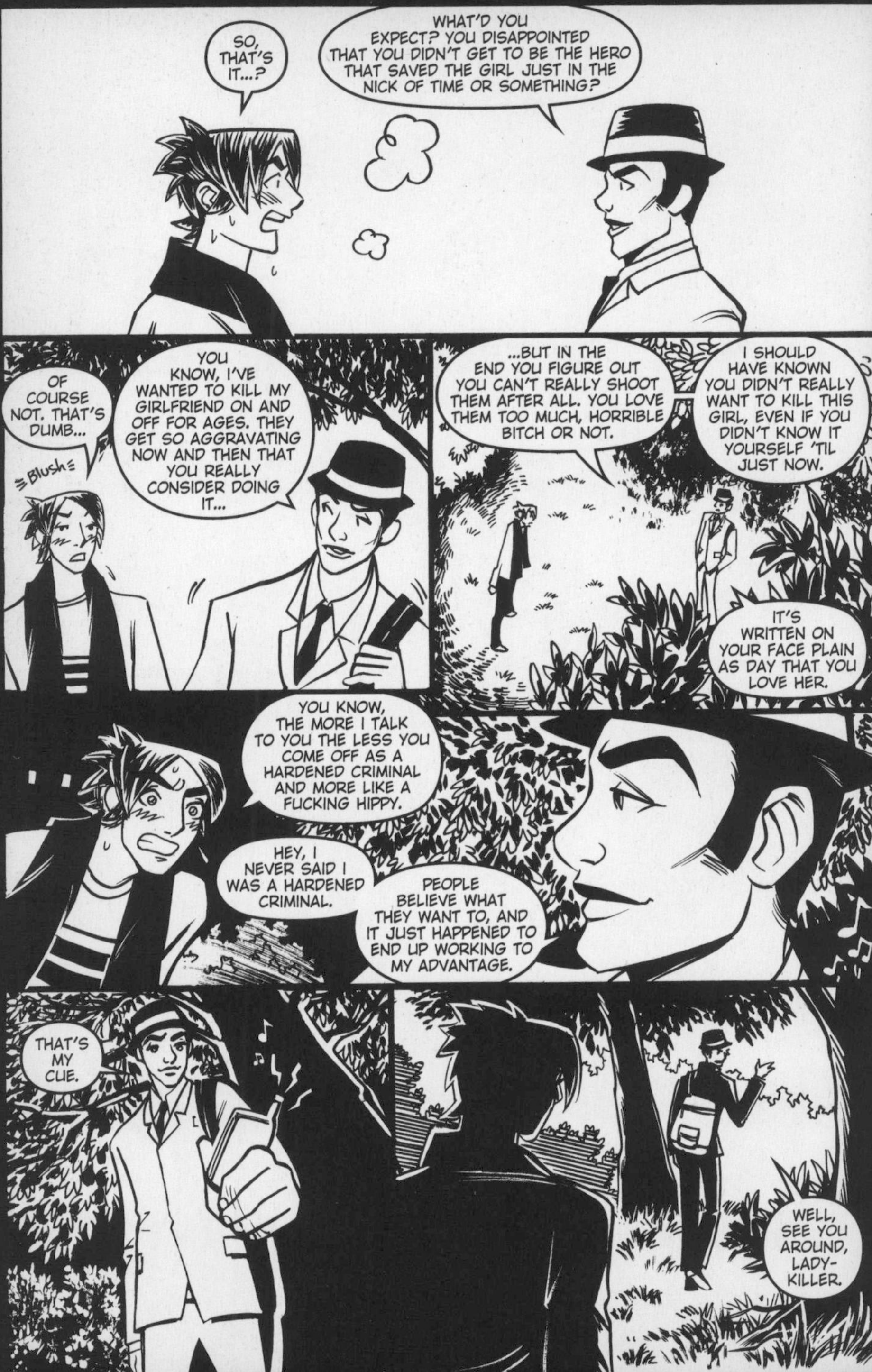
SO, THAT'S IT...?
WHAT'D YOU EXPECT? YOU DISAPPOINTED THAT YOU DIDN'T GET TO BE THE HERO THAT SAVED THE GIRL JUST IN THE NICK OF TIME OR SOMETHING?
OF COURSE NOT. THAT'S DUMB...
Blush
YOU KNOW, I'VE WANTED TO KILL MY GIRLFRIEND ON AND OFF FOR AGES. THEY GET SO AGGRAVATING NOW AND THEN THAT YOU REALLY CONSIDER DOING IT...
...BUT IN THE END YOU FIGURE OUT YOU CAN'T REALLY SHOOT THEM AFTER ALL. YOU LOVE THEM TOO MUCH, HORRIBLE BITCH OR NOT.
I SHOULD HAVE KNOWN YOU DIDN'T REALLY WANT TO KILL THIS GIRL, EVEN IF YOU DIDN'T KNOW IT YOURSELF 'TIL JUST NOW.
IT'S WRITTEN ON YOUR FACE PLAIN AS DAY THAT YOU LOVE HER.
YOU KNOW, THE MORE I TALK TO YOU THE LESS YOU COME OFF AS A HARDENED CRIMINAL AND MORE LIKE A FUCKING HIPPY.
HEY, I NEVER SAID I WAS A HARDENED CRIMINAL.
PEOPLE BELIEVE WHAT THEY WANT TO, AND IT JUST HAPPENED TO END UP WORKING TO MY ADVANTAGE.
THAT'S MY CUE.
WELL, SEE YOU AROUND, LADY-KILLER.

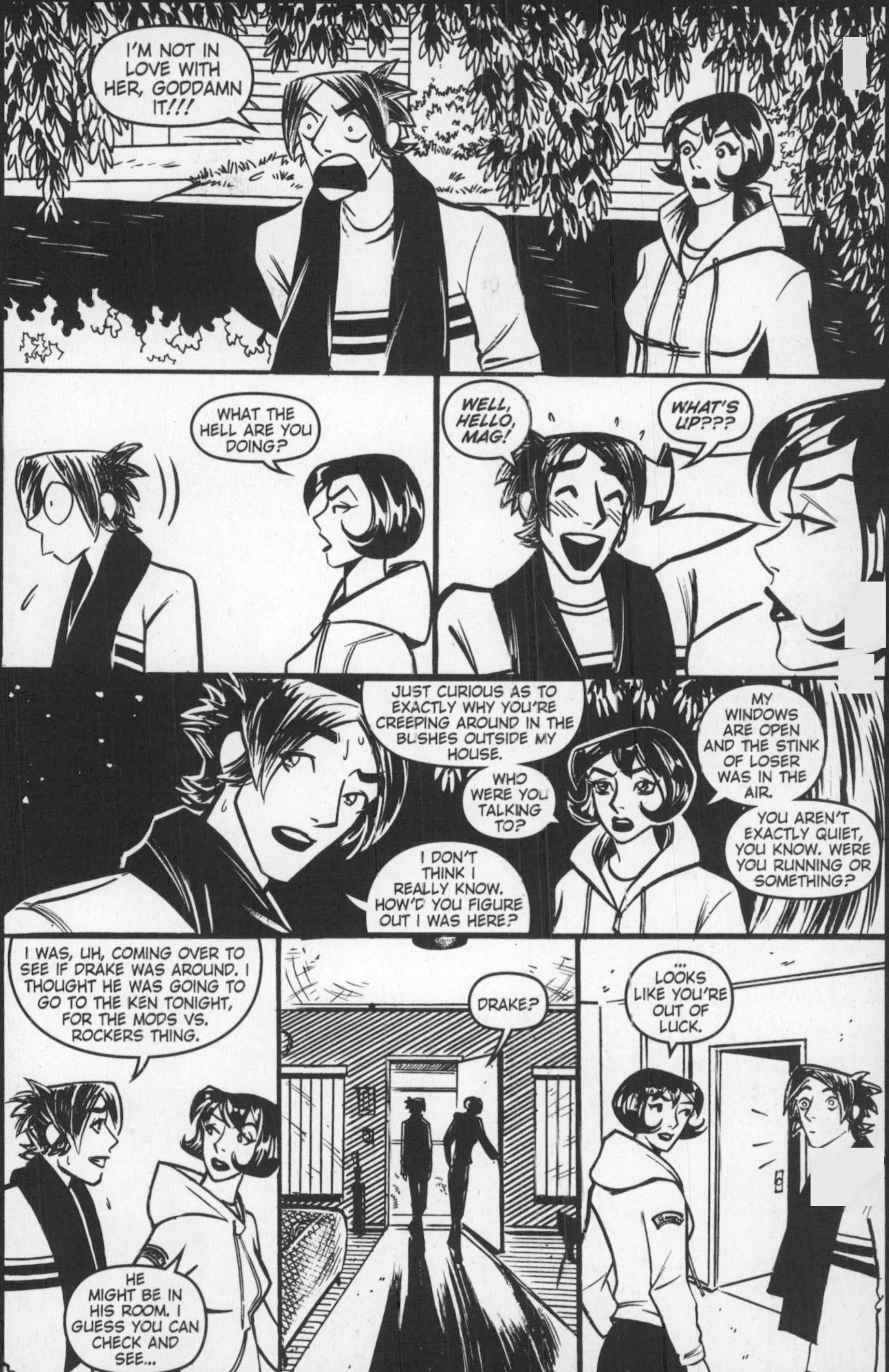
I'M NOT IN LOVE WITH HER, GODDAMN IT!!!
WHAT THE HELL ARE YOU DOING?
WELL, HELLO, MAG!
WHAT'S UP???
JUST CURIOUS AS TO EXACTLY WHY YOU'RE CREEPING AROUND IN THE BUSHES OUTSIDE MY HOUSE.
WHO WERE YOU TALKING TO?
I DON'T THINK I REALLY KNOW. HOW'D YOU FIGURE OUT I WAS HERE?
MY WINDOWS ARE OPEN AND THE STINK OF LOSER WAS IN THE AIR.
YOU AREN'T EXACTLY QUIET, YOU KNOW. WERE YOU RUNNING OR SOMETHING?
I WAS, UH, COMING OVER TO SEE IF DRAKE WAS AROUND. I THOUGHT HE WAS GOING TO GO TO THE KEN TONIGHT, FOR THE MODS VS. ROCKERS THING.
HE MIGHT BE IN HIS ROOM. I GUESS YOU CAN CHECK AND SEE...
DRAKE?
... LOOKS LIKE YOU'RE OUT OF LUCK.

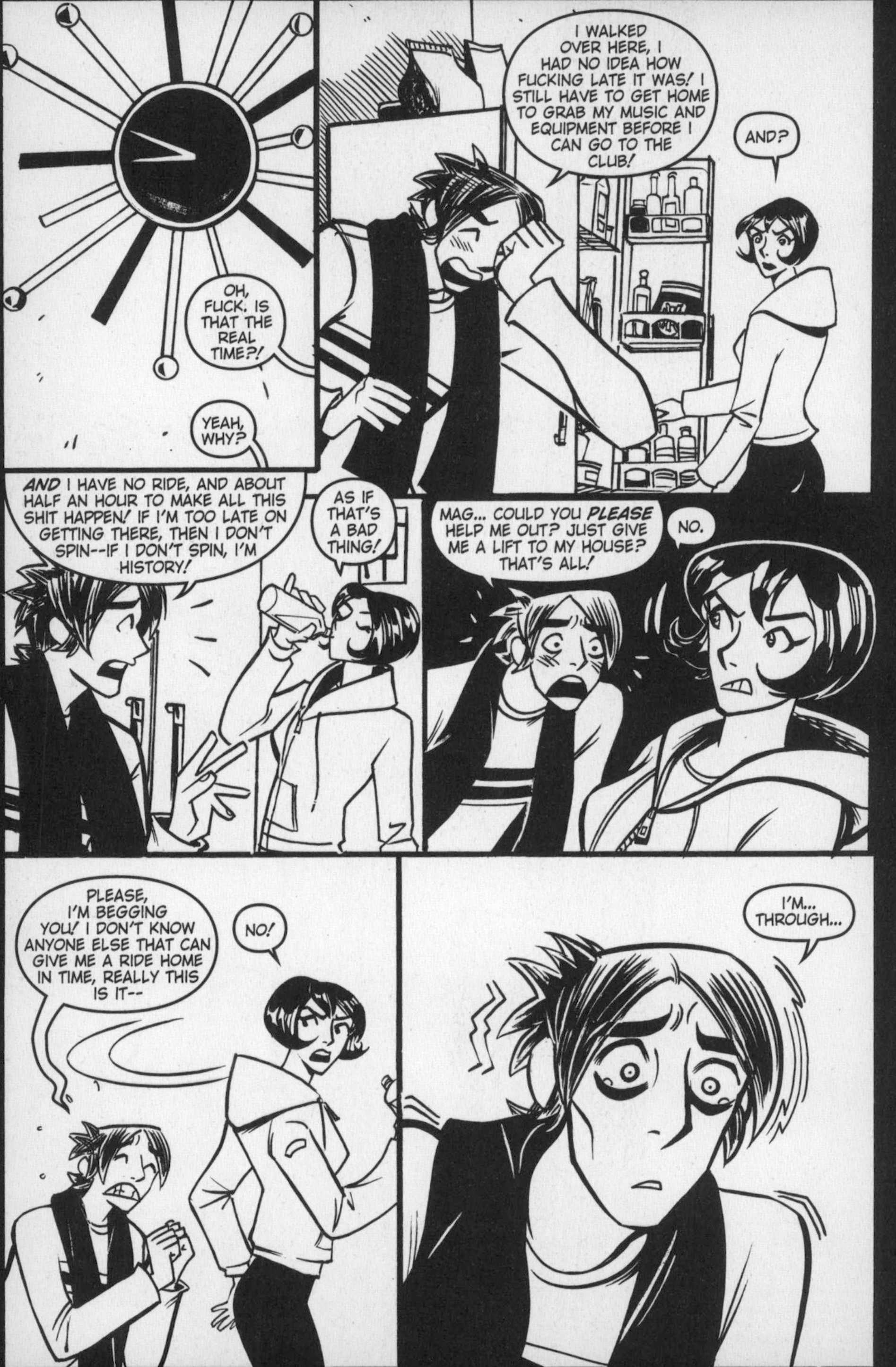
OH, FUCK. IS THAT THE REAL TIME?!
YEAH, WHY?
I WALKED OVER HERE, I HAD NO IDEA HOW FUCKING LATE IT WAS! I STILL HAVE TO GET HOME TO GRAB MY MUSIC AND EQUIPMENT BEFORE I CAN GO TO THE CLUB!
AND?
AND I HAVE NO RIDE, AND ABOUT HALF AN HOUR TO MAKE ALL THIS SHIT HAPPEN! IF I'M TOO LATE ON GETTING THERE, THEN I DON'T SPIN--IF I DON'T SPIN, I'M HISTORY!
AS IF THAT'S A BAD THING!
MAG... COULD YOU PLEASE HELP ME OUT? JUST GIVE ME A LIFT TO MY HOUSE? THAT'S ALL!
NO.
PLEASE, I'M BEGGING YOU! I DON'T KNOW ANYONE ELSE THAT CAN GIVE ME A RIDE HOME IN TIME, REALLY THIS IS IT--
NO!
I'M... THROUGH...

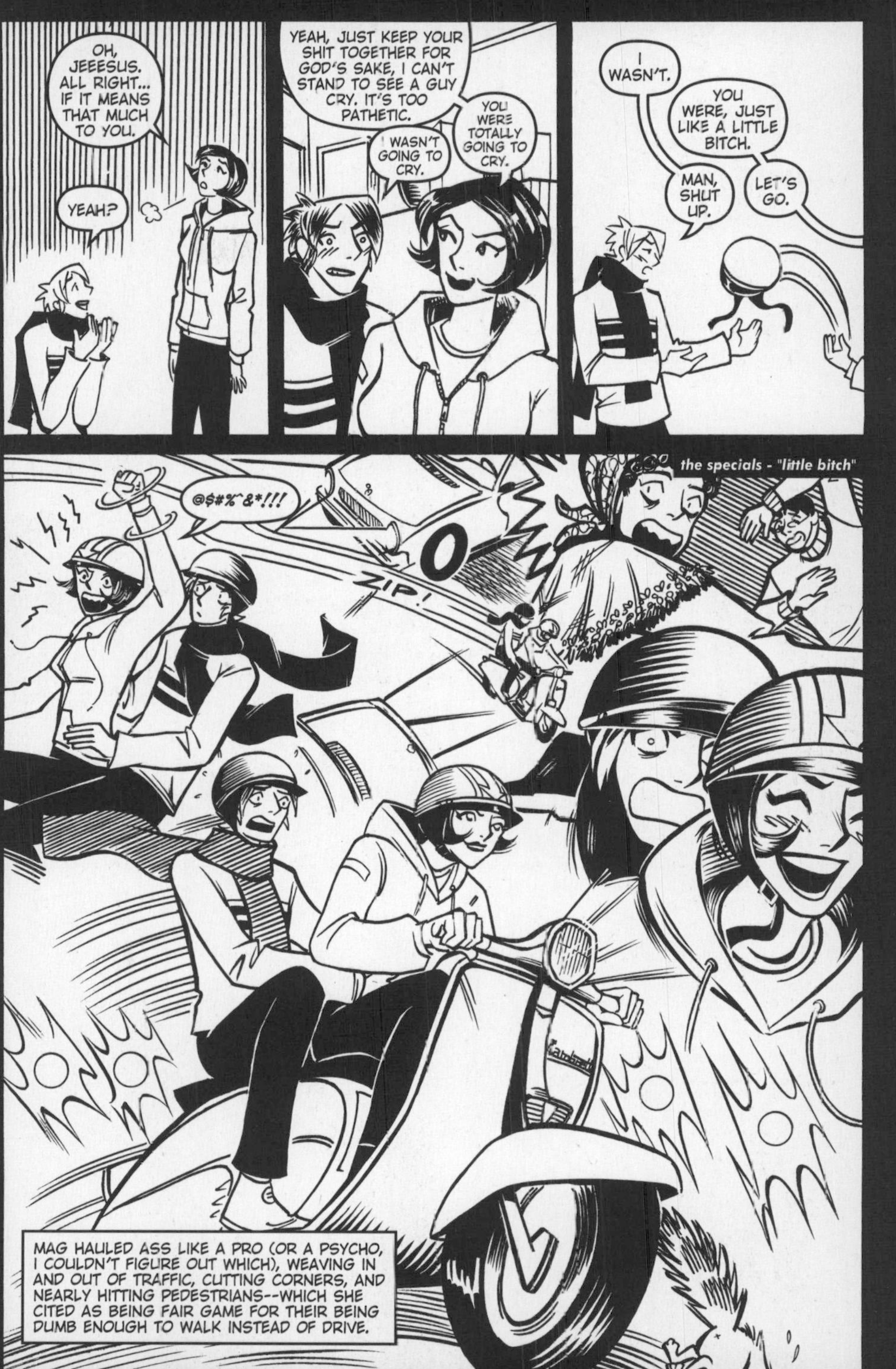
OH, JEEESUS. ALL RIGHT... IF IT MEANS THAT MUCH TO YOU.
YEAH?
YEAH, JUST KEEP YOUR SHIT TOGETHER FOR GOD'S SAKE, I CAN'T STAND TO SEE A GUY CRY. IT'S TOO PATHETIC.
I WASN'T GOING TO CRY.
YOU WERE TOTALLY GOING TO CRY.
I WASN'T.
YOU WERE, JUST LIKE A LITTLE BITCH.
MAN, SHUT UP.
LET'S GO.
the specials - "little bitch"
@$#%^&*!!!
ZIP!
MAG HAULED ASS LIKE A PRO (OR A PSYCHO, I COULDN'T FIGURE OUT WHICH), WEAVING IN AND OUT OF TRAFFIC, CUTTING CORNERS, AND NEARLY HITTING PEDESTRIANS--WHICH SHE CITED AS BEING FAIR GAME FOR THEIR BEING DUMB ENOUGH TO WALK INSTEAD OF DRIVE.

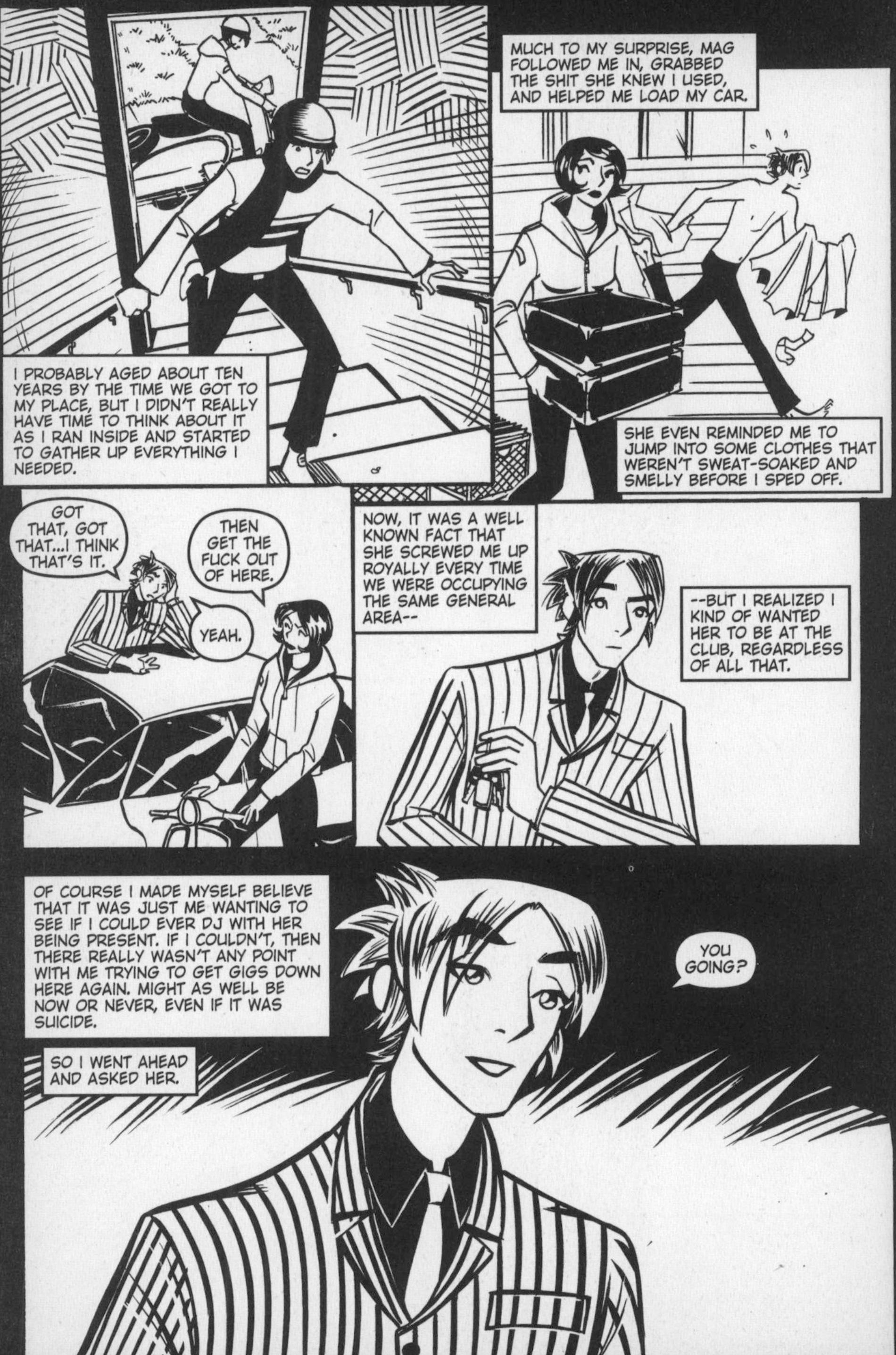
I PROBABLY AGED ABOUT TEN YEARS BY THE TIME WE GOT TO MY PLACE, BUT I DIDN'T REALLY HAVE TIME TO THINK ABOUT IT AS I RAN INSIDE AND STARTED TO GATHER UP EVERYTHING I NEEDED.
MUCH TO MY SURPRISE, MAG FOLLOWED ME IN, GRABBED THE SHIT SHE KNEW I USED, AND HELPED ME LOAD MY CAR.
SHE EVEN REMINDED ME TO JUMP INTO SOME CLOTHES THAT WEREN'T SWEAT-SOAKED AND SMELLY BEFORE I SPED OFF.
GOT THAT, GOT THAT...I THINK THAT'S IT.
THEN GET THE FUCK OUT OF HERE.
YEAH.
NOW, IT WAS A WELL KNOWN FACT THAT SHE SCREWED ME UP ROYALLY EVERY TIME WE WERE OCCUPYING THE SAME GENERAL AREA--
--BUT I REALIZED I KIND OF WANTED HER TO BE AT THE CLUB, REGARDLESS OF ALL THAT.
OF COURSE I MADE MYSELF BELIEVE THAT IT WAS JUST ME WANTING TO SEE IF I COULD EVER DJ WITH HER BEING PRESENT. IF I COULDN'T, THEN THERE REALLY WASN'T ANY POINT WITH ME TRYING TO GET GIGS DOWN HERE AGAIN. MIGHT AS WELL BE NOW OR NEVER, EVEN IF IT WAS SUICIDE.
SO I WENT AHEAD AND ASKED HER.
YOU GOING?

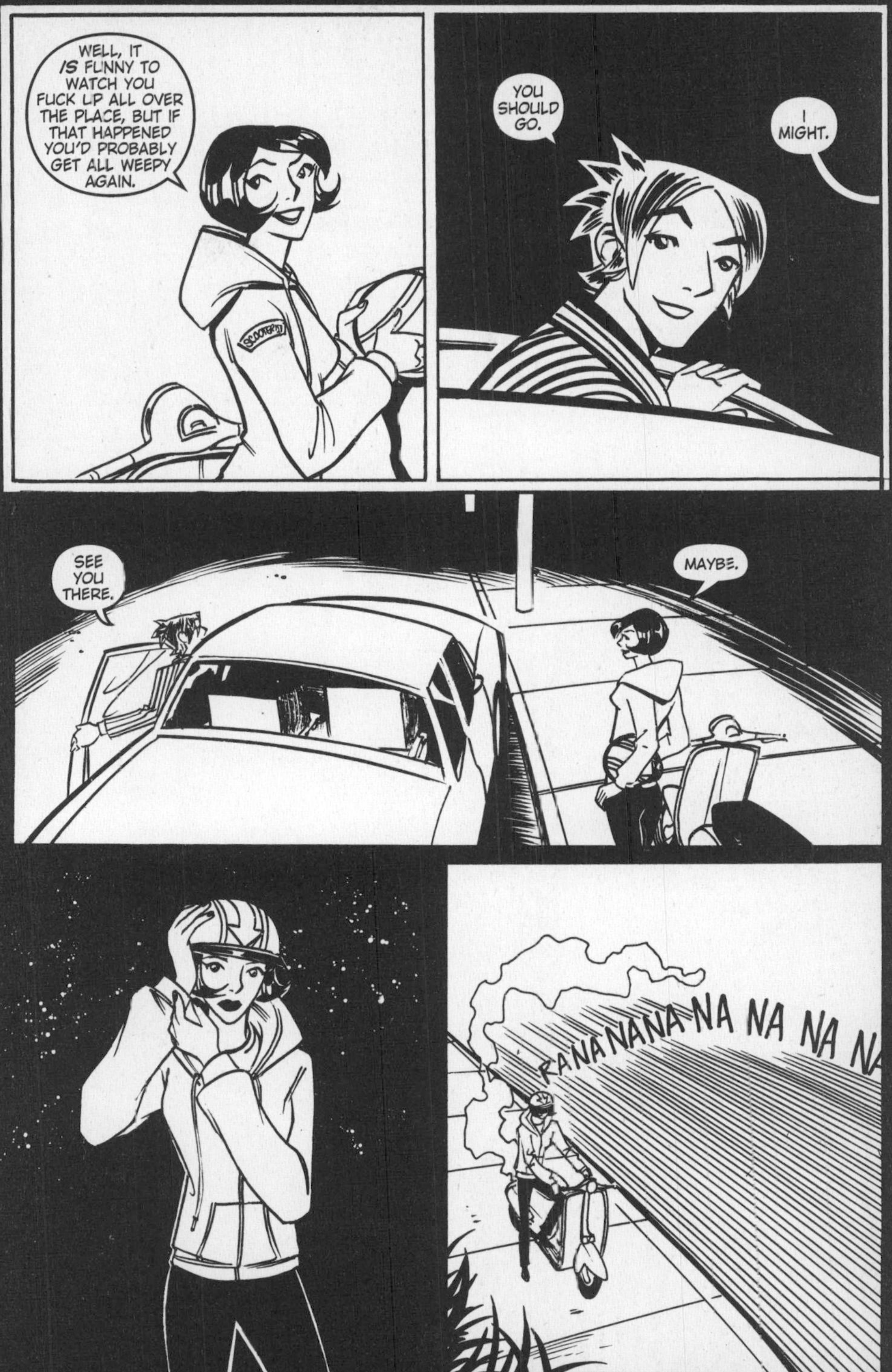

WELL, IT *IS* FUNNY TO WATCH YOU FUCK UP ALL OVER THE PLACE, BUT IF THAT HAPPENED YOU'D PROBABLY GET ALL WEEPY AGAIN.
SCOOTER
YOU SHOULD GO.
I MIGHT.
SEE YOU THERE.
MAYBE.
RANANANANA NA NA NA NA

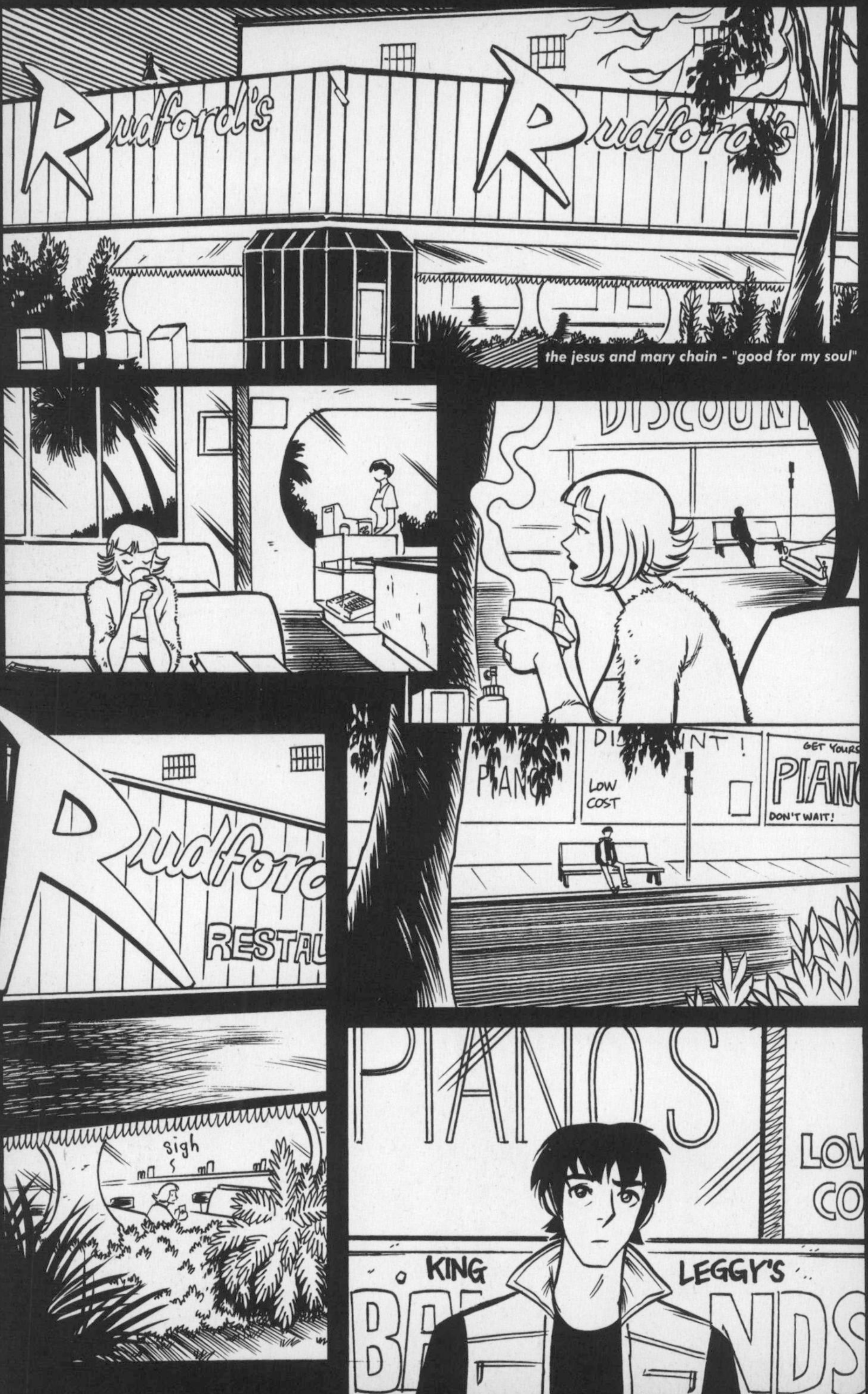

Rudford's
Rudford's
the jesus and mary chain - "good for my soul"
LOW COST
GET YOURS
DON'T WAIT!
sigh
KING
LEGGY'S

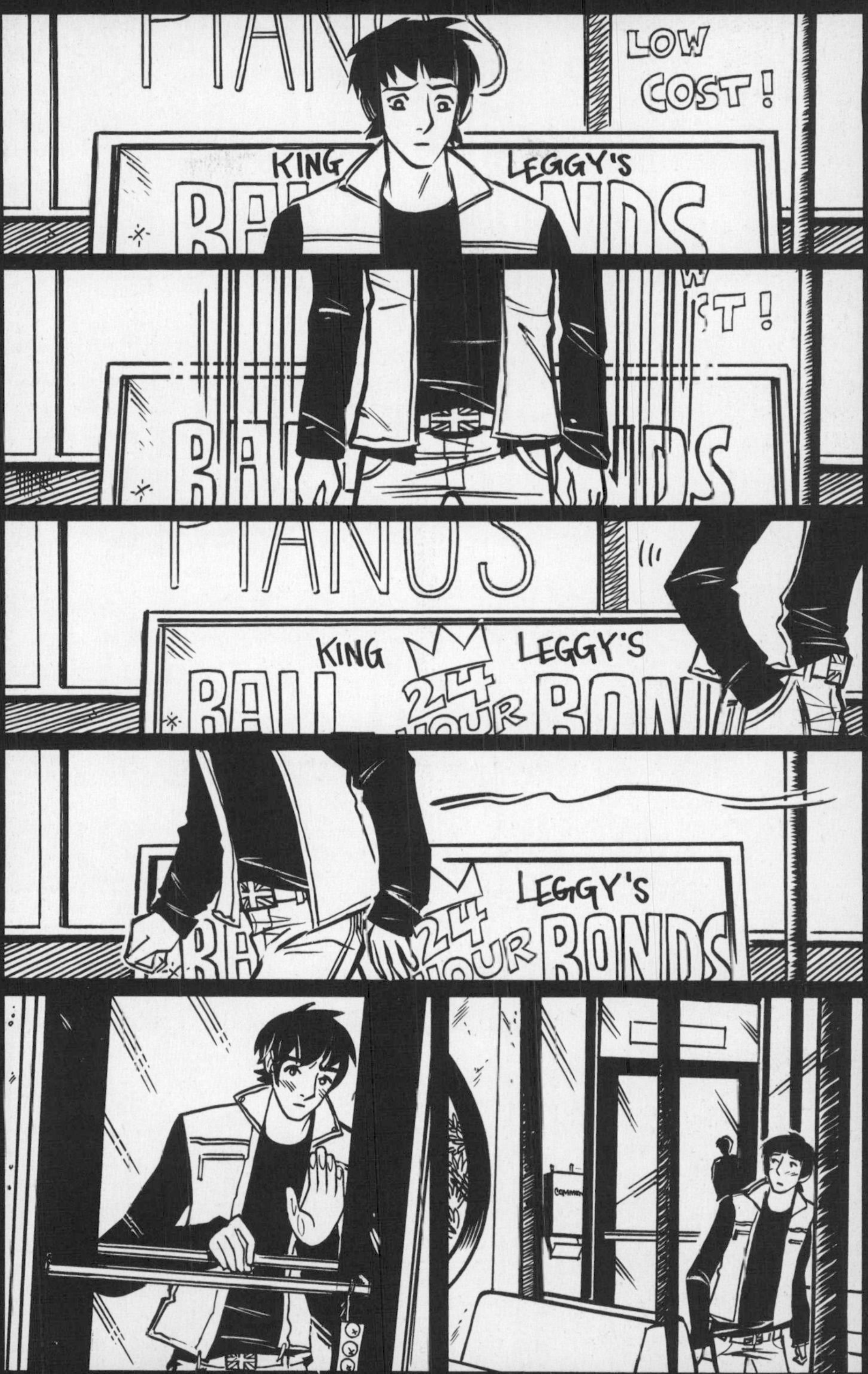
LOW
COST!
KING
LEGGY'S
PIANOS
KING
LEGGY'S
LEGGY'S
BONDS

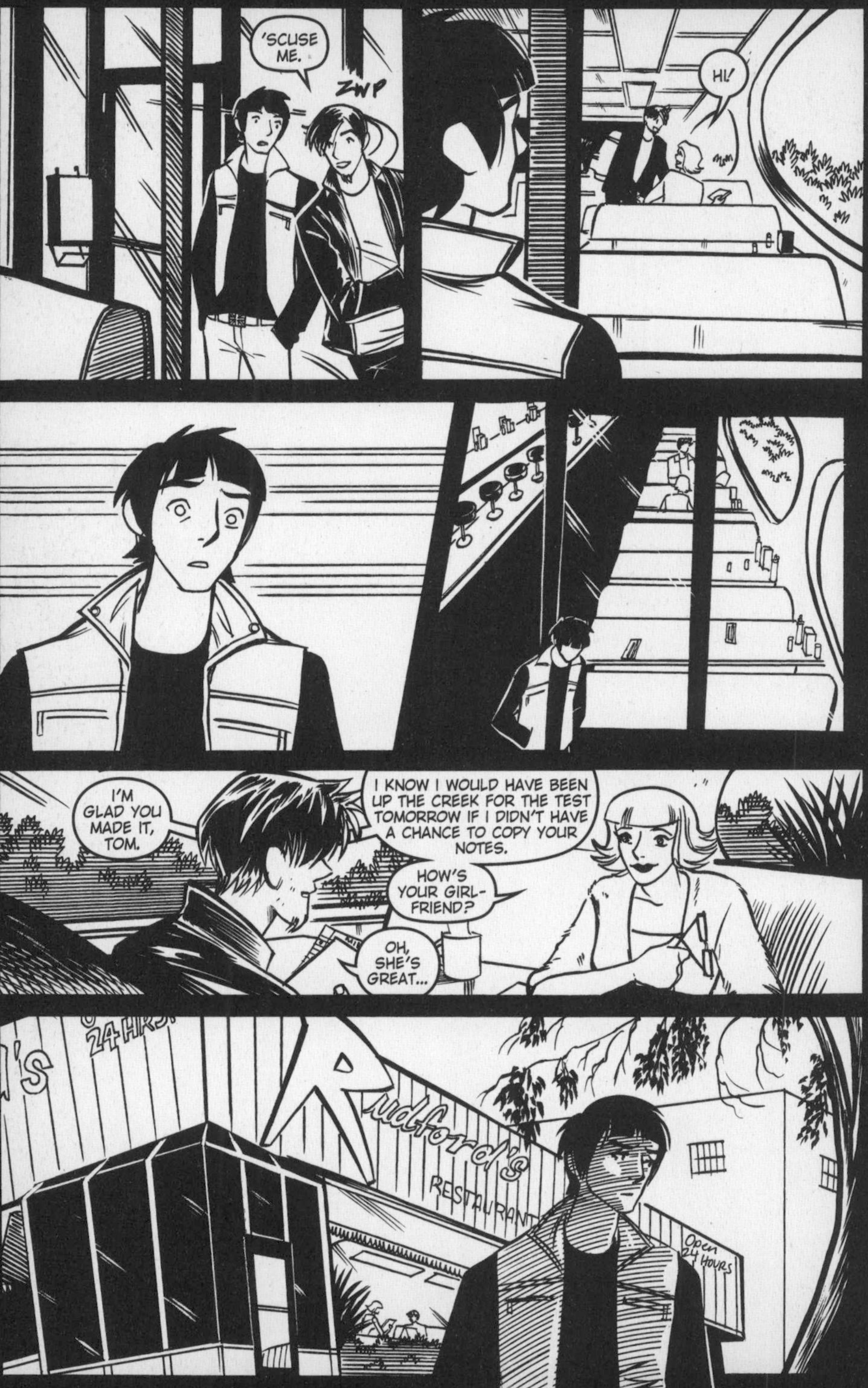
'SCUSE ME.
ZWP
HI!
I'M GLAD YOU MADE IT, TOM.
I KNOW I WOULD HAVE BEEN UP THE CREEK FOR THE TEST TOMORROW IF I DIDN'T HAVE A CHANCE TO COPY YOUR NOTES.
HOW'S YOUR GIRL-FRIEND?
OH, SHE'S GREAT...
24 HRS
udford's
RESTAURANT
Open 24 Hours

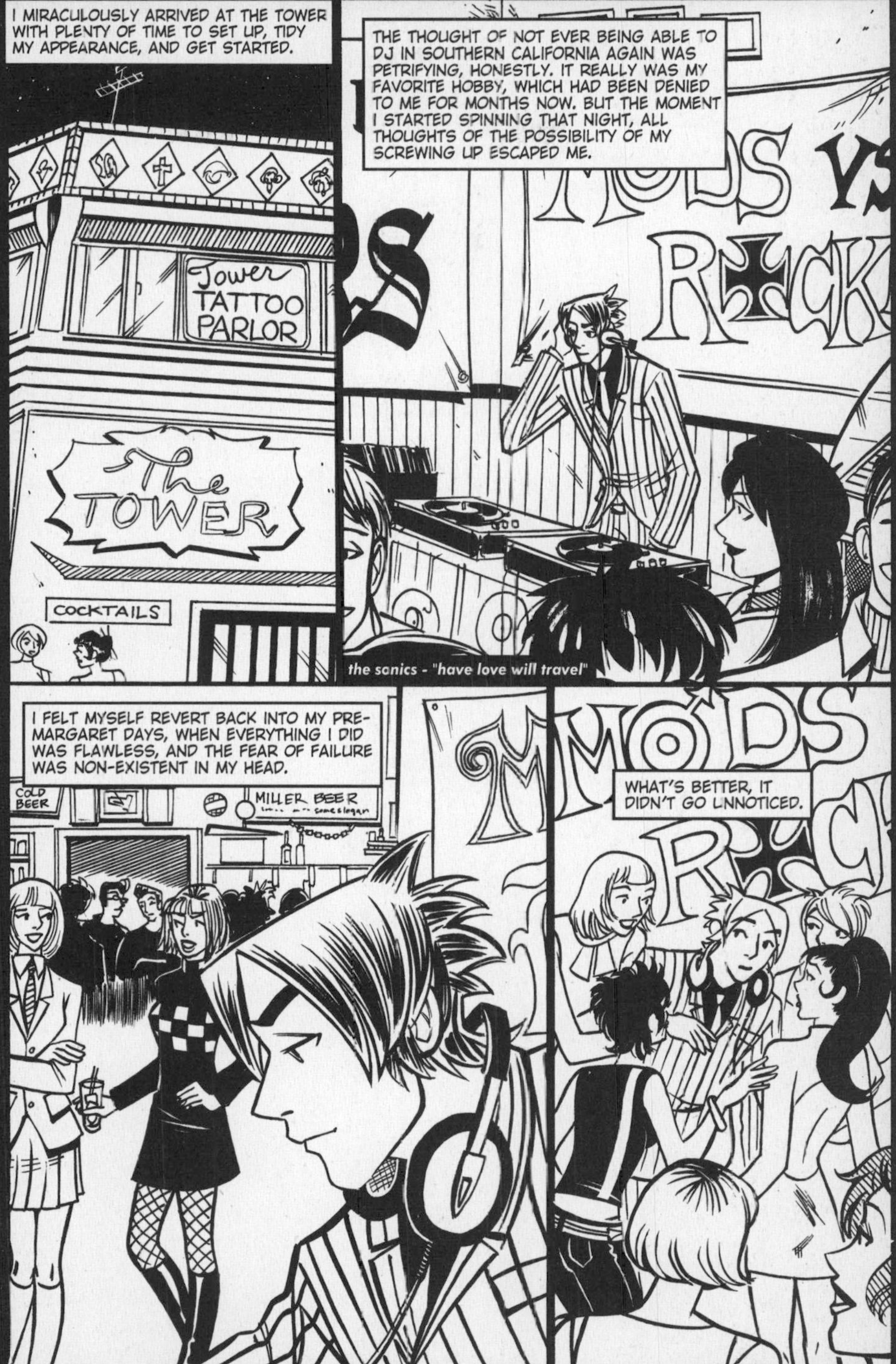
I MIRACULOUSLY ARRIVED AT THE TOWER WITH PLENTY OF TIME TO SET UP, TIDY MY APPEARANCE, AND GET STARTED.
Tower TATTOO PARLOR
The TOWER
COCKTAILS
THE THOUGHT OF NOT EVER BEING ABLE TO DJ IN SOUTHERN CALIFORNIA AGAIN WAS PETRIFYING, HONESTLY. IT REALLY WAS MY FAVORITE HOBBY, WHICH HAD BEEN DENIED TO ME FOR MONTHS NOW. BUT THE MOMENT I STARTED SPINNING THAT NIGHT, ALL THOUGHTS OF THE POSSIBILITY OF MY SCREWING UP ESCAPED ME.
MODS VS
the sonics - "have love will travel"
I FELT MYSELF REVERT BACK INTO MY PRE-MARGARET DAYS, WHEN EVERYTHING I DID WAS FLAWLESS, AND THE FEAR OF FAILURE WAS NON-EXISTENT IN MY HEAD.
COLD BEER
MILLER BEER
MODS
WHAT'S BETTER, IT DIDN'T GO UNNOTICED.

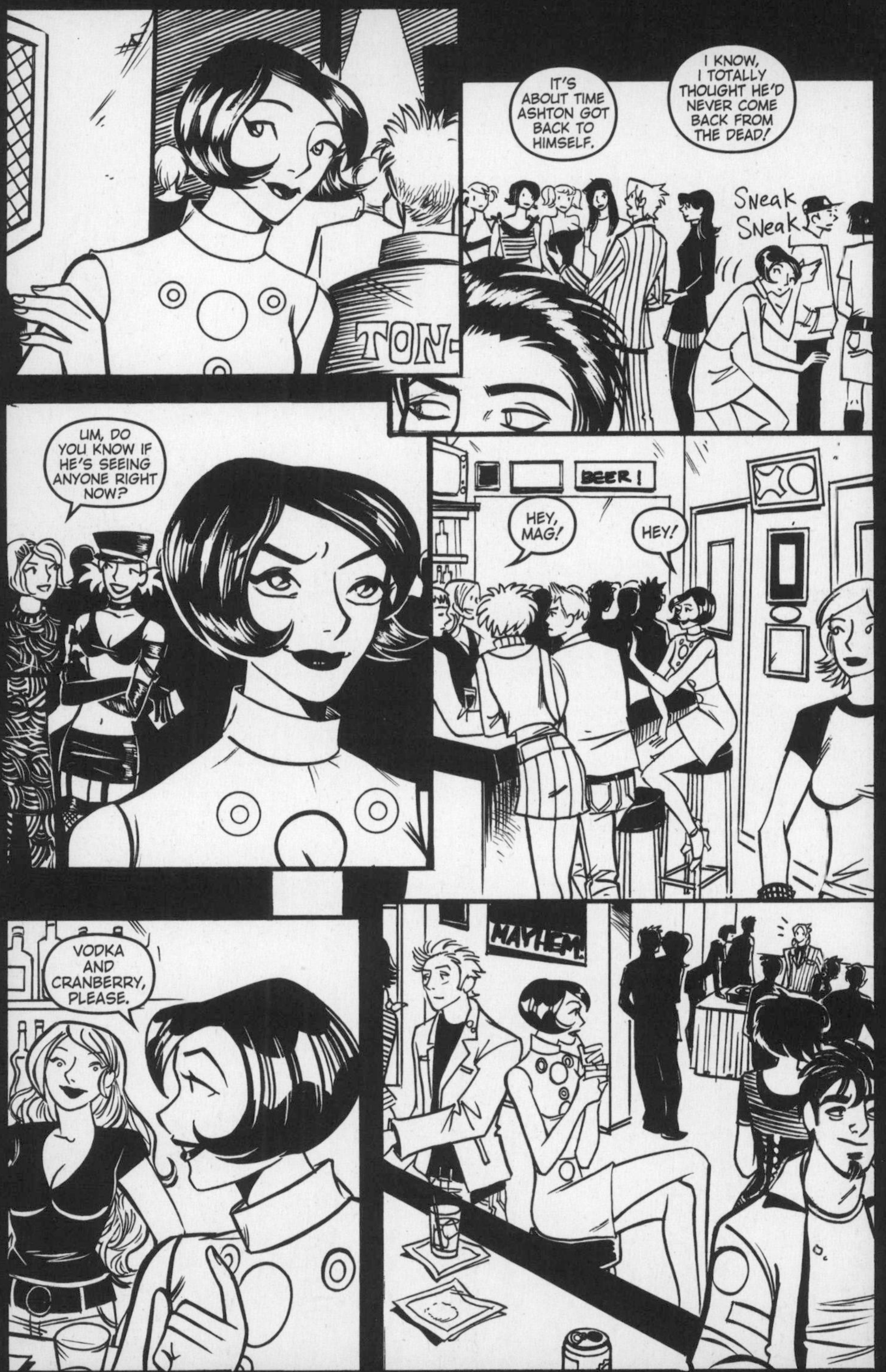
TON-
IT'S ABOUT TIME ASHTON GOT BACK TO HIMSELF.
I KNOW, I TOTALLY THOUGHT HE'D NEVER COME BACK FROM THE DEAD!
SNEAK SNEAK
UM, DO YOU KNOW IF HE'S SEEING ANYONE RIGHT NOW?
BEER!
HEY, MAG!
HEY!
VODKA AND CRANBERRY, PLEASE.
MAYHEM!

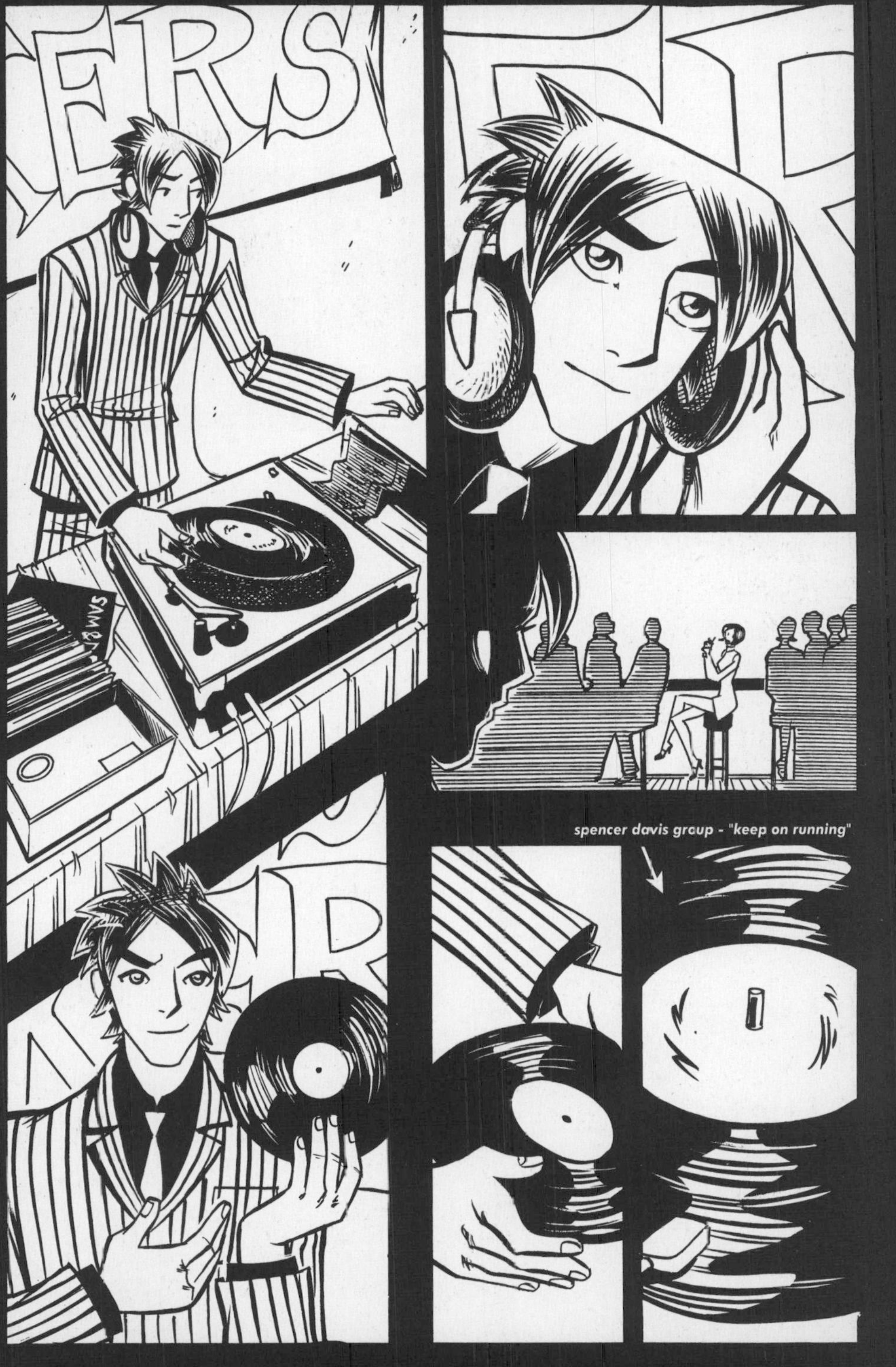
spencer davis group - "keep on running"

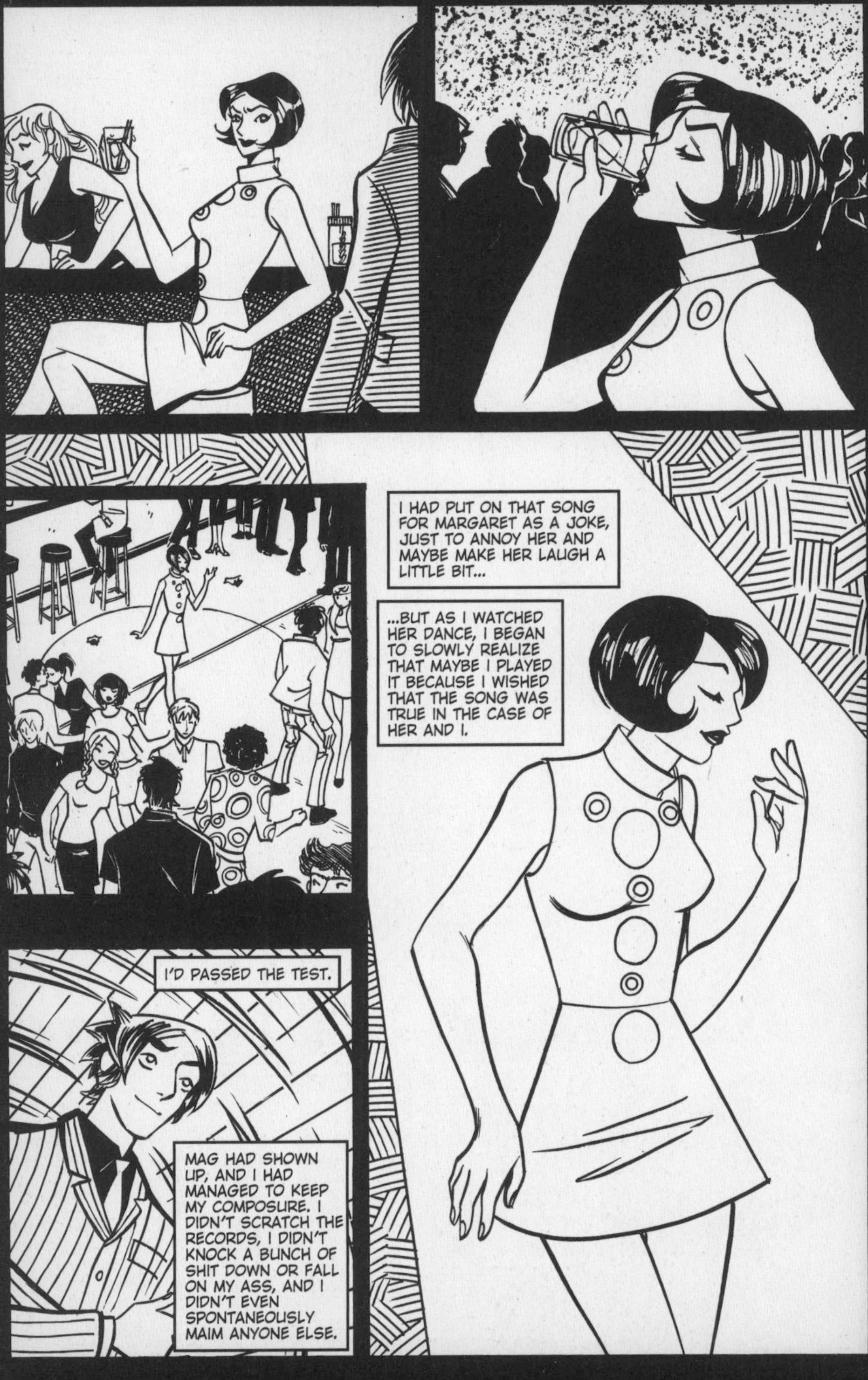
I HAD PUT ON THAT SONG FOR MARGARET AS A JOKE, JUST TO ANNOY HER AND MAYBE MAKE HER LAUGH A LITTLE BIT...
...BUT AS I WATCHED HER DANCE, I BEGAN TO SLOWLY REALIZE THAT MAYBE I PLAYED IT BECAUSE I WISHED THAT THE SONG WAS TRUE IN THE CASE OF HER AND I.
I'D PASSED THE TEST.
MAG HAD SHOWN UP, AND I HAD MANAGED TO KEEP MY COMPOSURE. I DIDN'T SCRATCH THE RECORDS, I DIDN'T KNOCK A BUNCH OF SHIT DOWN OR FALL ON MY ASS, AND I DIDN'T EVEN SPONTANEOUSLY MAIM ANYONE ELSE.

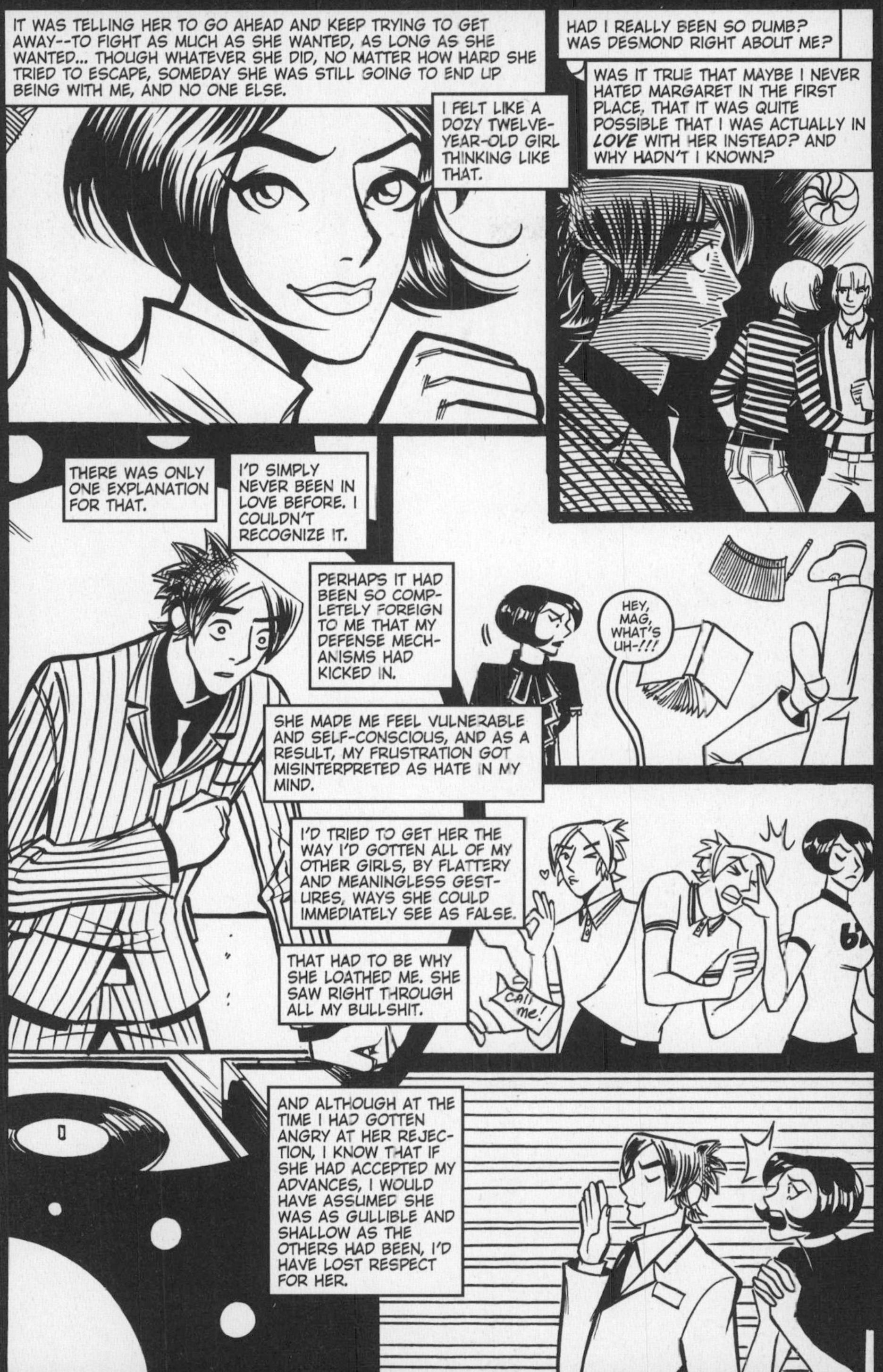
IT WAS TELLING HER TO GO AHEAD AND KEEP TRYING TO GET AWAY--TO FIGHT AS MUCH AS SHE WANTED, AS LONG AS SHE WANTED... THOUGH WHATEVER SHE DID, NO MATTER HOW HARD SHE TRIED TO ESCAPE, SOMEDAY SHE WAS STILL GOING TO END UP BEING WITH ME, AND NO ONE ELSE.
I FELT LIKE A DOZY TWELVE-YEAR-OLD GIRL THINKING LIKE THAT.
HAD I REALLY BEEN SO DUMB? WAS DESMOND RIGHT ABOUT ME?
WAS IT TRUE THAT MAYBE I NEVER HATED MARGARET IN THE FIRST PLACE, THAT IT WAS QUITE POSSIBLE THAT I WAS ACTUALLY IN LOVE WITH HER INSTEAD? AND WHY HADN'T I KNOWN?
THERE WAS ONLY ONE EXPLANATION FOR THAT.
I'D SIMPLY NEVER BEEN IN LOVE BEFORE. I COULDN'T RECOGNIZE IT.
PERHAPS IT HAD BEEN SO COMPLETELY FOREIGN TO ME THAT MY DEFENSE MECHANISMS HAD KICKED IN.
HEY, MAG, WHAT'S UH-!!!
SHE MADE ME FEEL VULNERABLE AND SELF-CONSCIOUS, AND AS A RESULT, MY FRUSTRATION GOT MISINTERPRETED AS HATE IN MY MIND.
I'D TRIED TO GET HER THE WAY I'D GOTTEN ALL OF MY OTHER GIRLS, BY FLATTERY AND MEANINGLESS GESTURES, WAYS SHE COULD IMMEDIATELY SEE AS FALSE.
THAT HAD TO BE WHY SHE LOATHED ME. SHE SAW RIGHT THROUGH ALL MY BULLSHIT.
Call me!
AND ALTHOUGH AT THE TIME I HAD GOTTEN ANGRY AT HER REJECTION, I KNOW THAT IF SHE HAD ACCEPTED MY ADVANCES, I WOULD HAVE ASSUMED SHE WAS AS GULLIBLE AND SHALLOW AS THE OTHERS HAD BEEN, I'D HAVE LOST RESPECT FOR HER.

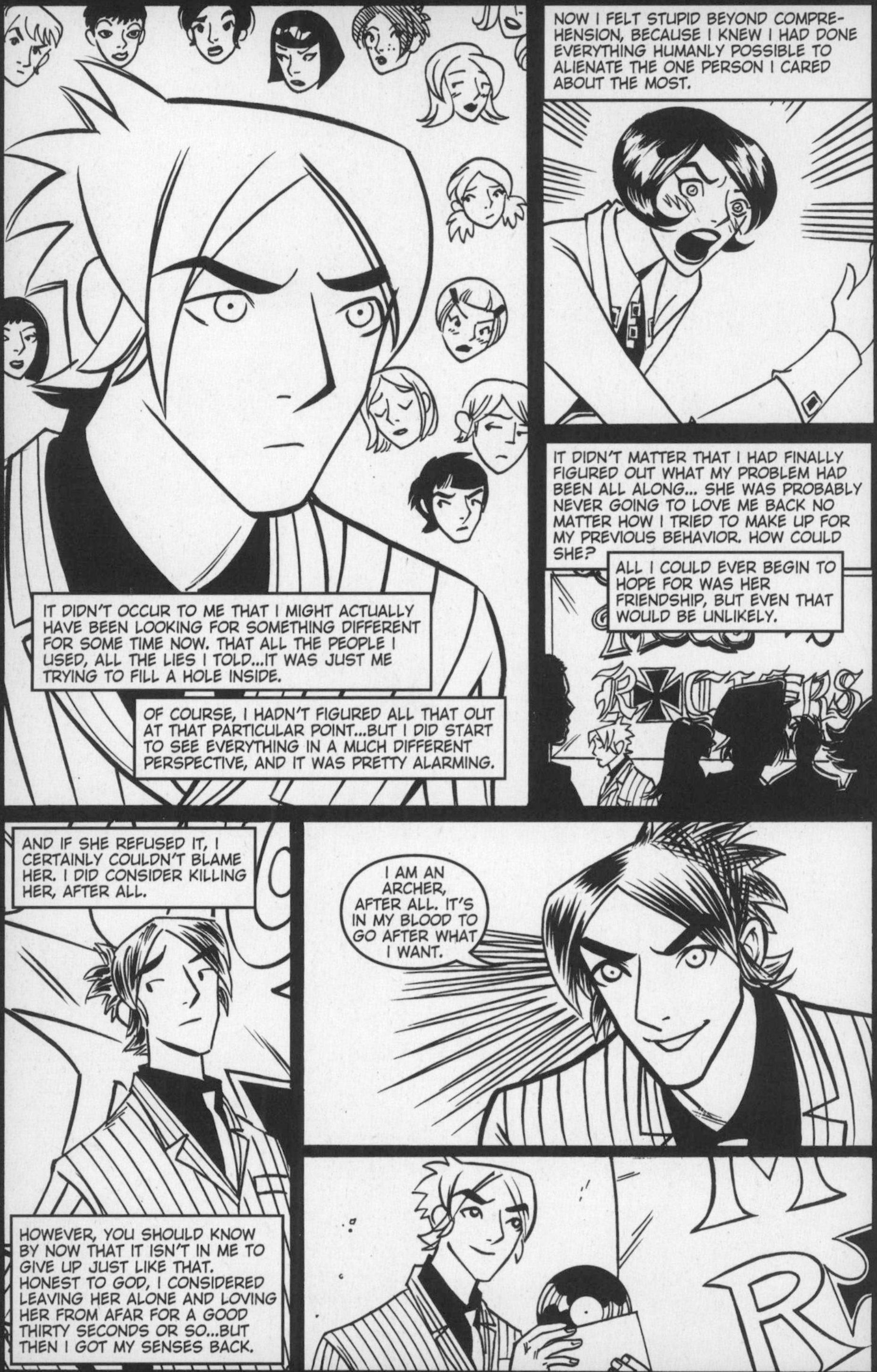

IT DIDN'T OCCUR TO ME THAT I MIGHT ACTUALLY HAVE BEEN LOOKING FOR SOMETHING DIFFERENT FOR SOME TIME NOW. THAT ALL THE PEOPLE I USED, ALL THE LIES I TOLD...IT WAS JUST ME TRYING TO FILL A HOLE INSIDE.
OF COURSE, I HADN'T FIGURED ALL THAT OUT AT THAT PARTICULAR POINT...BUT I DID START TO SEE EVERYTHING IN A MUCH DIFFERENT PERSPECTIVE, AND IT WAS PRETTY ALARMING.
NOW I FELT STUPID BEYOND COMPREHENSION, BECAUSE I KNEW I HAD DONE EVERYTHING HUMANLY POSSIBLE TO ALIENATE THE ONE PERSON I CARED ABOUT THE MOST.
IT DIDN'T MATTER THAT I HAD FINALLY FIGURED OUT WHAT MY PROBLEM HAD BEEN ALL ALONG... SHE WAS PROBABLY NEVER GOING TO LOVE ME BACK NO MATTER HOW I TRIED TO MAKE UP FOR MY PREVIOUS BEHAVIOR. HOW COULD SHE?
ALL I COULD EVER BEGIN TO HOPE FOR WAS HER FRIENDSHIP, BUT EVEN THAT WOULD BE UNLIKELY.
AND IF SHE REFUSED IT, I CERTAINLY COULDN'T BLAME HER. I DID CONSIDER KILLING HER, AFTER ALL.
HOWEVER, YOU SHOULD KNOW BY NOW THAT IT ISN'T IN ME TO GIVE UP JUST LIKE THAT. HONEST TO GOD, I CONSIDERED LEAVING HER ALONE AND LOVING HER FROM AFAR FOR A GOOD THIRTY SECONDS OR SO...BUT THEN I GOT MY SENSES BACK.
I AM AN ARCHER, AFTER ALL. IT'S IN MY BLOOD TO GO AFTER WHAT I WANT.

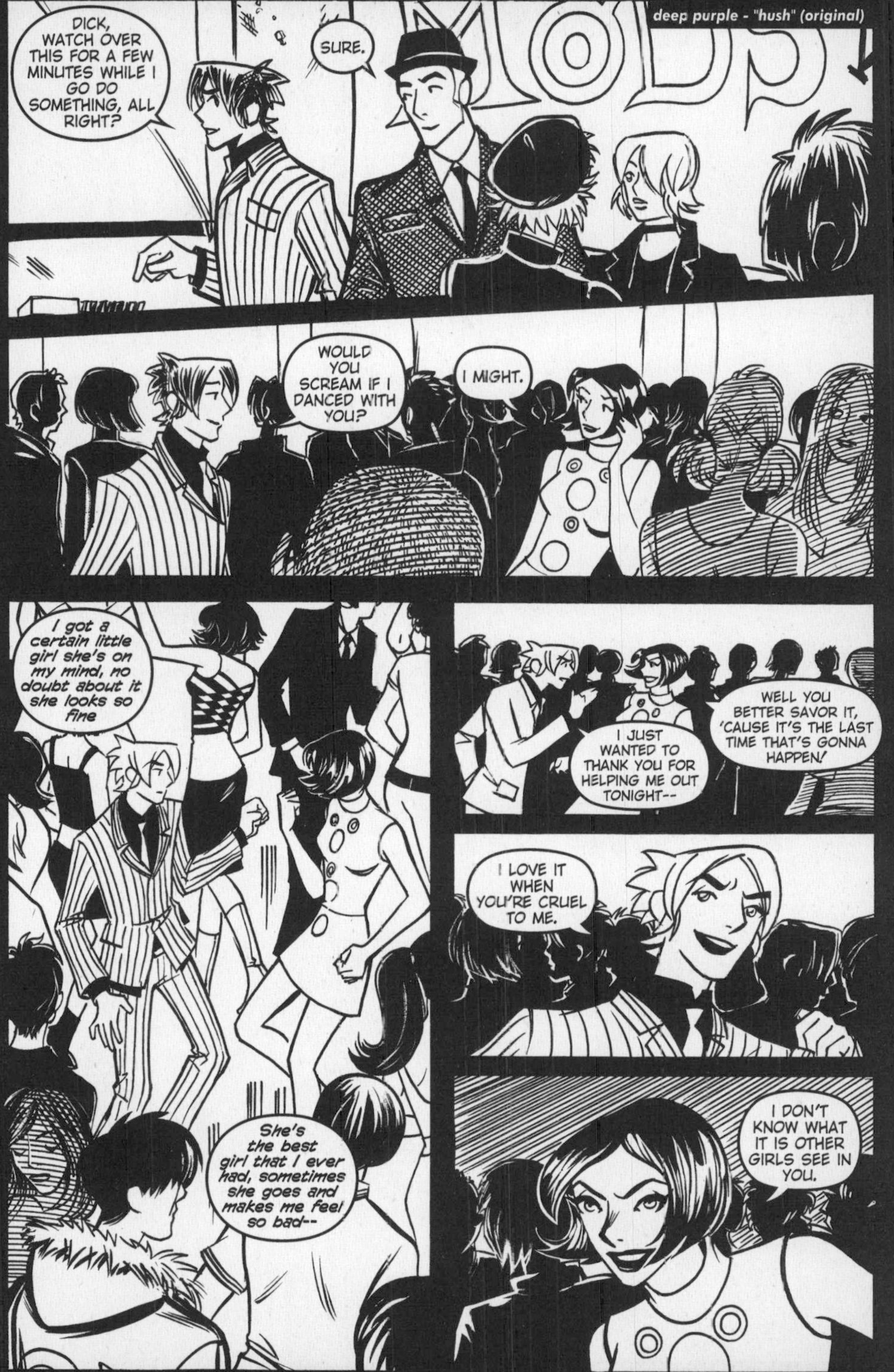
MODS!
DICK, WATCH OVER THIS FOR A FEW MINUTES WHILE I GO DO SOMETHING, ALL RIGHT?
SURE.
WOULD YOU SCREAM IF I DANCED WITH YOU?
I MIGHT.
I got a certain little girl she's on my mind, no doubt about it she looks so fine
I JUST WANTED TO THANK YOU FOR HELPING ME OUT TONIGHT--
WELL YOU BETTER SAVOR IT, 'CAUSE IT'S THE LAST TIME THAT'S GONNA HAPPEN!
I LOVE IT WHEN YOU'RE CRUEL TO ME.
She's the best girl that I ever had, sometimes she goes and makes me feel so bad--
I DON'T KNOW WHAT IT IS OTHER GIRLS SEE IN YOU.

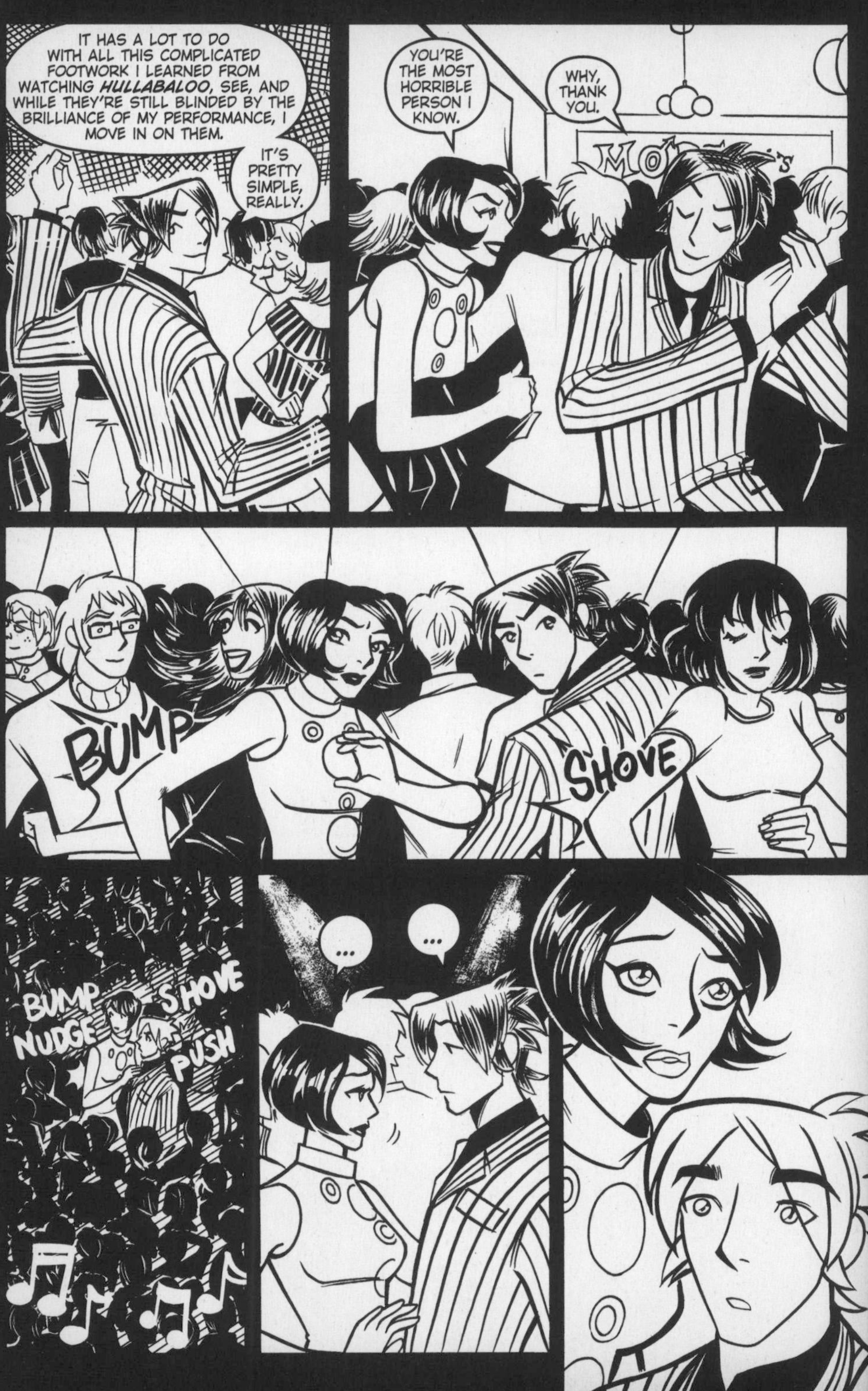

IT HAS A LOT TO DO WITH ALL THIS COMPLICATED FOOTWORK I LEARNED FROM WATCHING HULLABALOO, SEE, AND WHILE THEY'RE STILL BLINDED BY THE BRILLIANCE OF MY PERFORMANCE, I MOVE IN ON THEM.
IT'S PRETTY SIMPLE, REALLY.
YOU'RE THE MOST HORRIBLE PERSON I KNOW.
WHY, THANK YOU.
BUMP
SHOVE
BUMP
SHOVE
NUDGE
PUSH
...
...

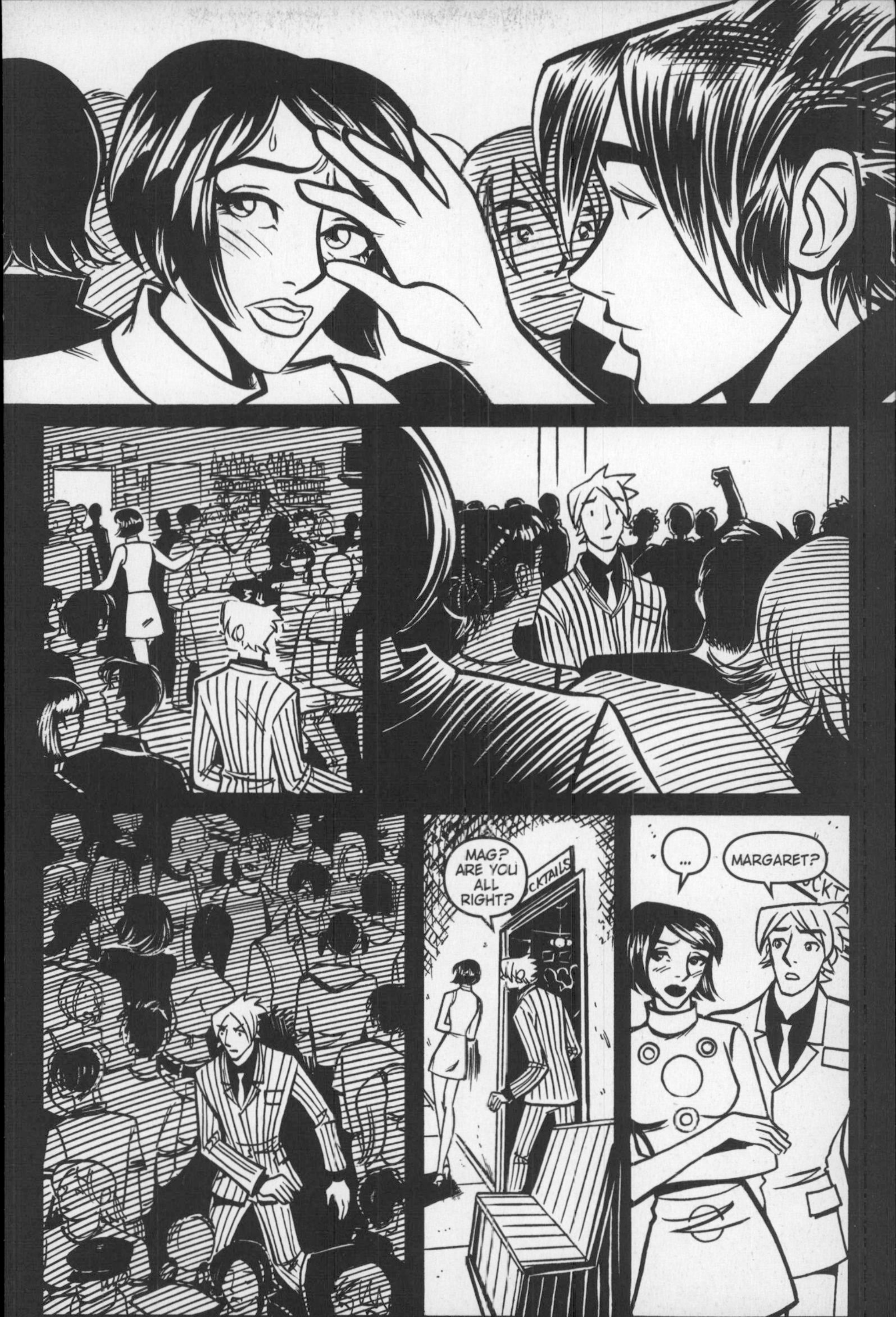
MAG? ARE YOU ALL RIGHT?
CKTAILS
...
MARGARET?

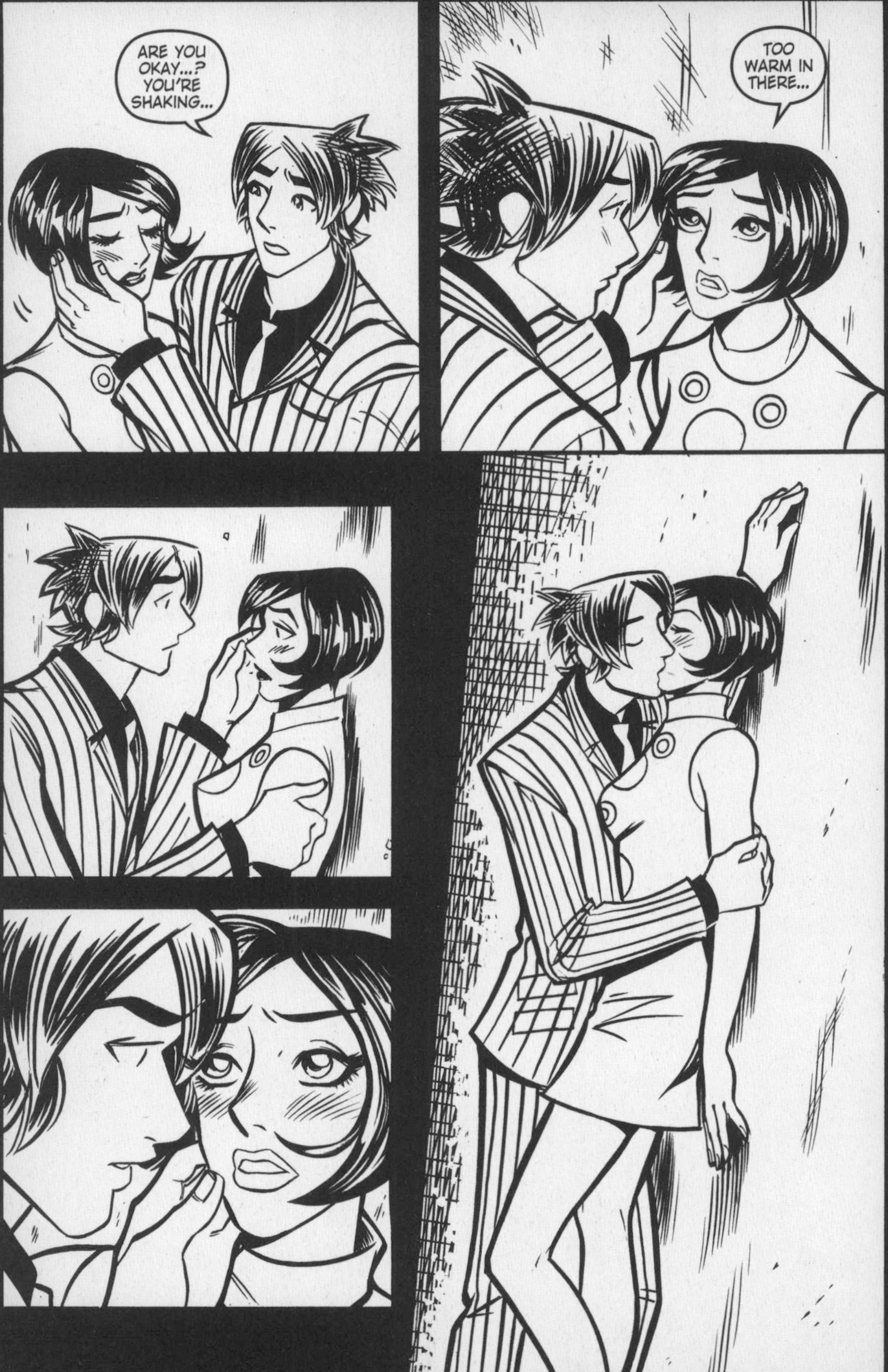
ARE YOU OKAY...? YOU'RE SHAKING...
TOO WARM IN THERE...

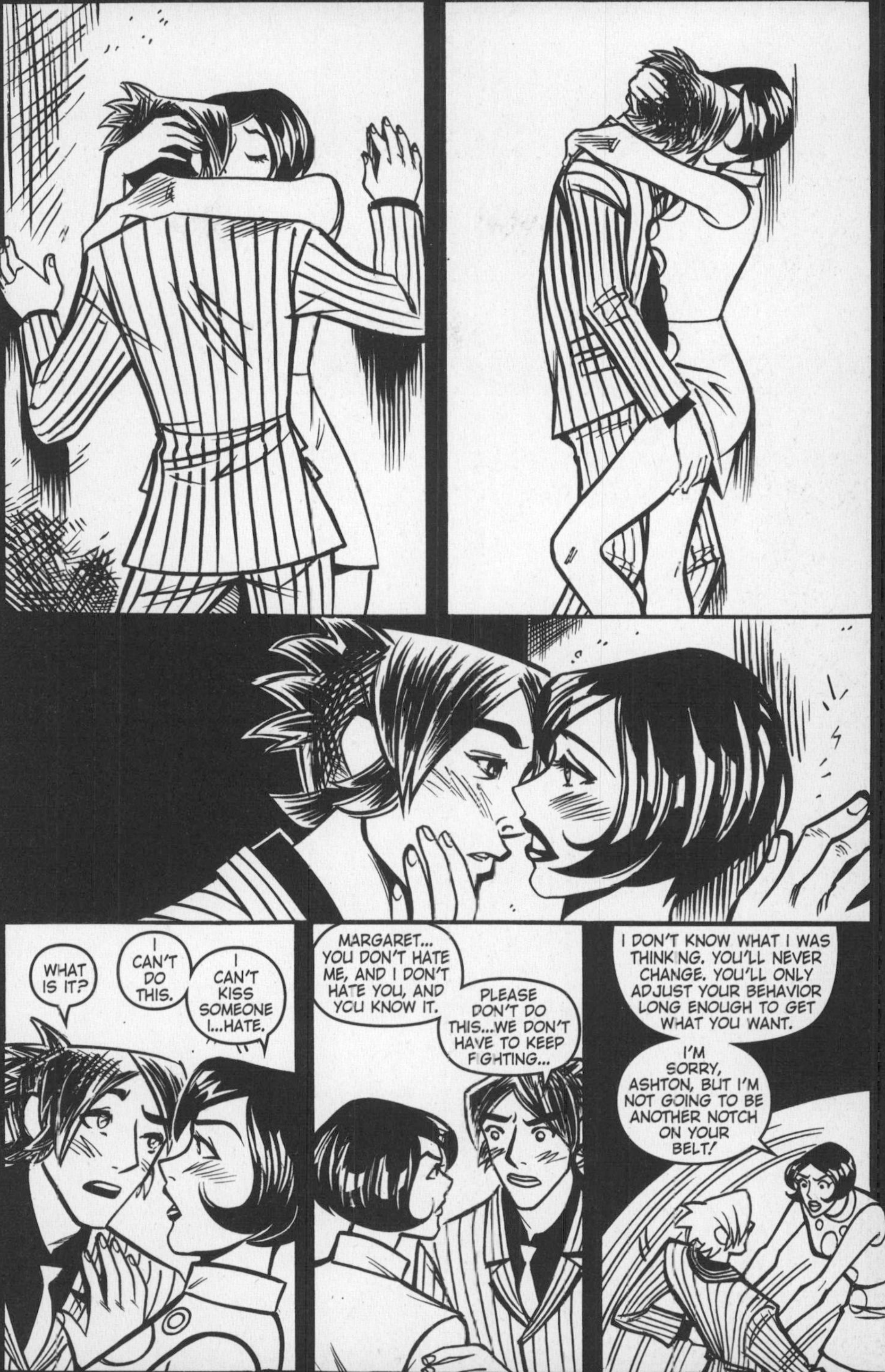
WHAT IS IT?
I CAN'T DO THIS.
I CAN'T KISS SOMEONE I...HATE.
MARGARET... YOU DON'T HATE ME, AND I DON'T HATE YOU, AND YOU KNOW IT.
PLEASE DON'T DO THIS...WE DON'T HAVE TO KEEP FIGHTING...
I DON'T KNOW WHAT I WAS THINKING. YOU'LL NEVER CHANGE. YOU'LL ONLY ADJUST YOUR BEHAVIOR LONG ENOUGH TO GET WHAT YOU WANT.
I'M SORRY, ASHTON, BUT I'M NOT GOING TO BE ANOTHER NOTCH ON YOUR BELT!

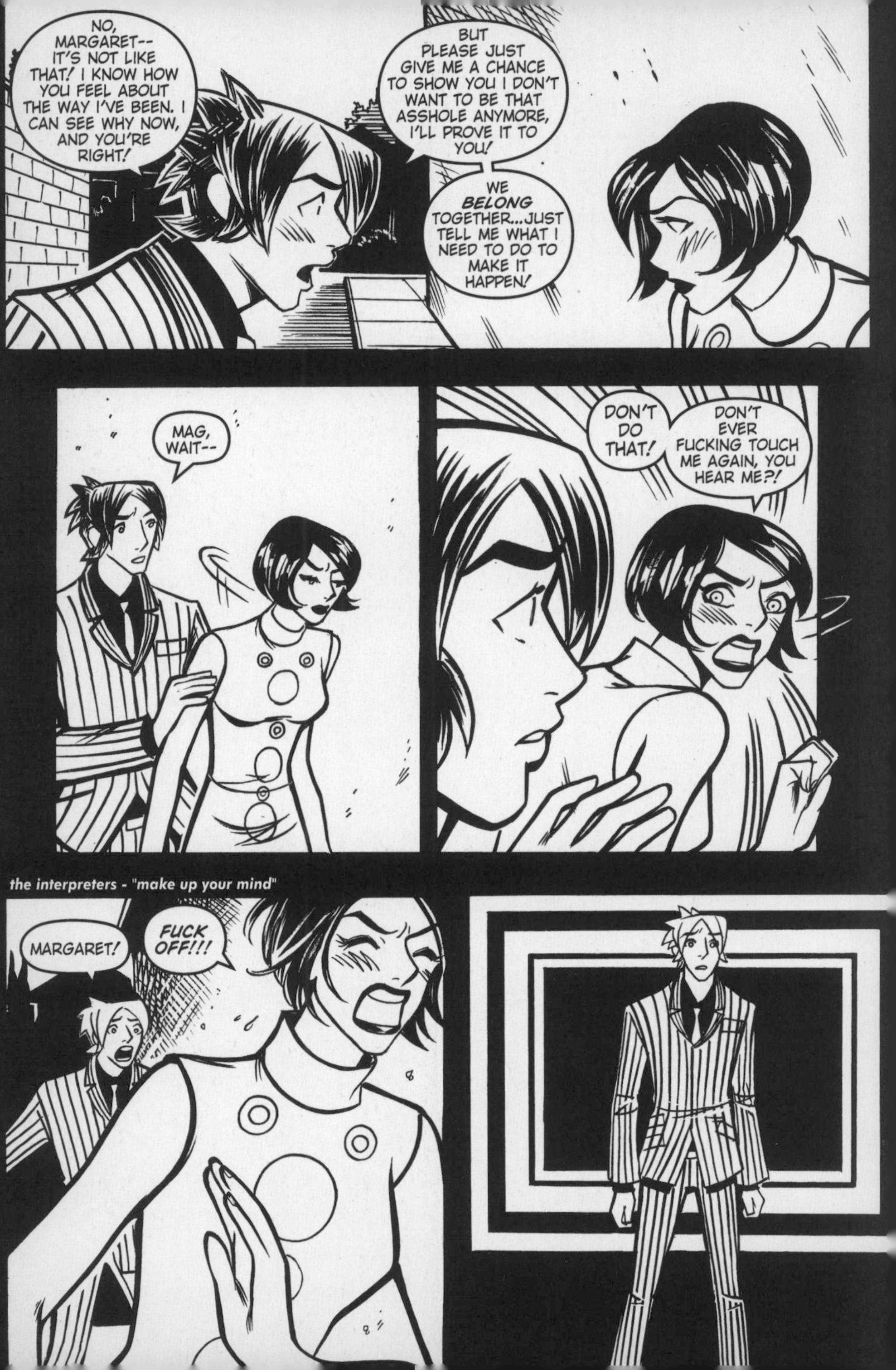

NO, MARGARET-- IT'S NOT LIKE THAT! I KNOW HOW YOU FEEL ABOUT THE WAY I'VE BEEN. I CAN SEE WHY NOW, AND YOU'RE RIGHT!
BUT PLEASE JUST GIVE ME A CHANCE TO SHOW YOU I DON'T WANT TO BE THAT ASSHOLE ANYMORE, I'LL PROVE IT TO YOU!
WE *BELONG* TOGETHER...JUST TELL ME WHAT I NEED TO DO TO MAKE IT HAPPEN!
MAG, WAIT--
DON'T DO THAT!
DON'T EVER FUCKING TOUCH ME AGAIN, YOU HEAR ME?!
the interpreters - "make up your mind"
MARGARET!
FUCK OFF!!!

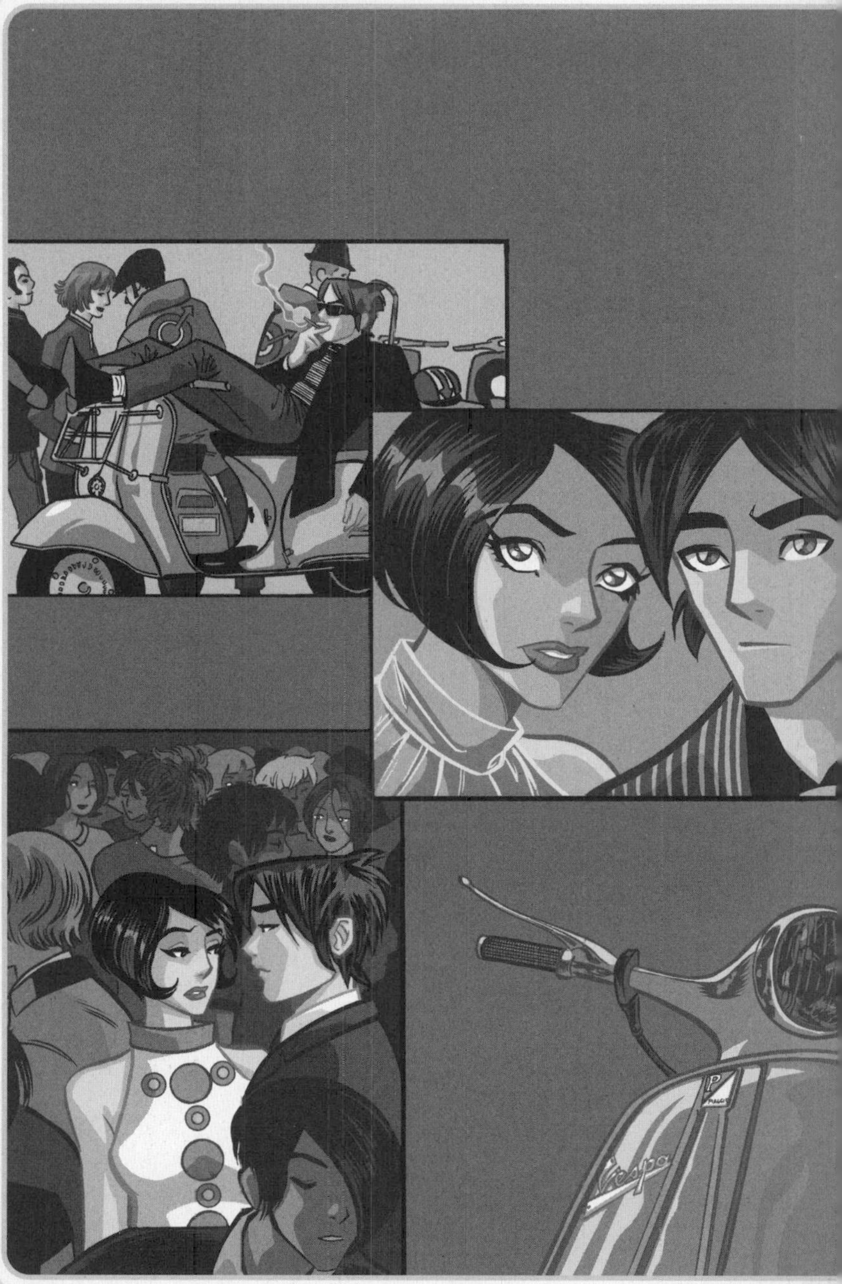
Vespa

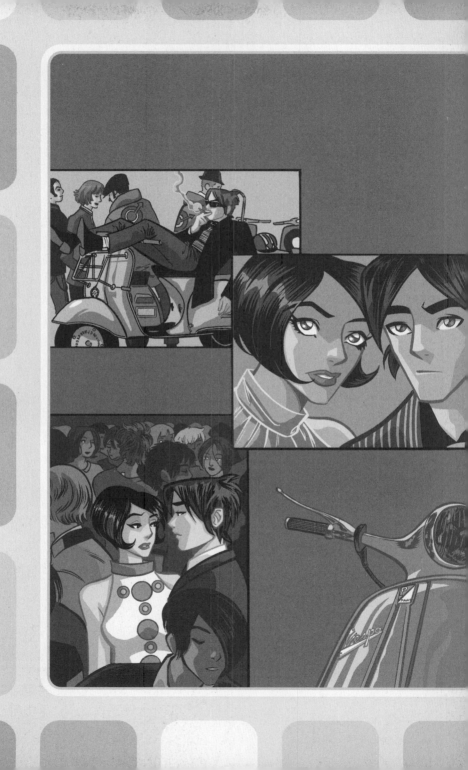

Chapter 6:
"Love Burns"

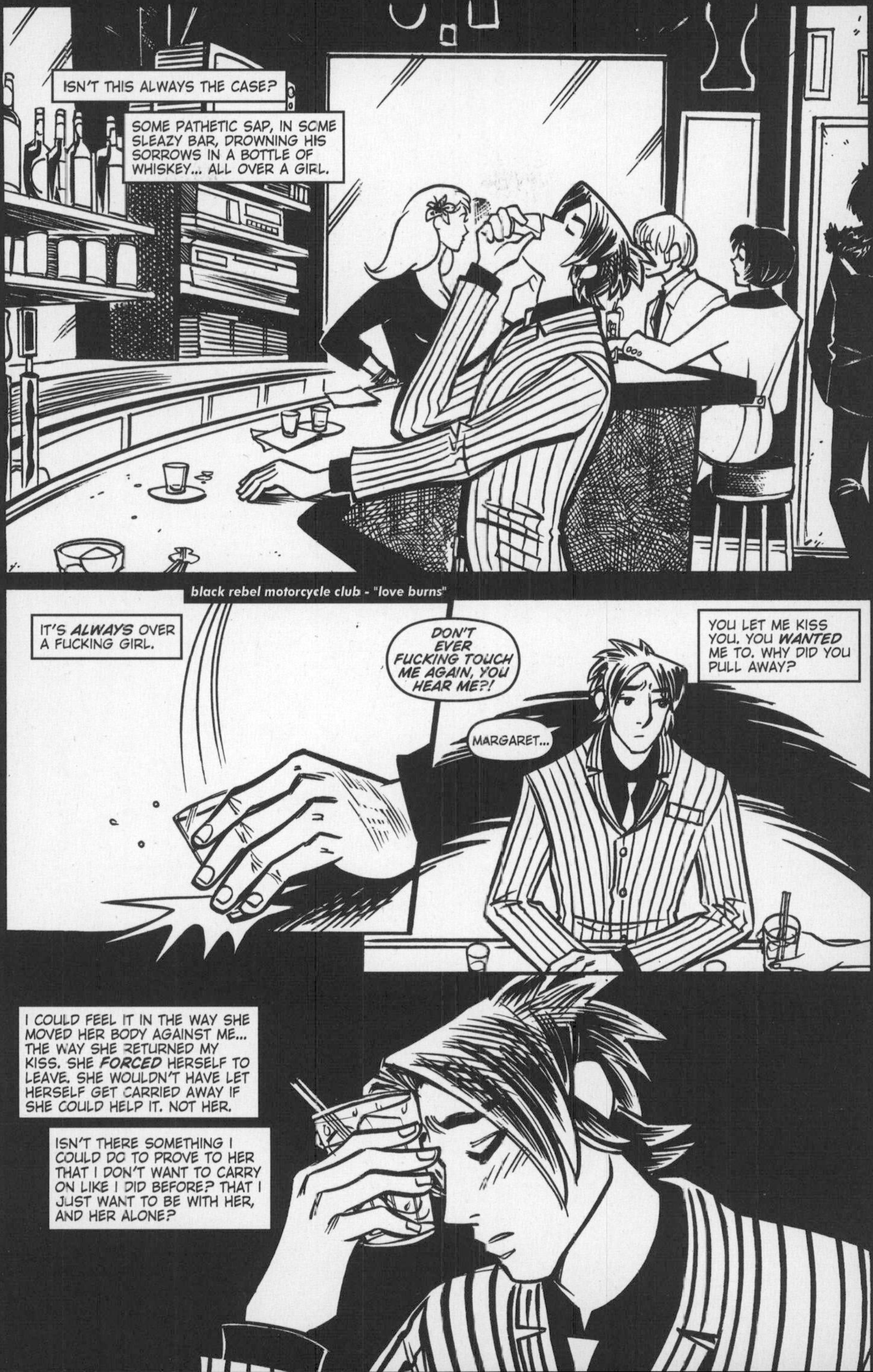
ISN'T THIS ALWAYS THE CASE?
SOME PATHETIC SAP, IN SOME SLEAZY BAR, DROWNING HIS SORROWS IN A BOTTLE OF WHISKEY... ALL OVER A GIRL.
black rebel motorcycle club - "love burns"
IT'S ALWAYS OVER A FUCKING GIRL.
DON'T EVER FUCKING TOUCH ME AGAIN, YOU HEAR ME?!
YOU LET ME KISS YOU. YOU WANTED ME TO. WHY DID YOU PULL AWAY?
MARGARET...
I COULD FEEL IT IN THE WAY SHE MOVED HER BODY AGAINST ME... THE WAY SHE RETURNED MY KISS. SHE FORCED HERSELF TO LEAVE. SHE WOULDN'T HAVE LET HERSELF GET CARRIED AWAY IF SHE COULD HELP IT. NOT HER.
ISN'T THERE SOMETHING I COULD DO TO PROVE TO HER THAT I DON'T WANT TO CARRY ON LIKE I DID BEFORE? THAT I JUST WANT TO BE WITH HER, AND HER ALONE?

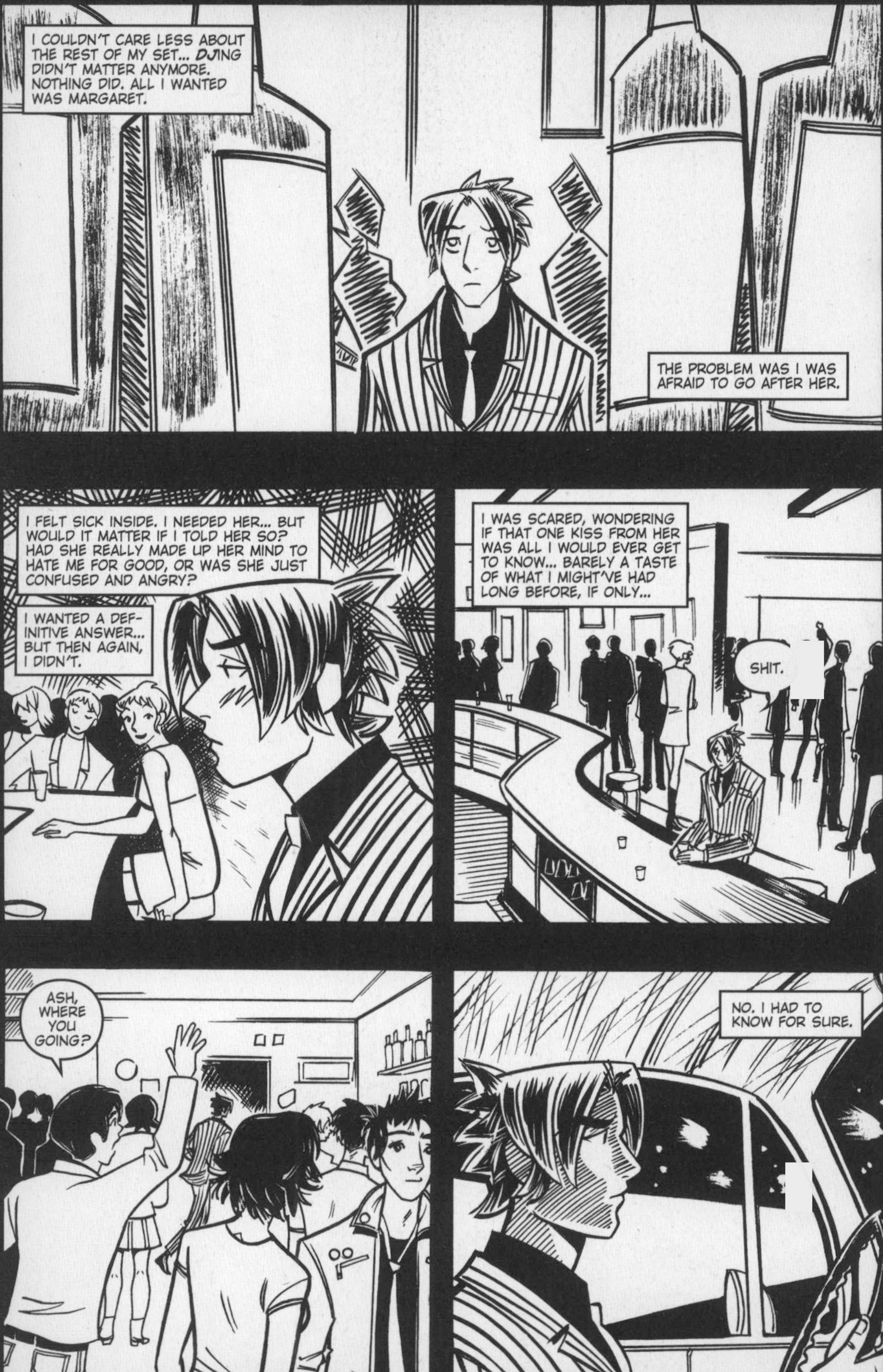
I COULDN'T CARE LESS ABOUT THE REST OF MY SET... DJING DIDN'T MATTER ANYMORE. NOTHING DID. ALL I WANTED WAS MARGARET.
THE PROBLEM WAS I WAS AFRAID TO GO AFTER HER.
I FELT SICK INSIDE. I NEEDED HER... BUT WOULD IT MATTER IF I TOLD HER SO? HAD SHE REALLY MADE UP HER MIND TO HATE ME FOR GOOD, OR WAS SHE JUST CONFUSED AND ANGRY?
I WANTED A DEFINITIVE ANSWER... BUT THEN AGAIN, I DIDN'T.
I WAS SCARED, WONDERING IF THAT ONE KISS FROM HER WAS ALL I WOULD EVER GET TO KNOW... BARELY A TASTE OF WHAT I MIGHT'VE HAD LONG BEFORE, IF ONLY...
SHIT.
ASH, WHERE YOU GOING?
NO. I HAD TO KNOW FOR SURE.

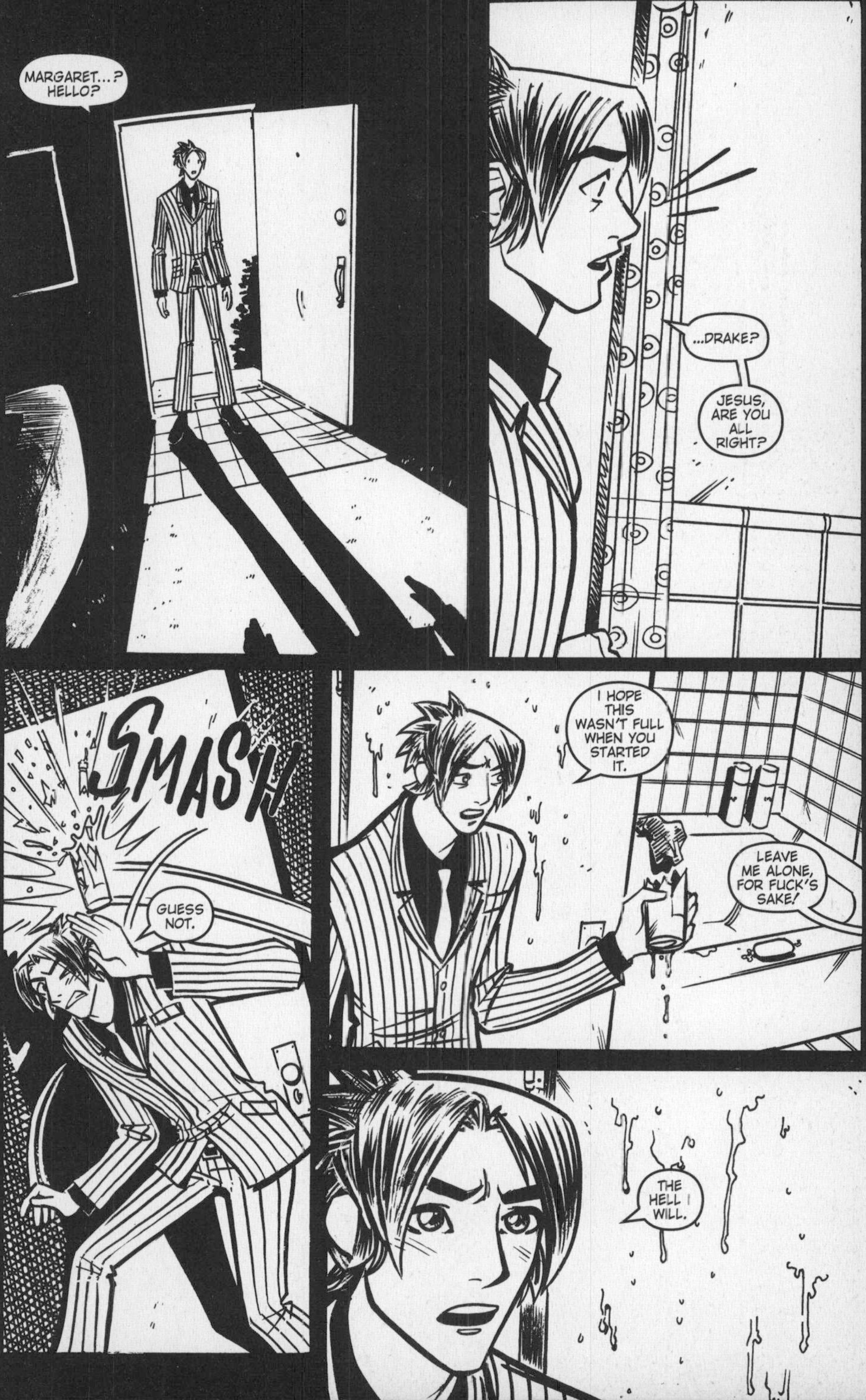
MARGARET...? HELLO?
...DRAKE?
JESUS, ARE YOU ALL RIGHT?
SMASH
GUESS NOT.
I HOPE THIS WASN'T FULL WHEN YOU STARTED IT.
LEAVE ME ALONE, FOR FUCK'S SAKE!
THE HELL I WILL.

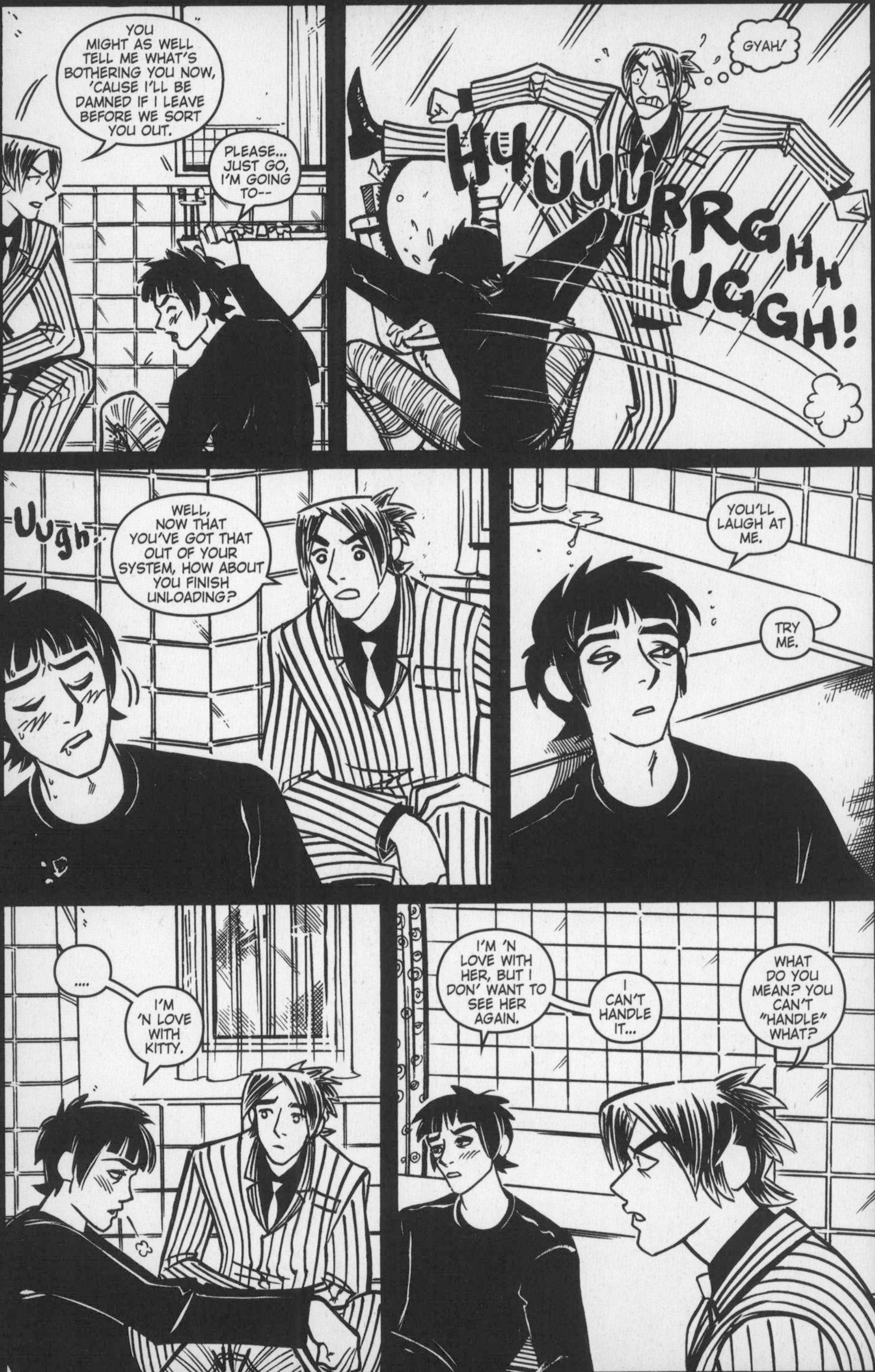
YOU MIGHT AS WELL TELL ME WHAT'S BOTHERING YOU NOW, 'CAUSE I'LL BE DAMNED IF I LEAVE BEFORE WE SORT YOU OUT.
PLEASE... JUST GO, I'M GOING TO--
GYAH!
HYUUURRGHH UGGH!
Uugh.
WELL, NOW THAT YOU'VE GOT THAT OUT OF YOUR SYSTEM, HOW ABOUT YOU FINISH UNLOADING?
YOU'LL LAUGH AT ME.
TRY ME.
....
I'M 'N LOVE WITH KITTY.
I'M 'N LOVE WITH HER, BUT I DON' WANT TO SEE HER AGAIN.
I CAN'T HANDLE IT...
WHAT DO YOU MEAN? YOU CAN'T "HANDLE" WHAT?

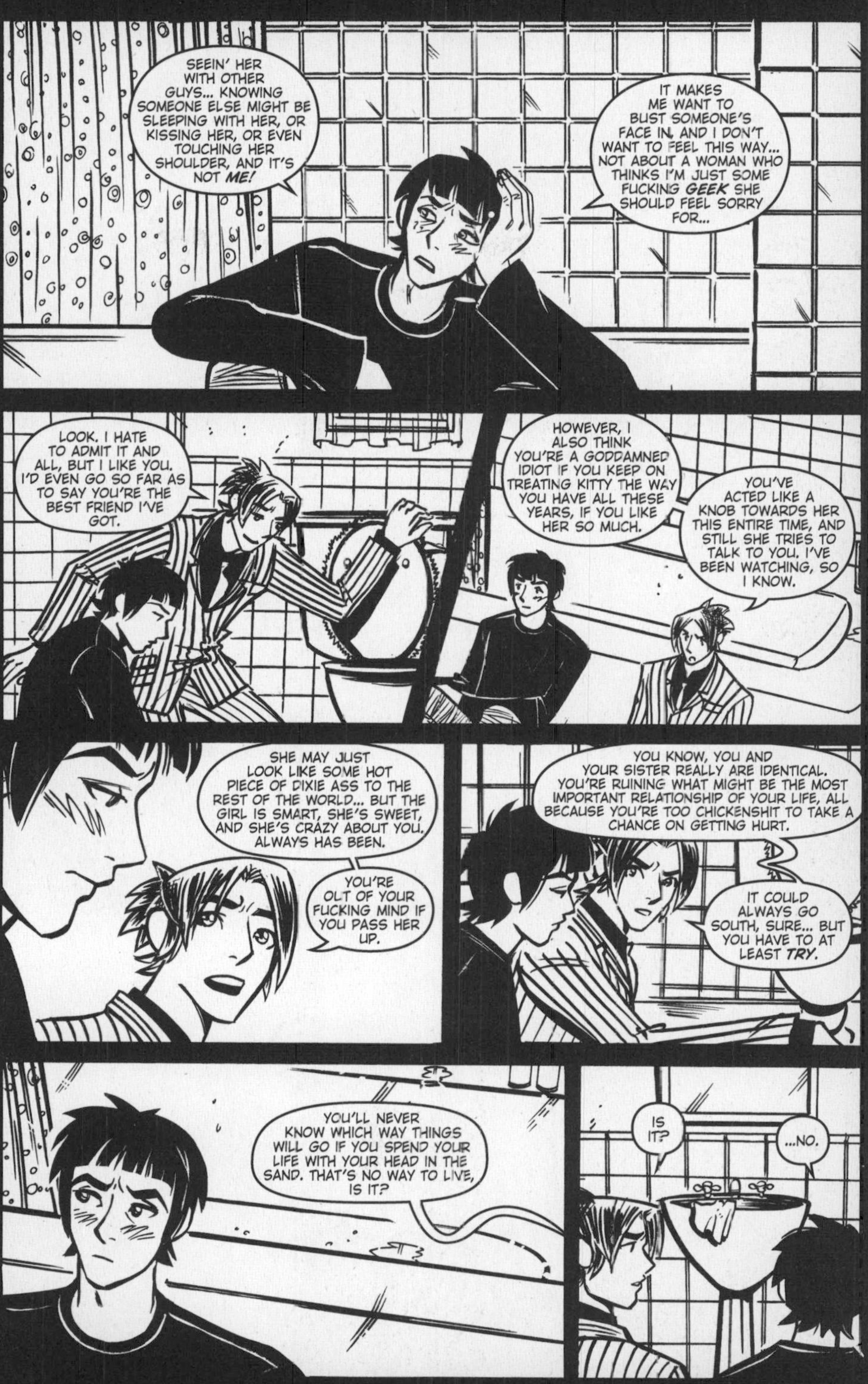
SEEIN' HER WITH OTHER GUYS... KNOWING SOMEONE ELSE MIGHT BE SLEEPING WITH HER, OR KISSING HER, OR EVEN TOUCHING HER SHOULDER, AND IT'S NOT ME!
IT MAKES ME WANT TO BUST SOMEONE'S FACE IN, AND I DON'T WANT TO FEEL THIS WAY... NOT ABOUT A WOMAN WHO THINKS I'M JUST SOME FUCKING GEEK SHE SHOULD FEEL SORRY FOR...
LOOK. I HATE TO ADMIT IT AND ALL, BUT I LIKE YOU. I'D EVEN GO SO FAR AS TO SAY YOU'RE THE BEST FRIEND I'VE GOT.
HOWEVER, I ALSO THINK YOU'RE A GODDAMNED IDIOT IF YOU KEEP ON TREATING KITTY THE WAY YOU HAVE ALL THESE YEARS, IF YOU LIKE HER SO MUCH.
YOU'VE ACTED LIKE A KNOB TOWARDS HER THIS ENTIRE TIME, AND STILL SHE TRIES TO TALK TO YOU. I'VE BEEN WATCHING, SO I KNOW.
SHE MAY JUST LOOK LIKE SOME HOT PIECE OF DIXIE ASS TO THE REST OF THE WORLD... BUT THE GIRL IS SMART, SHE'S SWEET, AND SHE'S CRAZY ABOUT YOU, ALWAYS HAS BEEN.
YOU'RE OUT OF YOUR FUCKING MIND IF YOU PASS HER UP.
YOU KNOW, YOU AND YOUR SISTER REALLY ARE IDENTICAL. YOU'RE RUINING WHAT MIGHT BE THE MOST IMPORTANT RELATIONSHIP OF YOUR LIFE, ALL BECAUSE YOU'RE TOO CHICKENSHIT TO TAKE A CHANCE ON GETTING HURT.
IT COULD ALWAYS GO SOUTH, SURE... BUT YOU HAVE TO AT LEAST TRY.
YOU'LL NEVER KNOW WHICH WAY THINGS WILL GO IF YOU SPEND YOUR LIFE WITH YOUR HEAD IN THE SAND. THAT'S NO WAY TO LIVE, IS IT?
IS IT?
...NO.

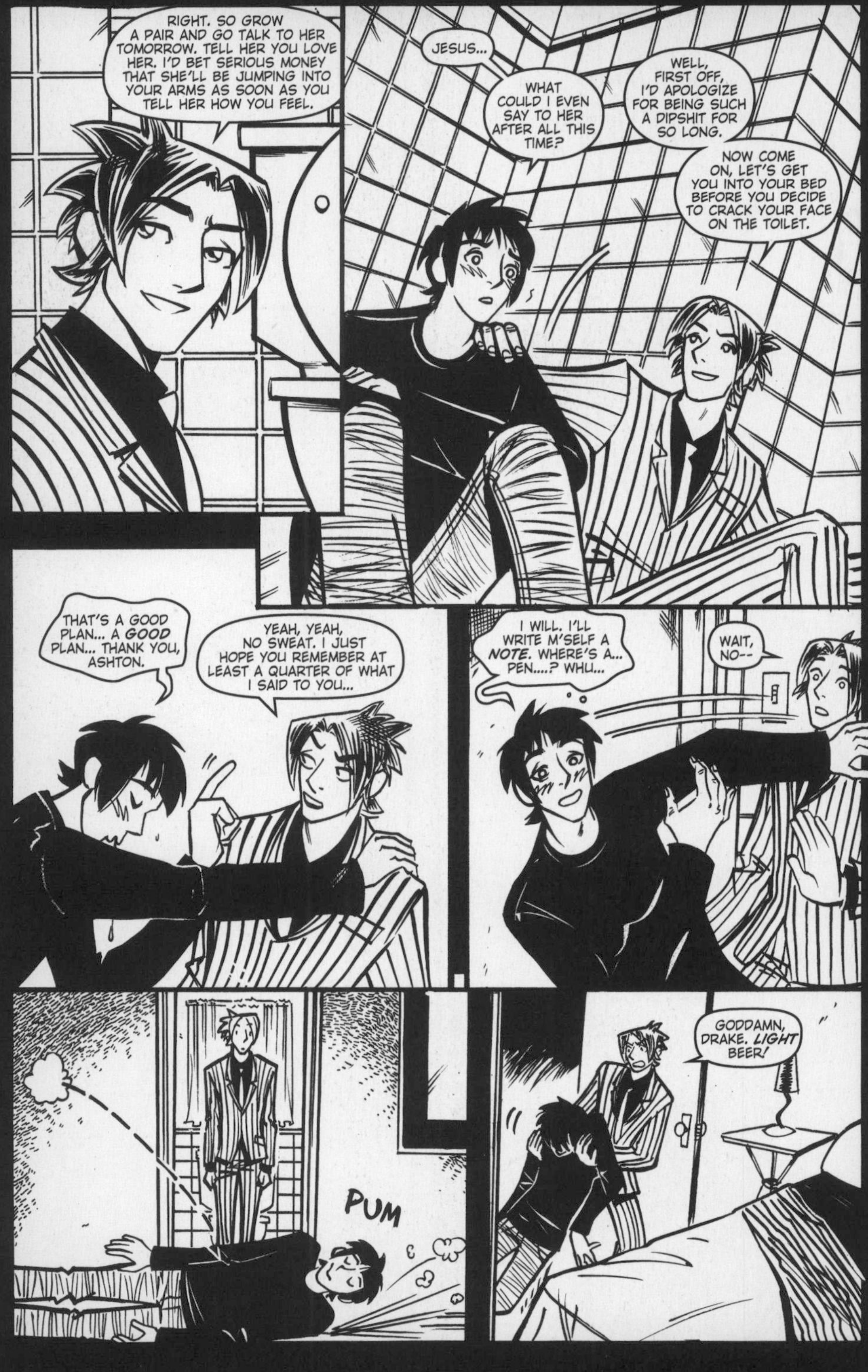
RIGHT. SO GROW A PAIR AND GO TALK TO HER TOMORROW. TELL HER YOU LOVE HER. I'D BET SERIOUS MONEY THAT SHE'LL BE JUMPING INTO YOUR ARMS AS SOON AS YOU TELL HER HOW YOU FEEL.
JESUS...
WHAT COULD I EVEN SAY TO HER AFTER ALL THIS TIME?
WELL, FIRST OFF, I'D APOLOGIZE FOR BEING SUCH A DIPSHIT FOR SO LONG.
NOW COME ON, LET'S GET YOU INTO YOUR BED BEFORE YOU DECIDE TO CRACK YOUR FACE ON THE TOILET.
THAT'S A GOOD PLAN... A *GOOD* PLAN... THANK YOU, ASHTON.
YEAH, YEAH, NO SWEAT. I JUST HOPE YOU REMEMBER AT LEAST A QUARTER OF WHAT I SAID TO YOU...
I WILL. I'LL WRITE M'SELF A *NOTE*. WHERE'S A... PEN....? WHU...
WAIT, NO--
PUM
GODDAMN, DRAKE. *LIGHT* BEER!

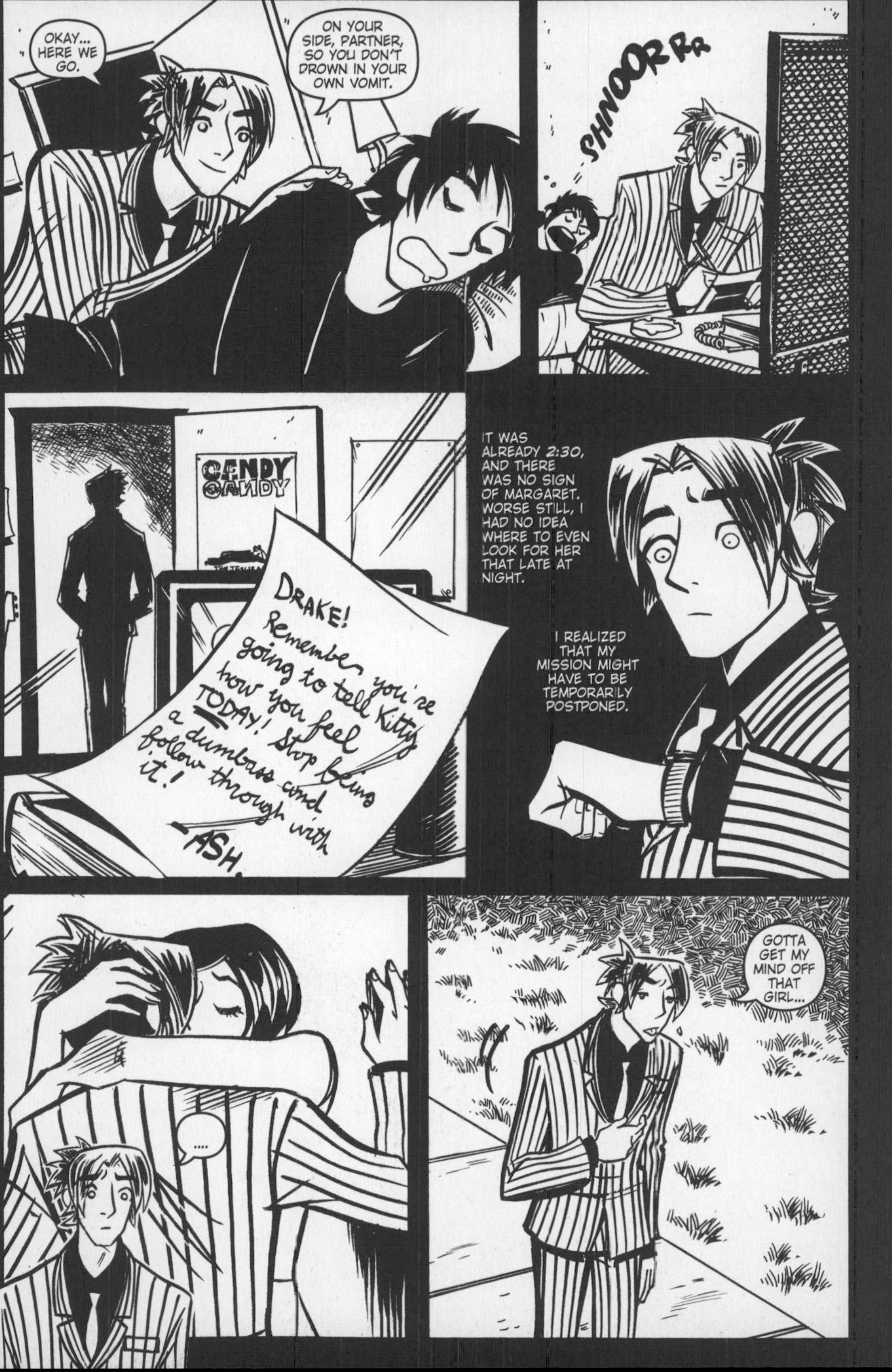
OKAY... HERE WE GO.
ON YOUR SIDE, PARTNER, SO YOU DON'T DROWN IN YOUR OWN VOMIT.
SHNOORRRR
CANDY CANDY
DRAKE! Remember you're going to tell Kitty how you feel TODAY! Stop being a dumbass and follow through with it! -ASH
IT WAS ALREADY 2:30, AND THERE WAS NO SIGN OF MARGARET. WORSE STILL, I HAD NO IDEA WHERE TO EVEN LOOK FOR HER THAT LATE AT NIGHT.
I REALIZED THAT MY MISSION MIGHT HAVE TO BE TEMPORARILY POSTPONED.
....
GOTTA GET MY MIND OFF THAT GIRL...

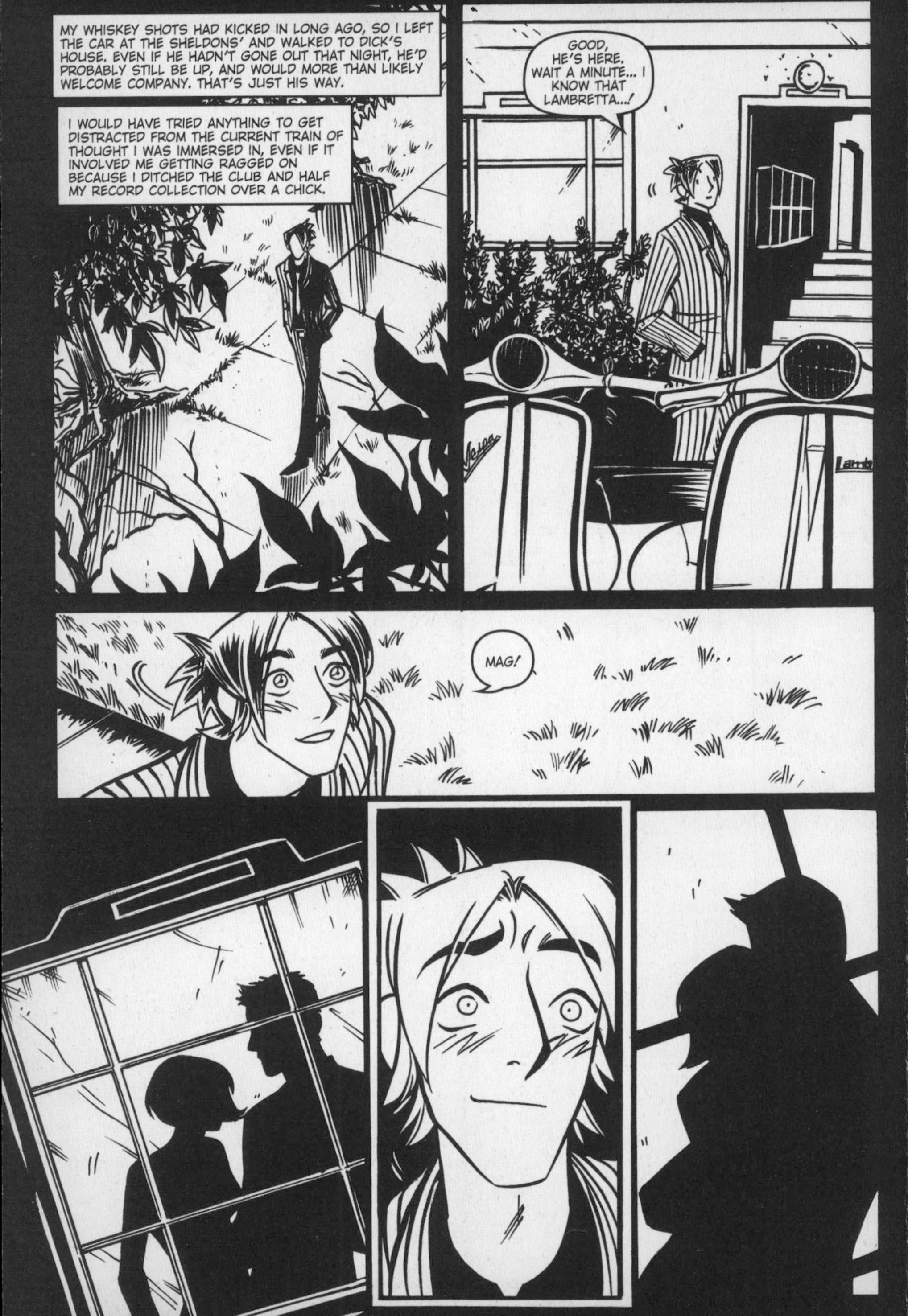

MY WHISKEY SHOTS HAD KICKED IN LONG AGO, SO I LEFT THE CAR AT THE SHELDONS' AND WALKED TO DICK'S HOUSE. EVEN IF HE HADN'T GONE OUT THAT NIGHT, HE'D PROBABLY STILL BE UP, AND WOULD MORE THAN LIKELY WELCOME COMPANY. THAT'S JUST HIS WAY.
I WOULD HAVE TRIED ANYTHING TO GET DISTRACTED FROM THE CURRENT TRAIN OF THOUGHT I WAS IMMERSED IN, EVEN IF IT INVOLVED ME GETTING RAGGED ON BECAUSE I DITCHED THE CLUB AND HALF MY RECORD COLLECTION OVER A CHICK.
GOOD, HE'S HERE. WAIT A MINUTE... I KNOW THAT LAMBRETTA...!
MAG!

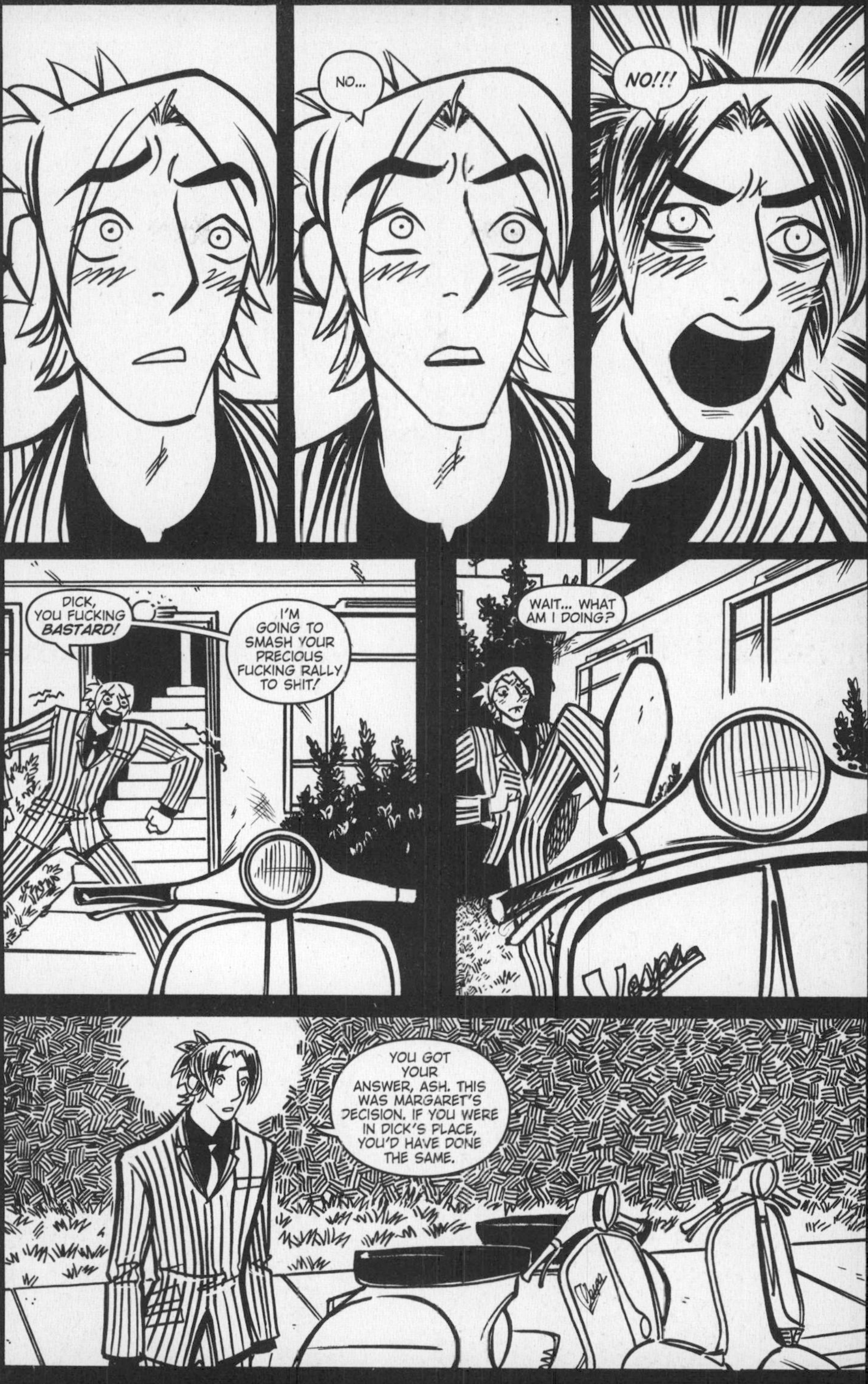
NO...
NO!!!
DICK, YOU FUCKING BASTARD!
I'M GOING TO SMASH YOUR PRECIOUS FUCKING RALLY TO SHIT!
WAIT... WHAT AM I DOING?
YOU GOT YOUR ANSWER, ASH. THIS WAS MARGARET'S DECISION. IF YOU WERE IN DICK'S PLACE, YOU'D HAVE DONE THE SAME.

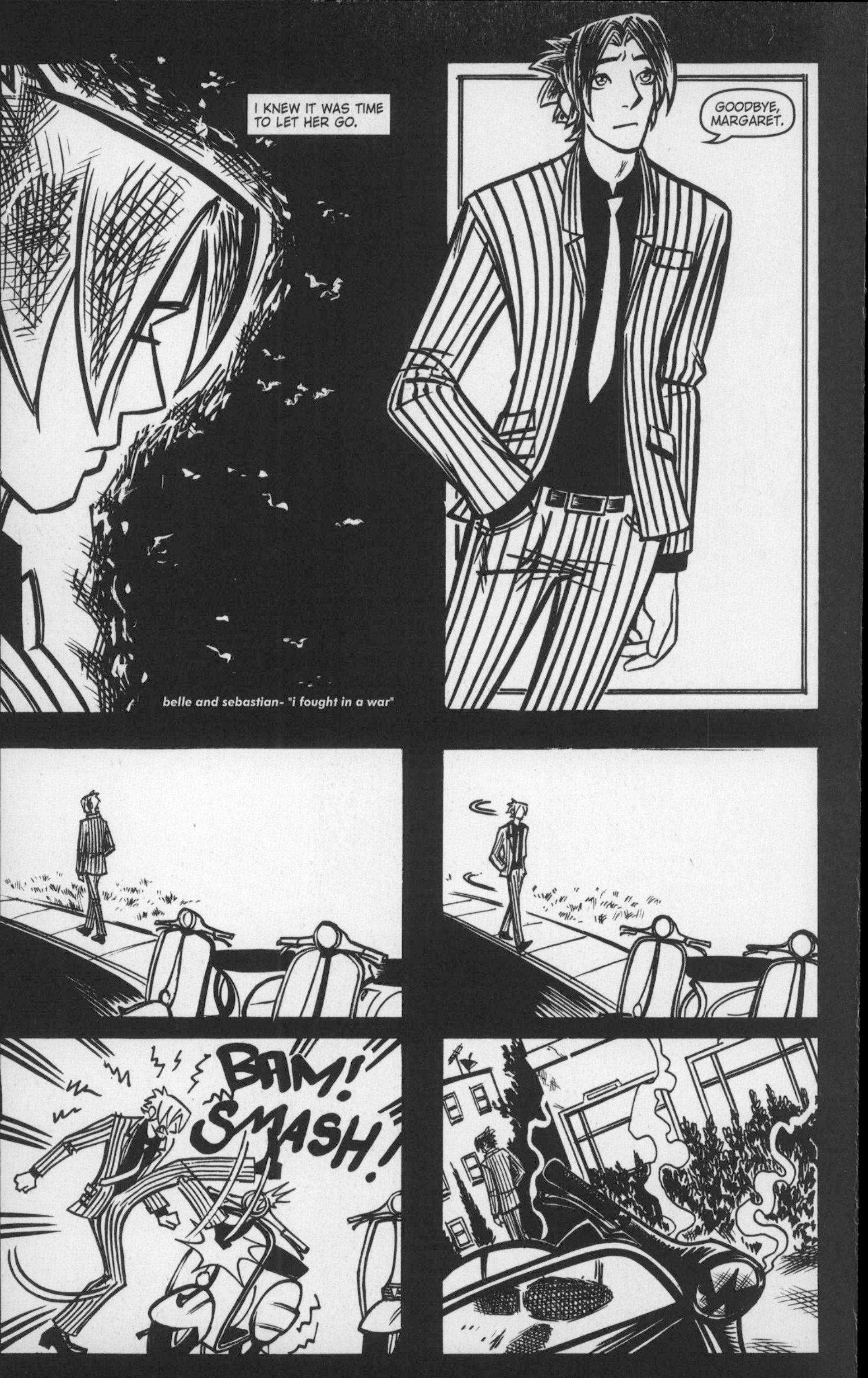

I KNEW IT WAS TIME TO LET HER GO.
GOODBYE, MARGARET.
belle and sebastian- "i fought in a war"
BAM!
SMASH!

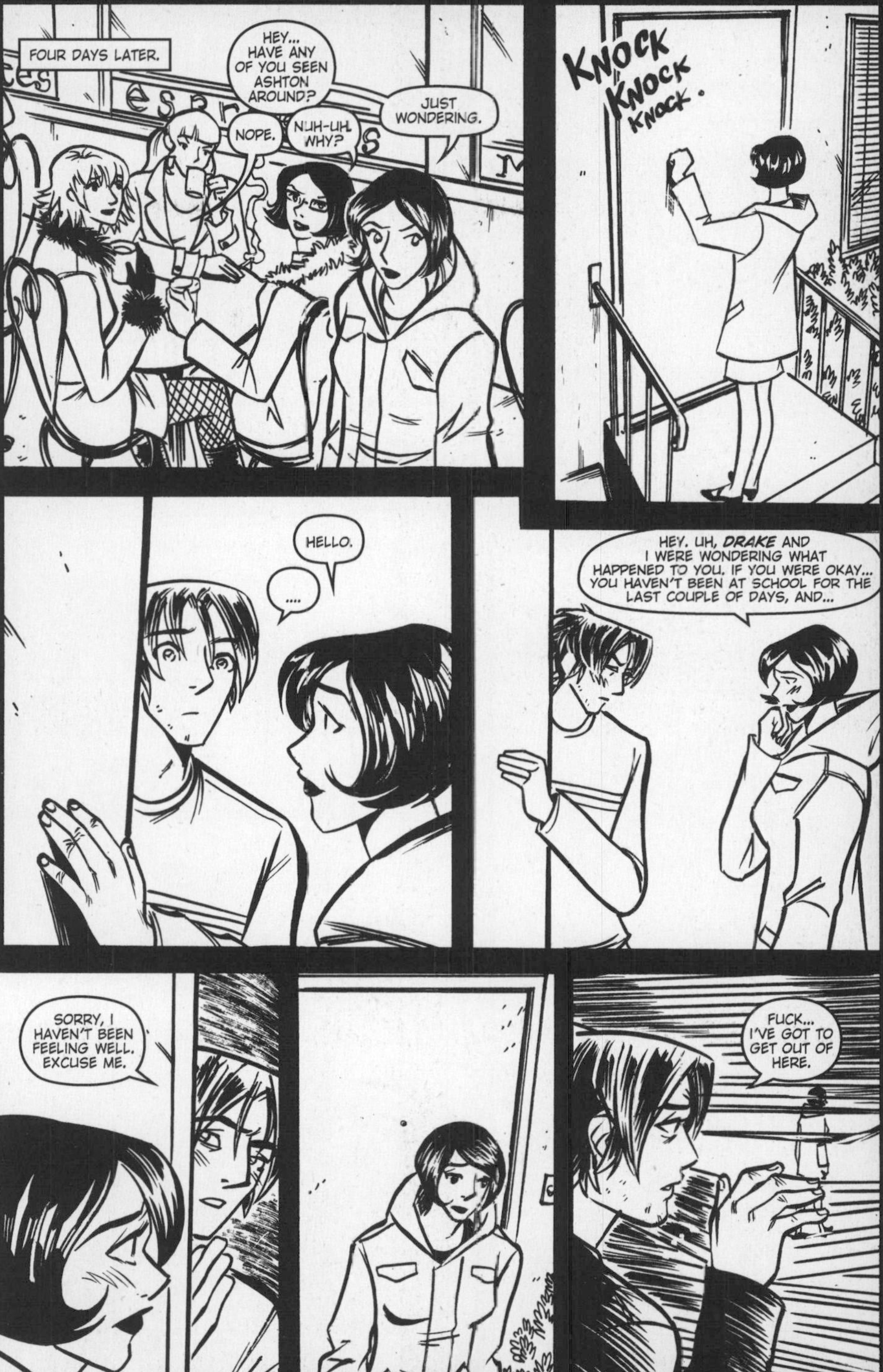
FOUR DAYS LATER.
HEY... HAVE ANY OF YOU SEEN ASHTON AROUND?
NOPE.
NUH-UH. WHY?
JUST WONDERING.
KNOCK KNOCK KNOCK.
HELLO.
....
HEY. UH, DRAKE AND I WERE WONDERING WHAT HAPPENED TO YOU. IF YOU WERE OKAY... YOU HAVEN'T BEEN AT SCHOOL FOR THE LAST COUPLE OF DAYS, AND...
SORRY, I HAVEN'T BEEN FEELING WELL. EXCUSE ME.
FUCK... I'VE GOT TO GET OUT OF HERE.

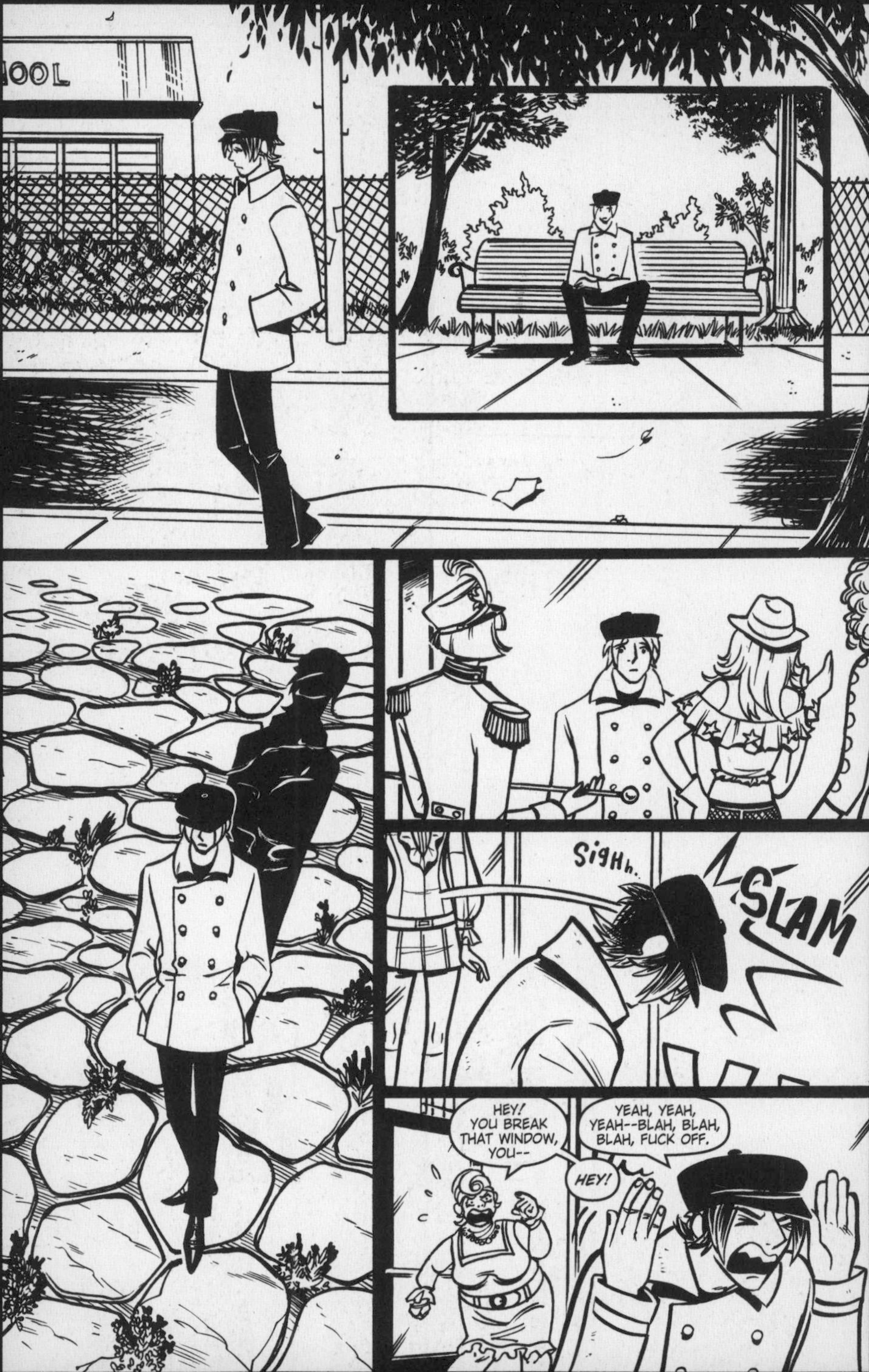

HOOL
SIGHh..
SLAM
HEY! YOU BREAK THAT WINDOW, YOU--
YEAH, YEAH, YEAH--BLAH, BLAH, BLAH, FUCK OFF.
HEY!

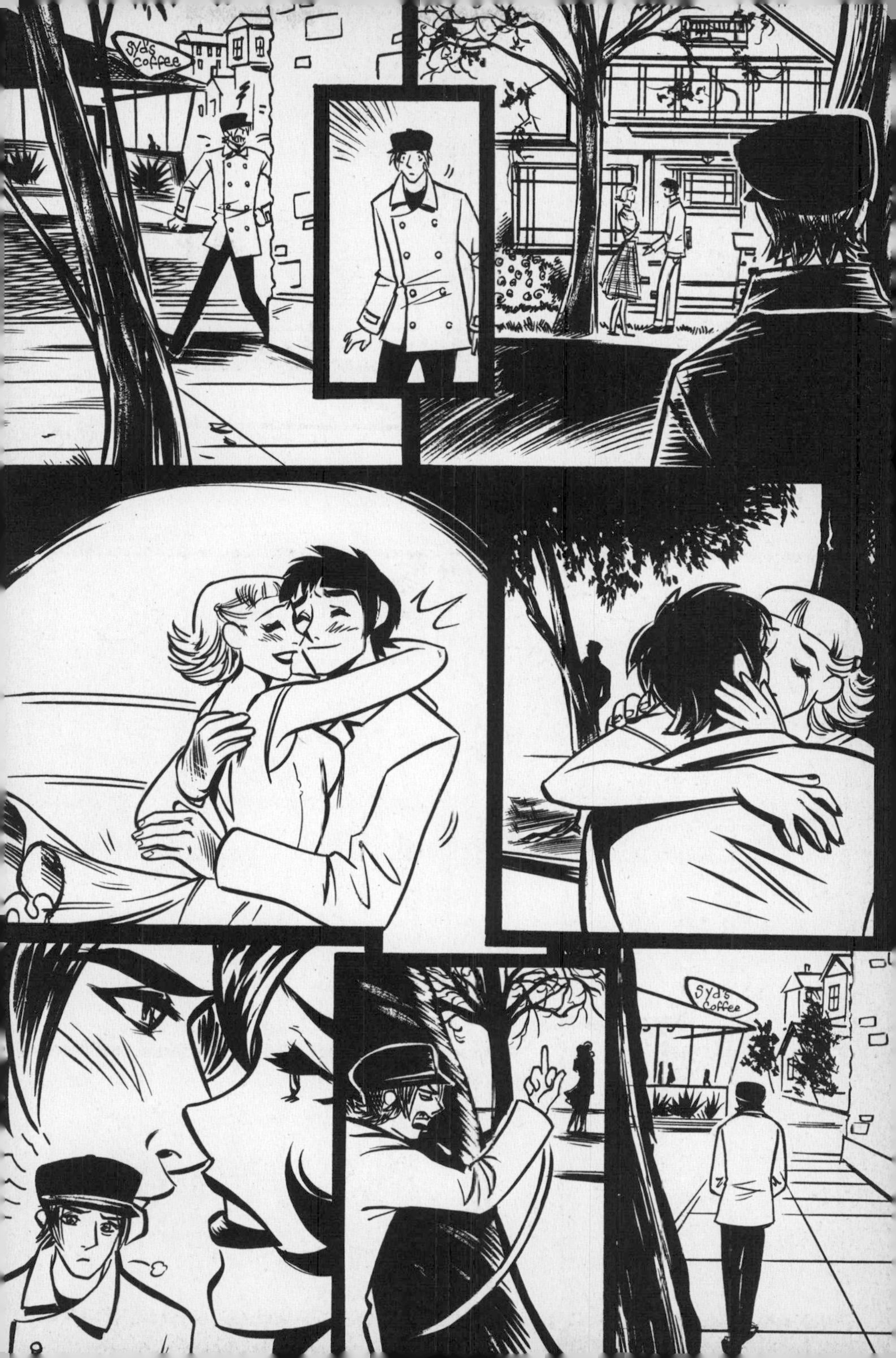
syd's coffee
syd's coffee

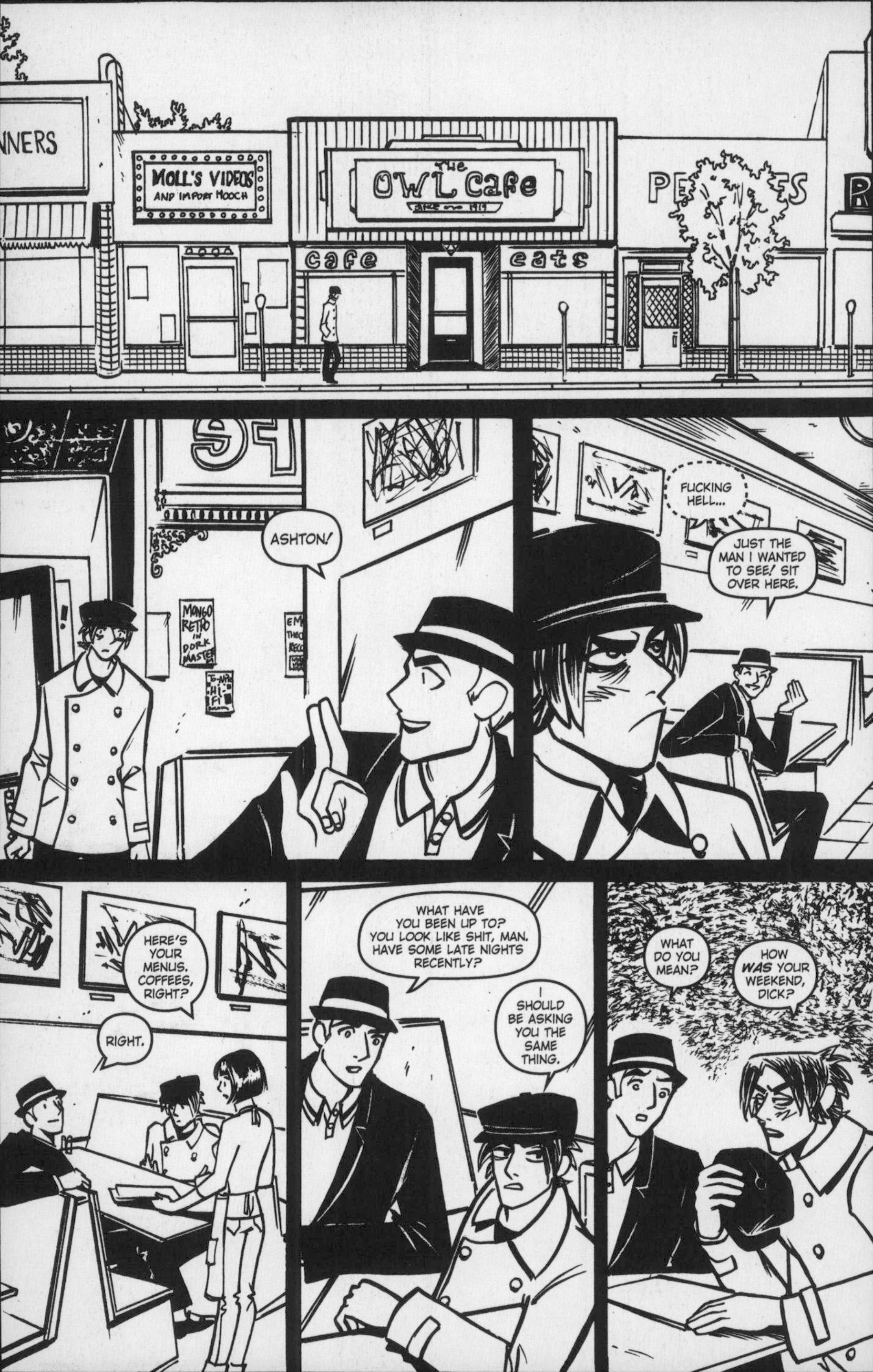
NNERS
MOLL'S VIDEOS
AND IMPORT MOOCH
THE OWL CAFE
cafe
eats
ASHTON!
MONGO RETRO IN DORK MASTER
FUCKING HELL...
JUST THE MAN I WANTED TO SEE! SIT OVER HERE.
HERE'S YOUR MENUS. COFFEES, RIGHT?
RIGHT.
WHAT HAVE YOU BEEN UP TO? YOU LOOK LIKE SHIT, MAN. HAVE SOME LATE NIGHTS RECENTLY?
I SHOULD BE ASKING YOU THE SAME THING.
WHAT DO YOU MEAN?
HOW *WAS* YOUR WEEKEND, DICK?

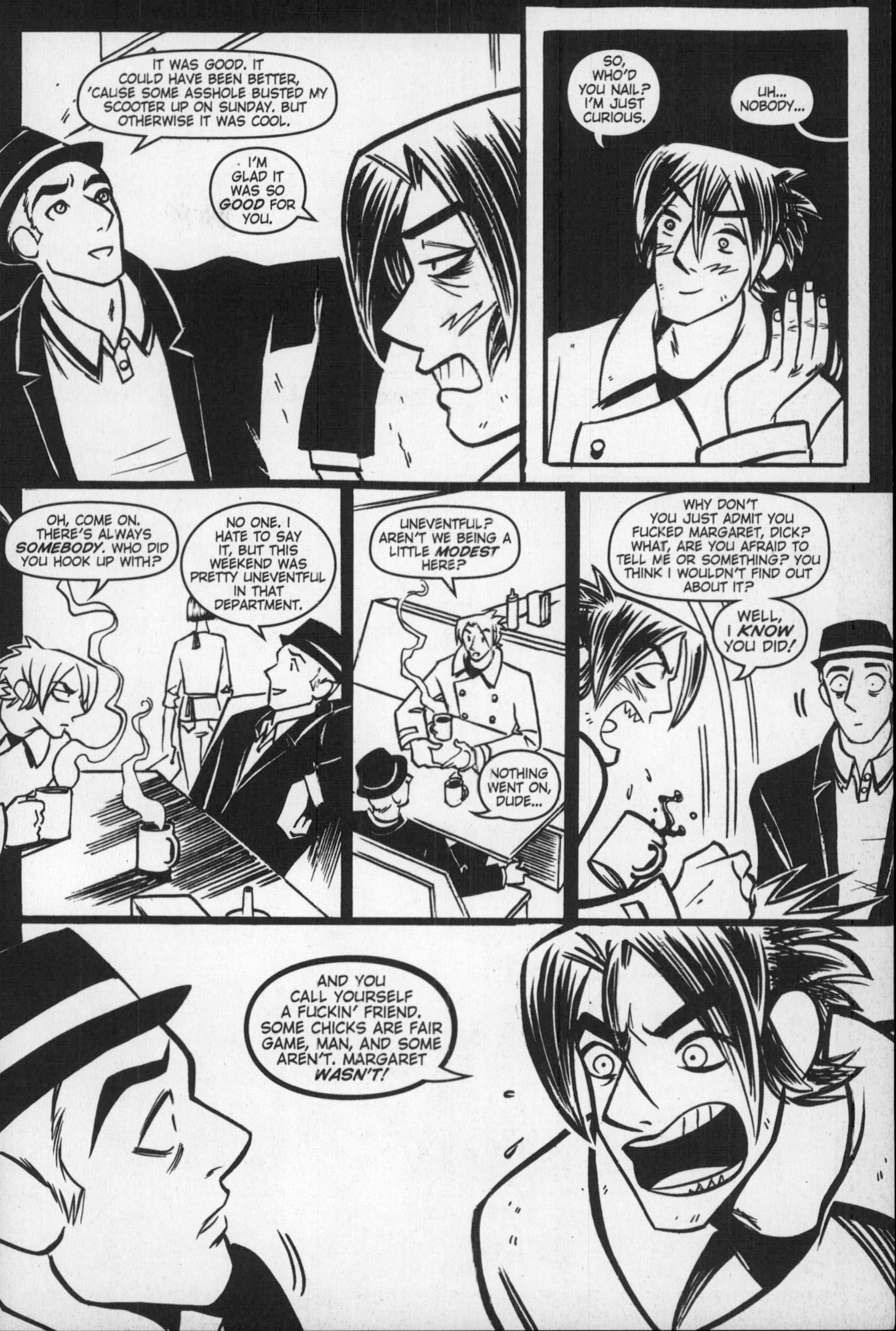
IT WAS GOOD. IT COULD HAVE BEEN BETTER, 'CAUSE SOME ASSHOLE BUSTED MY SCOOTER UP ON SUNDAY. BUT OTHERWISE IT WAS COOL.
I'M GLAD IT WAS SO GOOD FOR YOU.
SO, WHO'D YOU NAIL? I'M JUST CURIOUS.
UH... NOBODY...
OH, COME ON. THERE'S ALWAYS SOMEBODY. WHO DID YOU HOOK UP WITH?
NO ONE. I HATE TO SAY IT, BUT THIS WEEKEND WAS PRETTY UNEVENTFUL IN THAT DEPARTMENT.
UNEVENTFUL? AREN'T WE BEING A LITTLE MODEST HERE?
NOTHING WENT ON, DUDE...
WHY DON'T YOU JUST ADMIT YOU FUCKED MARGARET, DICK? WHAT, ARE YOU AFRAID TO TELL ME OR SOMETHING? YOU THINK I WOULDN'T FIND OUT ABOUT IT?
WELL, I KNOW YOU DID!
AND YOU CALL YOURSELF A FUCKIN' FRIEND. SOME CHICKS ARE FAIR GAME, MAN, AND SOME AREN'T. MARGARET WASN'T!

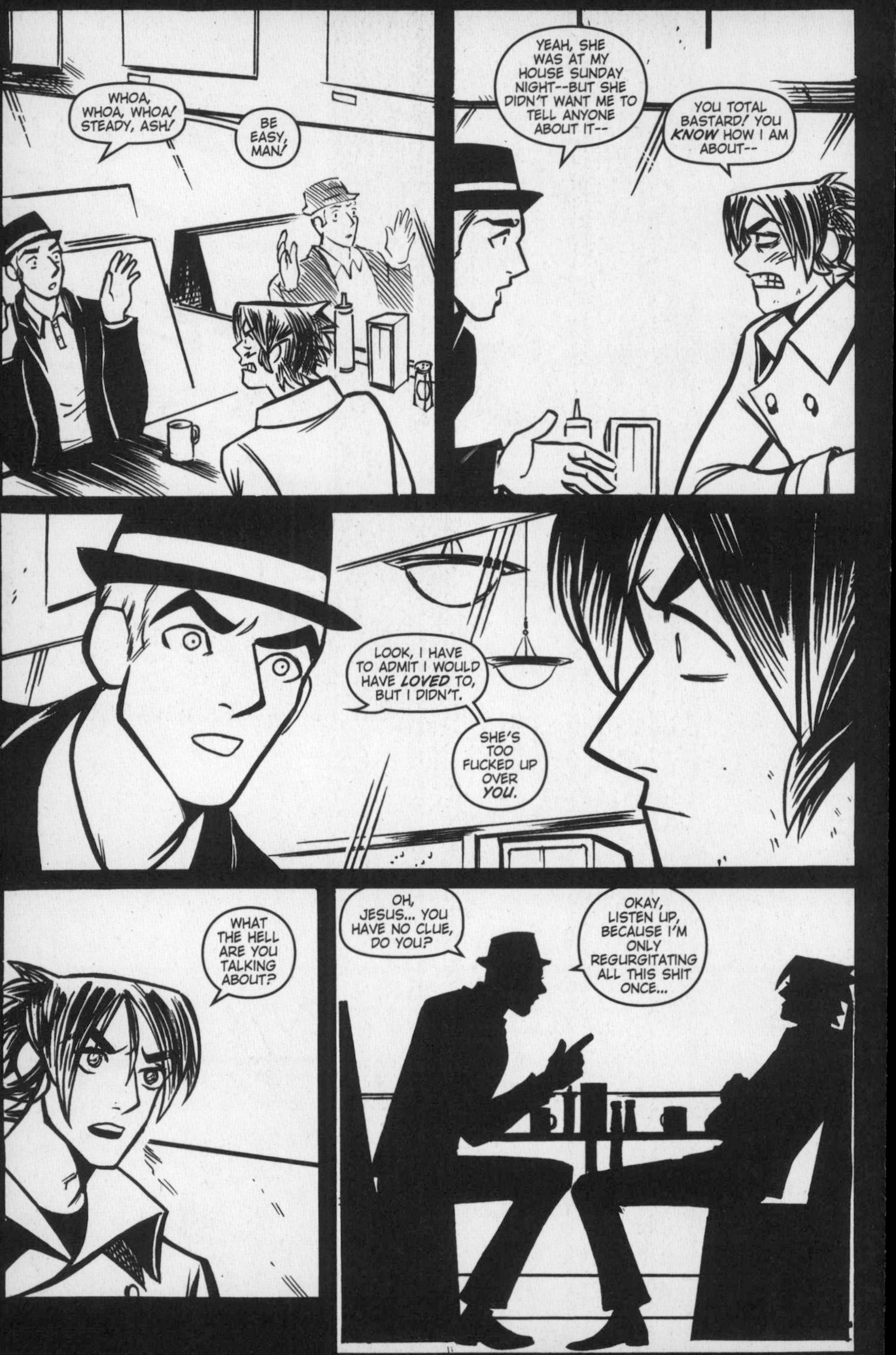
WHOA, WHOA, WHOA! STEADY, ASH!
BE EASY, MAN!
YEAH, SHE WAS AT MY HOUSE SUNDAY NIGHT--BUT SHE DIDN'T WANT ME TO TELL ANYONE ABOUT IT--
YOU TOTAL BASTARD! YOU KNOW HOW I AM ABOUT--
LOOK, I HAVE TO ADMIT I WOULD HAVE LOVED TO, BUT I DIDN'T.
SHE'S TOO FUCKED UP OVER YOU.
WHAT THE HELL ARE YOU TALKING ABOUT?
OH, JESUS... YOU HAVE NO CLUE, DO YOU?
OKAY, LISTEN UP, BECAUSE I'M ONLY REGURGITATING ALL THIS SHIT ONCE...

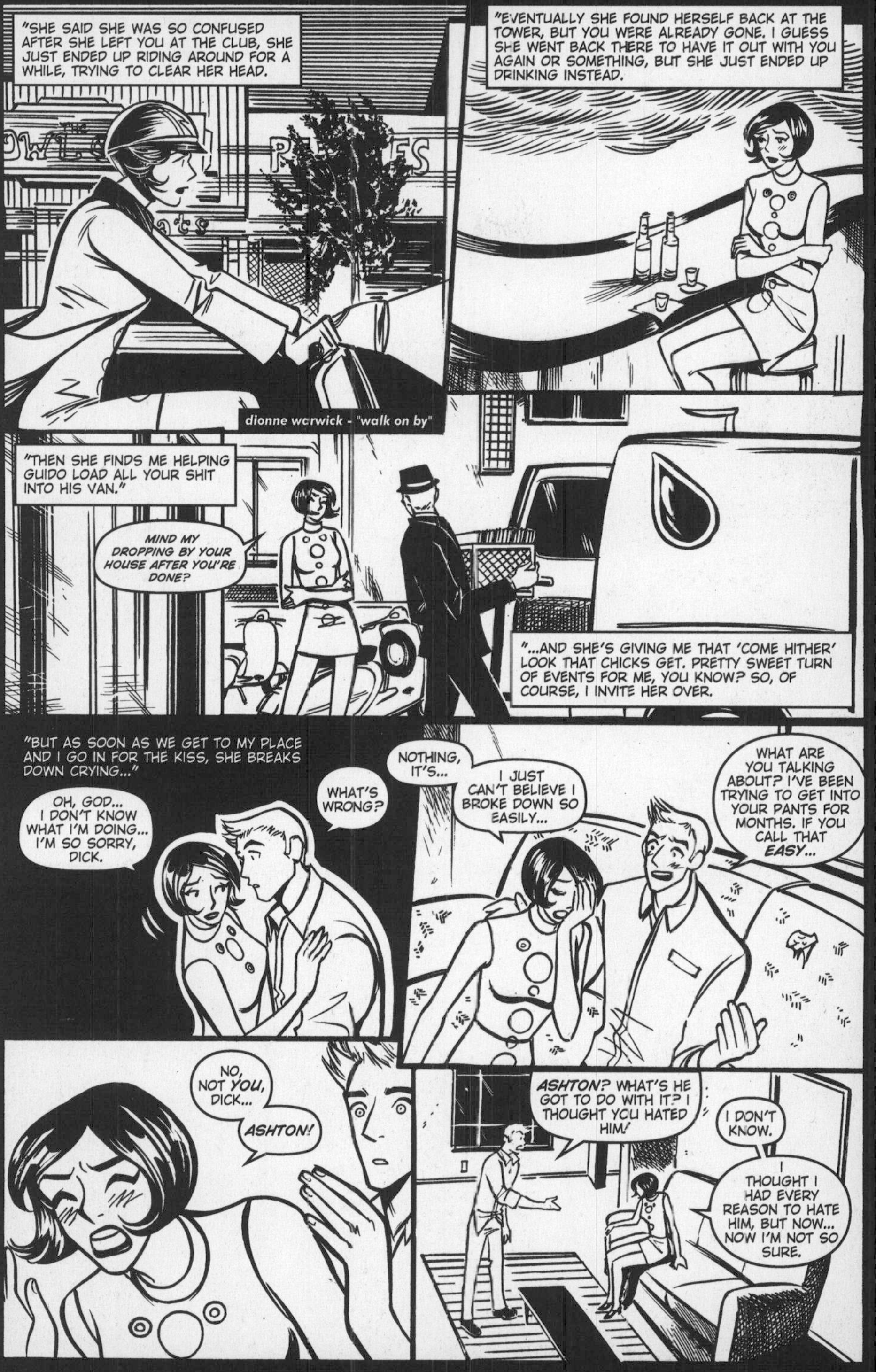
"SHE SAID SHE WAS SO CONFUSED AFTER SHE LEFT YOU AT THE CLUB, SHE JUST ENDED UP RIDING AROUND FOR A WHILE, TRYING TO CLEAR HER HEAD.
"EVENTUALLY SHE FOUND HERSELF BACK AT THE TOWER, BUT YOU WERE ALREADY GONE. I GUESS SHE WENT BACK THERE TO HAVE IT OUT WITH YOU AGAIN OR SOMETHING, BUT SHE JUST ENDED UP DRINKING INSTEAD.
dionne warwick - "walk on by"
"THEN SHE FINDS ME HELPING GUIDO LOAD ALL YOUR SHIT INTO HIS VAN."
MIND MY DROPPING BY YOUR HOUSE AFTER YOU'RE DONE?
"...AND SHE'S GIVING ME THAT 'COME HITHER' LOOK THAT CHICKS GET. PRETTY SWEET TURN OF EVENTS FOR ME, YOU KNOW? SO, OF COURSE, I INVITE HER OVER.
"BUT AS SOON AS WE GET TO MY PLACE AND I GO IN FOR THE KISS, SHE BREAKS DOWN CRYING..."
OH, GOD... I DON'T KNOW WHAT I'M DOING... I'M SO SORRY, DICK.
WHAT'S WRONG?
NOTHING, IT'S...
I JUST CAN'T BELIEVE I BROKE DOWN SO EASILY...
WHAT ARE YOU TALKING ABOUT? I'VE BEEN TRYING TO GET INTO YOUR PANTS FOR MONTHS. IF YOU CALL THAT EASY...
NO, NOT YOU, DICK...
ASHTON!
ASHTON? WHAT'S HE GOT TO DO WITH IT? I THOUGHT YOU HATED HIM!
I DON'T KNOW.
I THOUGHT I HAD EVERY REASON TO HATE HIM, BUT NOW... NOW I'M NOT SO SURE.

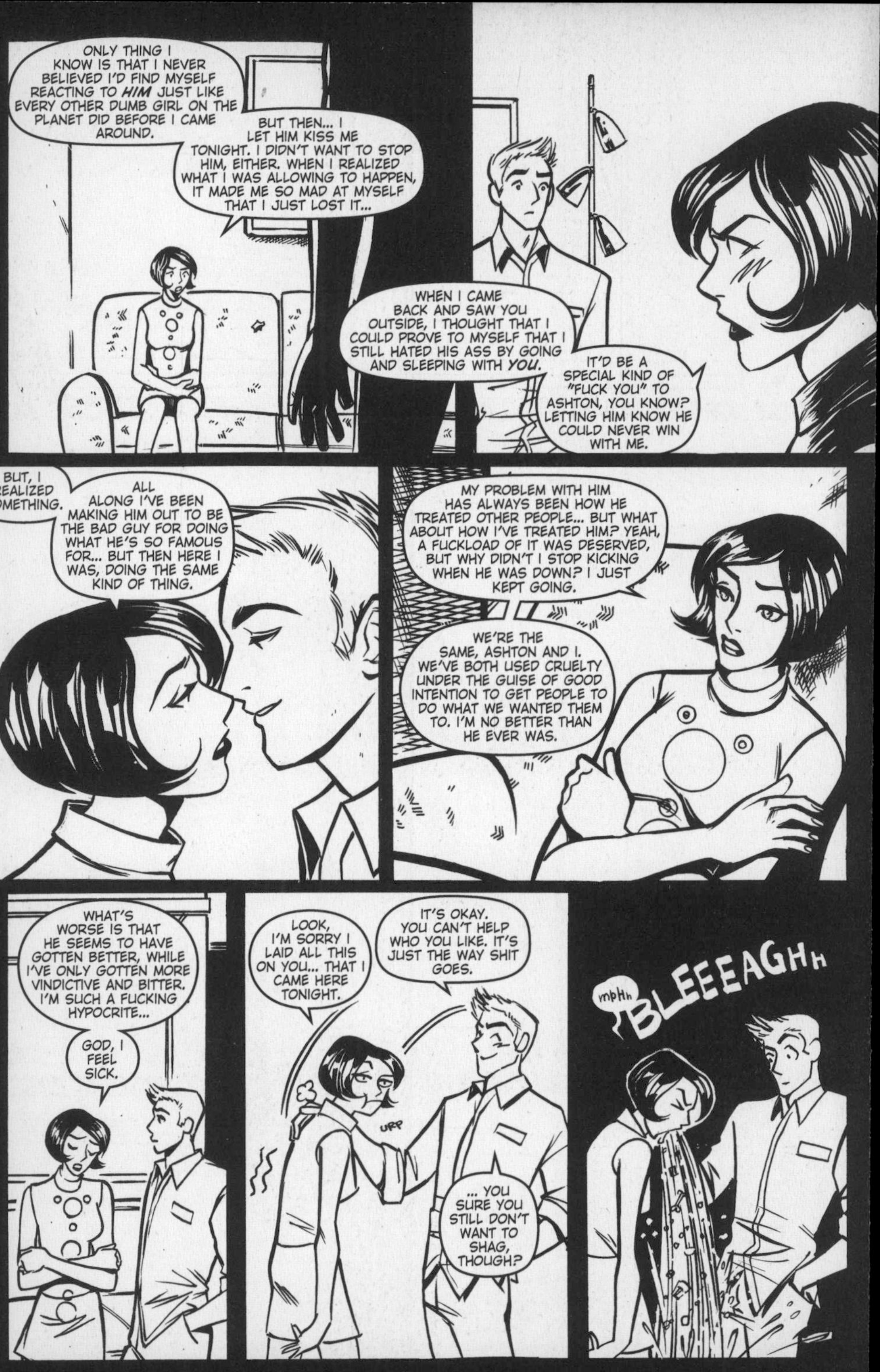
ONLY THING I KNOW IS THAT I NEVER BELIEVED I'D FIND MYSELF REACTING TO *HIM* JUST LIKE EVERY OTHER DUMB GIRL ON THE PLANET DID BEFORE I CAME AROUND.
BUT THEN... I LET HIM KISS ME TONIGHT. I DIDN'T WANT TO STOP HIM, EITHER. WHEN I REALIZED WHAT I WAS ALLOWING TO HAPPEN, IT MADE ME SO MAD AT MYSELF THAT I JUST LOST IT...
WHEN I CAME BACK AND SAW YOU OUTSIDE, I THOUGHT THAT I COULD PROVE TO MYSELF THAT I STILL HATED HIS ASS BY GOING AND SLEEPING WITH *YOU*.
IT'D BE A SPECIAL KIND OF "FUCK YOU" TO ASHTON, YOU KNOW? LETTING HIM KNOW HE COULD NEVER WIN WITH ME.
BUT, I REALIZED SOMETHING.
ALL ALONG I'VE BEEN MAKING HIM OUT TO BE THE BAD GUY FOR DOING WHAT HE'S SO FAMOUS FOR... BUT THEN HERE I WAS, DOING THE SAME KIND OF THING.
MY PROBLEM WITH HIM HAS ALWAYS BEEN HOW HE TREATED OTHER PEOPLE... BUT WHAT ABOUT HOW I'VE TREATED HIM? YEAH, A FUCKLOAD OF IT WAS DESERVED, BUT WHY DIDN'T I STOP KICKING WHEN HE WAS DOWN? I JUST KEPT GOING.
WE'RE THE SAME, ASHTON AND I. WE'VE BOTH USED CRUELTY UNDER THE GUISE OF GOOD INTENTION TO GET PEOPLE TO DO WHAT WE WANTED THEM TO. I'M NO BETTER THAN HE EVER WAS.
WHAT'S WORSE IS THAT HE SEEMS TO HAVE GOTTEN BETTER, WHILE I'VE ONLY GOTTEN MORE VINDICTIVE AND BITTER. I'M SUCH A FUCKING HYPOCRITE...
GOD, I FEEL SICK.
LOOK, I'M SORRY I LAID ALL THIS ON YOU... THAT I CAME HERE TONIGHT.
IT'S OKAY. YOU CAN'T HELP WHO YOU LIKE. IT'S JUST THE WAY SHIT GOES.
URP
... YOU SURE YOU STILL DON'T WANT TO SHAG, THOUGH?
mpHh
BLEEEAGHh

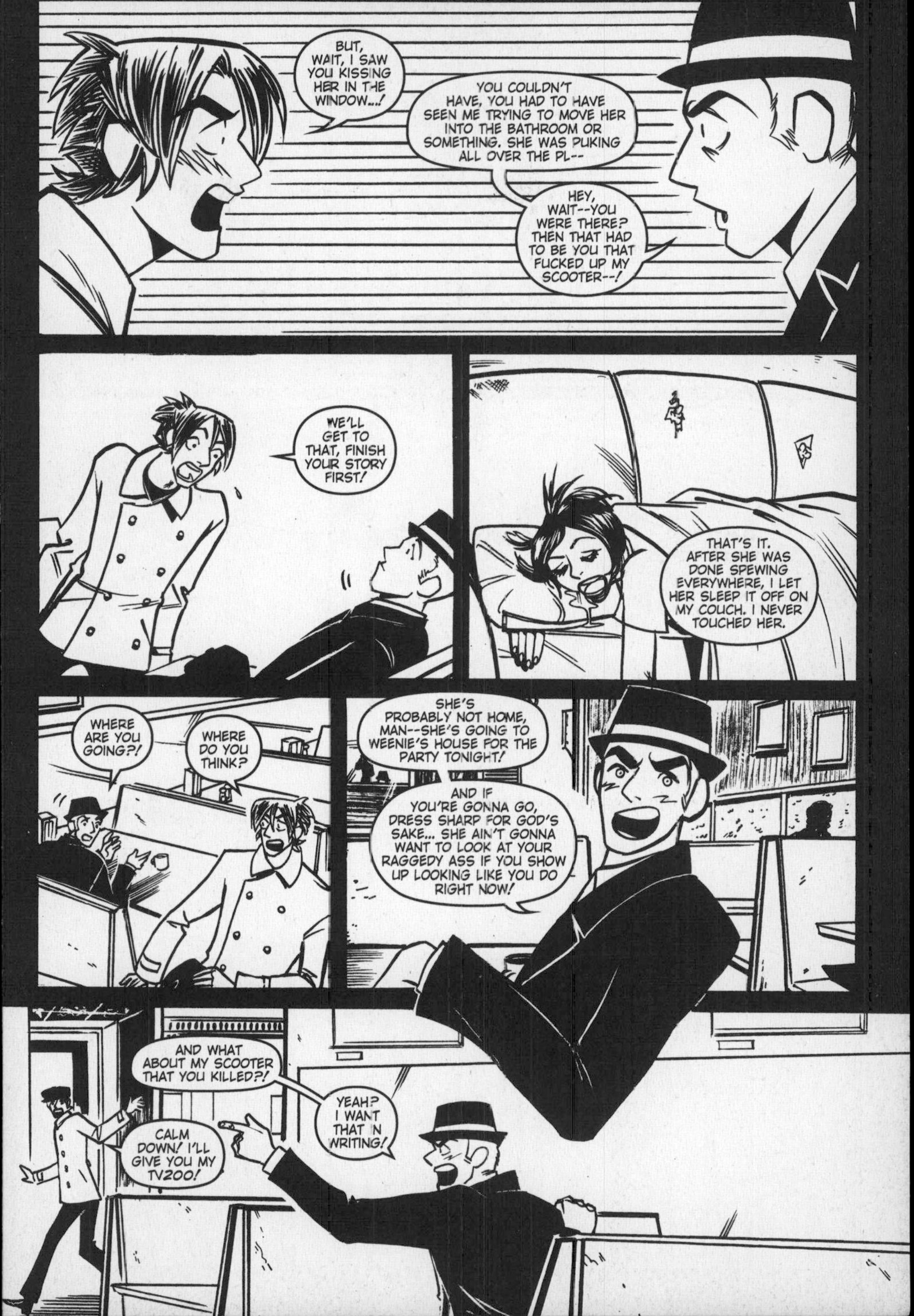
BUT, WAIT, I SAW YOU KISSING HER IN THE WINDOW...!
YOU COULDN'T HAVE, YOU HAD TO HAVE SEEN ME TRYING TO MOVE HER INTO THE BATHROOM OR SOMETHING. SHE WAS PUKING ALL OVER THE PL--
HEY, WAIT--YOU WERE THERE? THEN THAT HAD TO BE YOU THAT FUCKED UP MY SCOOTER--!
WE'LL GET TO THAT, FINISH YOUR STORY FIRST!
THAT'S IT. AFTER SHE WAS DONE SPEWING EVERYWHERE, I LET HER SLEEP IT OFF ON MY COUCH. I NEVER TOUCHED HER.
WHERE ARE YOU GOING?!
WHERE DO YOU THINK?
SHE'S PROBABLY NOT HOME, MAN--SHE'S GOING TO WEENIE'S HOUSE FOR THE PARTY TONIGHT!
AND IF YOU'RE GONNA GO, DRESS SHARP FOR GOD'S SAKE... SHE AIN'T GONNA WANT TO LOOK AT YOUR RAGGEDY ASS IF YOU SHOW UP LOOKING LIKE YOU DO RIGHT NOW!
AND WHAT ABOUT MY SCOOTER THAT YOU KILLED?!
CALM DOWN! I'LL GIVE YOU MY TV200!
YEAH? I WANT THAT IN WRITING!

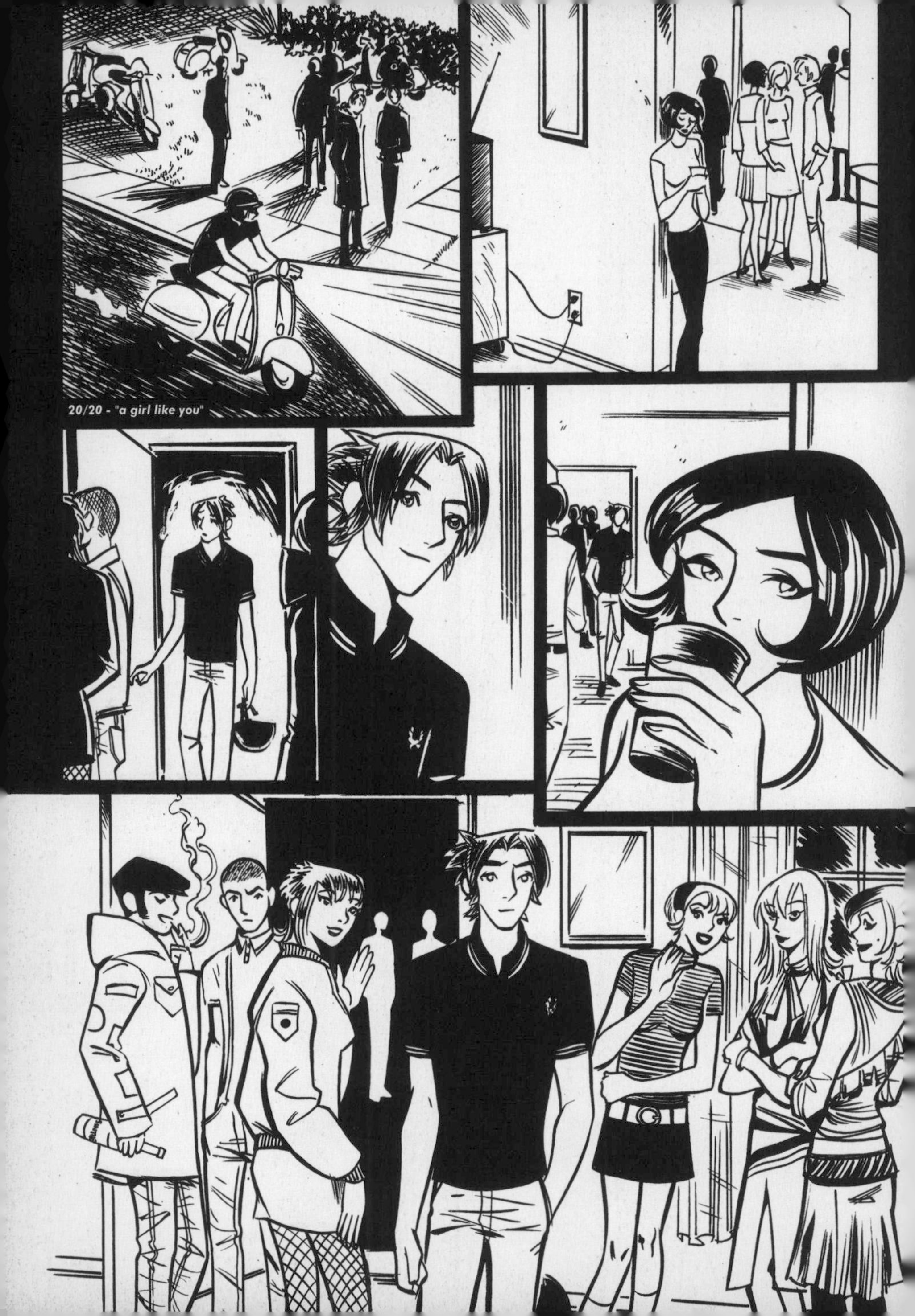
20/20 - "a girl like you"

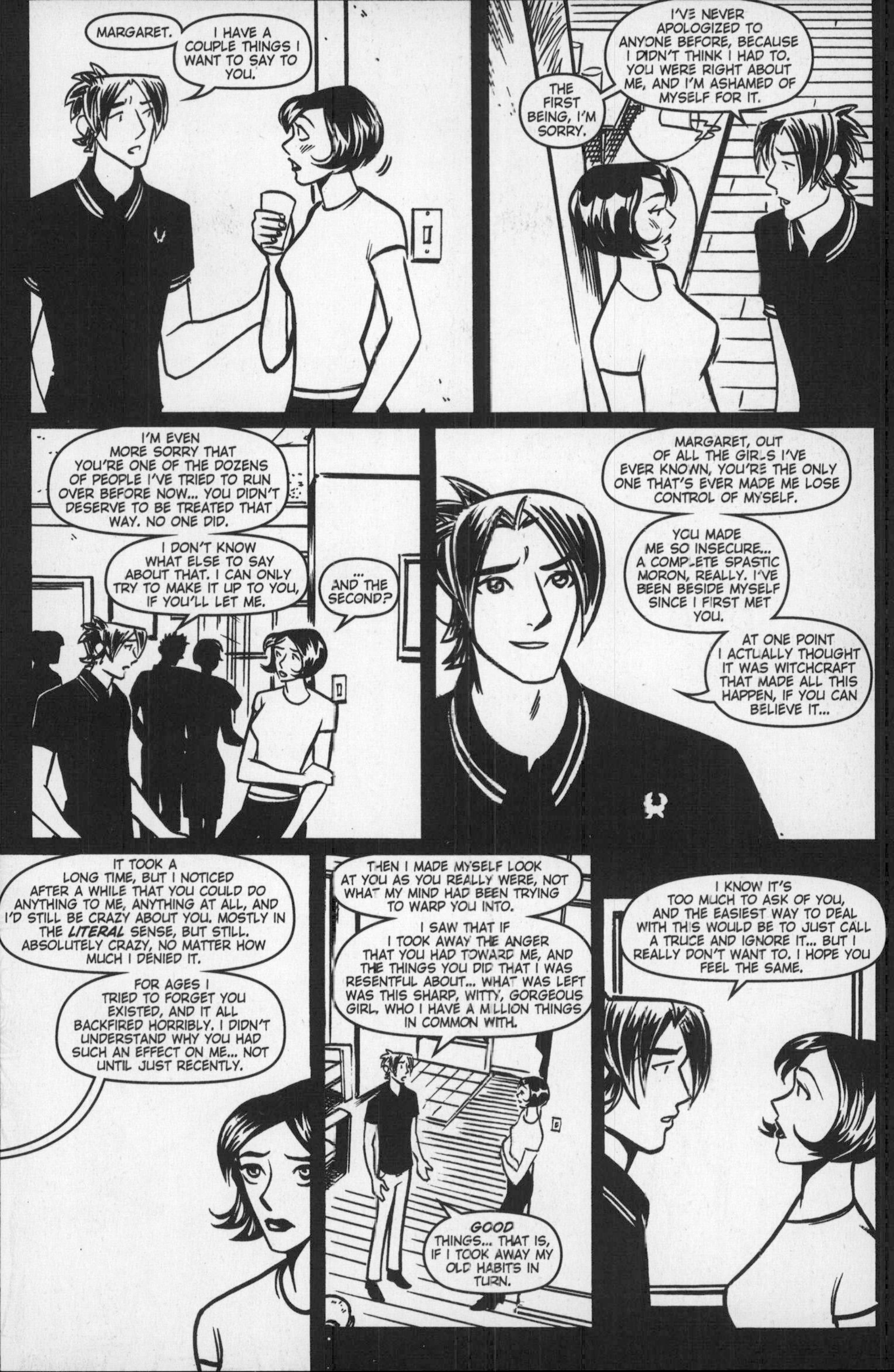
MARGARET.
I HAVE A COUPLE THINGS I WANT TO SAY TO YOU.
THE FIRST BEING, I'M SORRY.
I'VE NEVER APOLOGIZED TO ANYONE BEFORE, BECAUSE I DIDN'T THINK I HAD TO. YOU WERE RIGHT ABOUT ME, AND I'M ASHAMED OF MYSELF FOR IT.
I'M EVEN MORE SORRY THAT YOU'RE ONE OF THE DOZENS OF PEOPLE I'VE TRIED TO RUN OVER BEFORE NOW... YOU DIDN'T DESERVE TO BE TREATED THAT WAY. NO ONE DID.
I DON'T KNOW WHAT ELSE TO SAY ABOUT THAT. I CAN ONLY TRY TO MAKE IT UP TO YOU, IF YOU'LL LET ME.
...AND THE SECOND?
MARGARET, OUT OF ALL THE GIRLS I'VE EVER KNOWN, YOU'RE THE ONLY ONE THAT'S EVER MADE ME LOSE CONTROL OF MYSELF.
YOU MADE ME SO INSECURE... A COMPLETE SPASTIC MORON, REALLY. I'VE BEEN BESIDE MYSELF SINCE I FIRST MET YOU.
AT ONE POINT I ACTUALLY THOUGHT IT WAS WITCHCRAFT THAT MADE ALL THIS HAPPEN, IF YOU CAN BELIEVE IT...
IT TOOK A LONG TIME, BUT I NOTICED AFTER A WHILE THAT YOU COULD DO ANYTHING TO ME, ANYTHING AT ALL, AND I'D STILL BE CRAZY ABOUT YOU. MOSTLY IN THE *LITERAL* SENSE, BUT STILL. ABSOLUTELY CRAZY, NO MATTER HOW MUCH I DENIED IT.
FOR AGES I TRIED TO FORGET YOU EXISTED, AND IT ALL BACKFIRED HORRIBLY. I DIDN'T UNDERSTAND WHY YOU HAD SUCH AN EFFECT ON ME... NOT UNTIL JUST RECENTLY.
THEN I MADE MYSELF LOOK AT YOU AS YOU REALLY WERE, NOT WHAT MY MIND HAD BEEN TRYING TO WARP YOU INTO.
I SAW THAT IF I TOOK AWAY THE ANGER THAT YOU HAD TOWARD ME, AND THE THINGS YOU DID THAT I WAS RESENTFUL ABOUT... WHAT WAS LEFT WAS THIS SHARP, WITTY, GORGEOUS GIRL, WHO I HAVE A MILLION THINGS IN COMMON WITH.
GOOD THINGS... THAT IS, IF I TOOK AWAY MY OLD HABITS IN TURN.
I KNOW IT'S TOO MUCH TO ASK OF YOU, AND THE EASIEST WAY TO DEAL WITH THIS WOULD BE TO JUST CALL A TRUCE AND IGNORE IT... BUT I REALLY DON'T WANT TO. I HOPE YOU FEEL THE SAME.

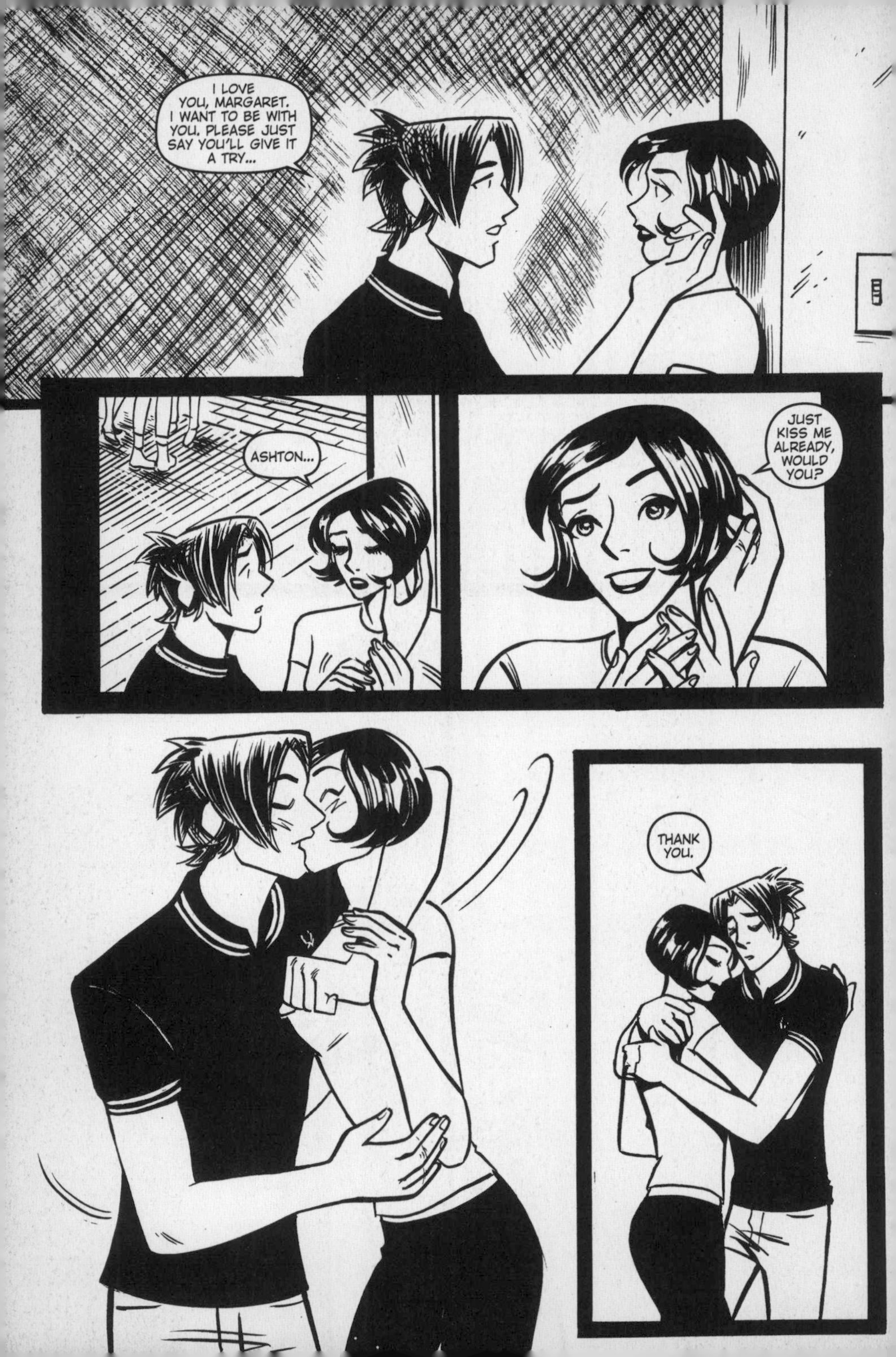
I LOVE YOU, MARGARET. I WANT TO BE WITH YOU. PLEASE JUST SAY YOU'LL GIVE IT A TRY...
ASHTON...
JUST KISS ME ALREADY, WOULD YOU?
THANK YOU.

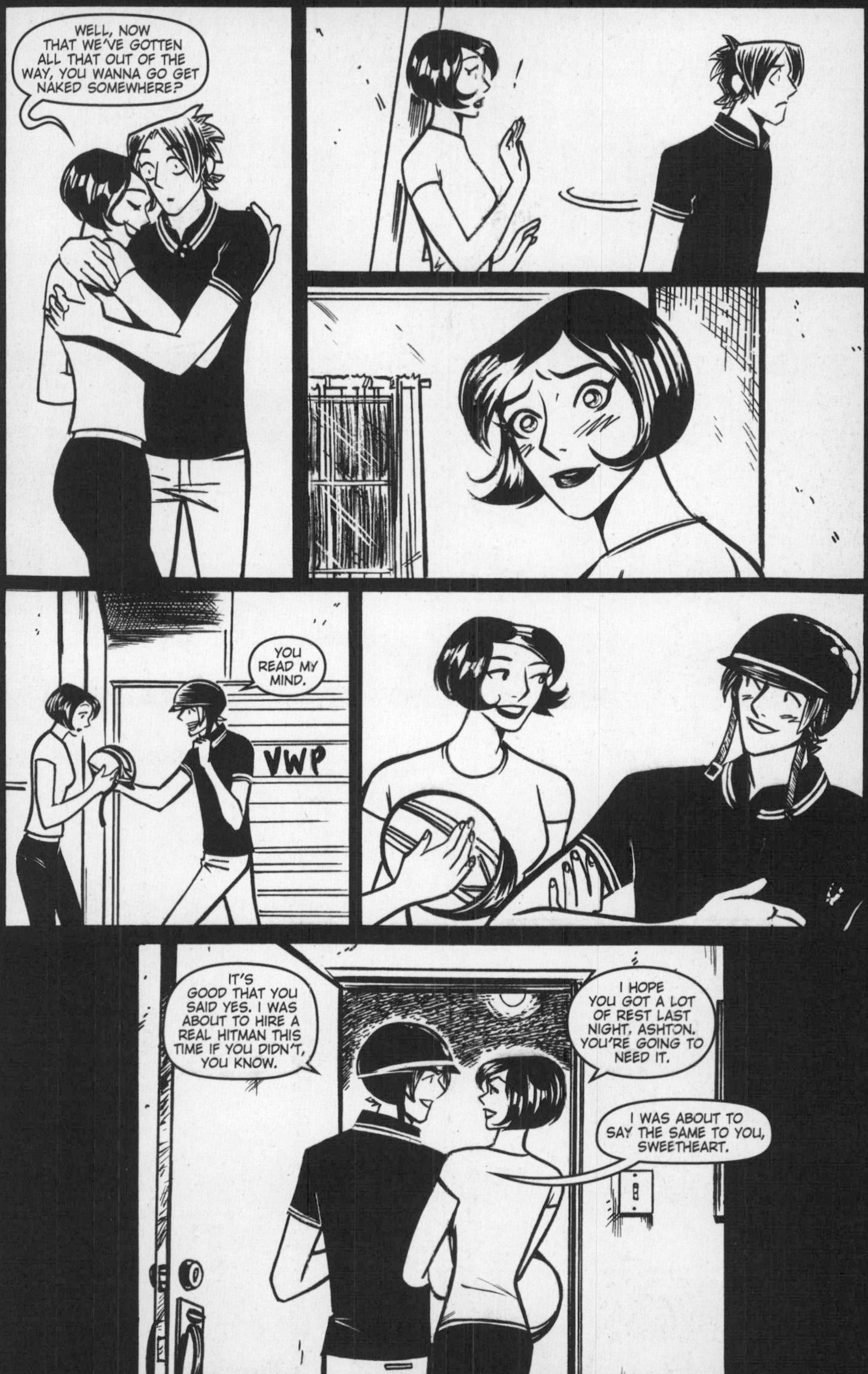
WELL, NOW THAT WE'VE GOTTEN ALL THAT OUT OF THE WAY, YOU WANNA GO GET NAKED SOMEWHERE?
!
YOU READ MY MIND.
VWP
IT'S GOOD THAT YOU SAID YES. I WAS ABOUT TO HIRE A REAL HITMAN THIS TIME IF YOU DIDN'T, YOU KNOW.
I HOPE YOU GOT A LOT OF REST LAST NIGHT, ASHTON. YOU'RE GOING TO NEED IT.
I WAS ABOUT TO SAY THE SAME TO YOU, SWEETHEART.

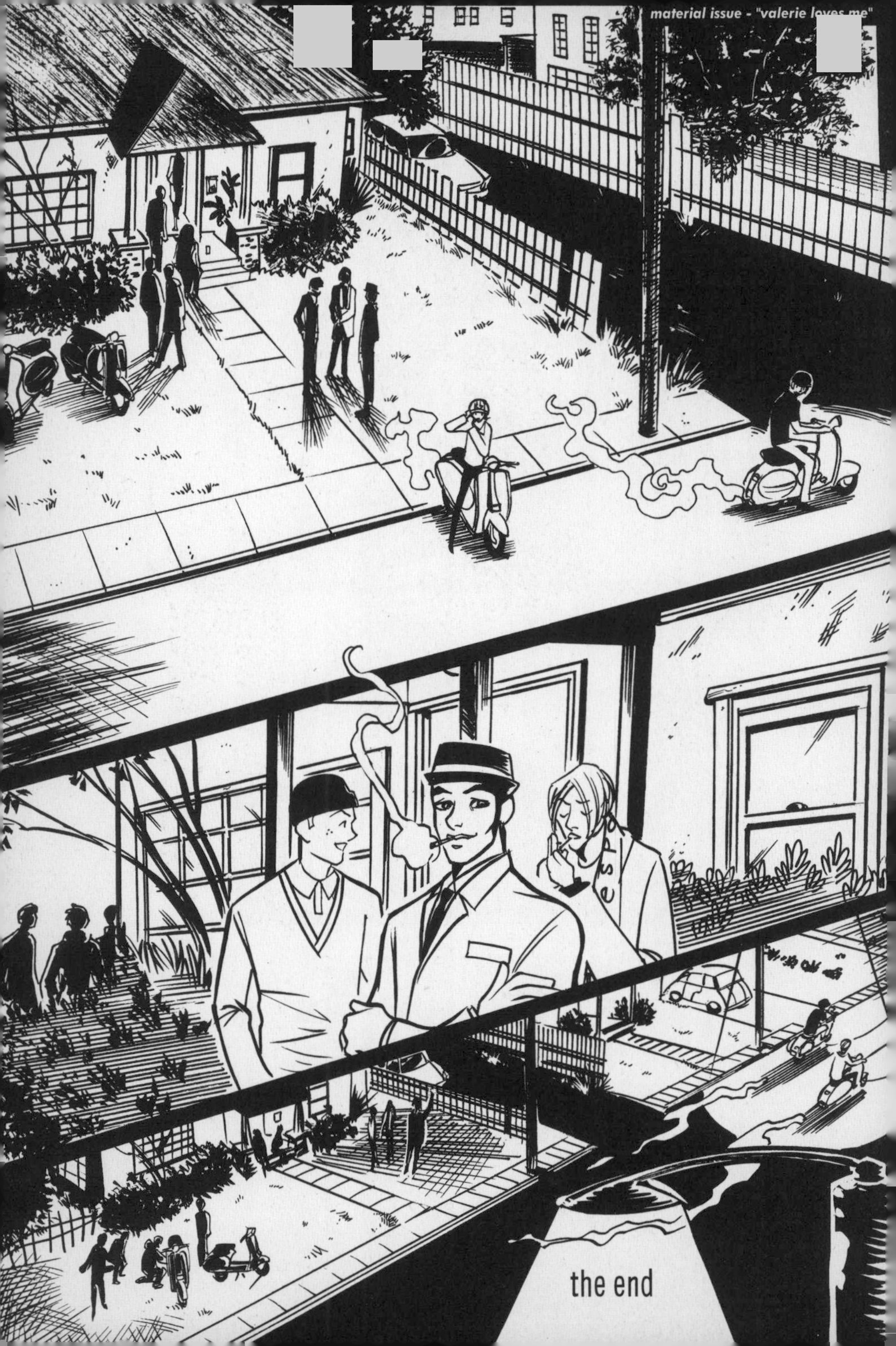
material issue - "valerie loves me"
the end

Extras

The original, rejected cover to issue #3. Most notably, Kitty's hairstyle changed between this being drawn and her actual appearance in the book.

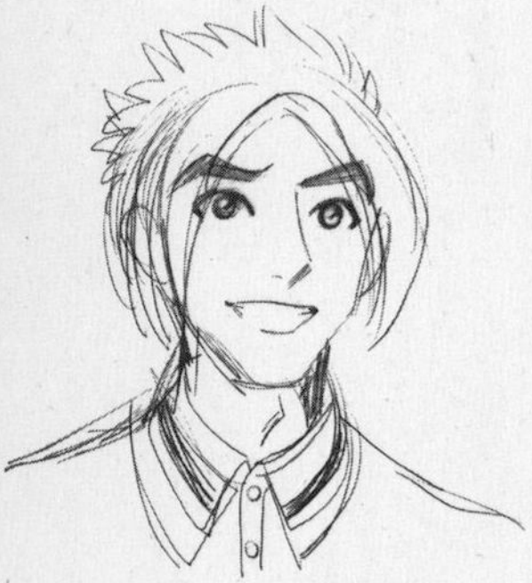

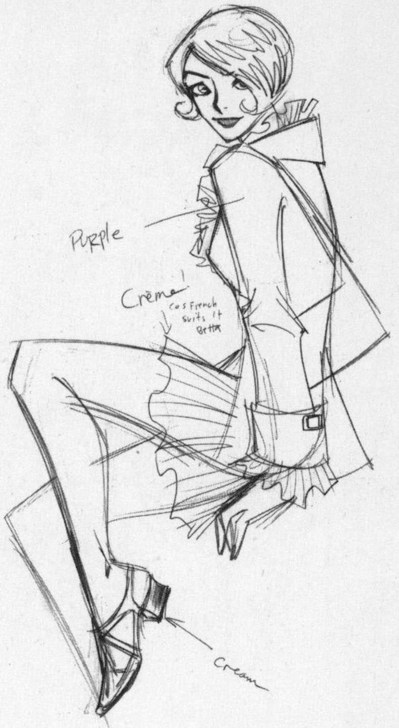
Purple
Crème!
Cos French suits it Betta
Cream

T-shirt design for the October 2003 First Annual All Girls Love-em' and Leave-em' Scooter Rally in Palm Springs, California.

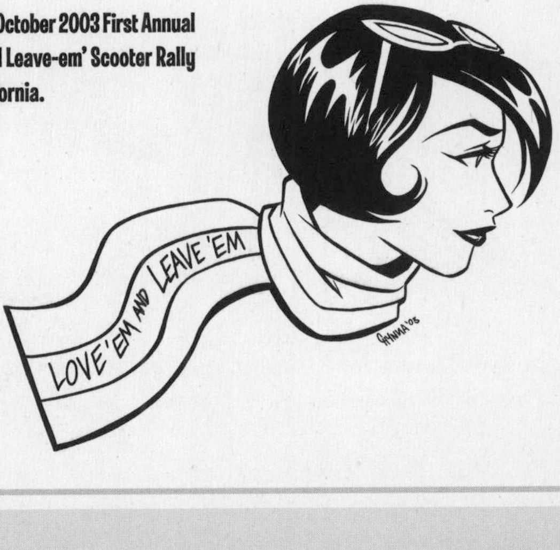
LOVE 'EM AND LEAVE 'EM

issue #1 deleted scene

Now a small crowd is standing around, admiring his scoot.

Kid/1: This one's my favorite. It's totally gonna win "best of" again, it's so cherry.

Kid/2: Whydoncha stick your dick in the exhaust pipe if you love it so much?

Kid/1: I can't, I burned it off last time.

Girl: Oh, so you weren't born with that little nub you got? Poor you, that's quite a step down...

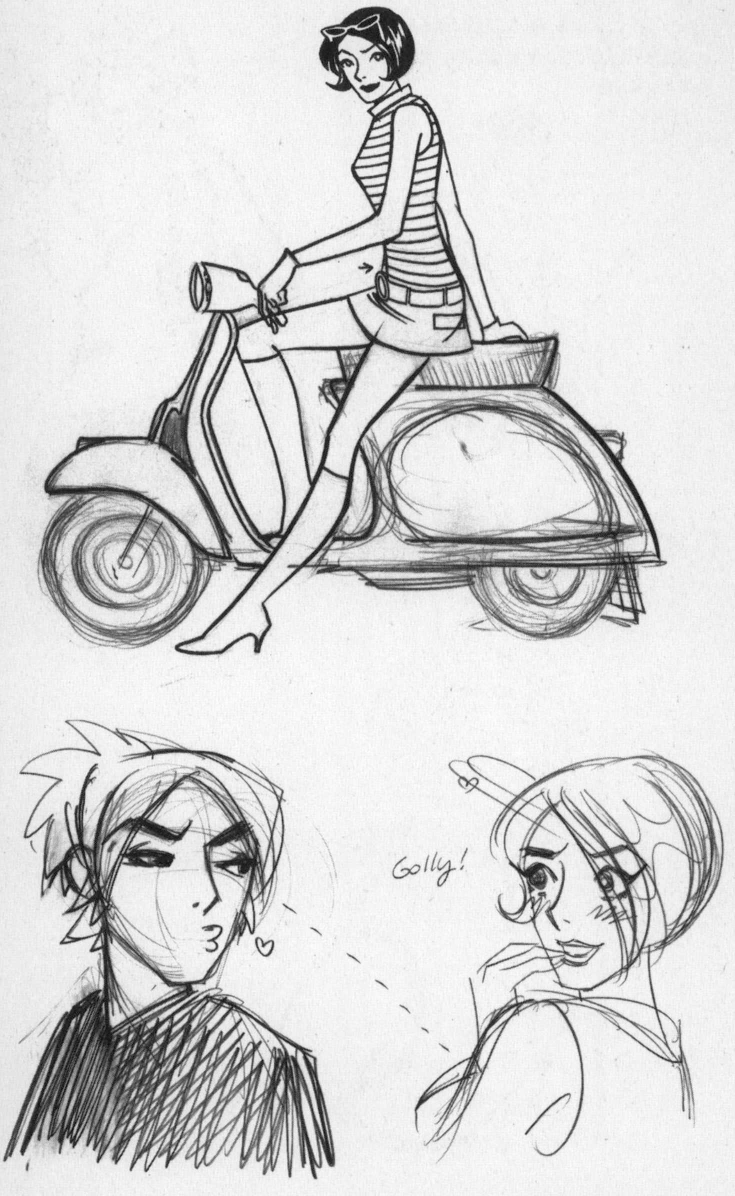
Golly!

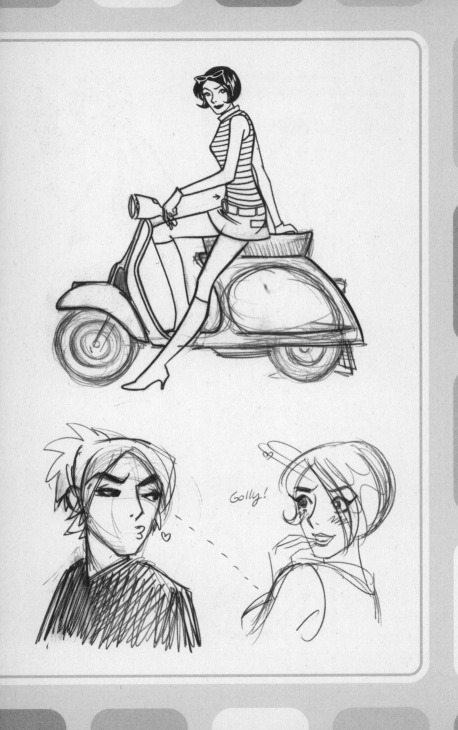

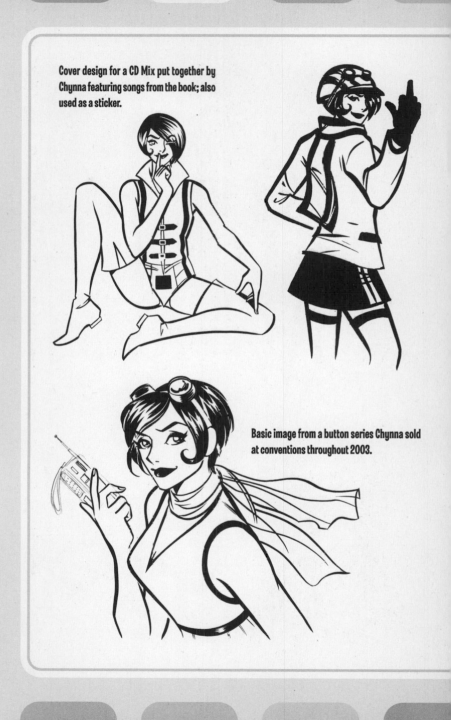

Cover design for a CD Mix put together by Chynna featuring songs from the book; also used as a sticker.

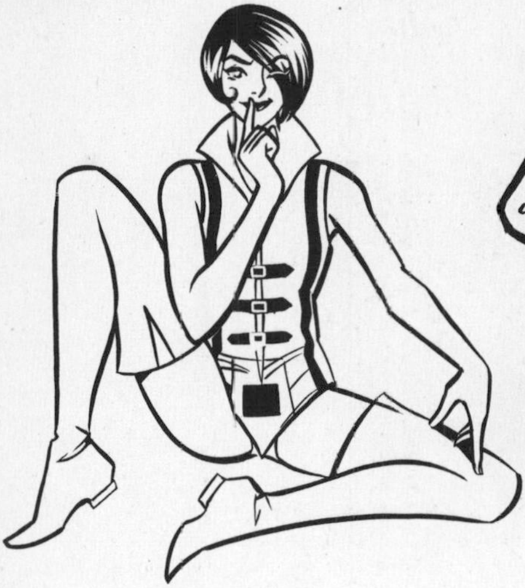

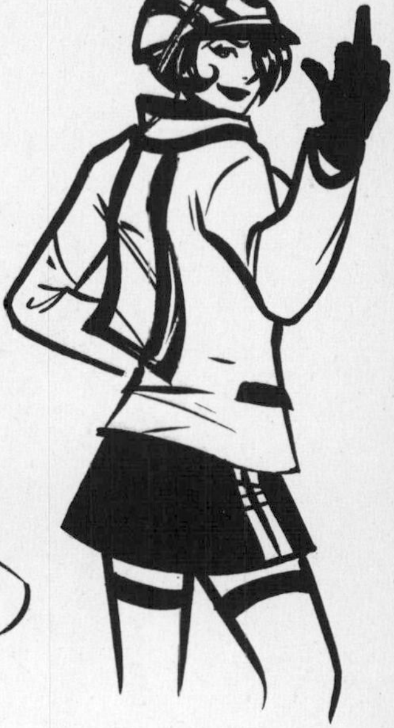

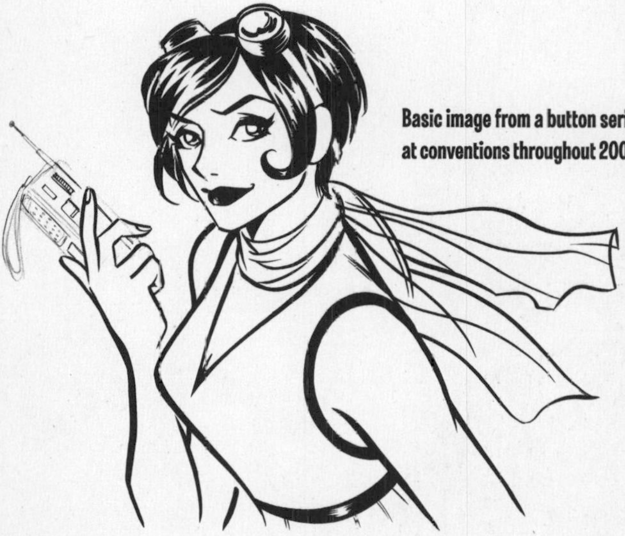

Basic image from a button series Chynna sold at conventions throughout 2003.

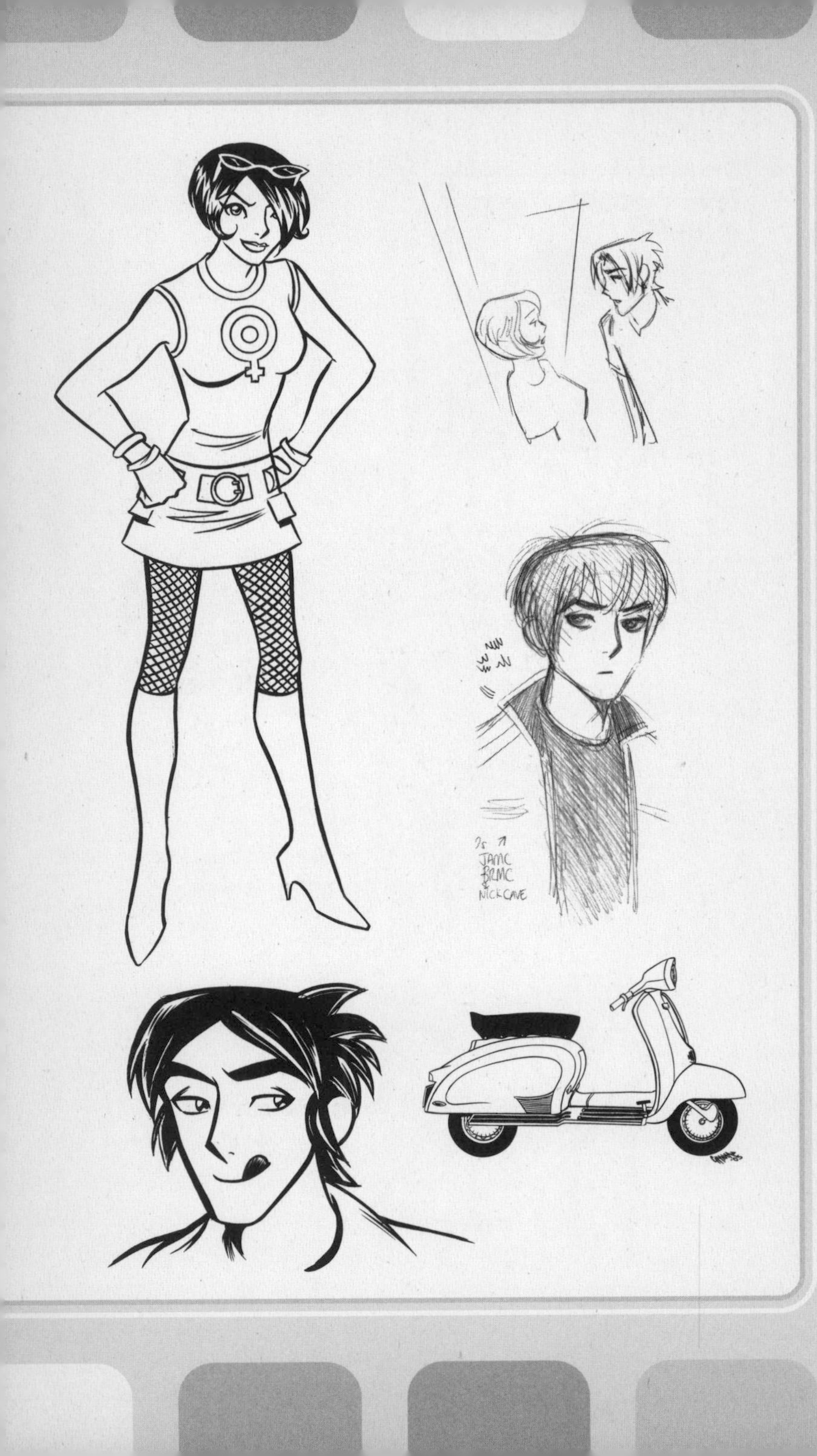

JAMC
BRMC
&
NICK CAVE

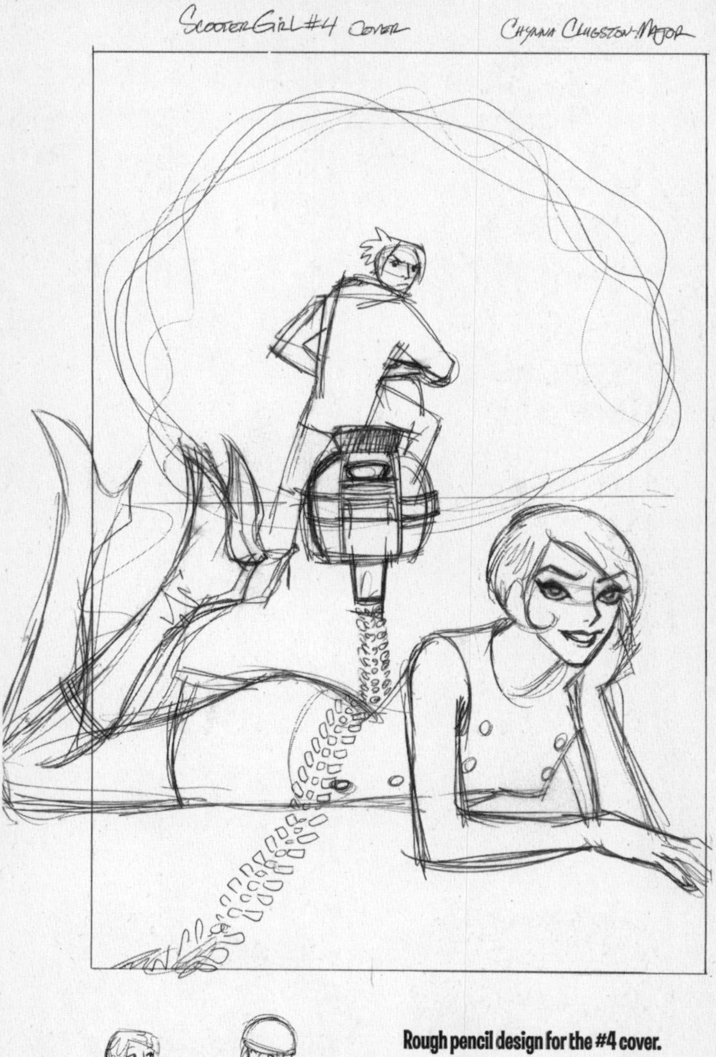
ScooterGirl #4 Cover
Chynna Clugston-Major

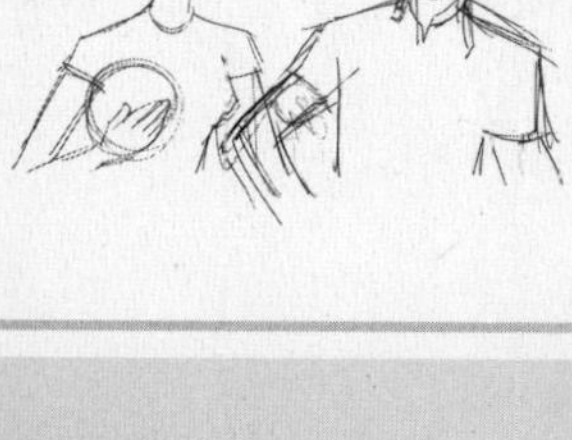

Rough pencil design for the #4 cover.

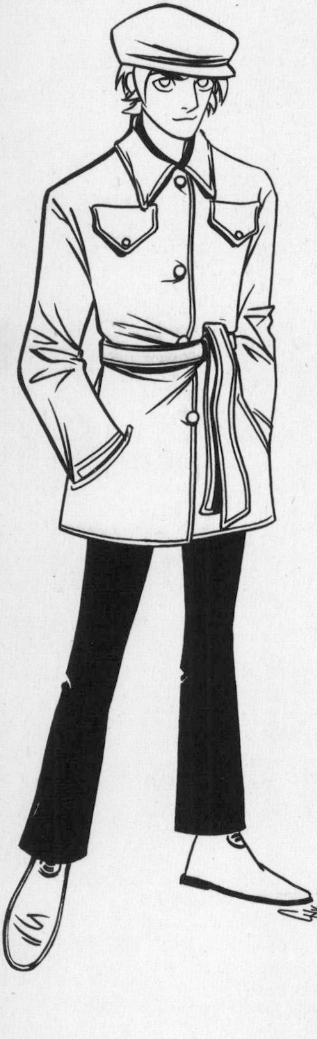

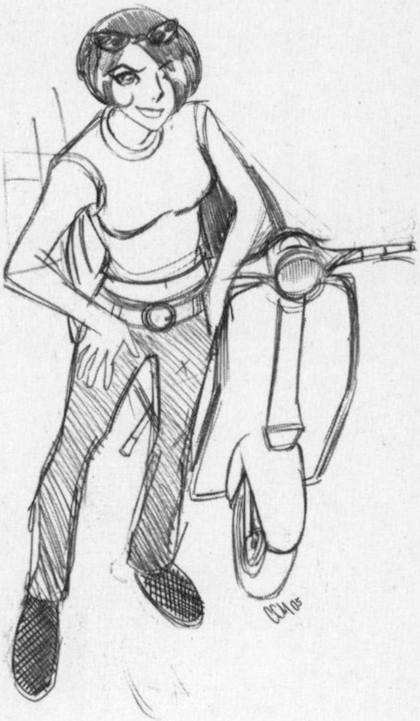

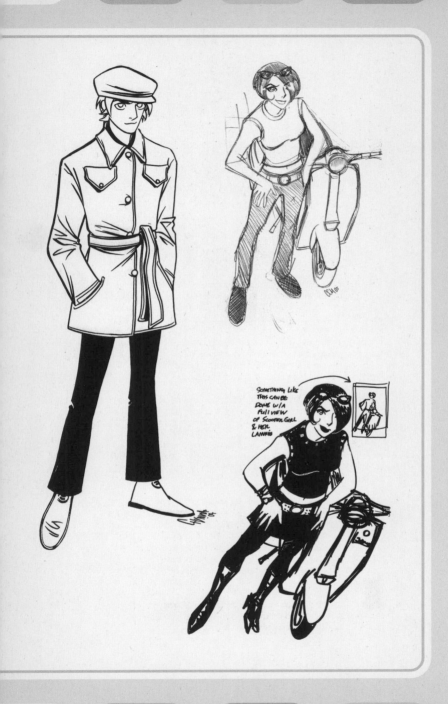

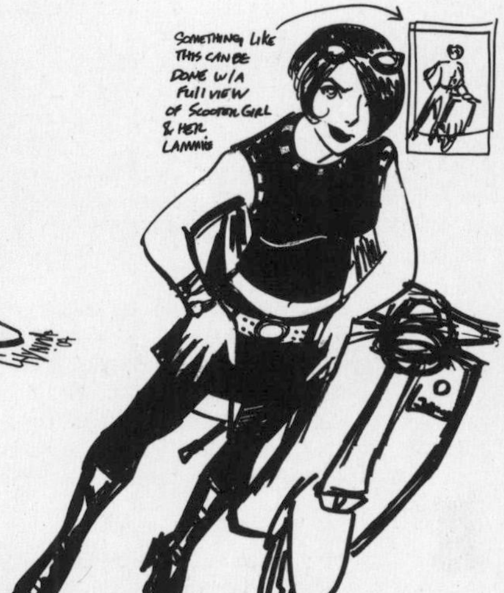
SOMETHING LIKE THIS CAN BE DONE W/A FULL VIEW OF SCOOTER GIRL & HER LAMMIE